Middle English Lyrics

Middle English Lyrics
New Readings of Short Poems

Edited by

Julia Boffey and Christiania Whitehead

D. S. BREWER

© Contributors 2018

All Rights Reserved. Except as permitted under current legislation
no part of this work may be photocopied, stored in a retrieval system,
published, performed in public, adapted, broadcast,
transmitted, recorded or reproduced in any form or by any means,
without the prior permission of the copyright owner

First published 2018
D. S. Brewer, Cambridge
Paperback edition 2021

ISBN 978 1 84384 497 6 hardback
ISBN 978 1 84384 592 8 paperback

D. S. Brewer is an imprint of Boydell & Brewer Ltd
PO Box 9, Woodbridge, Suffolk IP12 3DF, UK
and of Boydell & Brewer Inc.
668 Mt Hope Avenue, Rochester, NY 14620–2731, USA
website: www.boydellandbrewer.com

A catalogue record for this book is available
from the British Library

The publisher has no responsibility for the continued existence or accuracy of URLs for
external or third-party internet websites referred to in this book, and does not guarantee
that any content on such websites is, or will remain, accurate or appropriate

This publication is printed on acid-free paper

*Dedicated to
Thomas G. Duncan, with affection*

Contents

List of Illustrations	ix
List of Contributors	xi
Acknowledgements	xv
Abbreviations	xvi

Introduction: Julia Boffey and Christiania Whitehead — 1

1. Editing Issues in Middle English Lyrics — 12
   Thomas G. Duncan

Part I: Affect — 29

2. Moving Lights: An Affective Reading of *On leome is in þis world ilist* and Church Wall Paintings — 31
   A. S. Lazikani

3. Blood and Chocolate: Affective Layering in *Swete Ihesu, now wil I synge* — 45
   Daniel McCann

4. Textual and Affective Stability in *All Other Love is Like the Moon* — 57
   Michael P. Kuczynski

Part II: Visuality — 71

5. The Unlikely Landscapes of *On God Ureisun of Ure Lefdi* — 73
   Annie Sutherland

6. 'Adreynt in shennesse': Blood, Shame and Contrition in *Quis est iste qui uenit de Edom?* — 87
   Hetta Elizabeth Howes

7. *Ihesus woundes so wide* and the *fons vitae*: Text, Image and the Manuscript Context — 99
   Natalie Jones

8. 'Written in gold upon a purple stain': Mariological Rhetoric and the Material Culture of Aureate Diction — 109
   Anne Marie D'Arcy

Contents

9   Textual Lyricism in Lydgate's *Fifteen Joys and Sorrows of Mary*   122
    Mary Wellesley

Part III: *Mouvance*, Transformation   139

10 Voice and Response: Lyric Rewriting of the Song of Songs   141
    Anne Baden-Daintree

11 Compiling the Lyric: Richard Rolle, Textual Dynamism and   158
    Devotional Song in London, British Library, Additional
    MS 37049
    Katherine Zieman

12 Lyric Interventions in *Troilus and Criseyde*   174
    Elizabeth Robertson

13 Poems that Speak Volumes: Lydgate's *Thoroughfare of Woe*,   189
    and Lyric as Epitome
    Julia Boffey

14 'Short song is good in ale': Charles d'Orléans and Authorial   201
    Intentions in the Middle English *Ballade 84*
    Denis Renevey

Part IV: Words, Music, Speech   211

15 All Adam's Children: The Early Middle English Lyric Sequence   213
    in Oxford, Jesus College, MS 29 (II)
    Susanna Fein

16 Musical and Poetic Form in *Stond wel, moder, under rode*   227
    Christiania Whitehead

17 Tutivillus and the Policing of Speech in Oxford, Bodleian   240
    Library, MS Douce 104
    Mary C. Flannery

18 Have This in Mind: Word and Image in Audelay's Writing   251
    Jane Griffiths

19 'The Dance of the Intellect among Words': Wyatt's *In eternum*   261
    and Late Medieval Lyric Practice
    Joel Grossman

Afterword: The Study of Medieval Lyrics in 1960s Oxford and Today   273
    John C. Hirsh

Bibliography   285
Index of Manuscripts   303
General Index   305

Illustrations

1   Editing Issues in Middle English Lyrics
    Thomas G. Duncan
    Figure 1: An edited version of the words and music of *Miri it*   16
       is while sumer i-last.
    Figure 2: Cambridge, Trinity College, MS O. 2. 40, detail   26
       of fol. 58v. Reproduced by kind permission of the Master and
       Fellows of Trinity College, Cambridge.

4   Textual and Affective Stability in *All Other Love is Like the Moon*
    Michael P. Kuczynski
    Figure 1: Windsor, Eton College, MS 36, fol. 238rb, *All Other Love*   60
       is Like the Moon. Photo by the author and reproduced by
       permission of the Provost and Fellows of Eton College.
    Figure 2: Windsor, Eton College, MS 36, fol. 238b (detail in raking   61
       light), *All Other Love is Like the Moon*, lines 9–24. Photo by
       the author and reproduced by permission of the Provost and
       Fellows of Eton College.

9   Textual Lyricism in Lydgate's *Fifteen Joys and Sorrows of Mary*
    Mary Wellesley
    Figure 1: Cambridge, Trinity College, MS R. 3. 21, fol. 238r.   134
       Reproduced by kind permission of the Master and Fellows
       of Trinity College, Cambridge.

11   Compiling the Lyric: Richard Rolle, Textual Dynamism and
    Devotional Song in London, British Library, Additional
    MS 37049
    Katherine Zieman
    Figure 1: © The British Library Board. London, British Library,   162
       Additional MS 37049, fol. 36v.

Figure 2: © The British Library Board. London, British Library,   163
       Additional MS 37049, fol. 37r.
Figure 3: © The British Library Board. London, British Library,   169
       Additional MS 37049, fol. 52v.

The editors, contributors and publishers are grateful to all the institutions and persons listed for permission to reproduce the materials in which they hold copyright. Every effort has been made to trace the copyright holders; apologies are offered for any omission, and the publishers will be pleased to add any necessary acknowledgement in subsequent editions.

Contributors

Anne Baden-Daintree is Teaching Fellow in English at the University of Bristol. She has published on *Pearl*, Charles d'Orléans, and the alliterative *Morte Arthure*. Current projects include an edition of a fifteenth-century lyric anthology, Lambeth Palace, MS 853; a *Reader's Guide to Essential Criticism: Medieval English Literature*; and a study of the reception of the Song of Songs in medieval English literature and culture.

Julia Boffey is Professor of Medieval Studies in the Department of English at Queen Mary University of London. Her interests include Middle English verse, especially lyrics and dream poetry; and the relationships between manuscript and print in the late fifteenth and early sixteenth centuries.

Anne Marie D'Arcy is Associate Professor of Medieval and Renaissance Literature and Language in the School of Arts at the University of Leicester. Her research interests lie in the areas of medieval and Renaissance wisdom literature; iconology and political theology; the patristic sources of Old and Middle English literature, and nineteenth- and twentieth-century medievalisms, especially James Joyce. In addition to *Wisdom and the Grail: The Image of the Vessel in the Queste del Saint Graal and Malory's Tale of the Sankgreal* (Dublin, 2000), and *Joyce and the Irish Middle Ages: Saints, Sages, and Insular Culture* (London and New York, 2019), she is currently completing *The Artifice of Eternity: Mariology in the English Poetic Tradition* (Oxford, forthcoming), and working on a long-standing book project on Chaucer and the Crusades.

Thomas G. Duncan is Honorary Senior Lecturer in English Language and Literature in the School of English, St Andrews University. His edited publications include *The Middle English Mirror: Sermons from Advent to Sexagesima*, with Margaret Connolly (Heidelberg, 2003); *Medieval English Lyrics 1200–1400* and *Late Medieval English Lyrics and Carols 1400–1530* (Harmondsworth, 1995, 2000), both reissued in a revised, single-volume edition *Medieval Lyrics and Carols* (Cambridge, 2013), and *A Companion to the Middle English Lyric* (Cambridge, 2005).

Susanna Fein is Professor of English at Kent State University and editor of *The Chaucer Review*. Her research is in medieval English literature and manuscripts. Her most recent books include a three-volume edition and translation of the contents of MS Harley 2253 (2014–15) as well as the essay collections *The Auchinleck Manuscript: New Perspectives* (York, 2016) and *Chaucer: Visual Approaches* (Pennsylvania, 2016; with David Raybin). She is currently preparing an edition of the lyrics in Oxford, Jesus College, MS 29.

Mary C. Flannery has held posts at the J. Paul Getty Museum, Queen Mary University of London, and, most recently, the University of Lausanne. Her publications include *John Lydgate and the Poetics of Fame* (Cambridge, 2012), *The Culture of Inquisition in Medieval England* (Cambridge, 2013, ed. with K. Walter) and *Spaces for Reading in Later Medieval England* (New York, 2016, ed. with C. Griffin), as well as articles on medieval English literature and on the history of emotions. She is currently completing a book on shame and female honour in Middle English literature.

Jane Griffiths is Fellow and Tutor in English at Wadham College, Oxford. She has written two monographs, *John Skelton and Poetic Authority* (Oxford, 2006) and *Diverting Authorities: Experimental Glossing Practices in Manuscript and Print* (Oxford, 2014). Her most recent collection of poetry, *Silent in Finisterre* (Hexham, 2017) is a Poetry Book Society Recommendation.

Joel Grossman is an Associate Lecturer at Queen Mary University of London. He recently completed his doctoral project on secular poetry in the court of Henry VIII. His research concerns poetic form and poetic manuscripts in the late medieval and early modern periods. He has recently published on poetic games in the Devonshire Manuscript, and has forthcoming work on John Stow's antiquarianism in London, British Library, Harley MS 367.

John C. Hirsh is Professor of English and American literature at Georgetown University. His interests include Chaucer, the medieval lyric, and the devout and religious writing that inform these texts, and he has also worked in urban literacy. His recent publications include 'The Twenty-Five Joys of Our Lady: An English Marian Rosary of the Fifteenth Century', *Traditio* 71 (2016) and *Vygotsky's Children: Georgetown and Oxbridge Students meet Urban Youth* (Washington, DC, 2017).

Hetta Elizabeth Howes is Lecturer in Medieval Literature at City, University of London and a BBC/AHRC New Generation Thinker. She has published on crying and cleansing in Aelred of Rievaulx's writings for women, and the role of sight in alliterative verse. She is currently working on a monograph examining the role of water as a literary metaphor in devotional prose.

Contributors

Natalie Jones is Lecturer in Medieval Literature at University College London. Her research focuses primarily on Middle English religious literature, iconology and medieval theology, and she also has a particular interest in the relationship between text and image throughout the medieval period. She has published on the use of religious iconography in the Middle English carols and is currently completing a monograph on the Middle English religious lyric.

Michael P. Kuczynski is Professor and Chair of English at Tulane University in New Orleans. He publishes on medieval manuscripts and codicology, the circulation and use of the Psalms in late medieval England, and glosses in Wycliffite Bible manuscripts. He is currently completing an edition of a glossed Wycliffite psalter in the Bodleian Library.

A. S. Lazikani is Stipendiary Lecturer in Old and Middle English at the University of Oxford. She specializes in devotional and spiritual writing of the High Middle Ages, and is the author of *Cultivating the Heart: Feeling and Emotion in Twelfth- and Thirteenth-Century Religious Texts* (Cardiff, 2015).

Daniel McCann is the Simon and June Li Fellow in Old and Middle English at Lincoln College, University of Oxford. His research interests focus on medieval religious texts, medicine, psychology and grammar. More broadly, he also carries out research in the interdisciplinary fields of medical humanities and emotion studies. He is in the final stages of completing a monograph from his postdoctoral project, entitled *Soul-Health: Therapeutic Reading in the Middle Ages*.

Denis Renevey is Professor of Medieval English Language and Literature at the University of Lausanne. He is author and editor of several books (a monograph, edited collections and a critical edition) on mystical and devotional literature. Some of his most recent publications explore the interface between the late medieval French-speaking world and England, with particular attention paid to the Savoy, Othon de Grandson and Charles d'Orléans.

Elizabeth Robertson is Professor and Chair of English Language at the University of Glasgow. She publishes primarily on gender and medieval religion in early Middle English religious prose, Chaucer and Langland. She is currently completing a long-standing book project: *Chaucerian Consent: Religion, Women and Subjection in Late Medieval England*.

Annie Sutherland is Associate Professor in English at the University of Oxford, and a tutorial fellow at Somerville College, Oxford. She has published widely on devotional literature and biblical translation, and is currently working on an edition of the *Wooing Group* prayers.

Mary Wellesley worked until recently in the department of Ancient, Medieval and Early Modern Manuscripts at the British Library. She gained her doctorate in 2017 from University College London on the manuscripts of John Lydgate's *Life of Our Lady*. She recently co-edited (with Michael Bintley et al.) *Stasis in the Medieval West: Questioning Change and Continuity* and has published three articles in *Pecia* and *Notes and Queries*. She also regularly writes and reviews for a non-academic audience: her work has appeared in *The Literary Review*, *The London Review of Books* and *The Times Literary Supplement*, amongst others.

Christiania Whitehead is Professor of Middle English Literature in the Department of English and Comparative Literary Studies at the University of Warwick, and is also currently seconded to the University of Lausanne as Senior Research Fellow for a three-year project on northern English saints. She has published widely on religious allegory, devotional texts and lyrics, and insular hagiography, and is completing a monograph on the textual afterlife of St Cuthbert of Lindisfarne.

Katherine Zieman is the author of *Singing the New Song: Literacy and Liturgy in Late Medieval England* (Philadelphia, 2008) and articles on liturgy, literacy, poetics and religious writing, with a current focus on the works of Richard Rolle. She has taught at various institutions in the US and the UK, including the University of Notre Dame, University of Oxford, and Birkbeck, University of London.

Acknowledgements

We are grateful to Queen Mary University of London for providing funding and administrative support for the one-day 'Lyrics' workshop in 2014, at which the initial discussions on new methodologies for approaching the Middle English lyric took place between several of the contributors to this volume. We are also grateful to the congress committees of the International Medieval Congresses at Kalamazoo and Leeds for hosting a number of subsequent sessions in 2015 dedicated to the lyric, and to the audiences who attended those sessions and contributed to our developing conversations.

Many of the essays in this volume arise from close engagement with a single manuscript or manuscripts, and we would like to thank the very large range of specialist libraries and their staff, including the British Library; Cambridge University Library; the Bodleian Library, Oxford; the librarians of many individual Oxford and Cambridge Colleges; and Eton College, Windsor, who provided access to their collections and helped us with enquiries, reproductions and permissions. We would also like to thank the editorial board of the Early English Text Society, and Boydell & Brewer, for permission to reproduce poems included in their published editions and anthologies.

Finally, we are indebted to the anonymous reader of the book proposal for this collection for his/her helpful suggestions; and likewise to Caroline Palmer and the editorial team at Boydell & Brewer, for their expertise and encouragement throughout the evolution of this volume.

Abbreviations

AH	Dreves, G. M., C. Blume and H. M. Bannister, eds, *Analecta Hymnica Medii Aevi*, 55 vols (Leipzig, 1886–1922)
Benson	Benson, L. D., ed., *The Riverside Chaucer*, 3rd edn (Oxford, 1988).
BL	London, British Library
BL online MS catalogue	http://searcharchives.bl.uk/
BnF	Paris, Bibliothèque nationale de France
BodL	Oxford, Bodleian Library
Brook	Brook, G. L., ed., *The Harley Lyrics: The Middle English Lyrics of Ms. Harley 2253*, 4th edn (Manchester, 1968)
Brown *XIII*	Brown, C., ed., *Religious Lyrics of the Thirteenth Century* (Oxford, 1932)
Brown *XIV*	Brown, C., ed., *Religious Lyrics of the Fourteenth Century*, 2nd edn, revised by G. V. Smithers (Oxford, 1952)
Brown *XV*	Brown, C., ed., *Religious Lyrics of the Fifteenth Century* (Oxford, 1939)
CCSL	Corpus Christianorum Series Latina
CSEL	Corpus Scriptorum Ecclesiasticorum Latinorum
CUL	Cambridge University Library
DIMEV	Mooney, L. R., D. W. Mosser and E. Solopova, *Digital Index of Middle English Verse*. Online: http://www.dimev.net
Douay-Rheims	Douay-Rheims/Douay-Challoner Bible. *The Holy Bible, Douay Version: Translated from the Latin Vulgate (Douay, A.D. 1609: Rheims, A.D. 1582)* (London, 1956). Online: www.catholicbible.online
Duncan, *Companion*	Duncan, T. G., ed., *A Companion to the Middle English Lyric* (Cambridge, 2005)
Duncan	Duncan, T. G., ed., *Medieval English Lyrics and Carols* (Cambridge, 2013)
EETS	Early English Text Society
ES	Extra Series
EUL	Edinburgh University Library
Gray, *Selection*	Gray, D., ed., *A Selection of English Medieval Religious*

	Lyrics (Oxford, 1975; reprinted Exeter, 1992)
Gray, *Themes*	Gray, D., *Themes and Images in the Medieval English Religious Lyric* (London, 1972)
Greene	Greene, R. L., ed., *The Early English Carols*, 2nd edn (Oxford, 1977)
MED	*Middle English Dictionary*, ed. H. Kurath and S. M. Kuhn (Ann Arbor and London, 1952–). Online: http://quod.lib.umich.edu/m/med/
NIMEV	Boffey, J. and A. S. G. Edwards, *A New Index of Middle English Verse* (London, 2005)
NLS	Edinburgh, National Library of Scotland
NS	New Series
OED	*Oxford English Dictionary*
OS	Original Series
PG	Migne, J. P., ed. *Patrologiae Cursus Completus … Series Graeca* [*Patrologia Graeca*], 161 vols (Paris, 1857–66)
PL	Migne, J. P., ed., *Patrologiae Cursus Completus … Series Latina* [*Patrologia Latina*], 221 vols (Paris, 1844–55 and 1862–65)
PO	Graffin, R., et al., *Patrologia Orientalis*, 56 vols (Paris and Turnhout, 1903–)
Robbins *Hist.*	Robbins, R. H., ed., *Historical Poems of the Fourteenth and Fifteenth Centuries* (New York, 1959)
Robbins *Sec.*	Robbins, R. H., ed., *Secular Lyrics of the Fourteenth and Fifteenth Centuries*, revised edn (Oxford, 1952)
SS	Supplementary Series
Woolf	Woolf, R., *The English Religious Lyric in the Middle Ages* (Oxford, 1968)

Introduction

Julia Boffey and Christiania Whitehead

The aim of this collection of essays is to remind readers of the extraordinary richness of the body of Middle English poems conventionally, if not always unproblematically, held to be lyrics. 'The reader of Middle English lyrics need never want for variety', as Thomas G. Duncan noted in the introduction to the first of two anthologies of lyrics that he compiled for Penguin Classics.[1] Well over two thousand of these poems survive from the years between about 1066 and 1500, strikingly variegated in terms of subject matter, length and form, and constituting an important point of entry into an understanding of medieval English culture.[2] They illuminate religious teaching and pious practice, contemporary conditions and events, the history of feelings and emotions, and reveal much about the ways that speech, song, image and performance related to the written word. Outside the contexts of cultural and literary history, their modes invite analysis of some of the abiding concerns of poetics: voice and moment, shape and cadence. Surviving as inscriptions on tombstones, as graffiti, and on artefacts such as rings and jugs as well as in a variety of written forms in manuscripts, they are testimony to the range of functions fulfilled by medieval verse in many contexts, and to the value and significance that was attached to it.

The variety that characterises this body of poems has proved in the past to be something of an impediment to sustainedly productive scholarship and analysis. Although much industry went into the early collection and editing of ballads, when it came to lyrics most nineteenth-century editors of Middle English verse were understandably more attracted by the challenge of longer works than by the prospect of assembling anthologies from short poems scattered in a range of geographically dispersed witnesses. The earliest relevant collections produced for the Early English Text Society, Furnivall's *Political, Religious and Love Poems*

---

[1] T. G. Duncan, ed., *Medieval English Lyrics 1200–1400* (Harmondsworth, 1995), p. xxvii.
[2] The figure of two thousand is an approximation derived from Robbins *Sec.*, p. xvii. For an admirable conspectus of available editions of lyrics and of associated scholarship, see R. Greentree, *The Middle English Lyric and Short Poem*, Annotated Bibliographies of Old and Middle English Literature, 7 (Cambridge, 2001).

from Lambeth 306 and Other Sources and *Hymns to the Virgin and Christ and Other Religious Poems*, Kail's edition of the Digby lyrics and Murray's editions of variant texts of *Erthe upon erthe*, focused specifically on single manuscripts or small groups of witnesses, and in the last case on just a single poem.[3] The anthology of *Early English Lyrics* edited by E. K. Chambers and F. Sidgwick for publication in 1907 seems to have been the first attempt at a representative selection, and its categories of 'amorous, divine, moral and trivial' were to be influential on the focus of later collections, including Carleton Brown's three important editions of religious lyrics and R. H. Robbins's of secular ones.[4]

Early English Lyrics was a landmark in other ways. In grouping its texts together as 'lyrics' it gave currency to a useful and appealing catch-all term for the forms of short or shortish verse that earlier editors had simply called 'poems'. The term would be further authorised in the titles of Brown's and Robbins's anthologies, and in collections such as G. L. Brook's *Harley Lyrics*.[5] In addition, *Early English Lyrics* suggested ways of approaching these poems that were to be influential on shaping later critical trends. The essay 'Aspects of Medieval Lyric' provided for the anthology by Chambers had much to say on the one hand about the relationships of lyrics to music, minstrelsy and folksong, and on the other about their capacity to convey 'the emotions … which a man tells to his own heart in solitude'.[6] While neither of these approaches may now seem especially relevant to the many pragmatically handy or straightforwardly comic forms of short poem among the corpus of Middle English lyrics, they opened attractive possibilities for critical analysis addressing musicality and the lyric voice. In invoking in his essay the poetry of troubadours and *trouvères* Chambers also indicated profitable ways of contextualising Middle English lyrics in a wider continental corpus.

Although Chambers's emphasis on 'the folk' may have come to seem exaggerated,[7] the central preoccupations of his essay have in many respects proved both durable and productive. The musical dimensions of Middle English lyrics have been explored in studies of form, for example, especially of the carol; and in cultural analyses that relate their use and currency to social functions.[8] C. S. Lewis's characterisation of early Tudor lyrics as 'words for music' has been particularly influential, stimulating important studies of the conventions of

---

[3] F. J. Furnivall, ed., *Political, Religious and Love Poems from Lambeth 306 and Other Sources*, EETS OS 15 (London, 1866), and *Hymns to the Virgin and Christ and Other Religious Poems*, EETS OS 24 (London, 1867); J. Kail. ed., *Twenty-Six Political and other Poems*, EETS OS 124 (London, 1904); H. M. R. Murray, ed., *The Middle English Poem 'Erthe Upon Erthe'*, EETS OS 141 (London, 1911).

[4] E. K. Chambers and F. Sidgwick, eds, *Early English Lyrics* (London, 1907); Brown *XIII*, Brown *XIV* and Brown *XV*; Robbins *Sec.*

[5] Brook.

[6] Chambers and Sidgwick, eds, *Early English Lyrics*, p. 260.

[7] For recent discussion of the 'folk' elements of early lyric, see D. Gray, *Simple Forms: Essays on Medieval English Popular Literature* (Oxford, 2015), pp. 215–31.

[8] See for example the introductions to Greene and to Robbins, *Sec.*

short forms of courtly verse.⁹ Alongside these studies much energy has gone into making available the repertory of surviving musical settings found in manuscript copies with the texts of lyrics.¹⁰ This work has taken place in the context of a revival of interest in early music, which has given new prominence to medieval lyrics in both concert performance and recordings. At the same time, freshly accessible editions of the texts of Middle English lyrics, from Chambers and Sidgwick onwards, have made them available to successive generations of twentieth- and twenty-first-century composers and musicians: Vaughan Williams, Benjamin Britten and Steeleye Span are just a few of those for whom they have proved attractive.¹¹

The 'lyric voice' that exerted such a powerful appeal on Chambers has remained a matter of interest, if inflected in more recent discussion by newer preoccupations with the subject and the gaze. One dimension of this power derives, perhaps somewhat paradoxically, from the anonymity of many lyrics, and the associated fact that for twentieth-century readers of editions like that of Chambers and Sidgwick, the poems tend to be presented bare of annotation of constraining kinds. Critical energies were able to take free rein with these disembodied texts, using them occasionally as demonstration pieces. Leo Spitzer's 1951 essay '*Explication de texte* Applied to Three Great Middle English Poems' remains one of the classics of this genre.¹² Short, anonymous forms of verse turned out to be especially hospitable to twentieth-century new critical experiments with the poem as verbal icon or well-wrought urn.¹³

More recently, the formal turn in the study of poetics has directed attention in newer ways to the appealing range of stanzaic and metrical variety in the Middle English lyric corpus. Carols, Middle English variations on the French *formes fixes* of *ballade*, *rondeau* and *virelai*, and the pervasive use of alliteration in lyric forms have all been the subjects of study. These kinds of approach have necessarily

---

9   C. S. Lewis, *English Literature in the Sixteenth Century, Excluding Drama* (Oxford, 1954), p. 230; J. E. Stevens, *Music and Poetry in the Early Tudor Period* (London, 1961, repr. Cambridge, 1979), especially pp. 154–202.
10 E. J. Dobson and F. L. Harrison, *Medieval English Songs* (London, 1979); J. E. Stevens, ed., *Medieval Carols*, Musica Britannica 4 (London, 1958); *Music at the Court of Henry VIII*, Musica Britannica 18 (London, 1962), and *Early Tudor Songs and Carols*, Musica Britannica 36 (London, 1975); D. Fallows, *A Catalogue of Polyphonic Songs* (Oxford, 1999) and ed., *The Henry VIII Book (British Library, Add. MS 31922)*, DIAMM facsimiles 4 (Oxford, 2014).
11 See D. Fuller, 'Lyrics, Sacred and Secular', *A Companion to Medieval Poetry*, ed. C. Saunders (Chichester, 2010), pp. 258–76 (p. 272); for Steeleye Span and *Westron wynde* see https://mainlynorfolk.info/steeleye.span/songs/westronwynde.html (accessed 25/7/2017).
12 In *Archivum Linguisticum*, 3 (1951), 1–22, 157–65. The poems concerned are 'Ichot a burde in boure bryht', with refrain 'Blow northerne wynde' (NIMEV 1395, DIMEV 2325), 'Lestenyt lordynges boþe elde and ȝynge' (NIMEV 1893, DIMEV 3114) and 'I syng of a myden þat is makeles'(NIMEV 1367, DIMEV 2281).
13 Phrases from seminal books by W. K. Wimsatt, *The Verbal Icon: Studies in the Meaning of Poetry* (Lexington, KY, 1954) and C. Brooks, *The Well Wrought Urn: Studies in the Structure of Poetry* (New York, 1947).

worked comparatively, and in the light of as much understanding as possible of the particular contexts in which lyrics were conceived, copied and used, thus addressing form and function in combination. Even though the mid-twentieth-century tendency may have been to read lyrics as 'poems without contexts' (in John Burrow's memorable phrase),[14] most editions supplied, somewhere in their apparatus, information about textual witnesses from which a sense of context could be excavated; and the amounts of this made available have grown steadily more useful. R. L. Greene's edition of *The Early English Carols*, for example, while grouping its contents thematically, also supplied extensive information about textual witnesses, and his introduction explored at length the contexts in which carols may have been read, sung and circulated; Douglas Gray's smaller edition of selected religious lyrics offered detail of the same kinds.[15] It has become increasingly possible to perceive the dynamic features of these poems, and the range of contexts – instructional, devotional or social – in which they may have played a role. Editions devoted to the lyrics of single manuscripts, such as those making available John of Grimestone's sermon notes in Edinburgh, National Library of Scotland, Advocates' MS 18. 7. 21 or the poems of Oxford, Bodleian Library, MS Digby 102,[16] enable a still more detailed reconstruction of some of the circumstances in which these poems had a life.

Much criticism has responded to lyrics as if they somehow came into being without authorial intervention, and indeed an impressionistic glance at the Middle English corpus may suggest a body of largely anonymous poems. But substantial numbers are fairly firmly attributable to known authors, whose larger *oeuvres* supply other forms of productive contexts for understanding. William Herebert, James Ryman, John Audelay, Charles d'Orléans and John Lydgate were between them evidently responsible for large numbers of short poems; small clutches also survive from what may once have been larger bodies of lyrics produced by Minot, Chaucer, Hoccleve and Skelton.[17] Recent new editions of the works of Herebert, Audelay and Charles d'Orléans, and the scholarship they have prompted, have indicated the extent to which the arrangement and sequencing of short poems can be a significant part of their collective meaning.[18] Similarly, the relationship of lyrics to larger contexts in which they are embedded, as in some of the works of Richard Rolle, or in Chaucer's *Book of the Duchess* or Skelton's

14 J. A. Burrow, 'Poems without Contexts: the Poems of Bodl. Rawl. D. 913', *Essays in Criticism* 29 (1979), 6–32, reprinted in *Essays in Middle English Literature* (Oxford, 1974), pp. 1–26.
15 See Greene, and Gray, *Selection*.
16 E. Wilson, ed., *A Descriptive Index of the English Lyrics in John of Grimestone's Preaching Book*, Medium Aevum Monographs, NS 2 (Oxford, 1973); H. Barr, ed., *The Digby Poems: A New Edition of the Lyrics* (Exeter, 2009).
17 For details, see the subject index to NIMEV and the searchable 'Author' field in DIMEV.
18 S. R. Reimer, ed., *The Works of William Herebert* (Toronto, 1987); S. G. Fein, ed., *John the Blind Audelay, Poems and Carols* (Oxford, Bodleian Library MS Douce 302) (Kalamazoo, MI, 2009); M.-J. Arn, ed., *Fortunes Stabilnes: Charles of Orléans's English Book of Love: A Critical Edition* (New York, 1994).

Garland of Laurel, have generated productive insights. Some of the attributable bodies of lyrics are preserved with manuscript apparatus full of useful pointers about the Middle English terminology appropriate to short poems: authors and scribes used for this verse words like *dite*, *tretys* and *traitie*, *song*, *complaynt* and *balade*, sometimes drawing attention to formal features, elsewhere to discursive function.

That details of this kind are coming to the fore in lyric scholarship is in part a result of the material turn in literary studies – a move that has illuminated understanding of premodern literary production in particular. The appeal of this new turn is at one level quite straightforward: to find a lyric inscribed on a spare part of an administrative document, or noted in the margins of a service book, or incised above a doorway, is a discovery that makes suddenly very clear the fact that these poems were a part of life, actually used by individuals for their own purposes. At another level, new attention to the original recording of lyrics in legible form, whether scribally or by some other means, is also making apparent the textual challenges that they sometimes pose, and the larger insights about matters such as literary composition, scribal practice and transmission, reading and reception to be derived from unravelling these.

In many different ways, these short and often ephemeral-seeming poems are inviting, miniature testing grounds for investigating medieval cultural practice and production. Their potential in this regard was abundantly demonstrated in the books produced within a few years of each other by Rosemary Woolf and by Douglas Gray – *The English Religious Lyric in the Middle Ages* (Oxford, 1968) and *Themes and Images in the Medieval English Religious Lyric* (London, 1972) – which in differently inflected ways directed attention to the bodies of exegesis, instruction and practice to which lyrics make reference in characteristically compressed form. The important influence of these books has been reinforced by the availability of a range of new editions of lyrics by Douglas Gray, John Hirsh and Thomas G. Duncan,[19] in all of which the larger-informing contexts of medieval knowledge, instruction, literary form and convention are made prominent, and which supply necessary information about textual matters and the forms in which lyrics were recorded and transmitted. While there have been barely any book-length studies of the Middle English lyric over the last fifteen years, nonetheless, these lyrics have entered many textual conversations and made their presence felt in books and articles with other overall emphases. As such, it is possible to discern a number of distinctively new approaches towards them, some of which are picked up and developed by the essays in our collection.

First, with regard to late Middle English religiosity, *affect* has taken centre stage: the expression or incitement of feeling, most recently interpreted using tools from 'history of emotions' studies. Clearly, this focus lends itself well to

---

19 Gray, *Selection*; J. Hirsh, ed., *Medieval Lyric: Middle English Lyrics, Ballads, and Carols* (Oxford, 2004); T. G. Duncan, ed., *Medieval English Lyrics 1200–1400* and *Late Medieval English Lyrics and Carols 1400–1530* (Harmondsworth, 1995 and 2000), later followed by Duncan.

the expressions of pathos that dominate many religious lyrics and, accordingly, these kinds of poems have often been the subject of renewed attention, read with an eye to their affective impact both in public and solitary settings.[20] There are important issues at stake here differentiating *affect* within the medieval lyric from Romantic and post-Romantic perceptions, most fully laid out by Hegel, of the lyric as the textual place where the private subject voices his or her moods and passions, and makes sense of the emotions that populate their inner life. 'History of emotion' studies has alerted us to the 'situatedness' of the emotions and their expression – dolour in an Emily Dickinson lyric is probably not at all the same thing as dolour in a fourteenth-century Marian lament. More specifically, Sarah McNamer, Jessica Brantley and others have brought lyric affect into relation with performativity, and have posed the possibility that many lyrics may function as 'scripts for feeling', mapping an exemplary set of emotional responses to the crucifixion or the nativity, which may be 'played out' publicly from a pulpit or privately within a household or cell, by indefinite numbers of devout speakers and readers.[21] In this collection, the essays of A. S. Lazikani, Daniel McCann and Hetta Howes focus on affective complexity and the representation of 'shame', building on many of these recent insights.

The idea of 'devotional performance' might, on the face of it, seem not completely dissimilar to the tendency of postwar Anglo-American New Criticism to identify the lyric speaker as a fictional persona, essentially turning the lyric into a dramatic monologue. That tendency has been discredited in the most recent transhistorical discussions of lyric, and replaced with a non-fictive, non-mimetic understanding of its voice and genre.[22] Again, work needs to be done to differentiate the voice of medieval lyric 'performance' from twentieth-century notions of 'persona', but David Lawton offers a useful opening through his discernment of a 'public interiority' governing much vernacular secular and devotional poetry, that is, an 'I' voice, simultaneously intimate yet available for use by many, vocalising desire, self-loathing, contrition and the will to reform, in the confidence that those expressions will fulfil the affective requirements of a wide spectrum of devotees.[23] This 'public interiority' is something very different from post-Romantic perceptions of the individual subject, set against society, and its fictional derivative, 'persona'. Denis Renevey's essay in this volume, building

---

20 S. McNamer, *Affective Meditation and the Invention of Medieval Compassion* (Philadelphia, 2010), was one of the most influential studies in this field. More recent books maintaining the same affective focus include A. S. Lazikani, *Cultivating the Heart: Feeling and Emotion in Twelfth- and Thirteenth-Century Religious Texts* (Cardiff, 2015), which includes a chapter on the Passion lyrics.

21 J. Brantley, *Reading in the Wilderness: Private Devotion and Public Performance in Late Medieval England* (Chicago, 2007), examines the ways in which the lyrics, poems and prayer texts in the important religious anthology, BL, Additional MS 37049, were read performatively within the Carthusian cell.

22 J. Culler, *Theory of the Lyric* (Boston, 2015), maps and approves this critical change of direction.

23 D. Lawton, *Voice in Later Medieval English Literature: Public Interiorities* (Oxford, 2017).

on these debates, examines the construction of one particular 'I' voice, that of the authorial self, in Charles d'Orléans's English poetry, and notes the potential of the short poem to offer a space where authorial intentions can be asserted and discussed. Mary Wellesley, similarly focused on the authorial 'I', charts the way in which the writing process and the physical book are given pride of place as a spur to devotion in Lydgate's *Fifteen Joys and Sorrows of Mary*.

In addition to affect and performativity, recent attention has also turned to the relation of medieval verse to the visual and musical arts, and to the *visuality* of these texts: their ability to conjure a mental picture. There has been a new willingness to read lyric poetry alongside a variety of visual expressions of devotion: church wall paintings, stained-glass programmes, sculptures and manuscript illuminations, and to view them as complementary modes, capable of augmenting and modifying one another's meaning. Jessica Brantley's 2007 monograph, reading text alongside image in London, British Library, Additional MS 37049, offers a seminal example of this approach.[24] It is continued in this volume by Katherine Zieman's energising interpretation of lyrics and iconography within a single opening in BL, Additional MS 37049, by A. S. Lazikani's sensitive juxtaposition of *On leome is in þis world ilist* with thirteenth-century insular church wall painting, and by Anne Marie D'Arcy's exploration of aureated verse in praise of the Virgin in relation to dazzlingly ornamented plastic representations of Mary in fifteenth-century culture.

The relation of medieval poetry to music has proved, if anything, even more fruitful. Over the last fifteen years a lively interdisciplinary exchange has sprung up between literary scholars and musicologists, dedicated to restoring the sonic dimensions of the lyric and the literary qualities of song.[25] The new discipline of 'sound studies' has played an important role in this; we are now beginning to register and record the presence of 'soundscapes' within medieval texts, and to interrogate the relation between word and sound. Voice is receiving increasing attention. These new currents are represented in this volume by Christiania Whitehead's examination of the part played by liturgical music in determining the dialogic structure of a well-known Passion lyric.

Interest in the sonic qualities of short poems has gone hand in hand with a new attentiveness to poetic form, evident throughout the discipline as a whole. The effects of rhyme, rhythm, repetition and sound patterning through the use of homonyms and other linguistic tools, upon the construction of meaning, have all become renewed and adventurous topics of consideration. Jonathan Culler

---

24 Brantley, *Reading in the Wilderness*.
25 In relation to French lyric and music, see A. Butterfield, *Poetry and Music in Medieval France* (Cambridge, 2002); E. Dillon, *The Sense of Sound: Musical Meaning in France, 1260–1300* (Oxford, 2012); 'Unwriting Medieval Song', *New Literary History* 46 (2015), 595–622. In relation to English lyric and music, see H. Deeming, *Song in British Sources, c.1150–1300* (London, 2013), and more generally, E. E. Leach, *Sung Birds: Music, Nature and Poetry in the Later Middle Ages* (Ithaca, NY, 2007); H. Deeming and E. E. Leach, eds, *Manuscripts and Medieval Song: Inscription, Performance, Context* (Cambridge, 2015).

has recently called for more importance to be given to form, both in relation to how we determine a lyric genre and how we register a lyric's impact, although he tends to discern a long-standing tension between form and linguistic meaning, which may not always hold true for the medieval corpus under survey.[26] Cristina Cervone, in one of only two recent book-length studies of Middle English poetics, similarly centralises form, although in her case, she interprets form more generously to encompass complex figuration and patterns of imagery.[27] In this volume, the effects of rhyme, rhythm, sound patterning and wordplay upon lyric meaning are variously explored in the essays of Daniel McCann, Jane Griffiths and Joel Grossman, while Thomas G. Duncan passionately defends the importance of metre and syllabic count to editorial decision making.

Cervone's focus on figuration arises from her thesis that poetic language is capable of embodying theological complexities and paradoxes that fall outside the purview of 'plain' language. This acknowledgement of the intellectual sophistication underpinning some religious figuration stands as a welcome corrective to the priority accorded to affect over the last decade (which can sometimes be construed in opposition to the intellect). An equivalent respect for the sophistication of vernacular figures, with regard to their capacity to propound literary theories, also informs recent work by Nicolette Zeeman.[28] Such threads are represented in this volume by Denis Renevey's revelation of poetic forms configured as banqueting dishes in Charles d'Orléans's *Ballade 84*, and Joel Grossman's scrutiny of the intellectual formal play that underpins Thomas Wyatt's menacing love lyrics.

Through the twentieth century, anthologies of medieval lyrics tended to be monolingual, extracting lyrics from their frequently multilingual manuscript contexts, subordinating or suppressing variant versions, and organising them into categories: 'the love lyric', 'the religious lyric', and so on, which gave very little sense of the mixed textual environments from which they originated. Over the last ten years, this approach has been supplemented by a very welcome emphasis on the 'whole book': that is, by editions that *retain* the lyric within its manuscript environment, enabling a much more satisfying appreciation of its situated function, and original circumstances of reading and reception. The flagship edition in this respect is undoubtedly the monumental, three-volume edition of London, British Library, Harley MS 2253, published 2014–15,[29] which truthfully reproduces the trilingual contents of the manuscript in the order in which they

---

26 Culler, *Theory of the Lyric*.
27 C. M. Cervone, *Poetics of the Incarnation: Middle English Writing and the Leap of Love* (Philadelphia, 2012). There has also been a recent focus on alliterative metrics: A. Putter, J. Jefferson and M. Stokes, *Studies in the Metres of Alliterative Verse* (Oxford, 2007); J. Jefferson and A. Putter, eds, *Approaches to the Metres of Alliterative Verse* (Leeds, 2009).
28 N. Zeeman, 'Imaginative Theory', *Middle English*, ed. P. Strohm (Oxford, 2007), pp. 222–40.
29 S. Fein, ed. and trans., with D. Raybin and J. Ziolkowski, *The Complete Harley 2253 Manuscript, Volumes 1–3*, TEAMS (Kalamazoo, MI, 2014–15). I. Nelson's chapter on Harley 2253 in *Lyric Tactics: Poetry, Genre and Practice in Later Medieval England* (Philadelphia,

were copied (together with facing translations, which render the Latin and French texts more readily accessible), demonstrating how comprehensively short verse intermingled with longer poetry and prose in other genres (saints' legends, biblical narratives and so on), and revealing the differing themes and agendas embedded in distinct booklets of the manuscript, often expressed via a generically varied choice of both poetry and prose. The edition of Harley 2253 has perhaps excited most interest, but we should also note Jessica Brantley's earlier study of Additional 37049, which devotes similar attention to the 'whole book'; Susanna Fein's 2009 edition of Oxford, Bodleian Library, MS Douce 302: a collection of John Audelay's poems and prayers, apparently supervised by the author; and John Fox and Mary-Jo Arn's 2010 edition of Paris, Bibliothèque nationale de France, MS fr. 25458, the manuscript that contains Charles d'Orléans's personal collection of French lyrics composed by the duke, his household and friends.[30] Recent attention to the 'whole book' has brought into relief the textual sequences that may be embedded within it, and may travel between different manuscripts. Susanna Fein introduces us to one such sequence, extant in Oxford, Jesus College, MS 29, in her essay in this collection. It has also engendered a much greater awareness of interlinguistic relationships and exchanges. Languages may rub up against one another comfortably or contestively within a single manuscript. They can also do the same within a single poem, and Mary C. Flannery's reading of a short macaronic lyric in Oxford, Bodleian Library, MS Douce 104 reveals a jovial scenario in which Latin and Middle English alternate to reveal mutual linguistic and moral shortcomings.

The editors of Harley 2253 implore us to let go of category terms: political lyric, courtly love lyric, and so on. If we are not to convene essays on a single 'whole book' (and that has already been carried out very ably in relation to Harley 2253 and the Auchinleck manuscript),[31] then perhaps the best place to start is with the single poem. More than one recent writer upon medieval poetry has prioritised *close reading*, again a trend discernible well beyond medieval literary scholarship.[32] But what should this entail ? How has our close reading changed from the groundbreaking lyric readings of Woolf and Gray, to whom we remain indebted? Ardis Butterfield provides us with some fruitful suggestions in her important 2015 essay, 'Why Medieval Lyric?'[33] Citing the extraordinary changeability of the medieval short poem – its propensity to change shape, size, spelling and verse order every time it is copied – which she appraises in positive

---

2017), pp. 31–58, shows the influence of this recent trend, paying due attention to the manuscript's trilingual lyricism.

[30] Brantley, *Reading in the Wilderness*; Fein, ed., *John the Blind Audelay, Poems and Carols*; J. Fox and M.-J. Arn, eds, *The Poetry of Charles d'Orléans and his Circle: A Critical Edition of BnF MS Fr. 25458* (Tempe, AZ, 2010).

[31] S. Fein, ed., *Studies in the Harley Manuscript*, TEAMS (Kalamazoo, MI, 2000); S. Fein, ed., *The Auchinleck Manuscript: New Perspectives* (York, 2016).

[32] Cervone, *Poetics of the Incarnation*.

[33] A. Butterfield, 'Why Medieval Lyric?', *English Literary History* 82 (2015), 319–43, responding to J. Culler's 2010 Cornell lecture, 'Why Lyric?'.

terms as its 'textual dynamism', she urges scholars to discard outdated ideas of a preferred or authoritative version, and instead to 'observe the protean and mobile core of a verse cluster traverse the landscape of a medieval intellectual's memory', keeping also in mind its 'shadowy hinterland of additional textual ... material'.[34] This chimes well with a number of the reading practices in this collection, in particular those grouped under '*Mouvance, Transformation*'.[35] Anne Baden-Daintree charts the reorderings and repurposings of *Vndo þi dore*, a lyric derived from the Song of Songs, in its different manuscript versions; Katherine Zieman maps the way in which small text units drawn from diverse parts of the Rollean *œuvre* are stitched together to form new lyrics; Julia Boffey observes the ability of succinct lyric statements to allude to much larger bodies of textual materials beyond their immediate parameters.[36]

How, in addition, should we react to the lyric interpolated into the midst of writing of a different generic character altogether? How is it informed by the textual material that surrounds it, and how does it modify that material in turn? Elizabeth Robertson considers the effect of the serried lyric interventions in *Troilus and Criseyde*, Book 2, on our perception of Criseyde's surrender to love, noting how they encode submerged references to violence beyond the ken of the conscious purview of the narrative at this point. Natalie Jones attends to the textual 'hinterland' of *Ihesus woundes so wide*, examining its intercalation into a longer devotional prose treatise in the single manuscript in which it survives.

Finally, the intractable question of genre definition has once again returned to the fore. Jonathan Culler's influential book *Theory of the Lyric* (2015) attempts to settle the question by proposing various 'constants' of lyric voice, form and behaviour, through history. As is so often the case, though, his panoramic account effectively jumps straight from Pindar and Horace to the Renaissance, Romantic and modern corpus, marginalising the medieval lyric, whose practical and didactic purposes map particularly problematically onto this classically oriented grand narrative. Ingrid Nelson's *Lyric Tactics: Poetry, Genre and Practice in Late Medieval England* (2017), a book-length study devoted by contrast to the medieval lyric, takes a very different tack, heavily inflected by De Certeau.[37] Working against Culler's belief in transhistorical essences, she identifies the lyric genre as ad hoc, improvisatory and, above all, 'tactical', carving out 'makeshift pathways among institutional structures', and nimbly insinuating itself around longer texts.[38] Here, genre becomes not a set of identities but a type of *practice*,

---

34 Butterfield, 'Why Medieval Lyric ?', pp. 336, 329.
35 The term *mouvance* was first coined by Paul Zumthor in 1972 to describe the high levels of textual variation discernible between different manuscript versions of a single poem. Because of this mobility he argued that texts should not be seen as possessions of a single author in the modern sense, but as productions that might be indefinitely reworked by others: *Essai de poétique médiévale* (Paris, 1972).
36 See also, Whitehead, who charts the changing forms and uses of *Stond wel, moder*, and two related Middle English lyrics, in their extant manuscripts.
37 M. de Certeau, *The Practice of Everyday Life* (Berkeley, CA, 1984).
38 Nelson, *Lyric Tactics*, pp. 4, 11.

an agility, if you like, to squeeze into small spaces and take advantage of cracks and openings. This collection certainly attends to lyrics that seem to behave in this fashion: Mary C. Flannery's *Tutivillus* lyric appended to the end of the Douce *Piers Plowman*, Michael P. Kuczynski's *All Other Love* pencilled into a manuscript otherwise populated by Latin canon law and theology. However, many of our other short poems are markedly less tactical and adaptive, situated stably at the centre of author-based collections, and attributed to a named poet (Audelay, Lydgate, Chaucer, Charles d'Orléans), and it seems wisest to allow this diverse range of dispositions and behaviours to speak for themselves rather than seeking to limit the field one way or the other.

The essays in this volume and the lyrics that they expound offer a snapshot of the vernacular poets and groups of poems that seem to be commanding interest at the present time: the religious corpora of Rolle, Lydgate and Audelay, the love poems of Charles d'Orléans, Chaucer reread by Robertson and others as a lyric poet,[39] the poem *On God Ureisun of Ure Lefdi* that accompanies the *Wooing Group* texts, but has been largely excluded from their analysis. It is brought to light here by Annie Sutherland, and explored and enjoyed from a primarily literary perspective. In five or ten years time, this list will have changed, and the checklist of approaches will have shifted to reflect new ways of thinking about poems. This volume stands as a snapshot of the present time, dedicated to an inclusive definition of the short poem and to the value of exploratory close reading. We hope it will prove useful.

---

39 See also, Nelson's chapter on 'Antigone's Song' within Chaucer's *Troilus and Criseyde*, in *Lyric Tactics*, pp. 88–116.

1

Editing Issues in Middle English Lyrics

Thomas G. Duncan

In 1979, in his edition of *Medieval English Songs*, Eric Dobson castigated the established practice of the then chief lyric collections where:

> [T]he texts of the manuscripts, as read by the editors, are mostly printed without even the most obvious necessary changes: abnormal spellings, false forms, bad rhyme and worse metre, irregular or impossible accidence and syntax, and even sheer nonsense left uncorrected.[1]

Why this lamentable failure of editors to edit? The answer lay partly in the chaotically corrupt state in which Middle English lyrics have survived. However incredible it may seem, where these lyrics are found in multiple copies, in not a single instance are any two versions of any one lyric found to be identical. Textual variations in different copies of the same lyric frequently manifest differences in wording, in word order, in order of lines, and even in order of stanzas, differences sometimes so bizarre as to suggest that scribes must not only often have copied carelessly but may sometimes have done so from memory, and often from bad memory at that. Indeed, as in the instances where lyrics survive in shorter and longer versions, it is evident that rewriting sometimes entered into the transmission process. This state of affairs gave rise to the assumption that Middle English lyrics were, by and large, corrupt beyond repair, and that the traditional procedures of textual criticism revered by editors of previous generations were defeated from the start. In particular, it seemed impossible to analyse surviving manuscripts in terms of the stemmata of classical editorial procedure whereby manuscript superiority leading to the privileging of more authoritative readings could be established.

Yet another important requirement of traditional editorial practice was lacking. As E. T. Donaldson observed concerning Chaucer, 'it is impossible to edit at all without having in mind some fairly strong preconception concerning

---

For another essay in this volume similarly focused on editing issues, see Chapter 4, Michael P. Kuczynski, 'Textual and Affective Stability in *All Other Love is Like the Moon*', pp. 57–70.

1   E. J. Dobson and F. Ll. Harrison, *Medieval English Songs* (London, 1979), p. 27, b.

the metre'.² Whether one thinks of classical Latin poetry or, indeed, of *Beowulf*, metre has played a vital role in arriving at editorial decisions. In the case of Middle English lyrics, however, one will search the older standard editions in vain for any sustained discussion of metre. A notion commonly, albeit often tacitly, accepted was that lyric scansion was appropriately to be analysed in terms of the number of stresses per line. G. L. Brook, the editor of the standard edition of the *Harley Lyrics*, briefly outlined this view. According to Brook, in these lyrics, stressed and unstressed syllables 'alternate fairly evenly as in Modern English versification'. Nevertheless, some lines have 'fewer stresses than we should expect'; and although Brook accepts that 'some of these lines may be corrupt', he takes the view that it is 'better to regard the occasional substitution of a three-stress for a four-stress line as a form of licence to avoid monotony'.³ However, such an account of metre involves questionable assumptions. One is that a medieval reader would have entertained the same aesthetic responses as G. L. Brook. Yet, would a Middle English reader or poet necessarily have shared Brook's sense of 'monotony'? If anything, the evidence tells against any such view. Thus, in a poem so carefully crafted as the Harley lyric, *Weping hath myn wongës wet*,⁴ where each stanza concludes with a quatrain of 'three-stress' lines, it seems gratuitous to assume that out of twenty-four such lines one should happen to be a 'four-stress' line simply 'to avoid monotony'. Yet this anomaly, at line 59, was accepted by Brook without question or comment.

A second and equally dubious assumption was the notion that it was satisfactory to describe this verse simply in terms of the number of stressed syllables per line. Two obvious problems immediately suggest themselves. The first is that it is often unclear what is to count as a 'stressed syllable'; is it a syllable carrying 'natural' stress, or perhaps 'metrical', or perhaps 'rhetorical' stress? A second, and even more serious issue is that the question of unstressed syllables is left out of account. It had often been assumed that Middle English poets, accustomed to a measure of flexibility with regard to the number of unstressed syllables in traditional native alliterative verse, were happy with some variation in the syllable-count of their lines even when writing non-alliterative, stanzaic verse. However true of some looser verse, unsupported by any systematic analysis this view was hardly more than a sweeping generalisation. Inevitably, then, in the absence of some fairly strong preconception concerning the metre, it is not surprising that earlier editors often found it impossible, with any confidence, to resort to emendation *metri causa*.

Granted, then, that earlier scholars may have been inhibited by reservations as regards the applicability to Middle English lyrics of traditional editorial procedures and, furthermore, were severely limited by the lack of any adequate concept of metrical analysis, it is, perhaps, not surprising that what they offered were

2 E. T. Donaldson, 'The Manuscripts of Chaucer's Works and Their Use', *Writers and their Background: Geoffrey Chaucer*, ed. D. Brewer (London, 1974), p. 99.
3 Brook, p. 18.
4 Duncan, I, 27, pp. 78–9.

virtually diplomatic editions, that is to say, transcriptions of the manuscript texts in which attempts at editing were, at best, minimal and sporadic. Nevertheless, editions of this kind by such major scholars as Carleton Brown in the 1920s and 1930s, and G. L. Brook and Rossell Hope Robbins in the 1940s and 1950s, did indeed become 'standard' in so far as they were forerunners in their day and long continued to be the main source of the texts printed in subsequent anthologies and selections. Notably, however, in one such, the Norton Critical Edition of 1974, the editors, Maxwell S. Luria and Richard L. Hoffman, in acknowledging that their texts were mainly derived from Brown, Robbins and Brook, observed that 'a new edition, with variants, of the complete corpus of lyrics, based on modern editorial procedures, remains a *desideratum*'.[5]

What modern editorial procedures might Luria and Hoffman have had in mind? Doubtless one was the abandonment of recension as an indispensable part of the editorial process. By 1974, it was no longer the case that variant readings lacking the authoritative status derived from manuscript stemmata were automatically rejected as suspect or even worthless. Already in 1960, a radically new editorial approach had appeared in the 'Introduction' to George Kane's edition of the A-text of *Piers Plowman*.[6] It no longer mattered if, as in the case of Middle English lyrics surviving in multiple copies, it proved impossible to construct plausible stemmata. It was now open to an editor to take account of all extant readings in seeking to establish a 'good' text.

But what of the lack of a metrical hypothesis adequate to the editorial task? No advance had been made on this front. Two obvious obstacles stood in the way of arriving at such a hypothesis. First, no contemporary account of the metrical principles and practices of Middle English lyric poets has survived, if, indeed, any such treatise was ever written. Second, whereas it is clear to a present-day reader how many syllables are to be pronounced in a modern English text, in a Middle English text this is far from immediately self-evident. In seeking a defensible metrical hypothesis it has therefore been necessary in the first place to seek evidence independent of the actual written texts. Two such sources of evidence suggested themselves: one was the verse tradition from which Middle English stanzaic lyrics derived, French and Latin songs; the other was the music that survived with some Middle English lyrics.

In seeking a defensible metrical hypothesis it seemed reasonable to begin by considering the evidence of the verse tradition of French and Latin songs. A fundamental requirement of a song is that its words should fit the tune, and do so for all stanzas, a requirement that calls for a considerable degree of regularity. From a study of troubadour and *trouvère* songs, John Stevens concluded that in the matching of words and music the 'most important single controlling factor

---

5   M. S. Luria and R. L. Hoffman, eds, *Middle English Lyrics* (New York and London, 1974), p. ix.
6   G. Kane, ed., *Piers Plowman: The A-Version* (London, 1960).

is the number of syllables in any given line or stanza'.[7] It was, therefore, plausible to suppose that in English stanzaic lyrics within this tradition (whether surviving with music or not) the principal poetic constraint continued to be a matter of a syllabic match, line for line and stanza by stanza.

How well, then, does syllable-count fare as an operative poetic constraint in non-alliterative, stanzaic lyric verse when we turn to the evidence of Middle English lyrics themselves? Here, alas, major problems arise. First, whereas it is clear to a present-day reader how many syllables are represented in a modern English text, in Middle English not all the syllables in a line of verse as written were necessarily pronounced. The most obvious difficulty arises with the interpretation of the endings final '-e', '-est', '-eth', '-ed' and '-es'. For instance, it is evident, not least from Chaucer's verse, that not infrequently the verb endings '-est' and '-eth', written as full forms, conceal reduced pronunciations; and there is evidence to suggest that in the case of final '-ed' and '-es', the option of reduced endings was already available to poets even as early as the thirteenth century. As for the notorious problem of final '-e', it is evident that from early Middle English through to the fifteenth century poets had the metrical option of treating this '-e' as pronounced or silent. Furthermore, other syllables in a Middle English text *as written* may or may not have been pronounced, depending on the operation of phonetic principles such as elision, hiatus, synizesis, syncope and apocope, principles fundamental to any appraisal of metre. Elision, syncope, synizesis and apocope are processes of phonetic reduction operative within the spoken chain of speech, processes often masked by spelling in Middle English texts. Such phonetic operations may be illustrated by an analysis of the lyric *Miri it is while sumer i-last*,[8] a lyric surviving with music in Oxford, Bodleian Library, MS Rawlinson G. 22, fol. 1v. The first line, '[M]irie it is while sumer ilast' as written by the thirteenth-century scribe (the initial 'M' is not completed), appears potentially to number eleven syllables: /mi-ri-e-it-is-whil-e-sum-mer-i-last/. As pronounced within the chain of speech, however, it emerges as a line of seven syllables by virtue of the following phonetic operations.

First, by elision, which arose where a vowel at the end of a word was absorbed by an initial vowel (or 'h' plus vowel) of the following word, the final '-e' of *Mirie* would have been absorbed by the initial vowel of the following *it*. Second, by synizesis, a form of elision in which the vowel /i/ (in Middle English spelt 'i' or 'y') combines with a following vowel to become the corresponding semi-vowel /j/ (the sound of 'y' in 'yet'), /mir-i-it/ would be further reduced to /mir-yit/. Third, by apocope, which involves the suppression in Middle English verse of a final unaccented vowel before a following consonant to preserve the rhythmic pattern of one weak syllable between two accented syllables, the final '-e' of *while* is silent, leaving *whil* as a single weak syllable between the stressed syllables *is*

---

[7] J. Stevens, *The Old Sound and the New: An Inaugural Lecture* (Cambridge, 1982), p. 2. See also J. Stevens, *Words and Music in the Middle Ages: Song, Narrative, Dance and Drama, 1050–1350* (Cambridge, 1986).

[8] NIMEV 2163. Duncan, I, 36, p. 87.

Fig. 1: An edited version of the words and music of *Miri it is while sumer i-last*

and *sum* of *sumer*, i.e. giving the rhythm 'ís-whil-súm'. Fourth, by syncope, which frequently occurred where words ending in '-el', '-en' or '-er' were followed by a word beginning with a vowel (or 'h' plus vowel), the last two words in this line are to be read as three syllables (i.e. /sum-ri-last/) with the reduction by syncope of the second syllable of *sumer*. It may be added that a perplexed present-day reader might take comfort from the fact that the Middle English spelling of this line misled the medieval music scribe to add notes to cover all eleven syllables, thus destroying the syllabic and musical match of lines 1 and 3 and leaving an egregiously long first line completely at variance with a stanza form of seven lines, realised here in syllable count and rhyme as 7a, 4b, 7a, 4b, 7b, 7b, 5a.[9] The edited version of both music and words shown here clearly reveals the stanza structure and the essential syllabic match of the first and third lines.

One further issue has to be taken into account in assessing Middle English lyric metre. Middle English scribes tended to alter the language of the texts they copied to accord with the pronunciation and usage of their own dialects, and the spelling habits that prevailed in the schools or scriptoria where they had learnt to write. This common practice is known as 'linguistic revision' and gave rise to common variants such as: *havest / hast; haveth / hath; haveth / haven / have / han; haved / had; for to / to; upon / on; unto / to; other / or; also / so, as; muchel / much; loverd / lord; lavedy / lady; heved / hed; ne wot / not; never / ner*, and single *ne, nought* and double *ne ... nought* negatives.[10] Clearly metre was vulnerable to such scribal 'linguistic revision'. Chaucer was all too aware of this, as his famous plea at the close of *Troilus and Criseyde* makes clear:

And for ther is so gret diversite	*because; diversity*
In Englissh and in writyng of oure tonge,	
So prey I God that non myswrite the,	*thee*
Ne the mysmetre for defaute of tonge.[11]	*lack of skill in language*

Evidently Chaucer did suffer from a great deal of 'miswriting' and consequent 'mismetring'. E. Talbot Donaldson offers a telling illustration of the problem by detailing the eleven different versions of line 19 of the 'General Prologue' to *The Canterbury Tales*, found in twenty-seven authorities:

Bifel that in that sesoun on a day
Bifel that <u>on</u> that sesoun on a day
Bifel that in that sesoun <u>upon</u> a day
Bifel it in that sesoun on a day
Bifel ___ in that sesoun on a day
Bifel ___ in that sesoun <u>upon</u> a day
<u>And</u> fel ___ in that sesoun on a day
<u>It</u> bifel that in that sesoun on a day
<u>It</u> bifel <u>than</u> in that sesoun <u>upon</u> a day
<u>So</u> bifel <u>it</u> ___ that sesoun on a day
<u>So</u> <u>it</u> bifel ___ that sesoun on a day[12]

From the foregoing it is evident that metrical reading of Middle English verse depends crucially on taking these linguistic and scribal issues into account.

---

9   See T. G. Duncan, 'Two Middle English Penitential Lyrics: Sound and Scansion', *Late-Medieval Religious Texts and Their Transmission*, ed. A. J. Minnis (Cambridge, 1994), pp. 55–65 for a full discussion of the metre of this poem.
10 Numerous examples of 'mismetering' and spoilt rhymes caused by variants adopted by scribes other than the forms of the original authors are readily to be seen by comparing the texts of lyrics printed from more than one manuscript in Brown *XIII*. See also Duncan, I, 75. Commentary, line 14 n., p. 347.
11 Benson, *Troilus and Criseyde*, V, lines 1793–6, p. 584, with addition of glosses.
12 Donaldson, 'Manuscripts of Chaucer's Works', p. 99.

However, when read in the light of these considerations, it turns out that many stanzaic lyrics do indeed reveal a marked consistency in syllable count, a consistency confirming the legitimacy of this syllabic metrical hypothesis. In essence, syllable count is clearly as fundamental a principle of Middle English lyric verse as it is of troubadour and *trouvère* songs and, indeed, of Chaucer's decasyllabic line.

Granted, then, radical changes in editorial theory since the middle of the last century, a plausible hypothesis concerning metre (a tool so essential to the editorial task), an informed awareness of phonetic principles operative in the speech-chain of Middle English verse, and a recognition of the kinds of variant readings especially characteristic of Middle English scribes, not least those arising from 'linguistic revision', there is no longer any justification – even faced with the corruption so endemic in the surviving copies of Middle English lyrics (whether corruption of metre, rhyme, order of lines, loss of lines, stanza structure, stanza order, wording, word order, grammar, syntax, or, indeed, sense) – for shirking the editorial task of seeking, wherever possible, to remove such corruptions by emendation. The editor's obligation is, as Dobson put it, not 'to reproduce the texts given by the scribes, but to recover as far as might be the text written by the original author'.[13] In doing so, the editor must re-examine the source manuscripts and, whenever emendation is attempted, supply a textual apparatus recording the original readings of the base manuscript and of other relevant manuscripts. Moreover, in defending emendation, full account should be taken of such traditional scribal errors as haplography, dittography, letter confusion, eyeskip and the like. What follows offers sample instances of a range of essential emendations hitherto overlooked.

In the standard lyric collections of the twentieth century such evident corruptions as spoilt rhymes were often left standing even where plausible emendation readily suggests itself. For instance, the lyric *My folk, now answerë mei*,[14] from Edinburgh, National Library of Scotland, Advocates' MS 18. 7. 21, fol. 125, is written in four-line stanzas rhyming a, b, a, b. The eighth stanza of this poem is printed by Brown as:

A kingges yerde i the be-tok	king's scepter I granted you
til thu were al be-forn;	until; above all (others)
& thu heng me on rode tre,	
& corounnedist me with a thorn.[15]	crowned

The obvious fault in the rhyme scheme here, the failure of the 'a' rhymes, is passed over in silence by Brown. This fault, however, may easily be corrected by reversing the order of the last two words of the first line, i.e. by changing *the be-tok* to *be-tok the*. Initially, this seemed to me a highly plausible emendation; scribes not infrequently inverted word order as they copied. In the event,

---

13 Dobson and Harrison, *Medieval English Songs*, p. 27, b.
14 NIMEV 2240; DIMEV 3598. Duncan, I, 100, pp. 152–3.
15 Brown *XIV*, no. 72, lines 29–32, with addition of glosses.

however, an examination of the manuscript proved gratifyingly rewarding. Close inspection revealed that the word *the* had been marked by double ticks for transposition. Even if Brown had failed to notice it, the scribe had in fact corrected his own mistake! This first line was indeed correctly to be read as: 'A kingges yerde i be-tok the', with *the* rhyming with *tre* in the third line.

If spoilt rhymes in Middle English lyrics were not infrequently ignored, in many instances metrical corruption was left standing even where there are plausible grounds for emendation. A blatant instance of editorial failure to restore corrupt metre is evident in the case of the lyric *Now I se blosmë sprynge*.[16] This poem survives in two manuscripts, London, British Library, Royal MS 2 F VIII, fol. 1v, and London, British Library, Harley MS 2253, fol. 76. Its scansion is very simple: ten-line stanzas with almost all lines of six syllables, and a sustained three-stress rhythm. It was printed from the Royal MS by Carleton Brown, by Bennett and Smithers, by Silverstein, and by Celia and Kenneth Sisam. All retained the metrically short Royal reading of the third line, 'A swete longinge', despite the Harley reading, 'A suete loue-longynge', with six syllables as metrically required. No account was taken of the fact that the Royal reading *longinge* has all the appearance of a corruption arising from the common scribal error known as haplography, that is, the writing of a letter, or series of letters, once instead of twice. Granted the potentially indistinguishable appearance of the minim letters 'u' (for 'v') and 'n', an original *louelongynge* (perhaps spelt without the first 'e' as *loulongynge*) has been miscopied with the omission of the initial syllable *lou / loue*, as *longynge*. Here, then, an obvious emendation *metri causa* has been ignored by earlier editors, and that despite the clear support of another, the Harley manuscript. The validity of the third line as emended following the Harley reading is evident to the ear from reading even the first four lines of the poem:

> Now I se blosmë sprynge,   *blossom flourish*
> Ich herde a foulës song,   *I heard a bird's song*
> A swetë love-longynge
> Myn hertë thurghout sprong. (lines 1–4)   *throughout; has sprung up*

There are many lyrics, however, where no other copy survives to offer support for metrical emendations. In such cases emendation *metri causa* is inevitably more problematic. Nevertheless, where such lyrics are, on the whole, evidently metrically regular, it is arguably inadequate to leave occasional lines limping where typical scribal errors of the kind discussed above are plausibly at fault. For instance, the lyric *Thayr ys no myrth under the sky*,[17] which survives uniquely in Oxford, Bodleian Library, MS Arch. Selden. supra 52, fols 168v–169v, has, from the first of its six stanzas, all the appearance of metrical regularity:

---

16 NIMEV 3963; DIMEV 6334. Duncan, I, 69, pp. 122–4.
17 NIMEV 3534; DIMEV 5580. Duncan, II, 20, pp. 201–2.

	Thayr ys no myrth under the sky,	*no pleasure*
	Harpyng, lutyng, nor mery dance,	
	That may put owt my swet lady	*may oust*
	All fro my daly remembrance.	*entirely from my daily*
5	Yie be the birde of all plesance,	*you are the mistress of all delight*
	My lady gent with love inbraste,	*my gracious lady embraced with love*
	Full comly ys youre countenance –	*comely*
	Be trew, lady, for I you truste. (lines 1–8)	*be true*

Only in the second line, where *nor* here replaces the manuscript reading *nor no*, a typical case of scribal reduplication, has emendation been required. However, despite the overall metrical regularity of this poem, three instances of faulty metre occur in the manuscript version of the final stanza, lines 41–8. In the edited version quoted below, emendations have been made as follows: 42 Medyscyne] And medyscyne MS; 45 may] that may MS; 47 on] apon MS. The rejected readings here have all the appearance of the kind of scribal variants commonly found as alternative readings where lyrics survive in multiple copies:

	Yie are the salyfe unto my sore,	*you are the ointment for my wound*
	Medyscyne to myne infirmité;	
	My tonge cane not expresse tharfor	*can*
	The secunde parte of youre beauté.	*half (lit. the second part)*
45	Ther yse no surrance may hurte me,	*no affliction*
	Nor no sorow bot I shall cayste,	*which I shall not cast out*
	When I think on your love so fre –	*so noble*
	By trew, lady, for I you truste. (lines 41–8)	

Note that *Medyscyne* in line 42 may, by syncope, be pronounced as two syllables; indeed, the reduced spelling 'medcin(e)' sometimes occurs in Middle English. Yet even if the restoration of so essential an aspect of lyric form as metre by such emendations (emendations that in no way alter the sense) is arguably a proper editorial duty, it cannot, of course, be claimed that the emended readings necessarily restore the original readings of the lyric as first composed. Emendation is always to some degree a speculative venture. However, an adequate textual apparatus, an essential part of any satisfactory edition, will readily make available the readings of the source manuscript to those who take a sceptical view of such emendations.

The misordering of stanzas is another common result of scribal error in Middle English lyrics. A conspicuous instance of this kind of corruption occurs in a lyric entitled by Carleton Brown *Penitence for Wasted Life*. Brown simply prints the final two stanzas of this poem as found in the manuscript, London, British Library, Additional MS 27909, fol. 2:

Leuedi sainte marie, understond nu seonne mine;	*dear, sins*
ber min erende wel to deire sune þine,	*petition*
hwas flech & blod ihalwed is of bred, of water, of wine,	*whose, consecrated*
þat us ischulde he eure fram alle helle-pine.	*the pains of hell*

Inne mete & inne drinke ic habbe ibeo ouerdede,	*excessive*
& inne wel sittende schon in pruttere iwede;	*shoes, clothing*
hwanne ich ihurde of gode speke ne hedd ich hwat me sede –	*when, I heeded not*
hwan ich hier-of rekeni schal, wel sore me mei drede.[18]	*take account*

The anomaly presented by the final stanza is thereby ignored.

This lyric has eleven stanzas. In stanza 1 the poet appeals to the Virgin for help as, in perplexity, he reflects on his sinful life. Stanzas 2–8 give an account of his sins. In stanza 9 he again addresses the Virgin, praying for her help to reform. He then asks Mary, in stanza 10, to bear his petition to Christ, in order that Christ, through the sacrament of his sacrifice, should protect us from hell. It is at this point, where the poem might have been expected to end, that another stanza follows, a stanza that does not fit any thought sequence and which makes for an odd and inappropriate ending to this penitential poem. The problem of this anomalous final stanza in the manuscript can, however, readily be solved if it is reconsidered in the context of the overall sense-development of the poem. At stanza 7, the poet turns to charitable deeds, which he defines as feeding the hungry, clothing the naked and guiding the ignorant. He ends this stanza with an injunction to love God ' … and of him habbe drede' (line 28). The anomalous stanza, found as the final stanza in the manuscript, would follow naturally at this point, for in it the poet confesses that, by contrast, he has overfed himself, overclad himself, and has thereby ignored God's word (i.e. to feed the hungry and clothe the naked mentioned in stanza 7). Therefore, he concludes, ' … wel sore me mei drede' (line 44).

How then did this stanza come to be misplaced at the end of the poem? In the manuscript this lyric is in fact written out as prose. Coloured initials, alternately green and red, mark the beginnings of the stanzas. These initials, of course, as effectively draw attention to the final word of each stanza. In the original stanza order, with the anomalous final stanza of the manuscript copy correctly following stanza 7, there would have been two successive stanzas ending with the same rhyme word *drede*. Obviously, a scribe, having copied the word *drede* at the end of stanza 7, has looked back to his exemplar to have his eye caught by *drede* at the end of the original stanza 8, and has simply moved on to copy the next stanza (the original stanza 9), thus omitting a stanza. Here, again, we have a classic instance of the common scribal error known as 'eyeskip'. On looking back over his finished copy, however, the scribe noticed his omission and then added the stanza he had left out at the end of the poem. With this final stanza of the manuscript copy restored to its rightful place, the second last stanza, with

---

18 NIMEV 1839; DIMEV 3029. Brown *XIII*, no. 2, lines 37–44, with added glosses. The letters 'wynn' and 'yogh' of Brown's transcription have been altered to 'w' in the version of his text quoted here.

its petition to the Virgin, emerges in its true role as the proper conclusion of this poem.[19]

The common scribal errors haplography and eyeskip gave rise to corruption in the sole-surviving copy of the well-known lyric *Adam lay i-bowndyn*.[20] This poem is sometimes printed in eight long lines (as written in London, British Library, Sloane MS 2593, fol. 11), and sometimes as sixteen short lines. In the short-line version, lines 7 and 8 (line 4 of the long-line version) are variously given as:

> As clerkes fyndyn wretyn
> in here book

or as:

> As clerkes fyndyn
> wretyn in here book.

One critic, Edmund Reiss, opens his discussion of the long-line version of this poem with the observation that:

> On the surface a naive, unsophisticated ballad-like piece, even revealing faulty meter – as in line 4 – this lyric still has a compelling quality that stems from its simple language and the combination of its rhythms and sounds.[21]

However, Reiss does not clarify his point about 'faulty meter'. Yet, if, as he claims, 'the combination of its rhythms and sounds' so significantly determines this poem's 'compelling quality', a metrical anomaly surely invites further comment. Another critic, Stephen Mannyng, speaks of lyrics that 'so relate sound and sense that the sound structure buttresses the sense'.[22] Since he offers the poet of *Adam* as his example of one who 'exacts this very quality from his meter precisely because he has penetrated the significance of his topic',[23] it would be reasonable to expect him to address himself to the metrical peculiarities in this poem. This, however, he does only briefly:

> In fact, [he observes] lines 7–8 and line 12 have to be squeezed into the meter, to be syncopated as it were, yet this is precisely what the poem demands.[24]

Yet, how this process of metrical squeezing works and why it is 'precisely what the poem demands' are matters that, alas, Mannyng leaves unexplained. What is clear is that Mannyng accepts, without question, the integrity of the text as it

---

19 A notable instance of stanzas copied in the wrong order is found in the sole surviving version of the lyric *A wayle whyte as whalles bon* in Harley 2253. The restored stanza order is given in Duncan, I, 2, pp. 55–6. See T. G. Duncan, 'Textual Notes on Two Early Middle English Lyrics', *Neuphilologische Mitteilungen* 93 (1992), 109–20.
20 NIMEV 117; DIMEV 215. Duncan, I, 108, p. 161.
21 E. Reiss, *The Art of the Middle English Lyric* (Athens, GA, 1972), p. 139.
22 S. Mannyng, *Wisdom and Number* (Lincoln, NE, 1962), p. 6.
23 Ibid., p. 6.
24 Ibid., p. 7.

stands in the manuscript. In the case of Middle English lyrics, however, such an assumption is, as we have seen, wholly unwarranted.

It was the practice of the scribe of Sloane 2593 to write his poems in long lines and sometimes to divide these lines into two parts by marking the end of the first unit with a point. Thus he copies this lyric in eight long lines, six of which he divides in this manner with points after *i-bowndyn* (line 1), *wynter* (line 2), *appil* (first occurrence, line 3), *wretyn* (line 4), *lady* (line 6) and *syngyn* (line 8). It is clear that this scribe was at pains to save space. The manuscript pages are small and in many poems he fills up his page by copying the last line of each stanza in the right-hand margin. Furthermore, each poem is divided off from the next not by a space but simply by a line drawn right across the page. It may be, therefore, that the scribe did not regard his written lines as units of structure as the word 'line' is now used with reference to poetic form. Rather it seems that his long lines may merely have been an economic way of combining two units to save space. In this case, this poem is more appropriately to be viewed as one of sixteen units or (expressed in modern terms) sixteen lines and, when economy of space is not at issue, more appropriately so to be printed.

Granted a sixteen-line arrangement, lines 7–8 are the first and second parts of the long line 4 of the manuscript copy. A point after *wretyn* indicates that the scribe took the first part of this line (up to *wretyn*) as a complete unit. Line 7 should, therefore, read:

As clerkes fyndyn wretyn.

It is line 8, 'in here book', which is evidently imperfect and calls for emendation. The required emendation readily suggests itself: lines 7–8 should read:

As clerkes fyndyn wretyn,
   wretyn in here book.

The addition of *wretyn* in line 8 not only restores the otherwise faulty metre but, crucially, it also complies with a striking characteristic of this poem, namely repetition, as in the repetition of *i-bowndyn* of line 1 as *bowndyn* in line 2, the repetition of *an appil* of line 5 in line 6, and of *the appil take ben* of line 9 in line 10. Moreover, the presumed omission of *wretyn* by the Sloane scribe (or in an earlier copy) would again have arisen from that previously mentioned common scribal error, haplography.

What Mannyng and Reiss failed to notice is the problem in the Sloane reading of line 9: 'Ne hadde the appil take ben'. As it stands, this line is also manifestly corrupt: ending with the word *ben*, it has one syllable too many, indeed, one stress too many, and introduces a rhyme with the following line (albeit a self-rhyme), which is at variance with the rhyme scheme of this poem. Again, a simple emendation is not far to seek – the omission of *ben* in line 9. Lines 9–10 should read:

Ne hadde the appil takë,
   the appil taken ben.

Thus emended, the metre is restored. The extra *ben* after *takë* in line 9 is readily to be accounted for as a mistake in copying, deriving from a scribe's eye having caught *taken ben* of the next phrase, i.e. another instance of 'eyeskip'. Telling confirmation of this emendation is found in considering the nature of repetition in this poem, which is characteristically partial and incremental. Thus, *i-bowndyn* of line 1 is repeated and completed as *bowndyn in a bond* in line 2, *an appil* of line 5 as *an appil that he took* in line 6, and now, *the appil takë* of line 9 as *the appil taken ben*, in line 10. This emendation restores this incremental characteristic here while also restoring metre and rhyme scheme. It is somewhat surprising that Mannyng and Reiss should have been so ready to advance aesthetic assertions with such confidence on the basis of questionable metre. It may be noted, however, that the following metrically restored version of this poem in effect strengthens Mannyng's contention that here 'the strong beat supports the sense of joy'[25] – and that, be it added, without recourse to ungainly squeezing and syncopating:

> Adam lay y-bownden,
> > bownden in a bond,
> Fower thousand wynter,
> > thought he not to long.
>
> And al was for an appil,
> > an appil that he took,
> As clerkës fynden writen,
> > writen in here book.   *their*
>
> Ne hadde the appil takë,
> > the appil takë ben,
> Ne haddë never our lady
> > have ben hevenë quen.   *queen of heaven*
>
> Blessëd be the tymë
> > the appil takë was,
> Therfore we mown singen,   *may*
> > 'Deo gratias'!   *Thanks be to God!*

Sense may sometimes be an issue to confront an editor, not, however, only 'common' sense but crucially 'poetic' sense. The fifteenth-century lyric *Whan netilles in wynter bere rosis rede*[26] employs the rhetorical figure known as *adynaton*. This device, which originated in classical literature, involves the stringing together of a series of impossibilities, a characteristic means of expressing the common medieval poetic topos of the 'world upside-down', i.e. the depiction of a crazy world in which absurdities prevail and, typically, roles are reversed: the ass plays the lute, the ox dances, the hare is bold, the

---

25 *Ibid.*, p. 7.
26 NIMEV 3999; DIMEV 6384. Duncan, II, 136, pp. 299–300.

lion timorous, and so on.[27] However, the thematic absurdity of the second stanza of this poem (i.e. that of fish as hunters) breaks down at lines 11–12 if either of the readings of the surviving sources (*grengese* in Oxford, Balliol College, MS 354, fol. 250v, or *goslynges* in Oxford, Bodleian Library, MS Eng. poet. e. 1, fols 43v–45 and London, British Library, Printed Book IB. 55242, fol. 477v) is retained. As found in the Balliol manuscript these lines read:

| And gornardes shote rolyons owt of a crosse bowe, | *gurnards; fish* |
| And grengese ride hunting the wolf to overthrowe. | *goslings* |

This defect is easily made good if it is assumed that a scribe has mistakenly transposed *grengese* and *rolyons* in lines 11 and 12. Thus emended as:

| And gornardes shote grengese owt of a crosse bowe, | *gurnards (fish) shoot goslings* |
| And rolyons ride huntyng the wolf to overthrowe, | *fish* |

'Poetic' sense is restored with the removal of the anomaly of goslings instead of fish as hunters. The resultant alliteration of *gornardes* and *grengese* in line 11 and *rolyons* and *ride* in line 12 supports this emendation. It would appear from the Bodleian manuscript reading – *rokes* (for *rolyons*) in line 11 – that at least one medieval scribe spotted the inconsistency of fish hunting fish in this stanza.

Scribes sometimes accidentally omitted lines. Error of this kind is found in the fifteenth-century lyric *Freers, freers, wo ye be!*[28] This poem takes the form of a sequence of quatrains rhyming a, b, a, b. However, it ends with a group of only three lines. Robbins, apparently aware of this anomaly, dealt with it by means of detaching the final line from the text as a whole and printing it separately under the poem as a kind of appendage, thus leaving the poem to end with a mere final couplet.[29] However, as written in the manuscript, Cambridge, Trinity College, MS O. 2. 40, fol. 58v, there is nothing whatsoever to suggest that this line, 'Omnes dicant "Amen"', is anything other than an integral part of the poem (see fig. 2).

Clearly the final quatrain is incomplete: the penultimate line (line 43) has accidentally been omitted. This missing line must have rhymed with *trinité* of line 41 and, as part of this Trinitarian conclusion, must have been something like 'Three in one and one in three'. The required rhyme, metre and sense are all met here by the line 'All one God and persones thre' borrowed from another Middle English lyric, *Almyghty God, fadir of hevene*.[30] Thus completed, the concluding quatrain reads:

---

27 See E. R. Curtius, *Literature and the Latin Middle Ages*, trans. W. R. Trask (New York, 1953), pp. 94–8.
28 NIMEV 871; DIMEV 1456. Duncan, II, 141, pp. 303–4.
29 Robbins *Hist.*, no. 67.
30 NIMEV 241; DIMEV 417. Duncan, II, 84, pp. 259–60, line 18. The poem is edited here from London, British Library, Harley MS 2406, fol. 8v.

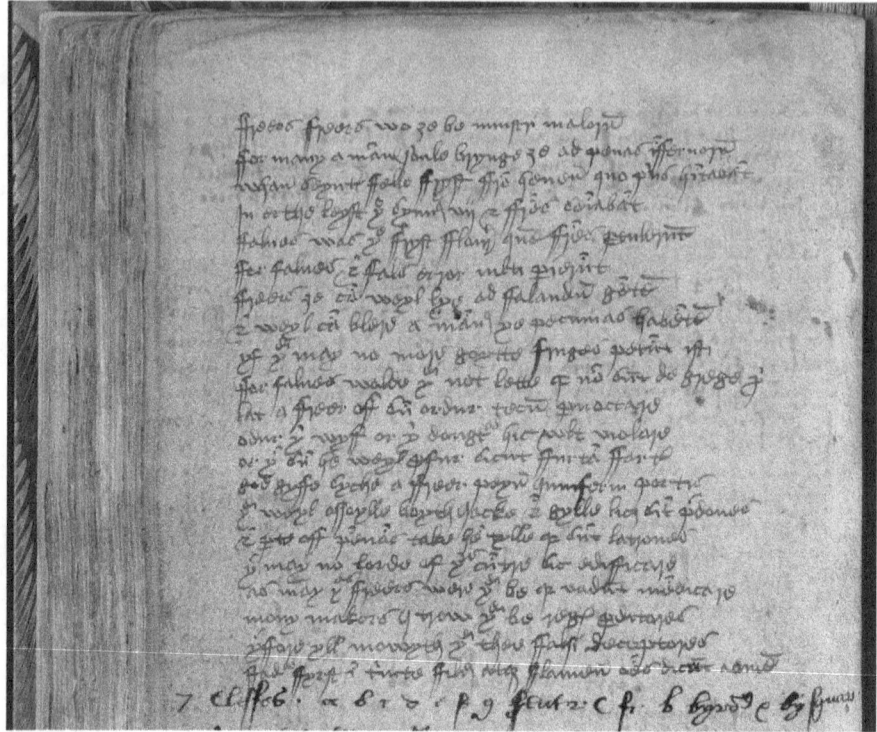

Fig. 2: Cambridge, Trinity College, MS O. 2. 40, detail of fol. 58v. By kind permission of the Master and Fellows of Trinity College, Cambridge

> Fader fyrst in trinité,
>   Filius atque flamen,   *Son and spirit*
> All one God and persones thre,
>   Omnes dicant 'Amen'.   *Let all say 'Amen'.*

Admittedly the supplying of a missing line is a conjectural procedure. An editor might indeed prefer to indicate such a lacuna simply by a series of dots. However, where, as here, rhyme, metre and sense can so convincingly be met, the case for supplying a missing line to complete the formal structure of the quatrain is defensible provided that a textual apparatus and commentary alert the reader to the emendation.[31]

---

31 Similarly, in the carol entitled *A Call for a Song* (NIMEV 1609), in C. Sisam and K. Sisam, ed., *The Oxford Book of Medieval English Verse* (Oxford, 1970), no. 259, p. 540, a line missing in the sole manuscript source, Oxford, Balliol College, MS 354, fol. 251v, is supplied to complete the first stanza. This line, which fits the rhyme scheme and makes appropriate sense, is adopted in *Is ther any good man here* (Duncan, II, 124, pp. 290–1, line 10). Again, where sense is not affected in any crucial way and the rhythm and flow

A 'new edition, with variants, of the complete corpus of lyrics, based on modern editorial procedures' as envisaged by Luria and Hoffman may remain some way off. As progress is made towards this ideal, it remains appropriate to pay tribute to the considerable contribution of such scholarly pioneers as Brown, Brook, Robbins and Greene. Nevertheless, the ultimate goal in the editing of literary texts must be the restoration of artistic integrity. It is to be hoped that further research, enlarging upon and refining the issues discussed above, may make a useful contribution towards reaching that goal.

of the stanza can thus be restored, it may be thought defensible to supply such a line, albeit purely by conjecture, rather than to leave a blank in the text. Alternatively, such a missing line may simply be indicated by a series of dots, as in Greene, no. 420, stanza 1.

Part I

AFFECT

2

Moving Lights: An Affective Reading of *On leome is in þis world ilist* and Church Wall Paintings

A. S. Lazikani

On leome is in þis world ilist (A light illumines this world)[1]

On leome is in þis world ilist,	*A light; illumined/illuminated*
þer-of is muchel pris;	
a-risen is god & þat is rist	*right*
from deþe to lif.	
5 Al for ure redempciun	
He þolede pine & passiun,	*suffered pain*
Derne wnden & greue;	*secret wounds and severe/grievous*
He broutte to saluaciun	*brought*
þe world þat was ibrot adun	*brought down*
10 þuru adam & eue.	
Of a meide he was iborin,	*born*
y-comin of heiye cunne;	*noble kind*
y-brout he hauit þat wes for-loren	*he delivered [they that] were lost*
þuru adames sunne.	
15 He hauit ibrout of pine,	*delivered from pain*
þat he weren ibunden inne	*bound*
wid serrue & herde bend,	*with sorrow and harsh bond*
To ioye þat brithe suinit	*brightly shines*
& neuer er ne finit,	*and will never finish*
20 World o butin hend.	*forever without end*
Al þat rouþe rouste	*sorrow/pity; took heed/cared for*
Wepen he misten heþe	*weep he may readily*
þo þe gyuis him bousten	*when the Jews; bought*
For to don to deþe –	

The focus on the visual representation of the crucifixion throughout this essay is continued in chapters 6 and 7 in this volume.

1   NIMEV 293; DIMEV 493. Reproduced from Brown *XIII*, pp. 34–7, with the addition of glosses. All subsequent references are to this edition, cited in the text by line number. For other editions, see T. Silverstein, ed., *Medieval English Lyrics* (London, 1971), pp. 15–17.

25	Boþen yung & holde	old
	Hardi he weren & bolde,	audacious they were
	A-wedde he weren y-nou.	enraged were they enough
	Ful feste he was iholden	
	þo iudas him solde	when Judas
30	Wid traisun & wid wou.	woe

	A reuli reid he funden,	pitiful counsel they found
	þe gyuis euer-uihon,	each of the Jews
	þo he ihesum beonden	when they bound Jesus
	To a pileir of ston;	
35	To him ha weren ful <t>ore,	they were very fierce,
	I-burst asse wedde bore,	furious as a raging boar
	So pilatis hem heit.	commanded
	Ha bueten him so sore	they beat
	His bodi barst a-more,	burst continuously/evermore
40	Þat blod ron to his fehid.	feet

	His bodi þat wes feir & gent	shapely
	& his neb suo scene	face so beautiful/gleaming
	Wes bi-spit & al to-rend,	defiled; rent
	His rude wes worþen grene.	face became green
45	Bufetes him weren iyeuene;	blows; given
	Of serue þer wes euene	of sorrow there was enough
	Þo he bigon to bleden.	when
	He bahit wid milde steuene	prayed; voice
	Þen suete feder of heuene	sweet father
50	fir-yewen hem heore mis-deden.	forgive them

	His suete bodi he stresten	sweet; stretched
	þe rode effer-long;	the cross lengthwise
	longius a spere bitaisten	Longinus; bit/slashed
	is herte he wor-stong.	his heart he pierced
55	Miracle he dude asse he deit drey;	as he endured death
	Of is blod as he heng hey,	
	To longius ron þe streim,	ran
	In-to is eyen asse he stoit ney.	stood nearby
	Is seisþe heueþe & sone he sey	his sight had and immediately he saw
60	þurru ihesu of bedleim.	through; Bethlehem

	From him ha weren to-dreuid	they; dispersed
	Is apostelis heuer-huic on,	every one
	Ful on he was bileuit	completely alone; remained
	Wid marie & Sein Iohon.	
65	Tuei þeues þer verrin a-hon,	two thieves there were hung up
	& þe oþer him beid on bon	bade him in prayer
	Wid rem & reuly cry:	wailing; woeful
	Wenne he come to is trone,	[that] when; his
	Þenchen up-hon him sone	to think
70	& habben of him mercy.	have mercy on him

	Hasse he biheuld þe rode,	as he beheld
	þe modir þat was of miste	power
	& þer I-sei al ablode	bloodied
	Hir sone þat her wes briste,	bright
75	Hisse tuo suete honden	
	Wid nailes al to-ronden,	rent/torn
	Is fehit iþurlid bo,	his feet pierced both
	Is suete softe side	his
	I-þurlit depe & wyde –	pierced
80	Wey, þat hire was wo!	Alas; to her
	Ha isei þe rode stonden,	
	Hire sone þer-to ibunden	
	Hoe wroinc hire honden,	she wrung
	Bi-heild his suete wunden.	
85	Þe gyues to him leden	the Jews led him
	On him for-to greden	to shout/shriek at
	Asse þat hoe weren wod.	as though they were mad
	Hire þucte a miste aweden,	She thought she may go mad,
	Hire herte bi-gon to bleden,	
90	Teres hoe wep of blod.	she
	Lauedi, flur of parradis, –	Lady, flower
	Nas neuir non so scene –	beautiful
	Ber hure herrinde if þi vil his,	Carry our praise, if it be your will
	Asse þu ard heuene quene,	as you are
95	To þine sone þat is so brit,	
	þat he us yeue strenþe & mist	power
	To seruen him wid wunne,	joy
	& to scenden þene vichit	put to shame; devil
	þat his humbe day & nicst	is busy day and night
100	To gabben us wid sunne.	deceive/reproach
	Biseich þine sone, asse he uel may,	beseech; as he well may
	þat he us alle yeme	keep
	Wenne he comit a domis day	Judgement Day
	Al folc forto demeN. [sic]	to judge all people
105	Wen huic mon for is owen dede	when each
	Sal þeir vnderfungen mede,	receive reward
	ful sore us may agrisen.	be afraid
	Wen vour engles bemen blouit,	angels blow trumpets
	Lef us him þenne to cnowen,	acknowledge/worship him
110	On his rist hond arisen.	
	Wenne he scauit is wndis	shows his wounds
	Þat reuful beet to seine,	that are pitiful to see
	Help us, leuedi, þe stunde	hour
	Wen he scauit is tenne.	shows his injury/suffering

115 'God, ye awariede in-to wo,	*condemn into woe*
To pine þat sal lesten OO.	*pain; last forever*
I-Greiþid hit was hou yore.'	*prepared [for] you a long time ago*
To loft up buven þat he seit to:	*to heaven above; he says*
'Comit, iblesede, in-to ro	*come blessed into peace*
120 þat lesten sal eueir more.'	

Infused with John 3: 19, the lyric *On leome is in þis world ilist* glows for its reader.[2] The meditator of this lyric can visualise images that are at once static and animated, stirring the heart towards this 'light … come to the world'. Even beyond the light–dark dualisms of Genesis and Exodus, there is much scriptural evidence for the Lord as luminescence: 'He revealeth deep and hidden things, and knoweth what is in darkness: and light is with him' (Daniel 2: 22).[3] From such a basis, medieval readers recognised a strong association between light and interior perception. In its most blinding form, light was also linked with superior insight during contemplation.[4] It is no surprise, then, that light has been at the centre of consciousness studies in recent decades: medieval authors acknowledged the relationship between light and conscious states many centuries earlier.[5]

The affective potency of this thirteenth-century lyric deserves attention. Like most earlier Passion lyrics, *On leome* has received less scrutiny than those of the fourteenth and fifteenth centuries. In this lyric, there are moments that anchor the speaker to the Passion narrative, enabling a near-scripted 'performance of feeling', to use Sarah McNamer's terms.[6] Elsewhere, however, she/he is freed from narrative constraints, meditating in stillness on the Passion; the speaker ruminates on each image in searing detail. This is a meditative practice in which visualisation is key: the eyes of the heart nourish the speaker's 'affective literacies',

---

2   'And this is the judgment: because the light is come into the world, and men loved darkness rather than the light: for their works were evil' (John 3: 19). All biblical references are to Douay-Rheims.
3   See also, for example, Job 12: 22 ('He discovereth deep things out of darkness, and bringeth up to light the shadow of death'), and Psalm 111: 4 ('To the righteous a light is risen up in darkness: he is merciful, and compassionate and just'). On Exodus and Genesis, see J. P. Fokkelman's chapters in *The Literary Guide to the Bible*, ed. R. Alter and F. Kermode (London, 1987), pp. 36–65 (especially p. 60).
4   See further, J. Hamburger, *Nuns as Artists: The Visual Culture of a Medieval Convent* (Berkeley, 1997), p. 129.
5   See S. Avery, *The Dimensional Structure of Consciousness: A Physical Basis for Immaterialism* (Lexington, KY, 1995), pp. 69–85; S. J. Hage, *Let There Be Light: Physics, Philosophy, and the Dimensional Structure of Consciousness* (New York, 2013), pp. 39–43; C. S. Hill, *Consciousness* (Leiden, 2009), pp. 128–68.
6   S. McNamer, *Affective Meditation and the Invention of Medieval Compassion* (Philadelphia, 2010), p. 26.

to invoke Mark Amsler's coinage.[7] Such strategies parallel those of church wall paintings, a growing but as yet understudied area.[8]

Meditative Vision

On leome is found on fols 32b–33a of Cambridge, Trinity College, MS B. 14. 39, with the uncommon form of the ten-line stanza.[9] The manuscript is datable to the mid- to late thirteenth century, and contains religious material in English, Anglo-Norman and Latin.[10] Trinity College B. 14. 39 was originally believed to be a 'preacher's notebook' or 'friar's miscellany', but Julia Boffey has since challenged such a description.[11] Given the manuscript's trilingual nature, it is important to remain cognisant of the multilingual milieu of *On leome*. This follows the research of Ardis Butterfield, who has documented the Latin and French 'hinterland' of lyrics concretised in Carleton Brown's editions.[12] Taking into account the broad audience of post-Norman Conquest lyrics, a wide readership can be assumed for *On leome*, encompassing the clerical and educated lay sectors. The meditator is likely to have possessed knowledge of English, French and possibly Latin.[13]

Christiania Whitehead and Sarah Stanbury have revealed the importance of vision in the lyrical mode.[14] But this remains a fruitful area of enquiry, given the recent surge of interest in historical optics and the 'spiritual senses'.[15] Most germane here are two writers on vision: patristic father Augustine of Hippo (354–430) and Archbishop Anselm of Canterbury (1033–1109), both of whom had a pervasive

---

7   M. Amsler, *Affective Literacies: Writing and Multilingualism in the Late Middle Ages* (Turnhout, 2011), p. 103. On the tradition of the 'eyes of the heart', see M. Carruthers, *The Book of Memory: A Study of Memory in Medieval Culture* (Cambridge, 1990), p. 31.
8   See R. Rosewell, *Medieval Wall Paintings in English and Welsh Churches* (Woodbridge, 2008), especially pp. 149–209, and A. S. Lazikani, *Cultivating the Heart: Feeling and Emotion in Twelfth- and Thirteenth-Century Religious Texts* (Cardiff, 2015), pp. 21–4.
9   Brown *XIII*, p. 182.
10 For a description, see M. R. James, *The Western Manuscripts in the Library of Trinity College, Cambridge: A Descriptive Catalogue*, 4 vols (1900–04), I, 438–99. For dating, see Brown *XIII*, p. xx n. 1, and K. Reichl, *Religiöse Dichtung im Englischen Hochmittelalter: Untersuchung und Edition der Handschrift B. 14.39 des Trinity College in Cambridge* (Munich, 1973), pp. 46–8.
11 J. Boffey, 'Middle English Lyrics and Manuscripts', Duncan, *Companion*, 1–18 (pp. 7–8, 13).
12 A. Butterfield, 'The Construction of Textual Form: Cross-Lingual Citation in the Medieval Insular Lyric', *Citation, Intertextuality and Memory in the Middle Ages and Renaissance: Text, Music and Image from Machaut to Ariosto*, ed. Y. Plumley, G. Di Bacco and S. Jossa (Exeter, 2011), pp. 41–57 (for the term 'hinterland', see p. 47).
13 On audience, see J. C. Hirsh, ed., *Medieval Lyric: Middle English Lyrics, Ballads and Carols* (Oxford, 2005), p. 5.
14 C. Whitehead, 'Middle English Religious Lyrics', Duncan, *Companion*, pp. 96–119 (especially pp. 107–8, 116), and S. Stanbury, 'The Virgin's Gaze: Spectacle and Transgression in Middle English Lyrics of the Passion', *PMLA* 106 (1991), 1083–93.
15 See V. Gillespie, 'The Colours of Contemplation: Less Light on Julian of Norwich', *The Medieval Mystical Tradition in England VIII*, ed. E. A. Jones (Cambridge, 2013), pp. 7–28; P. Gavrilyuk and S. Coakley, eds, *The Spiritual Senses: Perceiving God in Western Christianity* (Cambridge, 2012).

influence on devotional texts of the thirteenth century. In Book Eleven of *De trinitate* (*On the Trinity*), Augustine remarks: 'Visiones enim duae sunt, una sentientis, altera cogitantis' ('There are indeed two visions, one of which perceives, the other of which thinks/imagines'). The first is performed by the body, and the second by memory; the will (*voluntas*) guides both.[16] In Chapter Six of *De veritate* (*On Truth*), Anselm suggests that there is both an exterior and an interior sense (*sensus*) when processing colour.[17] As Mark A. Smith explains in his recent history of optical science, any mistakes on the part of this interior sense are 'rectified by the intellect in light of Truth, which is God Himself'.[18] In *On leome*, we find that the speaker's exterior perception of text and image is guided by the eyes of the heart – an 'interior' sight that is in turn clarified by God's direction of the will.

With visualisation at its core, *On leome* has remarkable affinity with devotional art.[19] As mentioned earlier, this lyric cannot be defined straightforwardly as either a performance 'script' or a collage of stationary images; it resides between these two poles. Since Erwin Panofsky's classic study of 1927, art historians have debated two impulses in Christological art: static icons versus contextualised narratives.[20] *On leome* is not formed solely of motionless icons: there is a progressing narrative. Nonetheless, the meditator does not only recite a narrativised script; the speaker also delves deeply into isolated images in her/his ruminative reading. As observed by Vincent Gillespie on later devotional texts, the 'abstracted image ... remains a signifier, but its signified is no longer determined by its immediate linguistic or narrative context'.[21] With these two impulses – narrative and abstraction – *On leome* generates a hermeneutic flexibility for the meditator.

This hermeneutic flexibility has potent resonances with church wall paintings. Far from being mere substitutes for texts, these paintings have their own affective puissance; like meditative lyrics, they enable a devotee to nurture compunction and compassion within the soul. Whilst a Passion cycle on a church's wall does form a narrative, individual scenes or figures can also be separated from this context – thus allowing the viewer to engage with the full signifying potential of each image. In the thirteenth-century cycle at St Mary's Church in Wissington, Suffolk, for example,

---

16 Augustine, *De trinitate*, ed. W. J. Mountain and F. Glorie, 2 vols (Turnhout, 1968), I, 353. See further, M. A. Smith, *From Sight to Light: The Passage from Ancient to Modern Optics* (Chicago, 2015), pp. 150–4.
17 Anselm, *De veritate*, in *S. Anselmi Cantuariensis Archiepiscopi Opera Omnia*, ed. F. S. Schmitt, 6 vols (Edinburgh, 1940–61), I, 183–5.
18 Smith, *From Sight to Light*, p. 237.
19 See further, R. Copeland, 'The Middle English *Candet Nudatum Pectus* and Norms of Early Vernacular Translation Practice', *Leeds Studies in English* 15 (1984), 57–81 (68–74).
20 See H. Belting, *The Image and its Public in the Middle Ages: Form and Function of Early Paintings of the Passion*, trans. M. Bartusis and R. Meyer (New Rochelle, NY, 1990), especially pp. 40–2. For Panofksy's original study, see E. Panofsky, '*Imago Pietatis*: Ein Beitrag zur Typengeschichte "Schmerzensmannes" und der "Maria Mediatrix"', *Festshrift für Max J. Friedlander zum 60 Geburstag* (Leipzig, 1927), pp. 261–308.
21 V. Gillespie, *Looking in Holy Books: Essays on Late Medieval Religious Writing in England* (Turnhout, 2011), p. 223.

scenes are divided by patterned lines, aiding such a meditative practice.[22] This cycle, painted in red ochre, is now heavily damaged; only a fraction remains visible. The divisions through horizontal and vertical ornamentation are nevertheless clear in their delineation/separation of the Last Supper and Christ Washing his Disciples' Feet. A thirteenth-century cycle at St Mary's Church in Fairstead, Essex is positioned over the chancel arch in pyramid tiers, painted in what would have been red and green pigment. The full Passion narrative – with its multitude of participants – is compressed into this triangular space. The Entry into Jerusalem forms the pinnacle; the Last Supper, the Betrayal, and the Arrest at Gethsemane come underneath; the Scourging, Mocking, Christ Before Pilate/Caiaphas, and the Road to Calvary form the tier below this. Finally, beneath the rood beam are two faded scenes, which may have been the Crucifixion and Deposition. With this layout, a viewer can trace the narrative, but she/he might also break down the chronological and semantic restrictions on the wall, extracting single moments for meditation. The viewer thus embraces a narrative context whilst also interacting with isolable images; such an affective dynamic is also at the heart of *On leome*.

Analysis of *On leome*

The opening stanza of *On leome* provides its doctrinal foundation: Christ's redemption of humanity. The Saviour's pained body is moored to his redemptive role from the start ('Al for ure redempciun / He þolede pine (*suffered pain*) & passiun', lines 5–6), in the same way as church walls like those in Wissington and Fairstead locate Christ's pain within salvation history. The lyric begins to take shape as a celebration of life for both Christ and his creation; from its opening, it is imbued with hope.[23] The soothing nature of such meditation is paralleled in the work of Anselm of Canterbury, a major source for Passion lyrics.[24] In his *Meditatio redemptionis humanae* (*Meditation on the Redemption of Humanity*), the speaker draws on imagery from the Canticles to express the delectability of contemplating the redemption.[25] Humanity's salvation is not a painless process. As the speaker of *On leome* asserts, 'Derne wnden & greue (*secret wounds and grievous*); / He broutte (*brought*) to saluaciun' (lines 7–8) – with the common adjectival intensifier of 'greue' attached to Christ's painfully wounded body; the description of his wounds as secret or hidden ('derne') is less common.[26] Both adjectives initiate the meditative focus on Christ's profound, unknowable anguish, which will reach its apex later in the lyric.

---

22 The approximate dates and colouring of all wall paintings follow those given by Anne Marshall in her online 'Painted Church' project accessed August 2016 but currently unavailable. For accessible references to all churches cited in the present essay, see the index in Rosewell, *Medieval Wall Paintings*, pp. 373–9.
23 See further, P. Tristram, *Figures of Life and Death in Medieval English Literature* (London, 1976), p. 194.
24 See P. Dronke, *The Medieval Lyric* (London, 1968), p. 65.
25 Anselm, *Orationes sive meditationes*, in *Opera Omnia*, ed. Schmitt, III, p. 84.
26 MED, 'derne (adj.)'.

From the basis of the Redemption, the speaker voices the miracle of the Incarnation: 'Of a meide he was iborin (*born*), / y-comin of heiye cunne (*noble kind*)'; the Saviour rescues humanity from the horrors engendered 'þuru adames sunne' (lines 11–14). In his embodiment, Christ offers healing from 'pine' – a noun with an extensive sematic range. 'Pine' can refer to an act of punishment, as well as painful sensation on skin; it also expands to include 'mental suffering, anguish, misery; displeasure, vexation'.[27] The speaker is invited to meditate upon such heavy 'pine' in these first two stanzas, apprehending the enormity of the Lord's suffering while he protected humanity from a painful doom. Christ's resurrection transmutes the 'pine' into 'joy' (lines 18–20). Such joy cannot be dwelt upon, however, as a deeper immersion in the Passion is first needed.

With the doctrinal foundation in place, the speaker is given a narrative anchor: a 'close-up' of the Lord's betrayal. It is an abrupt and painful shift, intended to prick the speaker into compunction:[28]

Ful feste he was iholden	
þo iudas him solde	*when Judas*
Wid traisun & wid wou. (lines 28–30)	*woe*

In its starkness, this view resembles the clear image of the Betrayal on the wall of St Andrews in Gussage, Dorset. This painting in red and yellow pigment depicts a group of figures gathered together, with Judas in the centre embracing Christ: a viewer is drawn to this painful act, whilst also observing the broader population surrounding Judas's duplicity. A medieval viewer's/speaker's relationship with Judas could be a vexed one, as evidenced in an Anglo-Norman Passion narrative also found in Trinity College B. 14. 39; it comes later than *On leome*, on fols 74ra–80vb.[29] In this verse-narrative, Judas laments that God will never care for him ('Ja n'averat Deus de mei cure'), evoking the audience's pity. But the audience must also critique his misapprehension; he does not realise that it is this very despair (*deseperance*) that results in his damnation.[30] Another Anglo-Norman meditative text found in London, British Library, Harley MS 2253 (c.1330–40) – known editorially as *Meditation of the Hours* – begins unconventionally with Compline, 'pur ce que a cel oure Judas Scarioth ly vendy' ('for this is the Hour when Judas Iscariot sold him'). At this Hour, the meditator must think deeply ('pensir devez mout ententivement') on Judas's act and her/his own, analogous guilt. At the Hour of Prime, the meditator again thinks upon Judas's sorrow and

---

27 MED, 'pine (n.)', especially definitions 1a–d and 2b.
28 'Compunction' should be distinguished from the more specific term 'contrition'; the latter indicates the perfect sorrow that facilitates remission of sin. See further, P. Adnès, 'Pénitence', *Dictionnaire de spiritualité: ascétique et mystique, doctrine et historique*, ed. M. Viller et al., 17 vols (Paris, 1984), XII, 943–1010 (p. 971).
29 T. Hunt, ed. and J. Bliss, trans., *'Cher alme': Texts of Anglo-Norman Piety* (Tempe, AZ, 2010), p. 199.
30 *Ibid.*, pp. 220–1.

despair (*deol, desesperance*). Meditation on Judas's act thus effects a mixture of distaste, compassion and painful identification.³¹

The fraught moment of the Lord's capture has been invoked for the speaker of *On leome*. The following stanza develops the narrative, whilst also shifting closer to Christ's impassioned body: he is bound to the 'pileir of ston' (line 34). Narrative details are provided not as constraints, but as reflexes for deeper meditation. Each moment of agony is itemised in the meditator's sight:

Ha bueten him so sore	*they beat*
His bodi barst a-more,	*burst continuously*
Þat blod ron to his fehid. (lines 38–40)	*feet*

The salvific blood swathes his body, with the speaker almost invited to bathe in this healing liquid running to his feet. The employment of the adverb 'a-more' is significant: it asserts the continuous, 'evermore' nature of Christ's distress. Although he suffered only once (Hebrews 9: 27–8), his is a repeating, circular anguish for the speaker.³² Awareness of such cyclicality would have been fortified for devotees through church walls like those in Wissington and Fairstead: the Passion narrative remains in cyclical play, with Christ's anguish inscribed into the church's structure, repeated in every act of meditation on the paintings.

From Christ's precious body, the meditator moves to his peerless visage. Devotion to the face is kindled; the lyric highlights Christ's face as the unique *imago Dei*, gesturing towards Psalm 83: 10.³³ The face is not revealed clearly: we are only given an obscured glimpse of 'his neb suo scene (*face so beautiful*)' (line 42). Through this blurred view, the speaker acknowledges that Christ's face dwells in the broken reflection offered by this world; the Son can never be a perfect likeness of the Father in the 'distortion of utter dissimilarity'.³⁴ Nonetheless, the speaker of *On leome* does voice the face's shining quality ('suo scene') and its changing colour, 'His rude wes worþen grene (*face became green*)', coming closer to the unknowable countenance (lines 42, 44). Christ's face is linked with his voice, a technique also evident in the longest of the *Wooing Group* meditations – a group of thirteenth-century English texts that have strong correspondences with the lyrical mode.³⁵ When Christ speaks in *On leome*, it is to voice mercy: 'He bahit (*prayed*) wid milde steuene (*voice*) / Þen suete feder (*sweet father*)

---

31 Ibid., pp. 254–6 (for manuscript description and dating, see p. 237; on Compline beginning the text, see p. 238).
32 'And as it is appointed unto men once to die, and after this the judgement: So also Christ was offered once to exhaust the sins of many; the second time he shall appear without sin to them that expect him unto salvation.'
33 See further, J-A. Robilliard, 'Face (dévotion à la Sainte Face)', *Dictionnaire de spiritualité*, ed. M. Viller et al., 17 vols (Paris, 1962), V, 26–33.
34 C. Schönborn, *God's Human Face: The Christ-Icon*, trans. L. Krauth (San Francisco, 1994), p. 5.
35 W. Meredith Thompson, ed., *Þe Wohunge of ure Lauerd*, EETS OS 241 (London, 1958), p. 31, lines 391–414; all subsequent references to *Wooing Group* texts are to this edition, unless stated otherwise.

of heuene / fir-yewen hem (*forgive them*) heore mis-deden' (lines 48–50). The mildness of his voice is crucial, for he remains the uncomplaining lamb of Isaiah 53: 7.[36] His voice is relayed through reported speech, preparing the meditator for the potency of the Saviour's direct address in the final stanza.

Hearing Christ's mercy, the meditator continues to focus on that ever-important flesh, tortured for humanity. The phrase 'His bodi' of the previous stanza is layered with the adjective 'suete' (line 51). This typical modifier identifies Christ's body as a source of nurturance; the adjective is suffused with eucharistic connotations. Seeing Christ's sweet flesh, the speaker also perceives his body stretched out ('bodi he stresten (*stretched*) / þe rode effer-long (*cross length-wise*)', lines 51-2) – his arms elongated in anguish yet also unfurled to cradle the meditator. This play of Christ's arms as opened both in pain and in embrace can be witnessed more obviously in the *Wooing Group* text *On wel swuðe god ureisun of god almihti* (p. 6, lines 58–62) and the pseudo-Anselmian meditation *De passione Christi*.[37] In *On leome*, the stretched arms facilitate a moment of stillness beyond the narrative context, as a Crucifixion wall painting within a cycle can be dwelt on in stasis: the meditator becomes stationary in front of Christ's tensile arms, poised to feel his 'pine' and his caress.[38]

Imagining Christ in this stretched position, the speaker sees the crucial moment at which Longinus pierces his side – part of a tradition that associated this act with access to Christ's heart and its mysteries.[39] The miracle resulting from this wound comes to the foreground, with Christ's medicinal blood curing the centurion's blindness: 'To longius ron (*ran*) þe streim, / In-to is eyen asse he stoit ney (*stood nearby*)' (lines 55, 57–8). This intent meditation on Longinus parallels wall paintings of the scene like those in Gussage St Andrews or St Botolph's Church in North Cove, Suffolk, where viewers can extract the soldier from a mass of Passion players. Focusing on him alone, the meditator can ruminate on the gateway to the Sacred Heart and the curative blood that flows from it.[40] The last line of this stanza in *On leome* then reasserts Jesus as a historical figure, 'of bedleim (*Bethlehem*)' (line 60), allowing narrative anchorage to secure the meditator before progressing further.

At this moment, the perspective transfers to the anguished observers, who become affective models for the meditator. The dispersing apostles are numbered each and every one, 'heuer-huic on (*everyone*)', establishing the scope of Christ's abandonment. There is then a focus on the remaining 'marie & Sein Iohon', a common coupling in textual and visual cultures from the twelfth century onwards

---

36 'He was offered because it was his own will, and he opened not his mouth: he shall be led as a sheep to the slaughter, and shall be dumb as a lamb before his shearer, and he shall not open his mouth.'
37 PL 158: 761B–762A.
38 See especially the Crucifixion painting in the thirteenth-century Passion Cycle in St Mary's Church of West Chiltington, Sussex.
39 See W. Riehle, *The Middle English Mystics*, trans. B. Standring (London, 1981), p. 46.
40 The North Cove painting is later in date, from the fourteenth century.

(lines 62, 64).[41] The speaker's affective literacies would have been enriched by a wealth of depictions of Mary and John on either side of the crucified body, such as the thirteenth-century paintings in the St Mary's churches of West Chiltington, Sussex and Great Tew, Oxfordshire. All would have aided a meditator's nurturance of compassion for the Mother and disciple, those notable figures of intercession. The speaker also visualises the enclosure of Christ between two thieves. Notably, the one thief who cries out for mercy ('beid on bon (*bade him in prayer*) / Wid rem (*wailing*) & reuly (*woeful*) cry') offers a mode of response for the sinful speaker; the thief's affective transformation is spoken by the meditator, encouraging a similar commitment within her/him (lines 66–70). Having been fixed on Christ's rent flesh, the speaker now travels outwards. Around the still body, the meditator sees the surrounding figures – each a paradigm of affective response.

The speaker then moves towards the most privileged perspective: that of the Virgin Mary. In embracing Mary's vantage point, *On leome* functions within a tradition epitomised by the thirteenth-century pseudo-Anselmian *Dialogus beatae Mariae et Anselmi de passione Domini* (*Dialogue of the Blessed Mary and Anselm on the Passion of the Lord*) and pseudo-Bernardine *Liber de passione Christi et doloribus et planctibus Matris ejus* (*Book of the Passion of Christ and the Sorrows and Laments of his Mother*).[42] Mary's optical and affective perception are brought together ('biheuld þe rode', 'I-sei al ablode', lines 71, 73). Crucially, she looks upon the portals on Christ's body carved 'depe & wyde'; the dual use of the past participle 'iþurlid' / 'I-þurlit (*pierced*)' further emphasises the depth of these wounds (lines 77, 79). His wounds are a voluminous sanctuary in which, following the post-Bernardine tradition, the dove of Canticles 2: 14 can find its repose.[43] As Jeffrey Hamburger has shown in his work on medieval German convents, wounds were bound with penetrative insight, as well as being crucial access points to the sacraments.[44] Through Mary's perspicacious eyes, the speaker can enter the wound-portals on her Son.

On the brink of such infiltration, the speaker visualises each aspect of Christ's woundedness:

Hisse tuo suete honden	
Wid nailes al to-ronden,	*rent*
Is fehit iþurlid bo,	*his feet pierced both*
Is suete softe side (lines 75–8)	*his*

Again, there is the insistent employment of the adjective 'suete', now bound with 'softe'. Both terms carry eucharistic significance for the meditator, who can move from the stillness of the sweet-soft flesh to an imagined consumption of it. Wall

---

41 See L. Gougaud, *Dévotions et pratiques ascétiques du moyen âge* (Paris, 1925), p. 77.
42 PL 159: 271A–289A; PL 182: 1133A–1142A.
43 See further, E. A. Matter, *The Voice of My Beloved: The Song of Songs in Western Medieval Christianity* (Philadelphia, 1990), p. 137.
44 Hamburger, *Nuns as Artists*, especially pp. 79, 128–9.

paintings could have intensified this effect, particularly when placed above the altar.⁴⁵

Almost tasting the Host, the speaker tries to achieve affective closeness to the flesh-giving mother (line 80), a move possibly aided by her close proximity to the body of her Son in Crucifixion paintings like that in West Chiltington. The lyric expands on Mary's standpoint: 'Ha isei þe rode stonden', and she 'Bi-heild his suete wunden' (lines 81, 84). The speaker thus attempts to reach her enhanced affective perspective of these 'wunden' – wounds that have been established as doorways to Christ's love. Mary's own affective wounding is then demonstrated for the meditator: 'Hire herte bi-gon to bleden, / Teres hoe (*she*) wep of blod' (lines 89–90). Such evocation of the Mother's extreme grief is inspired ultimately by her Sword of Sorrows (Luke 2: 35) and her Son's bloody sweat (Luke 22: 44).⁴⁶ Although there is the suggestion that the grieving Mary has an unstable mind (lines 87–8), her tears of blood also affirm her unique insight. The tear/blood-drops indicate the blinding clarity of her maternal gaze, unreachable for the meditator.

With bloodied eyes, the Mother remains a transparent receptacle of intercession. Addressing Mary directly ('Lauedi'), the speaker identifies her as the 'flur of parradis', an image that resonates with depictions of the Virgin as a resplendent flower-queen (lines 91–3).⁴⁷ As one example, floral associations with Mary are inscribed for devotees in the later Annunciation wall painting in St Peter ad vincula in South Newington, Oxfordshire (c.1330). Such imagery is also prominent in the thirteenth-century lyric *On God Ureisun of Ure Lefdi*, considered part of the *Wooing Group*, and discussed by Annie Sutherland in this volume.⁴⁸ The floral Mary is tied with the Son in her intercessory potency in *On leome*. Whilst the speaker imagines a continual serving of Christ with joy ('wunne'), the joy is charged with an awareness of sin; the devil is ever-present to deceive or reproach with sin ('To gabben us wid sunne', lines 97, 100). Mary, who saw the Crucifixion so clearly that she wept blood, must be reached so that she may act as conciliator between sinner and Son. Her intercession remains paramount in the following stanza, as the devastating Judgement is expanded upon. A plea is directed to the Mother, with the urgency of an imperative verb ('Biseich þine sone', line 101).

Fear is thus stirred alongside the imagined calm of Heaven. The verb 'agrisen', of Old English origin, is employed both to label and to provoke such fear. It has

---

45 See, for example, the fourteenth-century *Virgo lactans* image in St Mary's Church in Belchamp Walter, Essex.
46 'And thy own soul a sword shall pierce, that, out of many hearts, thoughts may be revealed' (Luke 2: 35). 'And his sweat became as drops of blood, trickling down upon the ground' (Luke 22: 44).
47 For a discussion of floral symbolism associated with Mary, see especially J. Mellon, *The Virgin Mary in the Perceptions of Women: Mother, Protector and Queen Since the Middle Ages* (Jefferson, NC, 2008), pp. 61–8.
48 *On God Ureisun of ure Lefdi*, Brown XIII, pp. 3–8 (especially p. 3, line 22; p. 4, lines 37–8, 53). See below, pp. 73–86.

the sense in Middle English not only of the 'emotion' of fear itself, but also the somatic response of shuddering.[49] Sight and sound are interwoven in the meditator's sensual apprehension of the Hereafter (lines 101–10); the angels blowing on trumpets ('engles bemen blouit', line 108), in particular, invokes Matthew 24: 31.[50] The trumpeting angels would have also been inscribed for medieval devotees on church walls, as testified in a thirteenth-century Doom painting in St Andrew's Church in Oddington, Gloucestershire. In Anselm's *Meditation I: Meditatio ad concitandum timorem* (*Meditation to Stir up Fear*), the speaker likewise evokes the horror of Judgement Day through visual and aural stimuli – including the cataclysmic trumpets. The Anselmian speaker also voices the need to 'tremble' before 'thunder' (*tremere, tonitrui*), which parallels the shuddering of our lyric.[51] Shuddering in fear in advance of Judgement Day, the meditator can arrive at the precious right hand of Christ ('On his rist hond arisen', line 110).

As the lyric draws to its close, Christ's wounded flesh and Mary's perspective of it are brought together in forceful unity:

Wenne he scauit is wndis	*shows his wounds*
Þat reuful beet to seine,	*that are pitiful to see*
Help us, leuedi, þe stunde	*hour*
Wen he scauit is tenne. (lines 111–14)	*shows his injury/suffering*

The wounds induce compassion whilst also gesturing towards their 'compassion-full' ('reuful') nature. With the revelation of these pitiful/compassionate wounds, Mary as intercessor is called upon directly: 'Help us, leuedi' (line 113) – a potentially reusable template for prayer. Help is requested for the precise time ('stunde') that Christ reveals his injury ('tenne') (lines 113–14). The use of 'stunde' recalls liturgical circularity, the adverb 'a-more' having earlier emphasised Christ's endless suffering. As seen with the Anglo-Norman prayer *Meditation of the Hours*, each liturgical hour has its own rich meditative promise.

Perception of Christ through Mary becomes the basis of terrifying revelation in this final stanza. The verb 'sheuen' (deriving from Old English 'sceawian') has the sense not only of disclosure, but also of penetration – inviting an onlooker towards hidden truths.[52] The verb, used twice, re-emphasises the essential link between seeing and wounding epitomised in Canticles 4: 9, and recalls the secret wounds of the first stanza.[53] Christ 'scauit (*shows*) is wndis' and 'scauit is tenne (*shows his injury*)' (lines 111, 114): phrases that recall depictions

---

49 See MED, 'agrisen (v.)', definition 1a.
50 'And he shall send his angels with a trumpet, and a great voice: and they shall gather together his elect from the four winds, from the farthest parts of the heavens to the utmost bounds of them.' See also Rev. 7: 1–3: 'After these things, I saw four angels standing on the four corners of the earth, holding the four winds of the earth, that they should not blow upon the earth, nor upon the sea, nor on any tree.'
51 Anselm, *Orationes sive meditationes*, in *Opera Omnia*, ed. Schmitt, III, 77.
52 See MED, 'sheuen (v.(1))', especially definitions 4 and 9.
53 See further, Hamburger, *Nuns as Artists*, p. 128.

of the Man of Sorrows laden with torture instruments.⁵⁴ It is also reminiscent of a thirteenth-century wall painting of the Judge Christ in St Clement's Church of Ashampstead, Berkshire; in this Doom painting, he opens his arms, allowing his robe to fall to reveal his wounds. In both lyric and painting, this is a moment of apocalypse, a terrible uncovering.⁵⁵ Through such revelation, the afflicted Christ becomes a source of torment for the lyric's speaker: 'God, ye awariede in-to wo' (line 115). The verb 'awarien', also of Old English origin, has the sense of a soul damned or condemned.⁵⁶ It relates back to 'agrisen' in the previous stanza, as well as the semantically broad terms of 'wo' and 'pine' (lines 6, 15, 80, 115–16). The crucial stirrings of fear and love are together nourished – but terror is not the closing note. At the end lies tranquility:

> Comit, iblesede, in-to ro   *come blessed into peace*
> þat lesten sal eueir more. (lines 119–20)

The lyric ends with Christ's voice, resounding and compassionate. His direct speech soothes the meditator while he speaks not of tribulation, but of 'ro': a noun signifying peace and repose, stemming from Old English 'row'.⁵⁷ Peace, uttered in Christ's voice, is the closing salve.

***

On leome shines for its meditators, facilitating affective sight in stasis and in motion. The speaker moves through the Passion narrative, and yet she/he also stands still among isolated images. This hermeneutic flexibility, based on both abstraction and narrative, has powerful correspondences with the 'reading' of church wall paintings. Such correspondences have been demonstrated through particular attention to churches in Wissington, Fairstead, Gussage, North Cove, West Chiltington, Great Tew, South Newington, Oddington and Ashampstead. In both image and lyric, elements of the Passion narrative give the speaker or viewer a firm anchor; but these elements can also be detached from their context to generate a boundless rumination. Vitally, the Lord's radiance may be felt through such meditative practice. As the Anselmian speaker declares in *Meditatio redemptionis humanae*, she/he had resided in darkness, but was illuminated (*illucere*) by Christ.⁵⁸ *On leome* enables such luminescence: it places the meditator's heart upon a candlestick, awaiting the hour when there is no need for lamp or sun.⁵⁹

---

54 See further, M. O'Kane, 'Picturing "The Man of Sorrows": the Passion-Filled Afterlives of a Biblical Icon', *Religion and the Arts* 9 (2005), 62–100; L. M. La Favia, *The Man of Sorrows: Its Origins and Development in Trecento Florentine Painting* (Rome, 1980), especially pp. 1–13.
55 For the origin of the word 'apocalypse' as 'uncover', see C. T. Onions ed., *The Oxford Dictionary of English Etymology* (Oxford, 1966), p. 42.
56 MED, 'awarien (v.)'.
57 MED, 'ro (n.(4))'.
58 Anselm, *Orationes sive meditationes*, in *Opera Omnia*, ed. Schmitt, III, p. 90.
59 Matt. 5: 15; Luke 8: 12; Luke 11: 33; Rev. 22: 5.

3

Blood and Chocolate: Affective Layering in *Swete Ihesu, now wil I synge*

Daniel McCann

Extract from *Swete Ihesu, now wil I synge*[1]
  Lines 105–56

105	Marie Mylde, freo and gent,	*noble*
	Preye for me – þou art present –	
	Whon my soule is from me went,	*when*
	Þat hit haue good Iuggement.	
	Ihesu, for loue þou soffredest wrong,	
110	Woundes sore and peyns strong;	
	Þi peens reuþful weore and long,	*pains; pitiful*
	Ne may me hit telle in spel ne song.	*prose tale*
	Ihesu, for loue þou suffredest so wo	*such*
	Þat bloodi stremes Ronne þe fro,	
115	Þi white bodi was bleyk and blo –	*black and blue*
	Vre sunnes hit made, weylawo!	*our sins*

---

[1] NIMEV 3238; DIMEV 5077. This extract from *Swete Ihesu, now wol I synge* (hereafter *Swete Ihesu*) is reproduced from C. Horstmann, ed., *Yorkshire Writers, Richard Rolle of Hampole, an English Father of the Church, and his Followers*, 2 vols (London and New York, 1895–96), II, 9–24, with the addition of glosses. All subsequent references are to this edition, cited in the text by line number. A slightly later edition is found in F. J. Furnivall, ed., *The Minor Poems of the Vernon Manuscript, Part 2*, EETS OS 117 (London, 1901; repr. 1973), pp. 449–62. In addition to these full editions, T. G. Duncan provides two smaller editions of lyrics that are clearly similar though they come from different manuscripts: Duncan, I, 67, p. 121 (NIMEV 3236; DIMEV 5075) and I, 68, pp. 121–2 (NIMEV 1747; DIMEV 2899). Each covers similar ground, and both represent distillations of the larger versions in Horstmann and Furnivall. However, while interesting in and of themselves, it is the larger Vernon version that is most interesting for my purposes. I do not support Furnivall's editorial division of this text into two separate lyrics. While the appearance of Mary may seem to suggest a separate lyric, a closer reading will show that the themes and images are merely overlaid upon each other: Mary is an extension, or means, of savouring the Holy Name. I therefore treat the lyric in the same way as the scribe of Vernon – as a single whole.

Ihesu, þi Coroune set þe sore,	was set painfully upon you
Þe scourgyng whon þow scourget wore;	were
Hit was for me – Ihesu, þin ore! –	mercy
120 Þe peynes þat þow þoledest þore.	endured there
Ihesu swete, þow heng on tre,	
Not for þi gult, but al for me,	
For sunnes and gult aȝeynes þe –	sins; against
Swete Ihesu, for-ȝif hem me.	
125 Ihesu, whon þow streyned wore,	were stretched out
Þi peynes woxen more and more.	grew
Þi Mooder euer wiþ þe was þore,	there
Wiþ serweful sikynges and wiþ sore.	sighs; pain
Ihesu, whi weore þou pyned so	tormented
130 Þat neuer wrouȝtest wrong ne wo?	carried out
Hit was for me, and moni mo,	many more
Þat þou so harde were bi-go.	beset so violently
Ihesu, whi weore þou so gelous,	jealous/ardent
So feruent and so disirrous	desirous
135 To buggen wiþ pris so precious	buy
Wrecche Mon so vicious?	
Ihesu, for vs þou henge on Rode,	the cross
For loue þou ȝeeue þin herte blode;	gave
Loue þe made vre soule foode,	
140 Þi loue vs brouhte to alle goode.	
Ihesu my lemmon, þou art so fre	beloved; generous
Þat al þou dedest for loue of me.	did
What schal I for þat ȝeelde þe?	give you back in return
Þow kepest not but þe loue of me.	take heed of nothing
145 Ihesu my god, my lord, my kyng,	
Þou askest me non oþer þyng	
But trewe loue and herte longyng	
And loue-teres and stille mournyng.	silent
Ihesu my deore, my loue, my liht,	
150 I wol þe louen, and þat is riht.	
Do me þe louen wiþ al my miht,	enable me to love you
And after þe Mourne dai & niht!	
Ihesu, do me so loue þe,	enable me so to love you
Þat my þouht ay on þe be;	always
155 Wiþ þin eȝen lok on me,	eyes
And Myldeliche my nede se.	

A woman who is very keen on chocolate once gave me some splendid chocolate, and saw me bite a great bit off, and said 'No, no, no, don't you know how to eat chocolate?' And I said, 'No, or at least I thought I did', and she said, 'No, you just take a tiny bit, put it on your tongue, ten minutes it will take, just let it melt, occasionally push it up against the roof of the mouth, and this great rainbow of flavours and textures melts in your mouth.' Now that's all poetry is in a sense.[2]

The medieval lyric must be savoured to be understood. Its poetic ligaments of form and metre, image and sound, must be masticated by the mind in the most sensitive of ways. Only through the process of rumination, itself a medieval metaphor for deliberative reading, can its complex blend of poetic flavours and tastes be unlocked. This is certainly the case with Middle English religious lyrics, and most emphatically with those that deal with devotion to the Holy Name. This grouping of texts draws inspiration from the anonymous *Jesu dulcis memoria*, a Cistercian hymn that deals with the 'sweetness' of Jesus and is preoccupied lexically and thematically with the taste of the Holy Name.

The most elaborate Middle English example is *Swete Ihesu, now wol I synge*, originally attributed to Richard Rolle by Carl Horstmann and found in its most extended form in the Vernon manuscript.[3] It is one of a number of similar, though much shorter, lyrics that all share the core purpose of 'savouring' the Holy Name. 'Ihesu' is all and everything, and this lyric plays with the language of love, but is not arch or overly stylised. It focuses on the taste of Jesus, on the sensory appreciation of His 'swete' name. Therein lies its subtle nuance and complexity, as savouring the quality of poetic 'sweetness' is far from a simple act.

As Mary Carruthers notes, throughout the period *dulcis* or sweetness has 'an essentially contrarian nature that includes within itself its opposites: bitter, salt, and sour'.[4] The sweetness of Jesus has a composite character, one that this lyric is completely aware of: his name evokes a complex taste, a blend of distinct and contrasting qualities that gradually unfold within the mouth of the mind. Its composite character also extends to its psychological attributes, as sweetness has both rational and affective aspects.[5] While all religious lyrics function as 'affective catalysts', those that deal with the sweetness of Jesus aim to do something more complex.[6] They seek to evoke not a shallow enthusiasm for Jesus, but a complex interior condition: a blend of contrasting affective states and modes of intersubjective awareness, a composite taste both delicious and disturbing – what *Swete Ihesu* calls 'loue longinge' (line 2).

The term 'loue longinge' is associated not only with secular love, but also with the highest levels of contemplative fervour. As Julian of Norwich notes, a

---

2   Interview with Stephen Fry, conducted by Jonathan Ross on the *Jonathan Ross Show* (BBC, London, October 2005).
3   Oxford, Bodleian Library, MS Eng. poet. a. 1, fols 298r–299r.
4   M. Carruthers, *The Experience of Beauty in the Middle Ages* (Oxford, 2013), p. 90.
5   Ibid., p. 98.
6   V. Gillespie, 'Moral and Penitential Lyrics', Duncan, *Companion*, pp. 68–95 (p. 70).

'trew longyng to God' is the most powerful medicine for the soul.[7] Its semantic range signals its intricacy. It primarily means 'to languish or pine in erotic or spiritual love'.[8] While this 'loue longinge' is the utmost expression of desire, it is a desire that is itself a combination of all other, contrasting, affective states. True 'loue longinge' is an affective complex, one that is so intense that it is painful, and contains as much fear of God and sorrow for sin as it does compassion and ardent love for the Divine.

A key theological treatise that clarifies the nature of this complex is the *De quatuor gradibus violentae caritatis* (*Four Degrees of Violent Love*) by Richard of St Victor.[9] It employs an expansive medical metaphor to delineate four levels of love for God. Each level is characterised by an increase in intensity and potency, and so the use of a medical register is not accidental: this love operates like a disease. The first three levels wound the soul, give it a fever and paralyse it.[10] The fourth is 'morbus irremediabilis et omnino desperabilis', a state of prolonged suffering 'ubi semper et remedium quaeritur, et nusquam invenitur, imo quidquid praesumitur ad remedium salutis, vertitur in augmentum furoris'.[11] This love destroys everything it touches. But that is how it should be: in its purest and highest form the love for God is a state of painful intensity.

It is this affective complex that *Swete Ihesu* seeks to evoke using vivid and rich poetic imagery. Both medieval psychology and poetic theory stress the ability of vivid imagery to generate affective reactions. Each poetic image is in practice a memory phantasm: a combination of verbally simulated sense data and the immediate psychological reaction to it.[12] When read or heard, each poetic image will evoke an affective reaction; the soul cannot behave otherwise. However, its psychological impact can be augmented through language. The

---

7   Julian of Norwich, *A Revelation of Love*, ed. M. Glasscoe (Exeter, 1976), p. 54.
8   MED, 'longen', senses 1a, b, and 2a.
9   Richard of St Victor, *De quatuor gradibus violentae caritatis*, PL 196: 1207C-24D; *Of the Four Degrees of Passionate Charity*, in *Richard of Saint Victor: Selected Writings on Contemplation*, trans. C. Kirchberger (New York, 1957), pp. 213-33. I follow Andrew Kraebel's translation of the title as *Four Degrees of Violent Love* rather than *Four Degrees of Violent Charity*. He, rightly to my mind, notes that the Latin is itself meant to seize attention, to offer a 'jarring' moment for the reader. See Kraebel's excellent introduction to the *Four Degrees of Violent Love*, in *On Love: A Selection of Works of Hugh, Adam, Achard, Richard, and Godfrey of St Victor: Victorine Texts in Translation Vol. 2*, ed. H. Feiss (Turnhout, 2012), p. 263 n. 2.
10 Richard, *Quatuor gradibus*, PL 196: 1209C-12C; *Four Degrees*, pp. 215-18.
11 Ibid., PL 196: 1212D; 'an incurable and wholly desperate sickness, in which a remedy is forever being sought and never found, in which indeed, whatever is considered remedial to health turns into an increase of the raging sickness', *Four Degrees*, p. 219.
12 M. Carruthers, *The Book of Memory: A Study of Memory in Medieval Culture* (Cambridge, 1990), pp. 57-60. V. Gillespie, 'Songs of the Threshold: Enargeia and the Psalter', *The Psalms and Medieval English Literature: From the Conversion to the Reformation*, ed. T. Atkin and F. Leneghan (Cambridge, 2017), pp. 271-97, and his 'The Senses in Literature: The Textures of Perception', *A Cultural History of the Senses in the Middle Ages*, ed. R. G. Newhauser (London, 2014), pp. 155-73 (p. 154).

lyrical form of *Swete Ihesu* works to amplify and modulate, controlling the passage of narrative time and accentuating the individual affective impacts of those images. At once bitter and sweet, this lyric is not concerned with a relentless focus on the crucified Christ, nor on his bloody body or pain. While such elements do appear, they are not the exclusive objects of focus. Mention of the Passion is thus tactical, enabling the lyric to evoke a layered affective state. Images do occur, but are not overabundant or lingered upon. Instead, they play off one another to generate composite aural and visual effects. Jesus is the ultimate, and so the lyric will constantly strive to present him in those superlative terms.

Many of the images and themes deployed harken back to biblical sources, such as the Song of Songs and the Psalms. As a result, the lyric's affective range is much more complex and complected than simply fear, penance, compassion or love. This text blends and mixes registers and images, thoughts and sensations, in a manner designed to evoke that state of 'loue longinge'. Its opening lines begin this process:

Swete Ihesu, kyng of blisse,	
Min herte loue, Min herte lisse:	*joy*
In loue, lord, þou me wisse,	*know*
And let me neuere þi loue misse. (lines 5–8)	

The reader here savours not the sweetness of Jesus but rather love itself, the word literally moved around the mouth time and again. The repetition of 'loue' in almost every line generates a recursive effect: the reader is encompassed about with talk of love, as the narrative voice loops round and round this central theme. The tactical use of possessives – 'Min herte loue' and 'þi loue misse' – works to connect the reader with Jesus: the thing we share with the Divine is the capacity for powerful love. The last line is almost but not entirely prayer-like. There is a sense of ambiguity and apprehension here, as the 'and let me neuere' places all agency within 'Ihesu's' hands. While this is a standard moment of humility, of giving due deference to the Divine, it nevertheless generates a change in tone. Desire shifts to pleading, and in so doing the line interposes a subtle sense of concern or anxiety into the stanza that adds much greater complexity to its overall tone and tenor.

This subtle shift continues in the next stanza, by a switch to a harsher form of end rhyme. Instead of soft and sibilant 'iss', this next stanza's lines end with 'liht / niht / miht / arhit' (lines 9–12). The result is that the reading process and the performance of the lyric begin to slow down – these words are not as easily or as softly spoken. The pace changes, as the reader is slowly compelled to savour the verse more. This continues in the next stanza:

Swete Ihesu, my soule bote,	*remedy*
In myn herte þou sette a Roote	
Of þi loue þat is so swote,	*sweet*
And weete hit þat hit springe mote! (lines 13–16)	*moisten; may grow*

Images of medicine and agriculture come together here in a rapid procession and reconfiguration. Jesus is not simply the remedy for the soul, but also its gardener – planting a root of his love within it that bursts forth. His operation within the soul is both regenerative and generative, but also far from gentle: his love has a definite force. He is also more emphatically sweet here – the word is repeated twice; once specifically in connection to the idea of God's love. Such images are given great space and focus, as the stanza employs a different and deeper end rhyme. The 'ote' sound is at once sonorous and meditative – the reader must adopt a specific posture, and must move through these simple patterns of sound in a more meditative and slow manner. The lyric, through its rhyme, is beginning to exert specific force upon the reader, augmenting the impact of its arresting images.

> Swete Ihesu, myn herte gleem,
> Brihtore þen þe sonne Beem:
> As þou weore boren In Bethleem,
> Þou make in me þi loue-dreem. (lines 17–20)

This is not simply stock language; it makes a very subtle theological point. The entire stanza is carefully undergirded with images of incarnation, of the ephemeral made flesh. The 'gleem' Jesus, brighter than all other light, becomes born in 'Bethleem'. Thus infleshed, he now becomes the fashioner of dreams: as light made flesh, he now makes the metaphysical 'loue-dreem' within the soul of the narrative voice. The intangible becomes tangible, and is forged through the work of the Light of the World.

From this point onwards, the tone of the text starts to change. The next stanza follows on from this talk of love, boldly asserting that anyone who hinders the narrative voice from loving Jesus will experience 'wo'. Yet, within the space of two lines, the narrative voice becomes penitential and humble, asking '3if me grace for to wepe / For my synnes teres wete' (lines 23–4). Immediately the emotional dimensions of the lyric change, as penitential thoughts and feelings become overlaid upon the 'loue' spoken of: the rhyme between 'swete' and 'wete' blends different affective registers together (lines 21, 24). This continues in subsequent stanzas:

> Swete Ihesu, me reweþ sore   *regret*
> Of my misdedes I haue don 3ore: *in the past*
> For-3if me, lord, I wol no more,
> But I þe aske Milce and ore. (lines 29–32)   *instead; mercy and grace*

Those penitential sentiments expressed earlier now come into a moment all of their own. The lines here extend and magnify that initial sense of sorrow for sin. Although very general, there is mention of misdeeds and of a great sorrow for sins committed. The stanza begins with the mention of Jesus's sweetness, but soon transforms into a penitential formula – a crafted cry for forgiveness and mercy. Time is subject to careful manipulation here, as the use of tense markers ('me reweþ', 'I haue don' and 'I wol no') generates a retrospective temporality to the stanza: it works to incorporate the prior sinful self into the present penitential moment. This allows the reader to be drawn much more directly into the narrative pattern of the lyric. Just as the past is brought into the present, so too the affective states the text describes are merged together. The loving address of 'Swete Ihesu' is now mixed and folded into a penitential moment, with the last line of the stanza functioning as another address to Christ that begs for pardon and mercy. Love and sorrow become interconnected as the text begins in earnest to evoke an affective complex within its reader.

Subsequent lines continue to beseech Christ, asking him: 'vndo myn herte and liȝte (*alight/dwell*) þerin / And saue me from wikked engyn (*schemes*)' (lines 35–6). Such affective development continues in the following stanza:

Swete Ihesu, lord good,	
For me þou scheddest þi blessed blod –	*shed*
Out of þin herte hit com þe flod –	
Þi Moder hit sauȝ wiþ druyri mod. (lines 37–40)	*saw; dreary feeling*

This is the first full and direct mention of the Passion, and it is presented in a series of imagistic fragments that increase in intensity and affective focus. Initially, the stanza presents Christ's blood, but before it does so it stipulates that the blood was shed 'Ffor me'. Such tactical use of the object pronoun connects the penitential states expressed earlier in the lyric directly to Christ's Passion.

From here the images become more intense, as the narrative gaze moves inwards to Christ's heart. It is the source of his blood, now described as a flood: the image is at once particular yet diffuse, focusing on a precise internal body part that is also the source of a vast expanse of blood. Rapid movement from Christ to his Mother adds to this effect. The narrative moves from the blood-flood to Mary's observation of it; perspective moves ever outwards, now considering the pain and suffering of Mary expressed in her face. End rhyme between 'blod / flod / mod' forges connections between these separate images, and maintains a meditative pace. This mention of her sadness makes the verse much more potent, and enhances its compassionate aspects by adding an intersubjective dimension: we not only see Christ suffer but Mary as well, all because of our sins. The images of the stanza oscillate between penance, the Passion and presentations of compassion, generating chains of association and affective evocation. The next stanza offers similar concatenated images. Jesus is the 'soule foode' – clearly a Eucharistic image, but one made affectively resonant by the subsequent use of rhyme: the food the narrator eats has first been hung 'vppon þe Roode' where it shed its 'swete blode' (lines 45–8).

Other aspects of Christ's life are also mined for their affective reach:

Swete Ihesu, Barn, Best,	*child*
Þi loue þou in myn herte fest;	*make fast*
Whon I go North, Souþ, Est or West,	
In þe al-one fynde I rest. (lines 49–52)	

The sudden change from the Passion to the Nativity allows its emotional aspects of tenderness and care to enter into the present narrative moment. This is a technique designed to augment and amplify the reader's affective engagement with the text: the Passion is now set beside the Nativity, as Christ the Child and Christ the Man of Sorrows blur into one. Affective states are becoming more clearly layered here, each one reiterated, contrasted and incorporated within others in structured shifts that orientate the reader's reactions. Yet this concentration of focus on particular events and moments in Christ's life is immediately contrasted with the strange image of Jesus being everywhere. The narrative perspective expands outwards from these precise events into a presentation of Jesus as omnidirectional. Such a shift generates a sudden sense of breathless immersion within Christ, and within the affective states that his life and death evoke.

The narrative begins to move beyond compassion here, and into something more intense. Subsequent lines make this clear, when the narrative voice asks 'Wiþ loue-cordes drauȝ (*drew*) þou me, / þat I may comen and wone (*dwell*) wiþ þe' (lines 55–6). This image of the 'loue-cordes' is rich in its suggestive range and potency. At once sublime and sinister, it conveys the sense not simply of love but also of menace: it is an image of imprisonment and constriction, one that echoes the 'loue-bonde' (line 28), and that similarly serves to draw the reader into unity with God. There is nothing easy or gentle about the image, but something immersive, inexorable and quietly forceful. It presents the multivalence of 'loue longinge': while Jesus is sweet, he is also powerful; suffering torture and aware of our sins, nonetheless he is also a figure to be desired. At this stage the lyric moves to one of its dominant structural patterns – a single stanza devoted to the Virgin Mary. This interposed reflection on Mary is used to break up the main narrative sections in the lyric. Yet it also has a further use: as Mary is usually associated with Christ's birth and death, mention of her can arouse all the tenderness of the Nativity alongside the compassionate awareness of her suffering at the Crucifixion. Those affective states are then used to enhance and magnify the following stanzas devoted to Christ. An affective complex, and indeed a sense of intersubjective awareness, is the result; one repeated at specific moments throughout the lyric:

> Ihesu, swete is þe loue of þe;
> Ne may no þing so swete be,
> Nouȝt þat mon may þenke or se,   *think of*
> Ne haue swetnesse aȝeynes þe. (lines 65–8)   *in comparison to*

This stanza propounds a poetics of negation, as Jesus and love are referred to in negative and exclusive terms. Essentially devoid of any real images, all that remains is the specification of Jesus as sweet and singular in his love. It is an open space, one that the reader occupies but now with all the imagistic and emotive freight generated by the preceding stanzas. Depth of feeling is what the lyric is striving for, and the reader now moves into a deeper engagement with Jesus.

As with the opening of the lyric, this stanza repeats 'swete' to make the reader savour the verse, but it is a taste that is becoming ever more complicated:

> Ihesu, no song mai be swettore,
> Ne þou3t in herte Blisfollere, *more blissful*
> Nou3t may be feeled lihtsomere *more readily/pleasantly*
> Þen þou, so swete a louyere. (lines 69–72)

The imagery of the stanza becomes more concrete. Emotional responses are also specified and patterned on these various images. Affective states thus begin to enter into the verse in a careful arrangement. We find here not one affective response to Christ but a series, articulated through a pattern of negation that works to lay emphasis on the sweetness of Christ. This layering continues, as a new affective note is struck:

> Ihesu þi loue was vs so fre *liberal*
> Þat hit from heuene brou3te þe,
> For love ful deore bou3test þou me,
> For loue þow henge on Roode-tre. (lines 73–6) *the cross*

After all this talk of the sweetness of Jesus, after the play of images of bliss and joy, the tones and colours of the Passion enter once again into the narrative. It is a gentle move, one delayed for as long as possible: only the last line mentions the 'Roode-tre'. Up until this point we are presented with allusions to the Passion. Love is the focus initially, the greatest love in the universe that made Christ come down from heaven and onto the cross. But this structured move to the Passion brings with it a range of additional ideas and images that add a different dimension to the affective states evoked up until now. From here the lyric enters into a small narrative retelling of the events leading up to the Passion (lines 76–85). This is a highly sophisticated move, as narrative time goes backwards: the reader leaves the 'Roode-tre', and moves not to its aftermath, but to the events leading up to it. Any expectations of narrative sequence are frustrated, yet such a technique allows extra details and affective states to be evoked: the reader can now return to specific moments with a heightened sense of their importance.

The emotional range of these subsequent stanzas covers sorrow and fear, yet not for the self, rather, it is the fear of the disciples at the apprehension of Jesus that is focused on. There is an intersubjective awareness developing here, one that is extended when the lyric renarrates the events in the Garden in Gethsemane and focuses on Christ's emotional turmoil (lines 86–104). However, instead of progressing further towards the Crucifixion, the narrative breaks to interpose a stanza on Mary (lines 105–9). This is essentially a prayer to Mary for help in the future when the narrator dies and is judged. While its presence may seem odd, it is a deliberate move. The stanza's function is to take the preceding lines on Christ's suffering, and the affective states they evoke, and convert that emotive energy into prayer. The past of Gethsemane, brought into the present moment by the lyric, is ultimately used to help safeguard the future judgement. It is, though, simply a prelude:

> Ihesu, for loue þou soffredest wrong.
> Woundes sore and peynes strong;
> Þi peynes reuþful weore and long, *pitiful*
> Ne may me hit telle in spel ne song. (lines 109–12) *prose*

From here on the lyric becomes darker, more striking, more complex. The narrative perspective changes to a loose focus upon Christ's 'woundes' and 'peynes'. Suffering, pain, and pity all coalesce here and are overlaid upon a direct mention of the Passion. The end rhyme, 'wrong / strong / long / song', works not only to provide extra detail about the nature of this event, but also generates connections here between the juridical, the powerful, the temporal, and the lyrical. The 'song' that the text presents itself as, covers, in effect, all these things. It is pain that acts as the focal point of the stanza – repeated twice – but used only to further the complex affective states that the lyric seeks to evoke. This can be seen in the last line with its use of negation. The 'ne song' is a phrase that echoes the earlier and more joyful stanzas, and it works to recall their affective range into this narrative moment, and to blend that joy with the pain and suffering mentioned now.

The reader's affective disposition is being carefully structured. No one affective state dominates – all must share space mentally and, indeed, within the stanza, with one another. The overall intensity is soon increased:

> Ihesu, for loue þou suffredest so wo, *such*
> Þat bloodi stremes Ronne þe fro,
> Þi white bodi was bleyk and blo – *black and blue*
> Vre sunnes hit made, weylawo! (lines 113–16) *our*

Such images of the Passion, though forceful and potent, are not lingered over. Each line adds new detail, but quickly moves the narrative gaze in a slightly different direction. It is that narrative movement that is key to understanding this lyric, as the whole stanza carefully layers affective states in each of its main parts. The initial mention of love and woe in the first line shifts into compassionate response in lines two and three, before entering into a penitential posture in the final line. Ending with the trisyllabic interjection 'weylawo', this line gives the stanza its full force and potency, as language breaks down under the emotional weight of the stanza into a single cry. But it is that precise movement that is key: the full range of affective states are covered here, each passion set upon the prior to create a lattice-like structure of affectivity and indeed self-reflexivity. This is the 'loue longinge' described, that blend of love and pain so necessary to reach God.

The following stanza focuses on the scourging and the crowning with thorns, and makes the explicit point that such pains are the result of the reader's sin (lines 117–20). It is a scene of intersubjectivity, creating a heightened awareness of the relationship between God and the self. The stanzas following this one offer similar moments: interspersed among specific and local observations on the Passion are the presence of Mary and her pain (lines 125–8). The emotional ambit of the lyric expands, as does the reader's scripted sense of awareness.

A series of rhetorical questions are then introduced (lines 129–32), each one designed to evoke specific forms of self-awareness. In a highly arresting moment, the narrative voice asks Christ 'what sauh þow (*did you see*) on me' (lines 133–6) to endure the Passion. Such rhetorical questions bring the whole weight of the Passion and its implications home to the individual reader.

From here, things become ever more extreme:

> Ihesu, for vs þou henge on Rode,
> For loue þou 3eeue þin herte blode;   *gave*
> Loue þe made vre soule foode,
> Þi loue vs brouhte to alle goode. (lines 141–4)   *all that is good*

Images, concepts and sensory states combine here in strange and arresting ways. Love is the focus of the stanza, but each line pairs that love with unusual associations. Love cannot be viewed or apprehended without the cross, without the 'herte blode', and without food. The first two lines situate love within the confines of the Passion, giving it a range of specific associations. Placed within the shadow of the cross, love becomes not simply self-sacrifice but also a form of torture: it is linked to violent pain and death. The third line adds yet greater complexity, as it moves the reader into a specific sensory realm: taste. This is a key moment in the verse, as the mention of 'soule foode' immediately recalls the idea of sweetness that opens and governs the entire lyric. The function of this line is to allow that bloody love of God mentioned earlier to enter into the mouth – to make the reader savour that complex taste of love in all its intense associations. The 'swete Ihesu' is now the aggregate product of pain, torture, death and nourishment: all these aspects to the love of God, and for God, are rendered as sweet to the palate. It is this complex love-taste alone that leads to the point of the last line, namely, that such love, such a blend of pain and delight, is entirely good.

The next stanza changes emphasis, posing the rhetorical question to Jesus, 'what schal I for þat 3eelde þe?' (line 147). This is a moment not of affect, but rather self-reflexivity, when the narrative voices pauses to reflect on the Passion and its implications, and to wonder what love could possibly repay Christ's. The lyric immediately offers an answer:

> Ihesu my god, my lord, my kyng,
> Þou askest me non oþer þyng
> But trewe loue and herte longyng
> And loue-teres and stille mournyng. (lines 149–51)   *silent*

What is required of the reader is a complex state of emotion: 'loue longinge'. This is not simply mentioned but also explained. Each line offers an insight into what loving God really entails. The 'trewe loue and herte longyng' are but half of the matter; 'loue-teres and stille mournyng' are also required. 'Loue longinge' is the aggregate product of these seemingly contrasting states. These are strange combinations: love to the point of crying; a grief that is 'stille'. The semantic range of this adjective is wide, and can mean silent, motionless, incessant, hidden and meek.[13] It is at once gentle and sinister, in the same way as the grief one should feel ought to be both silent and incessant, meek and motionless. The overall impression is one of arrested fixity, of grief so strong as to be a never-ending presence. 'Loue longinge' is something strange, something other; but also something divinely requested.

That, of course, is the whole point of the verse. The rest of the lyric operates in much the same way, but towards the end there is one stanza that describes exactly what the lyric hopes to achieve:

> Ihesu, mihtful Heuene-kyng,   *powerful*
> Þi loue beo al my lykyng,   *pleasure*
> Mi mournyng and my longyng,
> Wiþ swete teres wepyng. (lines 284–8)

Grief and sadness, sorrow and tears, are all part of the painful intensity of this form of love. It is not one thing but rather a combination of both pleasure and pain – a layered affective state that demands the utmost from the soul. The line 'swete teres wepyng' is at once sublime and extreme: it adds the sense of taste, itself now inflected with the horrors of the Passion from the previous stanzas, to the states of sorrow and love. The end rhyme between the present participles 'lykyng / mourning / longyng / wepyng', works to generate an arrested temporality, as each affect is coterminous with the others. The 'longyng' described here folds in all such states, taking them to ever higher levels of intensity. This is given powerful articulation by the mention of the taste of those tears: 'longyng' is a complex taste of 'sweteness', one comprised of a range of flavours that find their origin in the blood, sweat and tears of Christ, his mother, and the reader. For this lyric the point is clear: good poetry is like good chocolate – the darker the better.

---

13   MED, 'stille', senses 1–6.

4

Textual and Affective Stability in *All Other Love is Like the Moon*

Michael P. Kuczynski

All Other Love is Like the Moon[1]

    Al oþer loue is lych þe mone
    þat wext and wanet as flour in plein,   *flourishes and withers*
    as flour þat fayret and fawyt sone,
    as day þat [a]ddt and endt in rein.   *dawns (i.e. brightens)*

5   Al oþer loue bigint bi blisse,
    in wep and wo mak is hendyng: *ending*
    no loue þer nis þat oure halle lysse,   *restores our health*
    [Bot][2] wat areste in Evene-Kynge,   *the King of Heaven*

    Wos loue ys ai [and][3] eure grene,   *eternally*
10 and eure ful wythoute wanyyng;
    is loue suetyth wythoute tene,   *his; sweetens; pain*
    is loue is hendles and a-ring.   *everywhere*

    Al oþer loue Y flo for þe: *rejected*
    Tel me, tel me, wer þou lyst?   *reside*
15 'In Marie mylde an fre
    I schal be founde, ak mor in Crist.'   *but more*

For a broader essay on the issues faced by editors of medieval lyrics, see Chapter 1, Thomas G. Duncan, 'Editing Issues in Middle English Lyrics'.

1   NIMEV 196; DIMEV 353. I transcribe *All Other Love* here from Windsor, Eton College, MS 36, fol. 238rb, the unique manuscript witness, with the addition of glosses. I enclose my editorial interventions in square brackets and explain in the notes how my text differs from readings in the MS and from Carleton Brown's edition (Brown *XIV*, pp. 65–6, no. 49). I am grateful to Sally Jennings, Collections Administrator at Eton College Library, for arranging my examination of Eton College 36 and to the Provost and Fellows of Eton College for permission to reproduce photographs from the manuscript.
2   Brown *XIV*'s emendation; MS omits.
3   Brown *XIV* ' … and'; MS 'ai' and 'and' or the ampersand omitted.

> Crist me founde, nouht Y þe hast:
> hald me to þe with[4] al þi meyn. company
> Help geld þat mi loue be stedfast,[5] grant or assure
> 20 lest þus sone it turne ageyn.
>
> Wan nov hy[e]t[6] myn hert is sor,
> ywys hie spilt myn herte blod. i.e. Christ
> God sauue[7] mi lef, Y sei[8] na more – beloved one
> hyet Y hoppe hys wil be god. yet
>
> 25 Allas whai wole Y a Rome?
> Seye Y may in lore of loue: learning/experience in love
> 'Vndo Y am by manne[s][9] dome judgement
> bot he me help þat syt aboue!' unless; sits/reigns

Editors and anthologists of Middle English lyric poetry are often necessarily more concerned with stabilising the texts of their poems, in order to maximise accessibility and readability, than with presenting specific accounts of the poems' manuscript sources. In this chapter, I argue nevertheless that a detailed analysis of the manuscript context of an especially compelling fourteenth-century religious lyric, *All Other Love is Like the Moon* (hereafter simply *All Other Love*), is crucial to an accurate understanding of both its text and its affectivity or emotional dimension.[10] Ever since Wordsworth, in the preface to *Lyrical Ballads*, defined 'all good poetry' as 'the spontaneous overflow of powerful feelings', literary historians have been at pains to distinguish – in terms of kind – the aims and achievements of medieval lyric poets from their Romantic descendants.[11] E. K. Chambers's surprise at 'examples of individual lyric emotion disengaging itself' from common religious themes in a few Middle English lyrics points to a general distrust by critics of affective authenticity in the poems as a group.[12] To be sure, the authors of these poems, largely anonymous clerics, use a language of cliché and can be less adept at stylistic innovation than they are at recycling conventional themes and diction. However, when critics explore the manuscript circumstances of certain Middle English religious lyrics, they yield insights into

---

4   MS and Brown *XIV* 'wiht', which should probably be corrected as a simple transposition error. The scribe writes this word correctly twice in the preposition 'wythoute' earlier in the poem.
5   Brown *XIV* 'ste<d>fast', marking his conjecture, although Anglicana 'd' remains clear in the MS.
6   Brown *XIV*'s emendation; MS 'hyt'.
7   Brown *XIV* 'canne', mistaking a clear 's' in the MS for 'c'.
8   Brown *XIV* 'care' is not supported by what remains of the MS letterforms.
9   MS omits terminal 's' and Brown *XIV* does not provide it.
10 For the basic bibliography on *All Other Love*, see NIMEV 196 and DIMEV 353.
11 R. L. Brett and A. R. Jones, eds, *Wordsworth and Coleridge: Lyrical Ballads* (London, 2005), p. 291.
12 E. K. Chambers, ed., *Early English Lyrics: Amorous, Divine, Moral, and Trivial* (London, 1907), p. 286.

how the poets engaged some of their most important religious beliefs and their emotional implications. I have argued elsewhere that some shorter religious verse in Middle English is sophisticated as a medium for doctrinal statement and dispute.[13] Additionally, poems such as *All Other Love* indicate that their authors regarded theology both as a means of thinking about God and also of feeling his presence.

All Other Love survives in a single manuscript copy, written out in the bottom-right-hand quadrant of fol. 238rb of Windsor, Eton College, MS 36, a fourteenth-century theological compendium (see fig. 1). The main items in the volume are all Latin prose: a well-known alphabetic index of canon law by Martin of Troppau (d.1279); extracts from the *Quaestiones disputatae* of Thomas Aquinas (1225–74) – *De malo* ('Concerning Evil') and *De spiritualibus creaturis* ('Concerning Spiritual Creatures'); and a commentary on chapters 26–8 of St Matthew's Gospel, the Passion narrative, which cites frequently the exegeses of Bede and Rhabanus Maurus.[14] Moreover, Eton College 36 has extensive Latin (and some very brief English) annotation throughout, both in its margins and on its front and back flyleaves, done in a variety of hands that are contemporary with or slightly later than the handwriting of its main texts. It also contains a copy of a popular series of three Latin couplets on the nature of Christian honour (*Nobilitas hominis est mens deitatis ymago*, fol. 132vb). These verses are in the same hand as the Troppau and appear as a coda to that text.[15]

Carleton Brown was the first to edit *All Other Love*, in his groundbreaking 1924 anthology *Religious Lyrics of the XIVth Century*.[16] He confines his remarks on the poem's manuscript context to an endnote:

> These verses are written in pencil on a page left nearly blank at the end of the text of Vegetius, *De Re Militari*. The hand, in the opinion of Dr. James, Provost of Eton, is very little later than 1350. I am under the greatest obligations to Dr. James for his kindness in calling my attention to these verses and also for

---

13 M. P. Kuczynski, 'Theological Sophistication and the Middle English Religious Lyric: A Polemic', *Chaucer Review* 45 (2011), pp. 321–39.
14 For a detailed description of the manuscript, see N. R. Ker, *Medieval Manuscripts in British Libraries, II, Abbotsford-Keele* (Oxford, 1977), pp. 665–6. There is also a summary one in M. R. James, *A Descriptive Catalogue of the Manuscripts in the Library of Eton College* (Cambridge, 1895), p. 18.
15 See H. Walther, *Initia Carminum ac Versuum Medii Aevi Posterioris Latinorum* (Göttingen, 1959), p. 608, no. 11860.
16 I discuss in this chapter Brown's edition and those in two other important anthologies: C. Sisam and K. Sisam, eds, *The Oxford Book of Medieval English Verse* (Oxford, 1970), pp. 182–3; and J. C. Hirsh, ed., *Medieval Lyric: Middle English Lyrics, Ballads and Carols* (Oxford, 2005), pp. 91–2, no. 26. I do not, however, discuss the text in the popular Norton classroom edition by M. S. Luria and R. L. Hoffman, eds, *Middle English Lyrics* (New York, 1974), since the editors produce a conflated text from Brown and Sisam rather than offering their own readings.

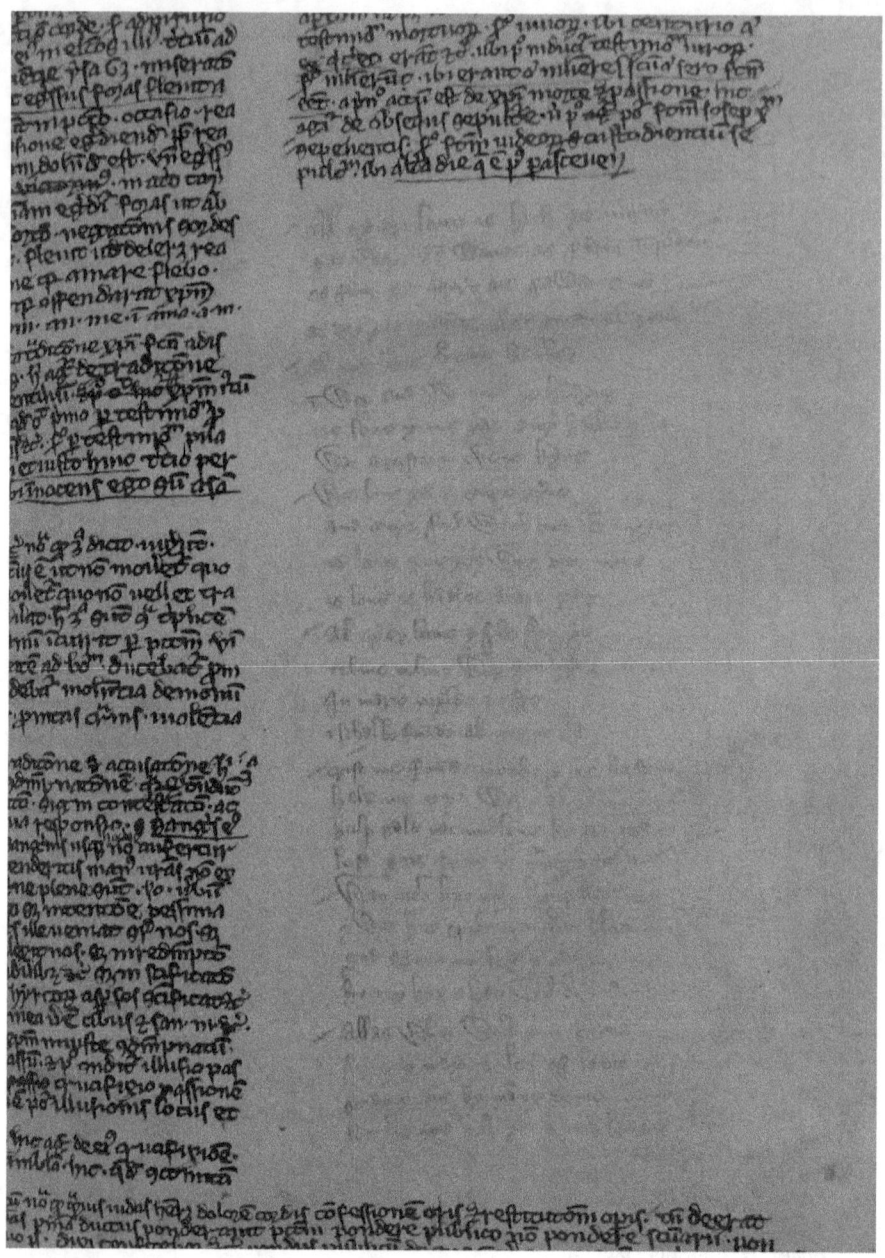

Fig. 1: Eton College, MS 36, fol. 238rb, *All Other Love is Like the Moon*. Photo by the author and reproduced by permission of the Provost and Fellows of Eton College

Fig. 2: Eton College, MS 36, fol. 238rb (detail in raking light), *All Other Love is Like the Moon*, lines 9–24. Photo by the author and reproduced by permission of the Provost and Fellows of Eton College

his patience in assisting me to decipher some of the lines which have become almost illegible.[17]

Some of this is accurate. The scribe has indeed written his text in what is a mid- to late- fourteenth-century Anglicana hand in pencil, with a sharp lead point. Much of his writing, especially down the right-hand side of the page, is rubbed heavily and nearly away in several places, where the parchment has buckled and been folded. This wear-and-tear has injured the text of the poem, although some of its damaged readings – many of them recovered with varying degrees of accuracy by Brown with the assistance of James – become even more legible under ultraviolet or in raking light (fig. 2).

It is not true, however, that the poem has been written on 'a page left nearly blank'. In fact, the first column of fol. 238r – not fol. 103r as Brown gives it in his edition, following an earlier foliation of the manuscript that numbers its three major textual components separately – is densely filled with Latin, as is the top third of the second column, in the bottom two-thirds of which *All Other*

---

17   Brown *XIV*, p. 263, no. 49. In his revised edition, published in 1952, G. V. Smithers makes no adjustments to Brown's endnote or to his text of the poem.

Love appears. Additionally, the bottom margin of fol. 238r is filled across the width of the page with Latin notes on the main text. While not his intention, Brown seems to imply in his endnote that *All Other Love* is one of a sub-class of Middle English lyrics – unlike, say, certain of the religious poems of Harley 2253 – recorded adventitiously on an endleaf or flyleaf of a manuscript by a scribe searching for empty parchment, rather than carefully and as a more integral part of a book, related in general or specific ways to some or all of the other texts in the volume.

Furthermore, *All Other Love* is not written at the end of a copy of *De re militari* ('Concerning Military Matters') by Vegetius, whose late Latin treatise is not among the contents of Eton College 36. Rather, the lyric appears immediately after an exegesis of St Matthew's account of Jesus's Last Supper, abduction, trial, crucifixion and burial – events that are of course immediately congruent with the Middle English poem's emphasis on the intensity and stability of God's love for the soul, as it is perfectly manifested by Christ. Brown's error about the Vegetius resulted, probably, from his use during his research of two different catalogues of Eton manuscripts, whose divergent numbering systems he confused, and from his not having read closely enough the Latin that surrounds the Middle English lyric on the page. Given his acknowledgement in his endnote of M. R. James's help in dating the hand of *All Other Love*, he must have worked with James's 1895 *Descriptive Catalogue*. This account superseded the hand-list of Eton manuscripts provided in Edward Bernard and Humfrey Wanley's two-volume *Catalogi librorum manuscriptorum Angliae et Hiberniae in unum collecti* (Oxford, 1697), 'the only attempt at a Catalogue', James notes in his preface, 'which has yet seen the light'.[18] Brown also had to have consulted, however, Bernard and Wanley's outdated catalogue. Whereas James assigns the theological compendium containing *All Other Love* the number 36 and the title 'TABULA MARTINI, ETC.,' Bernard and Wanley's number 36 is a different book altogether, a conflate manuscript containing, according to their hand-list, 'Cassiodori Hist. tripartite. | Martini Chron. | Veget. de re Militari'.[19] The name *Martini* in each catalogue entry and, possibly, references to *hostes* ('enemies') and *milites* ('soldiers') in the commentary on St Matthew's Gospel adjacent on the page to *All Other Love* presumably led Brown to confuse the two manuscripts and to mistake the Latin surrounding the lyric in James's MS 36 as Vegetius's treatise.[20]

Notwithstanding this error about context, Brown's edition of the poem itself is generally accurate, given the manuscript's multiple losses. Two major cruces demanded his attention and he alerts the reader to his engagement with them by symbols in his text. The first, at the start of line 8, is the scribe's omission of an adversative conjunction, which Brown provides in angled brackets: 'no loue

---

18   James, *Descriptive Catalogue*, vii.
19   E. Bernard and H. Wanley, *Catalogi librorum manuscriptorum Angliae et Hiberniae in unum collecti cum indice alphabetico*, 2 vols (Oxford, 1697), II, 47.
20   James's number 131, headed in his catalogue simply 'CASSIODORII HISTORIA TRIPARTITA, ETC.,' is the only Eton manuscript to contain Vegetius's text.

þer nis þat oure halle lysse, / <bot> wat areste in evene kyng' (lines 7–8). This emendation all subsequent editors of the poem adopt. The second crux, at the midpoint of line 9, Brown refrains from resolving, since it involves a missing word and, given the lack of another manuscript witness to the poem, would require a conjectural emendation. Here he inserts an ellipsis – 'wos loue ys … & eure grene' – and provides an explanatory note at the bottom of the page: 'A word is missing; no gap in MS.'[21] This crux, as we shall see, subsequent editors of *All Other Love* approach more adventurously.

In addition to these two interventions, Brown misreads the manuscript of the lyric in a few other places, where its words have become faint. For example, the last line of the first quatrain he transcribes unconvincingly: 'as day þat *scwret* (*showers*) and endt in rein' (my italics). Allowing that additional text may have been lost on the page since 1924, the space in which the scribe has written what Brown reads as 'scwret' could not have accommodated these graphs. I conjecture, instead, 'addt' – dawns or brightens.[22] The scribe's capital 'W' is easily confused with double-'d', the two graphs that are still clearly visible in the manuscript. Moreover, under ultraviolet light, 'a' emerges more clearly in the position immediately before 'ddt'. I discuss two other misconstrued readings by Brown that affect the poem's interpretation, these in the penultimate quatrain of the poem, below.

Dissatisfied with Brown's ellipsis and hesitancy to emend in line 9, Celia and Kenneth Sisam, the second editors to publish *All Other Love*, conjecture a reading for the missing word that amplifies the lyric's opening floral imagery. They do not mark their conjecture with symbols, but do identify it at the back of their anthology in a textual note:

> Whos love is *fresh* and evre greene   (my italics)
> And evre full without wanyng;
> His love sweeteth withoutë teene,
> His love is endless and a-ring. (lines 9–12)

---

9 *fresh* not in MS.[23]

Overall, the Sisam text is much cleaner – one is tempted to say fresher – than that found in Brown. The editors do not left-justify their lines, as Brown does in imitating the manuscript, where the rhymes are marked by braces; they indent every other one, presenting the lyric in modern verse format. They also regularise and modernise the poem's spelling (for example, expanding thorn to 'th' and the ampersand to 'and') and point its metre – note my use of an umlaut in the quotation above – so that the lyric's genuinely musical quality will not be missed. Brown printed, with only minor exceptions, a diplomatic transcript of

---

21 Brown *XIV*, p. 65.
22 MED 'adauen' (v.1), sense 1. (a) To dawn, become day; shine.
23 Sisam and Sisam, eds, *Medieval English Verse*, pp. 182–3 (text), p. 580 (note), respectively. That the Sisams worked from Brown's text rather than from the original manuscript is suggested by their duplication of his foliation error in their notes.

what he read and attempted to reconstruct from the unique manuscript witness. The Sisams print a more cosmetic edition of the poem, smoother both in terms of its appearance on the page and with respect to its language.

In his recent edition of *All Other Love*, John C. Hirsh follows a middle path, restoring the lyric's manuscript layout and its orthography but also emending conjecturally in a more expansive way than Brown does. Like the Sisams, he accepts Brown's emendation to the start of line 8 ('bot'). Hirsh rejects, however, both Brown's ellipsis and the Sisams' conjecture of 'fresh' at the middle of line 9, preferring an abstract adjective for their figurative one: 'Wos love ys *sure* and eure grene' (my italics).[24] Because Hirsh commendably indicates his interventions by way of notes that appear in the margins with his glosses of difficult words, he, like the Sisams, forgoes the use of symbols in the text itself. His conjecture of 'sure', however, while in keeping with the poem's overall theme, remains as subjective as the Sisams'.[25]

The manuscript evidence in Eton College 36 suggests a more likely alternative. All previous editors of the lyric assume that the scribe first omitted an adjective in line 9 of *All Other Love* and then wrote on the page some form of the word 'and', either the contraction 'ad' with a suspension line over it (the form he uses earlier, in line 2 of the poem) or the ampersand. Ultraviolet light confirms, however, that he first wrote 'ai' – the adverb 'always' – then, evidently, omitted the conjunction, probably due to eyeskip to the adverb's synonym, 'eure'. I restore the line thus and quote the full quatrain to indicate its relevant context in the lyric:

Wos loue ys ai [and] eure grene,	*always*
And eure ful wythoute wanyyng.	
is loue suetyth wythoute tene,	*his; sweetens; pain*
is loue is hendles and a-ring. (lines 9–12)	*everywhere*

The doublet 'ever and ay' or 'ay and ever' means, in theological contexts in Middle English, 'forever' or 'eternally' and emphasises here the endlessness of God's love. This transcendent love, which has existed towards his creatures always, even before they came into particular existence, is superior to all other earthly loves, which are bound by time.[26] Scripture mentions the point more than once (for example, 'Before I formed thee in the bowels of thy mother, I knew thee', Jer. 1: 5)[27] and it was a key principle of medieval theology, explained for example in the *Summa theologiae* of Thomas Aquinas, some of whose other works are collected in Eton College 36: 'Ad secundum dicendum quod, licet creaturae ab aeterno non fuerint nisi in Deo, tamen per hoc quod ab aeterno in Deo fuerunt ab aeterno Deus cognovit res in propriis naturis, et eadem ratione amavit.'[28] Line 10 adds

---

24 Hirsh, ed., *Medieval Lyric*, p. 92.
25 Hirsh, ed., *Medieval Lyric*, p. 91.
26 MED 'ai' (adv.), sense 4. Phrases and combs.
27 When I quote the Bible in English, I do so from the Douay-Rheims version, when in Latin, from Bonifatius Fischer's edition of the Vulgate.
28 'Though creatures have not been everlasting, except in God, yet because they are present from eternity in him, he knows them from eternity in their own proper nature, and from

to this point about the comprehensive nature of divine love by describing it as always complete ('ful'); and line 12, at the end of the quatrain, complements both of these observations when the speaker explains that Christ's affection is also 'a-ring', a Middle English word that is unique to *All Other Love* and likely means that God's love is, being eternal and complete, also limitless in space, extent or quantity – that is, beyond measure.[29]

The religious thoughts and feelings developed in *All Other Love*, then, are complex. The Sisams, however, simplify them by another major intervention in their text, this one to the lyric's structure. Frustrated possibly by the obscure sense of Brown's version of the poem's last three quatrains, they cut them entirely and acknowledge the abridgement only by a perfunctory note at the back of their anthology: 'Three verses omitted after l. 16.'[30] By deciding to end their version of the lyric prematurely, with the injunction of personified Love to the poem's speaker that true love can be found 'In Marie mylde an fre / ... ak more in Crist' (lines 15–16), they turn the poem into a more or less conventional lyric in praise of Jesus. The lyric's first quatrain consists of three clichés concerning earthly love's instability, which would have been familiar to any medieval reader: the flower that blooms and quickly fades; the day that brightens at dawn and ends in foul weather; the affair that begins happily but concludes in tears. This theme of love's passing seems to persist at the start of the second quatrain, when the speaker implies a complaint of lovesickness, but immediately shifts from an earthly to heavenly register once he identifies the cure for his illness as the love of Heaven's King. After he explains the nature of this sacred love in the poem's third quatrain, by defining it as all that profane love is not – eternal and infinite – he begins the fourth quatrain by forsaking all false loves for God's true love and pleading that Love tell him where this love can be found. Love directs him to the Blessed Virgin, the traditional *mediatrix* between sinful mankind and God, and more emphatically to Christ himself. With this appeal by the speaker and Love's instruction, the Sisam version concludes definitively with the name of the true lover, 'Crist'.

In its complete manuscript version, however, *All Other Love* becomes less rather than more emotionally settled after Love's advice to the speaker. The lyric's fifth and sixth quatrains dramatise the speaker's affective uncertainty and instability. This condition worsens despite the awareness he has developed of the essential difference between earthly and heavenly love and the preeminence of the latter. In the opening line of the fifth quatrain, for example, he admits his powerlessness to love God of his own volition: 'Crist me founde, nouht Y þe

eternity loves them', Prima Pars, Q. 20 (Love in God), art. 2, reply to objection 2. For the Latin text and facing English translation, see Thomas Aquinas, *Summa theologiae*, ed. and trans. M. Browne and A. Fernandez (New York, 1963), V, pp. 62–3.

29 MED cites only the word's use in *All Other Love*. OED cites an early seventeenth-century use of the preposition combined with the verb used as an adverb. See, for the latter, 'a-ring', *adv.*, In circumference (noted as rare).

30 Sisam and Sisam, eds, *Medieval English Verse*, p. 580.

hast' ('I didn't find you [i.e. Love], Christ found me', line 17) and pleads that Love 'hald me to þe with al þi meyn (*company*)' (line 18), since he knows that his love of God is unstable and may 'sone … turne ageyn' (line 20). Like the man in St Mark's Gospel, who has both faith and doubt – 'I do believe, Lord; help my unbelief' (Mark 9: 24) – the speaker of *All Other Love* is in crisis. His struggle is every Christian's earthly dilemma, only to be resolved in eternity. He wages the war within himself that St Paul describes in Romans 7: 23; he undergoes the torment that St Augustine recounts in Book 7 of his *Confessions* when, in the 'regio dissimilitudinis' ('region of unlikeness'), he both desires God but also maintains his attachment to creatures.[31] His soul knows itself to be in a state of spiritual conflict. He attempts to understand how it can cling, by way of affect, to a lesser love even as it aspires to the greatest. This psychology of affective dissonance is the real focus of *All Other Love*. It gives a rich emotional dimension to the lyric's theology, but is largely absent from the poem in the Sisams' truncated and more comforting version.

The penultimate stanza of the lyric adds emotional depth to the speaker's problem, as the poet adapts to his persona's situation one of the most powerful affective images in medieval art, the wound in Christ's side. Brown emends sensibly the first line of this quatrain, but then misreads two crucial words in its third line, occluding a key moment in the poem's affective development:

Brown's version:

Wan nov hy<e>t myn hert is sor,
ywys hie spilt myn herte blod.
God **canne** mi lef, Y **care** na more –
hyet Y hoppe hys wil be god.
(lines 21–4)

My version:

Wan nov hy[e]t myn hert is sor,
ywys hie spilt myn herte blod.
God **sauue** mi lef, Y **sei** na more –
hyet Y hoppe hys wil be god.

Brown's emendation of the manuscript's 'hyt' ('it') to 'hyet' ('yet'), adopted as well by Hirsh, helps the sense and seems to be sound.[32] In transcribing the second word of line 23, however, Brown mistakes a clear initial 's' for 'c', causing him then to misread the minims that follow as double-'n' rather than double-'u', thereby producing the erroneous reading 'canne' for 'sauue'. Four words later, probably under the inducement of this error and feeling alliterative, he lapses more egregiously, misreading the admittedly faint but still legible scribal word 'sei' as 'care'. Brown's mistaken version suggests that the speaker has relinquished all of his spiritual anxieties because of his faith in God's omniscience. The final line of the quatrain, however, which has to mean something like 'nevertheless, I hope that his [i.e. God's] will is good', implies doubt rather than faith. Moreover, the poet's powerful if conventional image of Christ spilling the speaker's heart-blood in the second line of the quatrain suggests that the emotional situation has become more intense rather than more settled. Brown's desire to see the lyric

---

31 See J. J. O'Donnell, ed., *Augustine: Confessions, Volume II; Commentary, Books 1–7* (Oxford, 2013), pp. 443–5.
32 Hirsh, ed., *Medieval Lyric*, p. 92.

moving from spiritual conflict to resolve is understandable – indeed is the same feeling that moved the Sisams to edit *All Other Love* aggressively by suppressing the poem's final three quatrains. An editor's affective impulses, however, are not always the same as a medieval poet's.

For although the speaker of *All Other Love* is ready to receive Christ's love, his heart is still 'sor' – it aches – because of its continuing earthly attachments. The lyric's speaker is not the clerical poet himself but a representative 'I' – perhaps the soul (*anima*) or the personification of Holy Church, the Bride (*sponsa*) of the heavenly Bridegroom (*sponsus*), or some collective Christian other. At this point, the speaker is in a passive condition and has to be wounded mystically if he or she wishes to achieve union with God. Barbara Kowalik argues that the poet intends the speaker's bleeding heart to be analogous with Christ's heart-wound on the cross, as if here the Bride is already somehow identified with the Bridegroom: 'He [i.e. Christ] has certainly spilled my heart-blood!' (translation of line 22).[33] The appeal to crucifixion iconography is only implied. Earlier, at line 11, the speaker explained that God's love 'suetyth wythoute tene' (*sweetens without pain*). This wounding, the synesthesia suggests, is one that never touches the senses and ought, therefore, to have no images of physical pain associated with it. The poet's language derives instead from the *fin amor* tradition and from the frank eroticism of the Song of Songs. He amplifies it in the second two lines of the quatrain, when the speaker (in the words of the poem as I restore them) expresses the intensity of his unexpected union with Christ by adopting the pose of a king's vulnerable and submissive lover: 'God sauue mi lef (*beloved one*), Y sei na more – / hyet (*yet*) Y hoppe hys wil be god' (lines 23–4).

This moment of sacred parody prepares the reader for the lyric's true resolution in its final quatrain, when the speaker asserts not confidence in but his absolute dependence upon God.[34] The quatrain's first two lines may refer both to some of the Latin prose texts in Eton College 36 and also to a major vernacular theological poem composed around the same time as *All Other Love* – *Piers Plowman*. For example, the speaker's rhetorical question concerning the futility of travelling to Rome for solace in love may recall Eton College 36's opening text, the papal-authorised treatise on canon law, as well as Langland's critique of 'Rome-renneres', corrupt priests who flee England and 'bere ... silver' to the papal court where they operate as agents, seeking pardons and preferment.[35] It also, as Hirsh suggests, may transfer authority in matters of love away altogether from the theology of the institutional Church, which by the fourteenth century was well known for its corruptions, to the conscience of the individual

---

33 See B. Kowalik, *Betwixt* engelaunde *and* englene londe: *Dialogic Poetics in Early English Religious Lyric* (Bern, 2010), p. 191.
34 On sacred parody, a phenomenon in early modern verse that has its roots in medieval allegorical readings of the Song of Songs, see L. Martz, *The Poetry of Meditation: A Study of English Religious Literature of the Seventeenth Century* (New Haven, 1954), pp. 184–93.
35 G. Kane and E. T. Donaldson, eds, *Piers Plowman: The B Version* (London, 1975), Passus IV, lines 128–9.

lover.36 The theme of ecclesiastical vice might seem a long way from the subject of *All Other Love*, unless one interprets capaciously the false loves rejected by the poem's speaker, to embrace any of the multiform types of cupidity or love of self – including the temptations of clerical status and authority – that are the antithesis of charity or love of God. The Troppau text organises on fols 133r to 135r a variety of topics alphabetically (for example, 'concupiscentia', 'dilectio' and 'fornicatio') that may be relevant here – including of course 'cupiditas' itself, under which heading the author prohibits to clerics both acquiring gold (*aurum*) and having a concubine (*consors*).

The Aquinas texts in Eton College 36 likewise take up in several places the theme of disordered affect. To take only one instance: in *De malo*, Aquinas observes that 'Sicut ergo amor et concupiscentia et delectatio quae sunt de vero bono sunt laudabilia; quae autem sunt de apparenti bono et non vere bono, sunt vituperabilia', laying out the essential conflict between true and false love that is at the heart of the Middle English lyric copied at the back of Eton College 36.37 An English glossator, recording an observation that the *All Other Love* scribe might have found confirmative, notes in the margin of fol. 155r in *De malo* how 'the fynd (*fiend*) leyth before mannys mynd or vnderstandyng, hys inward wyt and hys wytys, thyngys þat aperit gode' but that 'styryt and entysyt (*entice*) a man to yvyl'.38 The scribe of *All Other Love* may not necessarily have noticed these shared areas of theological and affective concern in the Aquinas texts, but he certainly could have done so.

The second line of the poem's final quatrain also invokes one of the key Latin texts in Eton College 36 and the world of *Piers Plowman*. Here the poet appeals to his 'lore of love' (*learning/experience in love*) (line 26) in dissociating himself from 'manne[s] dome' (*human judgement*) (line 27) and clinging to the help of 'he ... þat syt aboue' (*[God], who reigns in heaven*) (line 28). Love's lore, of course, is in its Ovidian sense a common trope in *fin amor* verse.39 It can also have here a non-erotic resonance, however. In Eton College 36, *All Other Love* appears immediately after a text that contains the 'lore' or teachings of Love himself, of Christ – a commentary on that part of St Matthew's Gospel that concerns Jesus's ultimate sacrifice for mankind, an act that sets the standard of selfless love for all Christians to follow. For example, the anonymous exegete explains how Christ's desire to eat the Paschal meal with his apostles, mentioned at Matthew 26: 18, reflected both his 'amore hominum desideratum' ('human desire for love') (fol. 236ra) and foreshadowed his own Passion, whereby he expressed his love for

---

36 Hirsh, ed., *Medieval Lyric*, p. 91.
37 'Love and desire and pleasure regarding a true good are praiseworthy, and love and desire and pleasure regarding an apparent but false good are blameworthy', Q. 11, art.1. For the Latin text, see Thomas Aquinas, *Quaestiones Disputatae, Volumen II* (Rome, 1965), p. 617. For the translation, see Thomas Aquinas, *On Evil*, trans. R. Regan (Oxford, 2003), p. 382.
38 Ker, *Medieval Manuscripts*, p. 665.
39 Cf. Brian Stone's translation of 'lore of love' in the final quatrain as 'words of courtly love' in his modern rendering of the lyric in *Medieval English Verse* (London, 1964), p. 44.

mankind supremely by dying on the cross. In Eton College 36, *All Other Love* provides possibly a fortuitous gloss on the St Matthew Gospel commentary – an amplification, in the contrapuntal voice of vernacular poetry, of the exegete's Latin prose. Indeed, the lyric poet's words echo those of a kindred vernacular literary spirit, the author of *Piers Plowman*, who in the final revision of his theological poem instructs his readers to 'Lerne to loue … and leef all othere' ('Learn how to love … and set aside every other concern').[40]

My reconstruction and analysis of the text of *All Other Love* is a hypothesis concerning its form, content and meaning that cannot be definitively proved. This hypothesis, however, is more sensible than Carleton Brown's mistaken view that the lyric, which survives in a single and much damaged manuscript copy, was written more or less cursorily on a nearly empty page at the back of a codex that contains one Latin prose work, a treatise on military strategy. By querying carefully the textual stability of *All Other Love is Like the Moon* in its editions, we can release anew this Middle English religious lyric's unique thought and feeling, its powerful affective theology.

---

40 G. Russell and G. Kane, eds, *Piers Plowman: The C Version* (London, 1997), Passus XXII, line 208. My translation.

Part II

VISUALITY

5

The Unlikely Landscapes of *On God Ureisun of Ure Lefdi*

Annie Sutherland

Extracts from *On God Ureisun of Ure Lefdi*[1]
Lines 1–16

Cristes milde moder seynte marie,
Mine liues leome, mi leoue lefdi,   *light of my life; beloved lady*
To þe ich buwe & mine kneon ich beie,   *bow; bend my knees*
And al min heorte blod to ðe ich offrie.
5 Þu ert mire soule liht & mine heorte blisse,   *light of a sinful soul*
Mi lif & mi to-hope, min heale mid iwisse.   *salvation, without doubt*
Ich ouh wurðie ðe mid alle mine mihte,   *should praise you*
And singge þe lofsong bi daie & bi nihte.   *a song of praise*
Vor þu me hauest iholpen a ueole kunne wise   *you have helped me in all kinds of ways*
10 And ibrouht of helle in-to paradise,
Ich hit þonkie ðe mi leoue lefdi,   *I thank you for it*
And þonkie wulle þe hwule ðet ich liuie.   *will thank you while I live*
Alle cristene men owen don ðe wurschipe,   *should*
And singen ðe lofsong mid swuðe muchele gledschipe,   *with very great rejoicing*

For further essays discussing lyrics addressed to Mary, see Chapter 8, Anne Marie D'Arcy, '"Written in gold upon a purple stain": Mariological Rhetoric and the Material Culture of Aureate Diction', and Chapter 9, Mary Wellesley, 'Textual Lyricism in Lydgate's *Fifteen Joys and Sorrows of Mary*'.

1   NIMEV 631; DIMEV 1031. Reproduced from Brown XIII, pp. 3–8, with the addition of glosses. All subsequent references are to this edition, cited in the text by line numbers. The *Ureisun of Ure Lefdi* has also been edited in R. Morris, ed., *Old English Homilies of the 12th and 13th Centuries*, 2 vols, EETS OS 29, 34 (Oxford, 1867, 1868; repr. 1988); J. Zupitza, ed., *Alt- und mittelenglisches Übungsbuch mit einem Wörterbuch*, 12th edn, ed. A. Eichler (Vienna and Leipzig, 1922); and J. Hall, ed., *Selections from Early Middle English, 1130–1250*, 2 vols (Oxford, 1920, repr. 1951). Most recently, it appears in C. Innes-Parker, ed. and trans., *The Wooing of Our Lord and the Wooing Group Prayers* (Claremont, 2015).

15 Vor ðu ham hauest alesed of deoflene honde   *freed from devils' hands*
   And isend mid blisse to englene londe.   *sent; the land of angels*

***

Lines 33–40

   Alle þine ureondes þu makest riche kings,   *friends*
   þu ham ȝiuest kinescrud, beies & gold ringes;   *royal robes; jewellry*
35 þu ȝiuest eche reste ful of swete blisse   *eternal rest*
   þer ðe neure deað ne come, ne herm ne sorinesse.   *never*
   Þer bloweð inne blisse blostmen hwite & reade,   *flowers*
   þer ham neuer ne mei snou ne uorst iureden,   *frost; harm*
   þer ne mei no ualuwen, uor þer is eche sumer,   *fade; eternal summer*
40 ne non liuiinde þing woc þer nis ne ȝeomer.   *weak; sorrowful*

***

Lines 59–74

   Mid ham is euer more dei wið-ute nihte,
60 Song wið-ute seoruwe & sib wið-ute uihte;   *harmony without hostility*
   Mid ham is muruhðe moniuold wið-ute teone & treie, *manifold joy; anger and pain*
   Gleo-beames & gome inouh, liues wil & eche pleie.   *harps; abundant delight; life's pleasure; eternal play*
   Þereuore, leoue lefdi, long hit þuncheð us wrecchen *it seems a long time to us wretches*
   Vort þu of þisse erme liue to ðe suluen us fecche; *until; this wretched life*
65 We ne muwen neuer habben fulle gledschipe   *may; happiness*
   er we to þe suluen kumen to þine heie wurschipe.   *before*
   Swete Godes moder, softe meiden & wel icoren,   *well-chosen*
   þin iliche neuer nes ne neuer more ne wurð iboren; *equal; never born*
   Moder þu ert & meiden cleane of alle laste,   *vice*
70 þuruhtut hei & holi in englene reste.   *throughout*
   Al englene were & alle holie þing   *troop of angels*
   Siggeð & singeð þet tu ert liues wel-sprung,   *sigh; well-spring of life*
   And heo siggeð alle þet ðe ne wonteð neuer ore,   *praises you; never lack mercy*
   ne no mon þet ðe wurðeð ne mei neuer beon uorloren. *may never be lost*

***

Lines 96–100

   Vor o ðe is al ilong mi lif & eke min heale.   *for on you depend entirely; also my salvation*

   Vor þine luue i swinke & sike wel ilome,   *labour; sigh very frequently*
   Vor þine luue ich ham ibrouht in-to þeoudome,   *I am brought into servitude*
   Vor þine luue ich uorsoc al þet me leof was   *I forsook all that was dear to me*
100 And ȝef ðe al mi suluen, looue lif, iþench þu þes. *you should consider this*

***

Lines 157-71

	Mi lif is þin, mi luue is þin, mine heorte blod is þin,	
	and ȝif ich der seggen, mi leoue leafdi, þu ert min.	*if I dare say it*
	Alle wurðschipe haue þu on heouene & ec on eorðe,	*also*
160	and alle gledschipe haue þu al-so þu ert wurðe;	*joy; as much as you deserve*
	Nu ich þe biseche ine cristes cherite	
	þet þu þine blescinge & þine luue ȝiue me.	*give*
	ȝeme mine licame ine clenenesse	*keep my body*
	God almihti unne me vor his mild-heortnesse	*grant me*
165	þet ich mote þe iseo in ðire heie blisse.	*I might see you*
	And alle mine ureondmen þe bet beo nu to-dai	*friends may be the better now*
	þet ich habbe i-sungen þe ðesne englissce lai.	*this English lyric*
	And nu ich þe biseche vor ðire holinesse	
	þet þu bringe þene Munuch to þire glednesse	*this monk; your joy*
170	þet funde ðesne song bi ðe, mi looue leafdi,	*devised*
	Cristes milde moder seinte marie. amen.	

On God Ureisun of Ure Lefdi has escaped critical attention for much of its life. Extant in a single manuscript (the early thirteenth-century London, British Library, Cotton MS Nero A XIV), it was included by Carleton Brown in his *English Lyrics of the Thirteenth Century*, but has not appeared in any other modern collection of Middle English verse. At least part of the reason for this critical neglect must be its length; at 171 lines of octosyllabic verse in rhyming couplets (with half of one couplet missing, as indicated by the odd number), it is considerably longer than many of the poems conventionally considered to be 'lyrics'.[2] But its neglect is also due, in part, to its position in Cotton Nero A XIV. Following immediately on (and sharing a folio with) an important early copy of *Ancrene Wisse*, it is succeeded by three prose meditations traditionally regarded as members of the *Wooing Group*, a series of prayers apparently intended for the use of female anchorites such as those to whom *Ancrene Wisse* itself is directed.[3]

---

[2] The missing line, which is not noted by Carleton Brown, seems to be that which should follow line 163 'ȝeme mine licame ine clenenesse'; a scribal annotation in the margin next to this line on fol. 123v indicates an omission here. One can see why the scribe might have become confused at this point, as the rhyme linking the couplet at lines 164 and 165 ('heortnesse' and 'blisse') is the same as that which should have linked line 163 ('clenenesse') with the missing line.

[3] It is copied by the same scribe as the other prayers (all are in a different hand from *Ancrene Wisse* itself). *On God Ureisun of Ure Lefdi* is followed immediately by *On Wel Swuðe God Ureisun of God Almihti* (fols 123v–126v). This is followed by another prose meditation to which Morris gave the title *On Lofsong of Ure Lefdi* (fols 126v–128r), which is followed by a third piece, to which Morris gave the title *On Lofsong of Ure Louerde* (fols 128r–131r). The final vernacular piece in the manuscript is a translation of an abbreviated version of the Creed (fols 131r–v). Noting affinities between Nero's prose meditations and a meditation entitled *þe Wohunge of Ure Lauerd* (extant in London, British Library, Cotton MS Titus D XVIII), Thompson gave the texts the collective title of the *Wooing Group*. See W. Meredith Thompson, ed., *þe Wohunge of Ure Lauerd*, EETS OS 241 (London, 1958 for 1955), p. xiv for discussion of the title.

Enjoying an uneasy relationship with these more illustrious companions, the *Ureisun* has been marginalised in readings of both lyric and anchoritic literature.[4] Yet, far from being a barrier to critical appreciation, its fundamental difference from its codicological neighbours – its *unlikeness* – might provide us with some productive ways of thinking about, and with, the poem.

For a text whose legitimate place in Cotton Nero A XIV has been so disputed, the *Ureisun* stakes a firm palaeographical claim to its position in the manuscript. Introduced by a title rubricated in red ('on god ureisun of ure lefdi', fol. 120v), its careful *mise-en-page*, with the initial majuscule letter of each line neatly isolated in the left-hand margin, suggests a scribe familiar with the conventions of verse layout and confident in their execution.[5] Yet this assured landscaping also highlights the *Ureisun*'s most obvious difference from its companions – it is verse while everything else in the manuscript is prose. And not only is it verse, but it is verse that is alert to its own formal qualities. Referring to itself as a 'lofsong' (*a song of praise*) (lines 8 and 14), a 'bene' (*a prayer*) (line 84), a 'song' (line 170) and an 'englissce lai' (*an English lyric*) (line 167), as well as defining itself as an 'ureisun', the poem is conscious of its own expressive potential. By means of such formal self-awareness, it distinguishes itself from the prayers that follow it; other than in its title, the *Ureisun of God Almihti* does not name or define itself at all, while the *Lofsong of Ure Lefdi* and *Lofsong of Ure Louerde* (both of which lack titles in Nero) simply call themselves 'bone[s]' (*Ure Lefdi*, lines 32, 70, 79; *Ure Louerde*, line 85).[6] While 'bone' obviously recalls 'bene' in the *Ureisun of Ure Lefdi*, 'lofsong' and 'lai' are rather different. 'Lof(t)song', meaning 'song of praise', is used in other thirteenth-century texts to refer specifically to psalmic or ecclesiastical prayer, which encourages a reading of this lyric as pseudo-liturgical, part of a routine of Marian devotion.[7] Indeed, Denis Renevey has suggested that the *Ureisun* poet was directly

---

[4] In the introduction to his edition of the *Wooing Group*, Thompson states that he does not include *On God Ureisun of Ure Lefdi* 'because it is in rhymed and metred couplets, and is in other ways very different from this group'. See Thompson, *Wohunge*, p.xiv n. 1. Chewning also excludes it from her discussion of the *Wooing Group* (see S. M. Chewning, ed., *The Milieu and Context of the Wooing Group* (Cardiff, 2009), p. 20 n. 13). As pointed out in fn. 1 above, Innes-Parker departs from Thompson and Chewning, including the *Ureisun of Ure Lefdi* in her 2015 edition of the *Wooing Group* prayers. Denis Renevey also discusses the poem in the context of the *Wooing Group* in his essay, 'Enclosed Desires: A Study of the Wooing Group', *Mysticism and Spirituality in Medieval England*, ed. W. F. Pollard and R. Boenig (Cambridge, 1997), pp. 39–62.

[5] For discussion of the layout conventions of medieval verse, see M. B. Parkes, *Pause and Effect: A History of Punctuation in the West* (Aldershot, 1992), pp. 97–114.

[6] This is not, however, to suggest that the prose prayers in Nero are not self-consciously literary. On the contrary, they are richly alliterative and carefully rhythmical. All quotations from the *Wooing Group* prayers (with the exception of *On God Ureisun of Ure Lefdi*) throughout this chapter are taken from Thompson, *Wohunge*, and cited in the text by page and line number. A partial version of the *Lofsong of Ure Lefdi* is extant in London, British Library, Royal MS 17 A XXVII, where it is given the title 'þe oreisun of seinte marie'.

[7] See MED, 'lof-song' (n.), 'A song of praise; esp. a hymn or psalm'.

inspired by the language of liturgical celebrations that focus on Mary.[8] And 'lai' has more specifically literary affiliations, suggesting that the poet was conscious of his prayer's aesthetic appeal. According to the Middle English Dictionary, this is the earliest occurrence of the Anglo-Norman term in English; it may well be that our poet is using it to advertise his artistic sophistication.[9] What both 'lofsong' and 'lai' have in common, however, is that they serve to highlight the poem's formal qualities in a manner that distinguishes them from the prayers that follow.[10] The *Ureisun of Ure Lefdi* further sets itself apart from its manuscript companions by containing reference to the vocation and gender of its maker. Two lines before its conclusion, the poet prays that the Virgin Mary might 'bringe þene Munuch (*monk*) to þire glednesse (*your joy*) / þet funde (*devised*) ðesne song bi ðe' (lines 169–70). The fact that none of the three prayers that follow the *Ureisun* in Nero make any reference to their originator(s) again emphasises this poem's unique awareness of its own status as composition.

Most obviously, however, the *Ureisun* demonstrates itself to be *unlike* the prayers that follow it by virtue of its markedly different tone and focus. It does not ignore Mary's identity as mother of Christ (indeed, its first and last lines refer to her as 'Cristes milde moder'), but the scene of his crucifixion, encompassing her role as grieving mother at the foot of the cross, is mentioned only once. Reminding Mary of the agony that she endured at Christ's death, the poet uses the occasion to appeal to her compassion:

> And ek ich ðe biseche uor ihesu cristes blode,
> þet for ure note was i-sched o ðere rode,   *benefit*
> Vor ðe muchele seoruwe ðet was o ðine mode   *in your mind*
> þo þu er ðe deaðe him bi-uore stode (lines 87–90)[11]

But this one reference aside, Mary the bereaved human parent is not foregrounded in the *Ureisun*. Instead, she is a figure of assured authority, who immediately elicits the poet's respect:

> To þe ich buwe & mine kneon ich beie,   *bow; bend my knees*
> And al min heorte blod to ðe ich offrie. (lines 3–4)

The Mary whom we encounter in this poem is the figure venerated in texts associated with the Cult of the Virgin, which, it is widely recognised, was 'exceptionally developed' in England even before the Conquest.[12] In keeping with the

---

8   See Renevey, 'Enclosed Desires', p. 49.
9   See MED, 'lai' (n.(2)) (a) A short narrative poem of love, adventure, etc., to be sung and accompanied on instruments, especially the harp; ~ of Britoun, a Breton lay; also, a tale; (b) a song, lyric.
10   While the *Ureisun of God Almihti* does not define itself in literary terms, its speaker is aware of attempting to speak using 'swete luue wordes' (p. 7 lines 86–7).
11   The poet also reminds us, on three occasions, that Christ is Mary's 'leoue sune' (lines 26, 76, 125). Further, he makes one conventional reference to 'Cristes fif wunden' (line 102).
12   For an introduction to the insular Marian Cult, see M. Clayton, *The Cult of the Virgin Mary in Anglo-Saxon England* (Cambridge, 1990). For this quotation, see p. 1.

emphases of this cult, the *Ureisun* poet draws our attention insistently to Mary's role as glorified queen of heaven, and to her paradisiacal situation:

> Heih is þi kinestol on-uppe cherubine,   *throne*
> Bi-uoren ðine leoue sune wiðinnen seraphine (lines 25–6)

She lives in heaven, where she rules over 'al ... godes riche' (line 32), makes her friends into 'riche kinges' (line 33) and is attended by a 'hird ... i-schrud mid hwite ciclatune' (*retinue ... clothed in white silken garments*) (line 51).

This hierarchy of focus is, however, upturned in the Nero prose prayers, which tend to prioritise an appreciation of Mary as bereaved parent. For example, although she first appears in the *Ureisun of God Almihti* as 'englene cwene of heouene: heouenliche leafdi . seinte marie' (p. 8, lines 130–1), the speaker's meditative energies in this prayer are directed towards the visualisation of Mary 'stondunge' at the foot of the cross, next to John, each 'weopinde ... wið sorhfule sikes' (p. 9, lines 154–5). Similarly, the *Lofsong of Ure Lauerd* is marked by vivid reference to 'þine moderes ream (*lamentation*) & sein i[o]hanes soruwe þo þu somnedest ham (*when you addressed them*) as sune & moder' (p. 10, lines 15–17). Of all three prose texts, it is the *Lofsong of Ure Lefdi*, an expansive translation of Marbod of Rennes's *Oratio ad Sanctam Mariam*, which is closest to the *Ureisun* in its characterisation of Mary as 'leafdi' (p. 16, lines 1, 18; p. 17, line 35; p. 18, line 84). Yet even here, the emphasis falls on a mother who has an intimate relationship with her 'eadi (*blessed*) sune' (p. 18, line 85), whose Passion the speaker evokes in an attempt to elicit Mary's compassion.

In its privileging of a regal, transfigured Virgin, the *Ureisun of Oure Lefdi* has greater affinities with contemporary Marian lyrics than it does with its prose companions in Nero. Mary the elevated 'heuene quene' is a consistent presence in thirteenth-century devotional verse, which praises her variously as 'feire ant brist', 'heie quen in parais',[13] 'leuedi brist (*bright*)', 'quene in heuene of feire blé (*beautiful countenance*)',[14] 'lauedi, ful of houene Blisse', 'swete flur of parais',[15] and as queen 'icumen of heʒe kunne (*descended from noble kin*)'.[16]

Not only is the *Ureisun*'s Mary regal and splendid, but she is also 'briht & blisful' (line 19), a 'leoue swete lefdi' (line 63), whom the poet addresses as one might a cherished lover: 'Þin ich am & wule beon nu & euer more' (line 113). In imbuing Mary with characteristics of a romance heroine, the *Ureisun* poet again draws on a dominant theme in contemporary lyric verse, which tends to visualise the divine in elevated human terms. The thirteenth-century lyric beginning 'Edi (*Blessed*) beo þu, heuene quene', for example, is explicit in its

---

13 Brown *XIII*, no. 17, lines 1, 4.
14 *Ibid.*, no. 18, lines 1, 3.
15 *Ibid.*, no. 55, lines 1, 2.
16 *Ibid.*, no. 60, line 41. This is not to say, however, that Mary the grieving mother does not appear in contemporary lyrics. See, for example, the famously enigmatic lyric beginning 'Nou goth sonne vnder wod' (Brown *XIII*, no. 1). See also that beginning 'On leome is in þis world ilist' (Brown *XIII*, no. 24) and that beginning 'Þe milde Lomb isprad o rode' (Brown *XIII*, no. 45).

evocation of the tropes of courtly romance; addressing Mary as 'heuene quene', the narrator praises her as a 'maide' and 'leuedi', 'swo fair, so sschene, so rudi, swo bricht'.[17] Characterising himself as Mary's 'knicht',[18] this narrator is in fact more fully immersed in the courtly metaphor than our poet, who refers to himself as her 'hine' (*servant*), but also retains his identity as 'Munuch' (*monk*) (line 169). Both, however, have in common a Mary who is romanticised by means of association with the surpassing beauty of the romance heroine. The affinities of the *Ureisun*'s Mary with the human object of romantic affection are, perhaps, most obviously foregrounded when the poet appeals to Mary with this anaphoric list:

Vor o ðe is al ilong mi lif & eke min heale.	*for on you depend entirely; also my salvation*
Vor þine luue i swinke & sike wel ilome,	*labour; sigh very frequently*
Vor þine luue ich ham ibrouht in-to þeoudome,	*I am brought into servitude*
Vor þine luue ich uorsoc al þet me leof was	*I forsook all that was dear to me*
(lines 96–9)	

As Carleton Brown points out, the structure of these lines, which by means of the repetition of 'vor þine … ' emphasise the speaker's absolute reliance on Mary, is very similar to that of a series of lines in London, British Library, Harley MS 2253's lyric beginning 'Blow, northerne wynd'.[19] Addressed to a secular lover, these lines rely on the anaphoric repetition of 'for hire loue' to emphasise the speaker's subjugation to his mistress.[20] Without claiming any close or direct link between the two lyrics, such a similarity can be seen as evidence of cross-fertilisation between thirteenth-century secular and devotional verse. Each borrows tropes and themes from the other, and exploits the expressive potential of speaking in terms other than their own.[21] Although Woolf observed that, until the end of the fourteenth century, poems that 'praise the Virgin in semi-secular style' are very 'narrowly diffused', there are enough to provide a meaningful context for the *Ureisun*.[22]

Like the romance heroine of secular lyric and the lofty queen of devotional verse, the *Ureisun*'s Mary lays claim to absolute uniqueness. As mother of Christ and queen of paradise, she is utterly *unlike* anyone else, entirely without parallel. While the aforementioned lyric beginning 'Edi beo þu, heuene quene' states:

Nis non maide of þine heowe	*complexion*
swo fair, so sschene, so rudi, swo bricht;[23]	

---

17 Brown *XIII*, no. 60, lines 1, 13–14.
18 *Ibid.*, no. 60, line 16.
19 Brown *XIII*, no. 83, lines 77–84.
20 For Carleton Brown's highlighting of this similarity, see Brown *XIII*, p. 167.
21 Carleton Brown also points to the similarities of both the *Ureisun* and 'The Loveliest Lady' with Imayne's words to her mistress regarding Ipomedon in the romance of *Ipomedon*: Brown *XIII*, p. 231.
22 Woolf, p. 114.
23 Brown *XIII*, no. 60, lines 13–14.

– our poet proclaims that:

> as nis no wummon iboren þet ðe beo iliche,   *who is like you*
> ne non þer ine þin efning wið inne heoueriche   *equal*
> (lines 23–4)

He goes on to reaffirm her singularity: 'Þin iliche neuer nes ne neuer more ne wurð iboren' (line 68). In making such claims, these Middle English authors are of course following in an established tradition of Marian devotion. For Anselm of Canterbury, long recognised as an important influence on English anchoritic literature, Mary is similarly incomparable; as he states in the third of his prayers to the Virgin, 'Nihil aequale MARIAE' ('[n]othing equals Mary'), going on to qualify this by pointing out that 'nihil nisi deus maius MARIA' ('nothing but God is greater than Mary').[24] Yet, while insisting on Mary's singularity (with the exception of God himself), Anselm finds it impossible to escape the language of comparison. In the same prayer, for example, he addresses Mary as 'domina magna et valde magna' ('great Lady, great beyond measure'), but precedes this with a description that relies on comparison, on measurement, labelling her as 'maior beatarum *MARIARUM* ... maxima *feminarum*' ('most blessed *of all Marys*, / greatest *among all women*') (my italics).[25] The impossibility of articulating uniqueness in a language that relies for meaning on a system of referentiality is also faced by our poet. For him, as for Anselm, Mary's singularity cannot be expressed without a paradoxical reliance on comparative terms. So, at the same time as proclaiming that there is nothing 'iliche' her, he invites us to assess her in relation to others:

> Þu ert briht & blisful *ouer alle wummen*,
> and god þu ert & gode leof *ouer alle wepmen* (lines 19–20) (my italics)

Her *unlikeness*, her singularity, can only be emphasised by reference to *likeness*, to plurality. Elevated to the heavenly realm, safe from the trauma of living and dying, Mary's detachment from the referential human world is beyond articulation.

Of course, upon finding that one cannot escape a system of referentiality, the poet's obvious course of action is to embrace it and exploit its expressive potential. This is exactly what our poet does, choosing to describe Mary by means of a sequence of metaphors. She is, variously, 'liues leome (*light of life*, line 2)'; 'soule liht' and 'heorte blisse' (line 5); 'lif', 'to-hope' and 'heale' (line 6); 'blostme bi-uoren godes trone (*throne*)' (line 22); 'liues wel-sprung' (*well-spring of life*) (line 72); and 'looue lif' (line 100). With the exception of 'blostme' and

---

[24] Anselm, *Oratio ad sanctam MARIAM pro impetrando eius et Christi amore*, in *S. Anselmi Opera Omnia*, ed. F. S. Schmitt, 6 vols (Edinburgh, 1940–61), III, p. 21. For the English translation, see B. Ward, ed. and trans., *The Prayers and Meditations of Saint Anselm with the Proslogion* (Harmondsworth, 1973), p. 120. The *Ureisun*'s incomparable Mary is also ambiguously lesser than her son: 'To þe one is al mi trust, efter þine leoue sune' (line 125).
[25] Anselm, *Oratio ad sanctam MARIAM*, III, p. 18; trans. Ward, *Prayers and Meditations*, p. 115.

'wel-sprung', each of these descriptions tends towards the abstract; it is difficult to visualise 'leome', 'liht', 'blisse', 'lif', 'hope' and 'heale', not least because they have no material quality. Such abstraction, combined with the poet's aforementioned insistence on her singularity, makes it hard to actually conceptualise the Mary who is the focus of the *Ureisun*. As Christiania Whitehead has observed of Mary in the medieval devotional lyric as a genre, she tends to remain somewhat abstract; her body is often 'either left unrealised or translated into a series of rapidly changing, compound, erudite metaphors that "resist fully satisfactory realistic visualization".'[26] While the *Ureisun*'s simple metaphors are not the erudite abstractions of later lyric, they operate similarly, concealing Mary's figure behind a series of non-bodily referents.

This shrouding of the *Ureisun*'s Mary works to compound our sense of her as somehow inaccessible, enthroned on her 'kinestol' and remote from human vulnerabilities. Admittedly, the poet does address her, on one occasion, as a 'softe meiden' (line 67) and does state that 'al þes middle-eard' is ful of her 'mild-heortnesse' (line 78). But this, on its own, is not enough to render her easily approachable, to mollify her hard edges. When, for example, he intercedes thus:

| þereuore ich ðe bidde, holi heouene-kwene, | *queen of heaven* |
| þet tu, ʒif þi wille is, iher mine bene. (lines 83–4) | *hear my prayer* |

– we are given no guarantee that she listens. Although he tells us that to '[i]lch mon þet to þe bisihð' (*each man who biseeches you*), she gives 'milce & ore' (*mercy and compassion*) (line 81), his plea that she should 'iher mine bene' remains unanswered within the poem. Her sealing off from the world of human experience is further emphasised by the fact that the poem begins and ends with repetition of the same line – 'Cristes milde moder seynte marie'. Such circularity of form creates the impression of a poem closed to its audience, and of a heavenly realm beyond its reach. The *Ureisun*'s Mary is to be admired at a formal distance, rather than held in an intimate embrace.

The paradise over which this remote Mary reigns is depicted vividly by our poet as a lofty realm of angelic beings. 'Cherubine', 'seraphine' and 'engles' appear to jostle for space before her throne:

Heih is þi kinestol on-uppe cherubine,	*throne*
Bi-uoren ðine leoue sune wiðinnen seraphine.	
Murie dreameð engles biuoren þine onsene,	*the angels happily rejoice; face*
Pleieð & sweieð & singeð bitweonen; (lines 25–8)	*sway*

This account of the angels' activity (they 'dreameð', '[p]leieð', 'sweieð' and 'singeð') is lulling in its repetition of the third-person present tense ending '-eð'. The heavenly existence of these celestial beings, it suggests, is nothing other than an

---

26 C. Whitehead, 'Middle English Religious Lyrics', Duncan, *Companion*, pp. 96–119 (p. 109). In her final phrase, Whitehead is quoting from H. Phillips, '"Almighty and al merciable Queene": Marian titles and Marian lyrics', *Medieval Women: Texts and Contexts in Late Medieval Britain*, ed. J. Wogan-Browne et al. (Turnhout, 2000), p. 85.

unvarying litany of praise and delight. Indeed, the poet goes on to state explicitly that the bliss of paradise is utterly unchanging, addressing Mary thus:

Þu ȝiuest eche reste ful of swete blisse	*eternal rest*
þer ðe neure deað ne come, ne herm ne sorinesse.	*never*
Þer bloweð inne blisse blostmen hwite & reade,	*flowers*
þer ham neuer ne mei snou ne uorst iureden,	*frost; harm*
þer ne mei non ualuwen, uor þer is eche sumer,	*fade; eternal summer*
ne non liuiinde þing woc þer nis ne ȝeomer. (lines 35–40)	*weak; sorrowful*

In itself, this description of heaven is by no means unusual. Inspired ultimately by Revelation 21: 4's prophetic words ('And God shall wipe away all tears from their eyes: and death shall be no more, nor mourning, nor crying, nor sorrow shall be any more, for the former things are passed away'), similar heavenly environments are imagined in much contemporary literature. A thirteenth-century lyric beginning 'Uuere beþ þey biforen vs weren' (*Where are those who came before us?*), for example, presents us with a paradisical landscape equally immune to threat and darkness:

Þere-inne is day wiþ-houten niȝt,	
Wiþ-outen ende strenkþe and miȝt,	*strength and might without end*
And wreche of euerich fo,	
Mid god him-selwen eche lif,	
And pes and rest wiþoute strif,	
Wele wiþ-outen wo.²⁷	

In their articulation of heavenly perfection, the biblical book of Revelation, the *Ureisun* and the aforementioned lyric all rely on extensive negation. Heaven is blissful precisely because it does not admit 'deað', 'herm' or 'sorinesse'. Its 'eche sumer' is marked by the absence of 'snou' and 'uorst', its eternal day by the absence of 'niȝt' and its 'pes' by the absence of 'strif'.

Yet in *Ureisun*, a poem so preoccupied with the distinction between heaven and earth, with their fundamental *unlikeness*, the description of heaven by means of repeated negation carries a particular weight, seeming paradoxically to tie the celestial realm to the mortal regions from which the poet works so hard to distance it. In the previously quoted lines from the lyric (lines 35–40), the three affirmative statements that the *Ureisun* poet makes with regard to heaven are that 'blostmen hwite & reade' bloom within it and that it is a place of 'eche blisse' and 'eche sumer'. In itself, this is a problematic description, the fundamental transience of 'blostme' sitting uncomfortably with the notion of an eternal summer. Affirmative statements, it seems, cannot quite accommodate heaven's essential otherness. Yet the extensive reliance on negation is equally problematic, demonstrating that it is simply impossible to describe heavenly perfection without reference to the earthly imperfection that it excludes and is fundamentally unlike. Elaborating on his description of the heavenly realm, the poet proceeds to address Mary and her retinue thus:

---

27   Brown *XIII*, no. 48, lines 49–54.

> Þi leoue sune is hore king & þu ert hore kwene.
> Ne beoð heo neuer i-dreaued mid winde ne mid reine;   *troubled*
> Mid ham is euer more dei wið-ute nihte,
> Song wið-ute seoruwe & sib wið-ute uihte; (lines 57–60)   *harmony without hostility*

Here once again, we find our poet stymied by the impossibility of articulating perfection without allusion to that which is imperfect. Eternal 'dei', 'song' and 'sib' cannot be evoked without reference to the exclusion of their respective opposites, 'nihte', 'seoruwe' and 'uihte'. Of course, a day without night is no more logically possible than an eternal summer. Day and summer are both inherently ephemeral; night follows and defines day, just as autumn follows and delineates the boundaries of summer. Yet such logical impossibilities are the stock in trade of the poet, whose challenge is the expression of the perfect in imperfect language. That the perfection evoked should be somewhat monochrome and sterile is, perhaps, an inevitability. A heaven without wind or rain might sound airless and arid, just as an eternal summer or a never-ending day might sound unsubtle and monotonous. But there seems to be no other way of articulating the distinction between perfection and imperfection, between eternity and ephemerality.

The difficulty of the task with which the poet is faced does not pass without comment. He is perfectly well aware of the challenge of his enterprise, remarking that:

> ne mei non heorte þenchen ne nowiht arechen,   *describe*
> neo no muð imelen ne no tunge tegen   *utter; tell*
> hu muchel god ðu ȝeirkest wið-inne paradise   *prepares*
> ham þet swinkeð dei & niht i ðine seruise. (lines 47–50)   *for those; labour*

Observing, from a distant vantage point, a community of 'cherubine', 'seraphine' and 'engles', whose bliss he cannot adequately describe, he is somewhat isolated, both as poet and as sinner. Although he states, close to the beginning of the *Ureisun*, that:

> ... þu [i.e. Mary] me hauest iholpen a ueole kunne   *in all kinds of ways*
> and ibrouht of helle in-to paradise (lines 9–10)

– the remainder of the poem indicates that he is not yet, in fact, sure of his place in paradise. Having turned his back on the world (presumably a reference to monastic enclosure of some sort):

> Vor þine luue ich uorsoc al þet me leof   *I forsook all that was dear to me*
> And ȝef ðe al mi suluen, looue lif, iþench þu þes.   *you should consider this*
> (lines 99–100)

he is acutely aware of his own vulnerability and fallibility; his soul is sullied with 'swuðe laðere lasten' (*such hateful defects*) (line 123) of sin. With this in mind, he begs Mary to preserve him from the horrors of hell:

> 3if þu milce nauest of me þet ich wot wel 3eorne   *if you do not have mercy on me; very well*
> þet ine helle pine swelten ich schal & beornen.   *perish; burn*
> (lines 103–4)

However, despite his isolation, he does not speak for himself alone. Referring, towards the end of the poem, to his 'ureondmen' (*friends*) (line 166) who stand to benefit from his song, he actually speaks on behalf of a wider community from an early point in the *Ureisun*:

> Wel owe we þe luuien, mi swete lefdi,
> wel owen we uor þine luue ure heorte beien.   *humble*
> (lines 17–18)

And along with this wider community, he awaits Mary's mercy, and transportation to the paradise over which she reigns as queen:

> Þereuore, leoue lefdi, long hit þuncheð us wrecchen   *it seems a long time to us wretches*
> Vort þu of þisse erme liue to ðe suluen ut fecche;   *until; this wretched life*
> (lines 63–4)

In the meantime, however, he and those on whose behalf he speaks, are in a state of suspended animation, caught on earth between the hope of heaven and the threat of hell:

> þe ne muwen neuer habben fulle gledschipe   *may; happiness*
> er we to þe suluen kumen to þine heie wurschipe.   *before*
> (lines 65–6)

In his ambiguous liminality – both solitary and in community, both mindful of hell and hopeful of heaven, he finds surprising common ground with Mary. At once incomparable yet assessed by means of comparison with other women (lines 19–20), all-powerful yet lesser than her son (line 125), and dwelling in heaven yet called to act on earth (line 81), she too is mired in equivocality. In fact, doctrinally speaking, she is the most liminal of biblical figures. As bearer of Christ and bridge between God and man, her importance is measured in terms of her function as intermediary. It is Anselm who expresses this aspect of her identity most powerfully in the third of his prayers to the Virgin, addressing her as 'porta vitae, ianua salutis, via reconciliationis' (*gateway of life, door of salvation, way of reconciliation*).[28] Functioning as 'porta', 'ianua' and 'via', she faces in the direction of both heaven and earth, both God and man. As depicted in the *Ureisun*, Mary is glorified in heaven, distinct from the human world and no longer subject to the vicissitudes of mortal life. But there still remains a likeness between her and humanity, a trace of the 'muchele seoruwe' (line 89) that she endured as mother of Christ, which serves to link her to the interceding poet.

---

28   Anselm, *Oratio ad sanctam MARIAM*, III, p. 20; trans. Ward, *Prayers and Meditations*, p. 117.

At the beginning of this chapter, I spoke about the *Ureisun*'s somewhat uncomfortable situation in Cotton Nero A XIV: its dissimilarity from its codicological neighbours, with which it does not seem entirely at home. This led to a broader discussion of likeness and unlikeness in the poem, and of its heavenly and earthly landscapes, at once utterly distinct from each other, yet each somehow marked by the other. Now that the chapter is reaching its end, a return to these motifs of landscape and environment seems appropriate.

In composing the *Ureisun*, the poet is very aware of the vernacularity of his enterprise, commenting, towards the end of the poem, on the language in which he has written:

And alle mine ureondmen þe bet beo nu to-dai	*friends may be the better now*
þet ich habbe i-sungen þe ðesne englissce lai. (lines 166–7)	*this English lyric*

Referring to the poem as an 'englissce lai', he seems acutely conscious of having imported a hitherto Anglo-Norman literary form into a straightforwardly domestic context. He composed and sung a deliberately literary song in a language that is accessible to his 'ureondmen', attempting (with varying degrees of success) to reproduce the octosyllabic lines of his continental models. The rhyme of 'to-dai' and 'lai' draws attention to the 'modernity', the innovativeness of what the poet has done; his poem manages to be contemporary in form and language, yet traditional in its elevation of a queenly Mary. In its foregrounded vernacularity, it might be said to highlight its links with the three prose meditations that immediately follow it in Cotton Nero A XIV, and from which it otherwise differs in so many ways. All of these texts, including the verse *Ureisun*, work together to make models of Marian and Christocentric devotion available to readers of 'Englissche'.

The *Ureisun*'s foregrounding of Englishness is not, however, an afterthought, something tagged on to the end of the poem. On the contrary, punning references to England and to Englishness appear early on in the poem. To revisit a previously quoted couplet, less than twenty lines into the lyric, the poet reflects thus on Mary's ability to save:

Vor ðu ham hauest alesed of deoflene honde	*freed from devils' hands*
And isend mid blisse to englene londe. (lines 15–16)	*sent; the land of angels*

The most obvious reading of this line (indeed, the reading proposed earlier in this chapter) is that the poet is distinguishing between heaven ('englene londe') and hell ('deoflene honde'). But another reading highlights the close aural similarity between 'englene londe' (*land of angels*) and 'engle-lond' (*land of the English*), a similarity famously noted by Gregory the Great in Bede's *Historia ecclesiastica*.[29] Conscious of importing an Anglo-Norman form into an English context, it

---

29 In Bede's original Latin, the pun is on 'Angli' (*the English*) and 'Angeli' (*angels*). See B. Colgrave and R. A. B. Mynors, eds. and trans., *Bede's Ecclesiastical History of the English People* (Oxford, 1969), pp. 132–5. For discussion of this episode, see K. Lavezzo, *Angels on*

seems possible that the poet is also playfully equating the English landscape with the landscape of heaven, in which Mary dwells.[30] Just as he perceives himself to be inaugurating a tradition of Marian 'lais' in English, so he might understand himself to be welcoming in a foreign Mary, establishing a new pattern of Marian devotion in his own country. The 'englene lond' in which she dwells is both the eternal paradise and, thanks to his pioneering poetic efforts, the homeland of the English.

Praising Mary at a slightly later point in the *Ureisun*, he states:

Moder þu ert & meiden cleane of alle laste,	*vice*
þuruhtut hei & holi in englene reste.	*throughout*
Al englene were & alle holie þing	*troop of angels*
Siggeð & singeð þet tu ert liues wel-sprung. (lines 69–72)	*sigh; well-spring of life*

Relying on the same pun, one might read this as suggesting that Mary is both at rest among the angels and in the land of the English ('in englene reste'), who are now equipped to praise her in fitting, contemporary verse. So, when the poet states that 'al englene were' extols the Virgin, it is tempting to speculate that this refers not only to a troop of angels, but also to the English nation as a 'were', a troop. Despite Mary's absolute otherness, her exaltation in the heavenly realm, the 'englissce lai' that our poet sings enables him and his 'ureondmen' to establish common ground with her, and to call on her as intermediary, as 'Cristes milde moder', in the hope that she might hear and respond.

---

the Edge of the World: Geography, Literature, and English Community, 1000–1534 (Ithaca and London, 2006), pp. 27–45.

30 In her edition of the *Wooing Group* prayers, Innes-Parker makes a similar observation, commenting: 'It is possible, given the author's pride in putting an Anglo-Norman verse form into English, that *englene londe* may be an implicit pun on *Engelonde*', Innes-Parker, *The Wooing of Our Lord*, p. 163 n. 4, p. 24.

6

'Adreynt in shennesse': Blood, Shame and Contrition in *Quis est iste qui uenit de Edom?*

Hetta Elizabeth Howes

Quis est iste qui venit de Edom?[1]

Questio angelorum:

1   'What is he, this lordling   *young lord*
      that comëth from the fight
   With blod-rede wedë   *blood-red garments*
      so grisliche y-dight,   *terribly arrayed*
5   So faire y-cointisëd,   *beautifully apparelled*
      so semlich in syght,   *fair to see*
   So stiflichë gangëth,   *Who so bravely advances*
      so doughty a knight?'   *valiant*

Responsio Christi:
   'Ich hit am, Ich hit am,   *It is I*
10   that ne spekë bute right,
   Champioun to helen   *save*
      mankinde in fight.'

The focus upon affective devotion in this chapter is continued in the chapters by A. S. Lazikani (Chapter 2), 'Moving Lights: An Affective Reading of *On leome is in þis world ilist* and Church Wall Paintings', and Daniel McCann (Chapter 3), 'Blood and Chocolate: Affective Layering in *Swete Ihesu, now wil I synge*'.

1   NIMEV 3906; DIMEV 6232; reproduced with permission from Duncan, I, 104, pp. 154–5, with Latin headings supplied from the edition in *The Works of William Herebert*, ed. S. R. Reimer (Toronto, 1987), p. 132, no. 16. In this chapter citations will be primarily from Duncan's edition, but because Reimer's edition gives a fuller sense of the manuscript context of the lyric and includes the dialogue within it, reference will occasionally be made to this. Other editions are in Brown *XIV*, pp. 28–9; R. T. Davies, ed., *Medieval English Lyrics: A Critical Anthology* (London 1964), pp. 94–5; C. and K. Sisam, eds, *The Oxford Book of Medieval English Verse* (Oxford, 1970), pp. 175–6; T. Silverstein, ed., *Medieval English Lyrics* (London, 1971), pp. 45–6; and M. S. Luria and R. L. Hoffman, eds, *Middle English Lyrics* (New York, 1974), pp. 204–5.

Questio angelorum:
'Why thenne is þy shroud red | thy clothing red
   with blod al y-meind, | all mingled
15 As treddares in wringe | like treaders in the winepress
   with must al bispreynd?' | with must all spattered

Responsio Christi:
'The wringe Ich have y-treddëd | winepress; trod
   al myself on, | myself all alone
And of al mankinde | for all mankind
20   ne was non other won. | no other hope
Ich hem have y-treddëd | them
   in wrathe and in grame, | in wrath and in anger
And al my wede is bispreynd | my clothing is spattered
   with here blod y-same, | with their blood together
25 And al my robe y-foulëd | garment defiled
   to here gretë shame. | to their great disgrace
The day of thilke wreche | of that vengeance
   liveth in my thought,
The yer of medes yeldyng | year of reward-giving
30   ne foryet Ich nought. | forget I not
Ich lokëd al aboute | looked all about
   som helpynge mon; | for someone to help (me)
Ich soughte al the route | searched all the crowd
   bote help nas ther non. | was there none
35 Hit was myn owne strengthe
   that this bote wroughte, | salvation wrought
Myn owne doughtynesse | own courage
   that help ther me broughte.
Ich have y-treddëd the folk
40   in wrathe and in grame, | in wrath and in anger
Adreynt al wyth shennesse, | drowned; ignominy
   y-drawe doun wyth shame.' | dragged down

Ista sunt uerba Iudeorum penitenciam | These are the words of the Jews
agencium: | doing penance
'On Godes milsfulnesse | mercifulness
   Ich wole by-thenche me, | I will bethink me
45 And herien Him in alle thing | and praise; everything
   that He yeldeth me.' | grants

Affective meditations on the Passion have been persuasively described as 'richly emotional, script-like texts'.[2] Sarah McNamer has argued that these works, which encourage their readers or listeners to imagine themselves at the scene of Christ's suffering and death, have 'serious, practical work to do' because, through literary affective performance, they can teach their audiences how to feel.[3] Whilst the fourteenth-century lyric *Quis est*

---

2   S. McNamer, *Affective Meditation and the Invention of Medieval Compassion* (Philadelphia, 2010), p. 1.

3   Ibid., p. 2.

iste qui uenit de Edom? cannot be straightforwardly described as an 'affective meditation' on the Passion, this chapter will draw attention to moments where it seems deliberately to allude to the Passion of Christ, in particular through an emphasis on blood and shame. In light of these allusions, the lyric can be read as an emotive, script-like text, specifically designed to provoke an array of responses – awe, dread, fear, pity, but most especially, shame. Through an emphasis on the performance of these feelings and emotions, a performance that is modelled in the lyric itself by the penitential Jews, *Quis est iste qui uenit de Edom?* teaches readers and listeners how to appropriately convert these emotional responses into something more productive: contrition and penitence.

Quis est iste qui uenit de Edom? is among the Middle English poems of the Franciscan friar, William Herebert.[4] The lyric, which appears in forty-six short lines, or twenty-three long ones, depending on editors' decisions about layout, is a relatively faithful paraphrase of Isaiah 63: 1–7, one of the *lectiones* traditionally read aloud on the Wednesday of Holy Week. It can be found in London, British Library, Additional MS 46919 (on fol. 210), a manuscript that contains a collection of treatises, poems and sermons in Anglo-Norman, Latin and English, copied by Herebert somewhere between 1300 and 1333.[5] The lyric is framed in the manuscript as a dialogue between a group of angels and the solitary figure of Christ, a doughty knight who enters the scene fresh from battle with blood-red garments, just like those worn by treaders of a winepress.[6] The original passages from Isaiah reveal that this figure has returned from Edom, where he has defeated the enemies of the Hebrews. They do not identify the figure as Christ, but medieval exegesis routinely made this connection and Herebert follows suit. He does not name Christ in the lyric itself, but the words of the blood-stained figure are marked with the tag '*Responsio Christi*'.[7] Although Herebert tends to keep closely to his source, he does make a few more small but meaningful changes.[8] He removes the specific references to Edom and Bosra – instead of 'Quis est iste qui uenit de Edom?' the opening question reads, 'What is he, this

---

[4] Reimer, ed., *The Works of William Herebert*, pp. 1–6, offers a useful, brief biography of Herebert's life and works. See also J. Boffey, 'Middle English Lyrics and Manuscripts', Duncan, ed., *Companion*, pp. 1–18 (p. 4).

[5] See Reimer, ed., *The Works of William Herebert*, pp. 7–25; Boffey, 'Middle English Lyrics and Manuscripts', p. 13; *The British Library Catalogue of Additions to the Manuscripts: 1946–1950*, 2 vols (London, 1959), I, pp. 197–206.

[6] Douglas Gray draws attention to this performative aspect of the lyric, which was previously either unnoticed or marginalised, in Gray, *Themes*, pp. 16–17. Reimer's edition of the lyric is the first to make the dialogue format clear; Carleton Brown, in Brown *XIV*, pp. 28–9, does not set out the lyric as dialogue, nor does he mention the marginal rubrics that indicate that the lyric is a dialogue.

[7] Reimer is the only editor to include these tags in his edition of the lyric.

[8] Reimer makes a case for Herebert's translational style in his lyrics, but acknowledges that he 'follows his sources, not so slavishly as to preclude embellishment and *amplification*, but closely enough that his chief editors and critics to date have been almost unanimous in considering this a major fault in his poetry'; Reimer, ed., *The Works of William Herebert*, pp. 18–19.

lordling (*young lord*) / that cometh from the fight?'⁹ He also slightly embellishes his source, twice inserting details about Christ's blood and the shame of those who refused to help the 'lordling' in battle. These additions, I suggest, serve to remind readers of the blood and shame associated with Christ's death, even as they simultaneously depict a scene from the Old rather than the New Testament.

To date, the fullest and most convincing analysis of *Quis est iste qui uenit de Edom?* is that of Douglas Gray. He argues that the lyric is a typological reading of its biblical source, as Herebert moves the 'celebration of the redemption of Israel' from its historical context and places it in 'a new Passion-tide context', and he describes this treatment of the source as 'a mild sort of popularization'.¹⁰ The dyed garments that appear in Isaiah become blood-red weeds, later drenched in blood, and the lines 'Champioun to helen (*save*) / Mankinde in fight' (lines 11–12) fuse the popular images of Christ as warrior and Christ as physician in a pleasing paradox.¹¹ Gray notes a number of embellishments to the source, namely the addition of 'grisliche' in line 4 and the references to blood in lines 3–4 and 13–14: 'With blod-rede wedë (*blood-red garments*) / so grisliche y-dight' and 'Why thenne is þy shroud red (*thy clothing red*) / with blod al y-meind?' He attributes both sets of changes to Herebert's preference for the concrete over the abstract and to his desire to make the ironic contrast between Christ as warrior champion and Christ as suffering redeemer more explicit. These are both persuasive explanations, but they do not take sufficient account of the emotional possibilities that these additions also introduce. Moreover, Gray does not explicitly address Herebert's insertion of 'shame' in lines 26 and 42 and 'shennesse' in line 41, or the implication of these embellishments. Taken together, these additions can be read as a means for eliciting a particular emotional response in the reader. The vivid details must, to a fourteenth-century Christian, contain echoes of Christ's bloody Passion. The references to 'shame' should remind such a reader of one appropriate emotional response to that event.

Reflecting on how the embellishments of shame and blood function in *Quis est iste qui uenit de Edom?* can also help to explain two aspects of the lyric that Gray finds troubling. First, Gray believes that Herebert reduced and 'blunted' one of the more striking images from his source, in his attempt at 'popularization'. The poet changes *inebriavi eos in indignatione mea* ('have made them drunk in my indignation') into the line 'Adreynt al with shennesse' (line 41),

---

9   On the removal of Edom and Bosra, R. T. Davies writes: 'the element of "strength" and "might" in the prophet's first verse is abstracted and developed into the traditional image of the Christ fighting the battle of redemption and the irrelevant references to Edom and Bozrah are omitted'; ed., *Medieval English Lyrics*, p. 319.
10 Gray, *Themes*, pp. 14–15, p. 16.
11 Gray, *Themes*, p. 16. For Christ as physician, see N. K. Yoshikawa, 'Mysticism and Medicine: Holy Communion in the *Vita of Marie d'Oignies* and *The Book of Margery Kempe*', *Poetica* 72 (2009), 109–22 (113). For Christ as warrior and champion, and how this image develops in the later Middle Ages, see R. Woolf, 'The Theme of Christ the Lover-Knight in Medieval English Literature', *Review of English Studies* 13 (1962), 1–16.

which Gray finds to be less exciting and complex.[12] Second, Gray suggests that the final couplet, which he reads as an affirmation of faith from the poetic voice, presents some difficulty because the contrition and penance described arrive too suddenly:

> [a]fter the verses which have preceded it this couplet almost inevitably sounds rather flat. The possibilities of the emotional encounter and of the dialogue form have not been completely realized. Two rather impersonal questions are not really a sufficient basis for a sudden, personal spiritual denouement.[13]

However, I will suggest that Herebert's new image of drowning in humiliation is central to his interpretation of Isaiah and to the lyric's function. The final lines are directly related to the introduction of shame and humiliation to the biblical source, and this conclusion should be read as a model for contrite and penitential behaviour, appropriately produced by an affective scene, which the lyric has deliberately sketched to this end. The conclusion should not come as a surprise, or fall flat; rather, these lines, voiced by penitent Jews, perform the proper response to the emotions provoked by the lyric's central spectacle: Christ striding into the foreground, drenched in blood.

One way in which Herebert makes allusion to the Passion, and begins to prompt an emotional response, is in his use of winepress imagery. Herebert twice inserts references to blood where the verses from Isaiah only imply it:

> [2] Quare ergo rubrum est indumentum tuum, et vestimenta tua sicut calcantium in torculari? [3] Torcular calcavi solus, et de Gentibus non est vir mecum: calcavi eos in furore meo, et conculcavi eos in ira mea: et aspersus est sanguis eorum super vestimenta mea, et omnia indumenta mea inquinavi.[14]

This archetypal image of the winepress underwent a significant change during the later Middle Ages. The Isaiahan trope of crushing slaughter became, by the later Middle Ages, 'a common medieval image that Christ trod the winepress in which he was trodden and conquered the Passion that he suffered'.[15] So in the *Fifteen Oes*, a set of fifteenth-century prayers, Christ is addressed as a 'verai and true plentevous vine' and the 'habundaunt shedynge of [his] blode' is noted, as if liquid from a winepress.[16] Herebert's references to the winepress, R. T. Davies argues, contain no suggestion of this more affective image, commonplace a century later, where Christ treads the

---

12   Gray, *Themes*, p. 16.
13   Gray, *Themes*, p. 17.
14   '[2] Why then is thy apparel red, and thy garments like theirs that tread in the winepress? [3] I have trodden the winepress alone, and of the Gentiles there is not a man with me: I have trampled on them in my indignation, and have trodden them down in my wrath, and their blood is sprinkled upon my garments, and I have stained all my apparel.'
15   D. Gray, 'The Medieval Religious Lyric', *The Blackwell Companion to the Bible in English Literature*, ed. R. Lemon, E. Mason, J. Roberts and C. Rowland (Chichester, 2009), pp. 76–84 (p. 83).
16   'The Fifteen Oes', *Women's Writing in Middle English*, ed. A. Barratt, 2nd edn (Oxford, 2013), pp. 175–82 (p. 182).

mystic winepress of the cross.¹⁷ The angels ask Christ why his robe is 'with blod al y-meind (*mingled*)', just like the garments of 'tredderes in wringe (*treaders in the winepress*)' (lines 14–15); Christ replies that he has trodden 'hem [...] in wrathe and in grame (*in wrath and in anger*)' (line 22) and his garments are therefore coated with their blood, 'to here (*their*) grete shame' (line 26). Though it is not made clear to whom specifically the words 'hem' and 'here' are referring here, we can infer from the biblical context that Christ means the enemies of the Hebrews. He later repeats the image in his dialogue towards the end of the poem: 'Ich have y-treddëd the folk / in wrathe and in grame' (lines 39–40). Aside from the two additional references to blood, these lines offer none of the attention given to the minutiae of Christ's body in the later *Fifteen Oes*. Only his blood-red weeds are described and the blood that dyes them such a vivid colour has come from the bodies of the enemies he has trampled, not from his own wounds.

Nevertheless, it is too simplistic to suggest that any reference to the Passion and the consequent redemption of humankind is absent from this lyric. As Davies himself notes, the removal of Edom and Bosra from the translation allows the 'fight' to be interpreted more broadly. The sufferings of the Passion may not be mentioned specifically, but the *glossa ordinaria* for these Isaiahan verses deliberately widened out their sense, so that they could be used to refer to all the sufferings of the Passion: *Torcular calcavi. Scilicet crucem et omnia tormenta passionis in quibus quasi prelo pressus ut etiam sanguis funderetur*.¹⁸ Herebert's bloody additions serve to draw attention to this more affective interpretation of the image and therefore, in his use of the winepress, Herebert captures an archetypal image in flux. Christ as fearsome warrior may be central to the lyric, which closely follows its Isaiahan source; however, the increasingly popular depiction of Christ himself as winepress, shedding blood for our sins on the cross, is also made present. This double preoccupation is further supported by the manuscript context of the lyric. Stephen Reimer notes that the other lyrics authored by Herebert, in BL, Additional MS 46919, portray both Christ as king and judge and Christ as suffering human:

---

17 Davies, ed., *Medieval English Lyrics*, p. 319. For further reading on the archetypal image of the winepress, see A. Timmerman, 'A View of the Eucharist on the Eve of the Protestant Reformation', *A Companion to the Eucharist in the Reformation*, ed. L. P. Wandel (Leiden, 2014), pp. 365–98 (pp. 384–6); R. M. Hillier, 'The Wreath, the Rock and the Winepress: Passion Iconography in Milton's *Paradise Regain'd*', *Literature and Theology* 22 (2008), 387–405; J. H. Marrow, *Passion Iconography in Northern European Art of the Late Middle Ages and Early Renaissance: A Study of the Transformation of Sacred Metaphor into Descriptive Narrative* (Kortrijk, 1979), pp. 82–90; T. H. Bestul, 'Chaucer's *Parson's Tale* and the Late Medieval Tradition of Religious Meditation', *Speculum* 64 (1989), 600–19 (pp. 608–9).
18 'I have trodden the winepress. That is, the cross, and all the torments of the Passion, in which I was squeezed as if in a press in order to push forth my blood'; as cited by Marrow in *Passion Iconography*, p. 85. See also Gray, *Themes*, p. 15.

The poems in general make an affective appeal, intended to produce in the hearers contrition and penitence. They focus on the Infancy and Passion of Christ, both emotionally appealing aspects of Christ's life. The Cross and the Blood of Christ are presented repeatedly, with a strong sense of pathos. Christ as King and Judge is also central, and Judgement and Hell are used to compel the hearer both to contrition and to moral improvement in this life.[19]

Central to Reimer's summary is the idea that these lyrics function as an instrument for affective appeal. With their plea to the emotions, and their reminders of the judgement to come, the lyrics in BL, Additional MS 46919, including *Quis est iste qui uenit de Edom?* can stir the reader/listener to transformation, specifically to contrition and moral improvement.

Another way in which Herebert stirs his reader/listener to transformation in *Quis est iste qui uenit de Edom?* is through an emphasis on the solitude of Christ. In some of the more striking, late-medieval depictions of the winepress, Christ is depicted as a figure alone, scorned and beaten by those around him. Aside from the specific image of the winepress, this rather pathetic solitude is a common feature of Passion narratives more generally, too. In Aelred of Rievaulx's *De institutione inclusarum*, a handbook for anchoresses that is often cited for including the first Passion meditation of its kind, Aelred heightens the pathos of his Passion scenes with descriptions that highlight Christ as one against many. In a fourteenth-century Middle English translation of the treatise, roughly contemporary with Herebert's lyric, Christ is followed through his sufferings by an 'acursyd companye of Iewes' and the reader is forced to watch whilst they 'defoyleþ [Christ's face] wit here foule spatelyngge (*spitting*)'.[20] Herebert's lyric similarly emphasises Christ's solitude, most particularly when he recounts Christ's experiences. The angels stand together to watch Christ's approach and through their questioning of each other – 'what ys he?' – they include the reader or listener in the performance of that watching. In reply, Christ declares, twice: 'Ich hit am' (line 9). The repetition is used to emphasise how Christ was forced to act alone, as the single hope of mankind, a sense that is only enhanced by the frequent possessive pronouns 'my' and 'myn' in the following lines. On the one hand, these details create an image of a conqueror: one man who has greater strength than all others, whose triumph is all the more impressive for the lack of assistance. They generate a feeling of awe, and distance readers/listeners from God. However, they can also be read as a deliberate engagement with affective piety.[21] The lines create pity for this man who no one else can help and who has

---

19 Reimer, ed., *The Works of William Herebert*, p. 22.
20 See J. Ayto and A. Barratt, eds, *Aelred of Rievaulx's 'De Institutione Inclusarum': Two English Versions*, EETS, OS 287 (Oxford, 1984), p. 47. The Passion meditation is identified as the first of its kind by B. P. McGuire, 'c.1080–1215: Culture and History', *The Cambridge Companion to Medieval English Mysticism*, ed. S. Fanous and V. Gillespie (Cambridge, 2011), pp. 29–47 (p. 44).
21 Duncan, p. 359, points out that the tone of these lines is similar to that of Psalm 68: 21: 'I looked for some to take pity but there was none; and for comforters, but I found none', a passage associated with the loneliness of Christ on the cross.

to suffer in order to save his people: 'Ich loked al aboute / Som helpynge mon (*for someone to help me*), / Ich soughte al the route (*crowd*) / bote helpe nas ther non' (lines 31–4). In Herebert's translation, *circumspexi* (I looked about) becomes 'Ich soughte al the route', with the addition of 'route' creating a backdrop of spectators who will not help him.[22] Where the anchoritic reader of *De institutione inclusarum* is encouraged to participate in the action and comfort Christ, the reader or hearer of *Quis est iste qui uenit de Edom?* is forced to remain a bystander, watching the dialogue from afar. They are encouraged to envision this scene in performative terms, because of the dialogue form, but they are simultaneously made impotent as spectators both of Christ's battle against his enemies and his more metaphorical battle for their own redemption.

In an essay on Middle English religious lyrics, Christiania Whitehead reminds readers that identification with Christ is designed to 'facilitate repentance and moral reformation, and, as such, was invariably envisaged as a salvatory mental stratagem'.[23] Further, she points out the pivotal role that spectacle and the emotions play in producing this repentance and moral reformation: 'by the fourteenth century, images and sights were also held to have unprecedented power to arouse the emotions, effectively enabling the viewer to "feel", and by "feeling" to resolve upon a programme of personal moral reform'.[24] In a similar vein, Kathryn A. Smith explores how interacting with images of the Passion can be not only a useful, but also an actively penitential, act. She notices how medieval devotional literature often affords sins the power to rewound Christ, citing an Anglo-Norman lyric from BL, Additional MS 46919 in which Christ asks readers to reflect on his wounds.[25] The severity of sin is lingered over in the lyric – those who sin do Christ great wrong and put him to death anew: 'E si autre fez cheiez, vous frez a moi grant tort, / Kar kant ke en vous est derechef me mettez a la mort'.[26] However, a remedy is offered. Meditating on the Passion, having pity on Christ and – as a result – acknowledging and repenting for those sins that wound Christ, can produce contrition, making good the wrong done. Smith concludes that, in light of the related ideas, 'contemplating an image of the Crucifixion or other Passion subject, reading a work of devotional literature on the Passion, or using a devotional book illustrated with Passion imagery could be a penitential act'.[27]

This is the context in which *Quis est iste qui uenit de edom?*, and specifically its final lines, should be read. I have already established that the late medieval

---

22 See Gray, *Themes*, p. 16.
23 C. Whitehead, 'Middle English Religious Lyrics', Duncan, *Companion*, pp. 96–119 (p. 100).
24 *Ibid.*, p. 108.
25 K. A. Smith, *Art, Identity and Devotion in Fourteenth-Century England* (London, 2003), p. 161.
26 'In additional sins you do me great wrong/for whatever it means to you, you put me to death anew'. See D. Jeffrey and B. Levy, eds, *The Anglo-Norman Lyric* (Turnhout, 1990), pp. 80–1, no. 13, lines 9–10.
27 Smith, *Art, Identity and Devotion*, p. 161.

version of a suffering Christ coexists alongside the more dreadful warrior in the lyric, and that allusions to the winepress, Christ's solitude and blood may well inspire pity for, and even identification with, Christ, who fights various battles without aid. However, alongside pity, this lyric encourages readers/listeners to experience another significant emotion: shame. The dialogue format of *Quis est iste qui uenit de Edom?* forces readers into the role of bystander rather than participant. Such casting highlights the solitude of Christ, as explored above, but it also highlights the shameful nature of the two spectacles that the lyric creates – the verbalised spectacle 'offstage', where Christ treads the winepress alone, and the more immediate spectacle of Christ recounting his experiences to the angels. Whether Christ has been engaged in a battle to defeat the enemies of his followers, or whether he has been waging a more universal war to redeem the sins of mankind (and I have argued that the lyric suggests both simultaneously) the devoted reader/listener plays the part of removed spectator – to their shame.[28] Reimer suggests that the lyrics in Herebert's manuscript, which also includes a number of sermons, may well have been used to illustrate preaching material, but he singles out *Quis est iste qui uenit de Edom?* as having a slightly different function. He suggests that the dramatic aspect of the lyric seems to require a number of voices for effective presentation.[29] However, even if Herebert's audience were encouraged to voice the angels, or Christ himself, they would surely feel most closely aligned with the only human voices in the lyric – the voices of the penitential Jews, who as a product of their shame collectively announce that they must be mindful of God and his mercy: 'On Godes milsfulnesse (*mercifulness*) / Ich wole by-thenche (*bithink*) me' (lines 43–4).

Shame, as recent research by a number of scholars has shown, is a complex emotion in medieval Christian thought.[30] Although shame was associated with postlapsarian weakness and the Fall – Adam and Eve become suddenly aware of their naked, exposed bodies and try to hide themselves from the eyes of God – it was also sanctified by its association with Christ's endurance of humiliation in the Passion, as well as the sufferings of Christian martyrs.[31] Moreover, medieval penitential literature shows how shame, in the right context, was considered to be a productive emotion, because it could encourage confession and, as a

---

28 It is worth noting that the emotion of shame is frequently linked with spectacle. For instance, Stephanie Trigg shows how experiences of shame in romance narratives, such as *Sir Gawain and the Green Knight* and Malory's *Morte d'Arthur*, involve external public affects and public recognition; see Trigg, *Shame and Honor: A Vulgar History of the Order of the Garter* (Philadelphia, 2012), p. 129 and pp. 131–3. For an overview of shame in literary criticism of medieval literature, see M. Flannery, 'The Concept of Shame in Late-Medieval English Literature', *Literature Compass* 9 (2012), 166–82, and for an exploration of shame and guilt in Chaucer, see A. McTaggart, *Shame and Guilt in Chaucer* (New York, 2012).
29 Reimer, ed., *The Works of William Herebert*, p. 22.
30 See footnote 28, above.
31 Flannery, 'The Concept of Shame', p. 172.

consequence, contrition and penitence.[32] For instance, Julian of Norwich depicts sorrow and shame at having defouled the fair image of God through sin 'as the emotional and physiological preconditions for successful penance, and as pleasing to God'.[33] Christians will be able to receive redemption if they account for their sins in confession with a contrite heart, and perform penance. However, there is a danger associated with shame. Penitential literature lists the emotion as both a facilitator of contrition and redemption and an obstacle to achieving it, and Anne McTaggart has argued that this genre actively tries to manage shame as a result.[34] Too much shame means a desire to conceal sins, rather than to expose them through confession; too little means a dismissal of them.

The final lines of *Quis est iste qui uenit de Edom?*, which follow on from the word 'shame', script the most productive reaction to this emotion; neither too much nor too little, the shame that Herebert adds to this lyric is just enough to cause the reader/listener to think on God's mercy and repent. Gray reads these lines as an affirmation of the lyric speaker, although a rubric in the manuscript attributes them to the penitent Jews. Whether they are supposed to come from the mouth of the redeemed Jews, the poet, or both simultaneously, these lines teach the correct response to the kind of shame that envisaging or hearing about Christ's solitary battles can provoke.

Reading *Quis est iste qui uenit de Edom?* in this light makes the final couplet seem less flat and more like a natural end to the lyric's emotional, devotional journey.[35] The penitence that readers or listeners are encouraged to perform, in imitation of the Jews in the lyric, has not appeared out of nowhere but has been carefully elicited by a combination of awe and fear – through the fearsome warrior figure of Isaiah – and the allusions to the Passion, which Herebert generates through embellishment of his source. Before this final couplet, Herebert includes three new references to shame in the lyric, deliberate prompts to the kind of reform and moral improvement scripted for reader/listeners in the final lines. If reading about the Passion, or looking at an image of Christ, can be a 'penitential act' as Smith suggests, then these lines are the most productive conclusion to the scenario we are given in *Quis est iste qui uenit de Edom?*.

Such a reading can also help to shed light on Herbert's introduction of the phrase 'Adreynt (*drowned*) al wyth shennesse (*ignominy*)' in the preceding line. Rather than being part of a popularisation, or even simplification of his Isaiahan

---

32 See McTaggart, *Shame and Guilt in Chaucer*, pp. 2–20.
33 Flannery, 'The Concept of Shame', p. 172.
34 McTaggart, *Shame and Guilt in Chaucer*, p. 16.
35 Gray is the first critic to notice the marginal note in the manuscript copy of Herebert's lyric, which suggests that lines 41–2 should be inserted before the final couplet (lines 43–6) rather than afterwards, following the verses of Isaiah. Earlier editions of the lyric that ignore this instruction have the poem ending with 'shame' rather than repentance, and these versions mean that the lyric seems to conclude with an unresolved, potentially dangerous emotion. Altering the order of lines as the manuscript suggests (the order that Reimer follows in his edition) means ending the lyric with the productive outcome of the emotion (penitence), rather than the emotion itself.

source, this phrase is integral to Herebert's new interpretation of the biblical verses. The concept of drowning is intimately connected with shame and sin in late medieval devotional literature. Aelred of Rievaulx describes how, in his youth, wicked company and fleshly love 'rauysschede [his] syke and feble age of childhood in-to manye foule vices, and dreynte [his] wrecchede soule in þe stynkynde flood of synne' and similar tropes endure well into the fifteenth century.[36] In the *Orcherd of Syon*, a Middle English translation of Catherine of Siena's *Dialogue*, sinful souls drown in the filthy flood of sin, and the sermon-series *Jacob's Well* describes wayward individuals as being full of corrupt water, which can not only infect but also drown their souls.[37] The word 'adreynt' in Herebert's lyric therefore uses the established association between sin and drowning to amplify the feeling of shame, which he makes explicit in his version of Isaiah.[38] However, like so many of the details considered thus far, the word can be read another way. Whilst the reference to water and drowning evokes sin it may also, in light of the affective hints throughout the lyric, remind readers of the rivers of blood that stream from Christ's body in many narratives of the Passion. In *De institutione inclusarum* the blood streams from Christ's side like 'fayre fressche rennyngge ryueres in a stoon' and in the fourteenth-century alliterative poem, *Pearl*, the river across which the dreamer and the pearl-maiden converse flows from Christ's wound.[39] Significantly, this streaming blood promises redemption and the kind of deeper relationship with God that affective piety aims to produce. Moreover, late medieval devotional literature frequently communicates such a relationship through bathing in, even metaphorically drowning in, Christ's blood.[40] The thirteenth-century anchoritic guide *Ancrene Wisse* describes three healing baths provided by God, one of which is made up

---

36 Ayto and Barratt, eds, *Aelred of Rievaulx's 'De Institutione Inclusarum'*, pp. 52–3.
37 Those who do not take to the bridge of Christ 'wilfully drenchen hemsilf' and consequently 'falle' into 'synnes and defautis'; P. Hodgson and G. M. Liegey, eds, *The Orcherd of Syon*, EETS, OS 258 (Oxford, 1966), p. 79. In *Jacob's Well*, an individual whose soul is full of such corrupt water must cry out: 'delyuere me, lord, fro þe depe watrys of cursys! […] þat þe tempestys of þe watrys of cursys drenche me noȝt, ne þat þe pyt of lustys, wyth his mowth of temptacyoun, drenche noȝt my soule'; A. Brandeis, ed., *'Jacob's Well': An English Treatise on the Cleansing of Man's Conscience*, Volume 1, EETS, OS 115 (London, 1990), p. 6.
38 This association exists in biblical sources, too. The Old Testament tells us that God sent a flood to wipe out the sinful, survived only by Noah and his family (Genesis 5: 32–10: 1).
39 Ayto and Barratt, eds, *Aelred of Rievaulx's 'De Institutione Inclusarum'*, p. 49, and 'Pearl', in M. Andrew and R. Waldron, eds, *The Poems of the Pearl Manuscript: 'Pearl', 'Cleanness', 'Patience', 'Sir Gawain and the Green Knight'*, 5th edn (Exeter, 2007), pp. 53–110 (p. 104, lines 1055–60).
40 For a fuller exploration of such tropes, see L. H. McAvoy, 'Bathing in Blood: The Medicinal Cures of Anchoritic Devotion', *Medicine, Religion and Gender in Medieval Culture*, ed. N. K. Yoshikawa (Cambridge, 2015) pp. 85–102; and H. E. Howes, 'In Search of Clearer Water: An Exploration of Water Imagery in Late Medieval Devotional Prose', unpublished Ph.D. thesis, Queen Mary University of London, 2016, pp. 128–30.

of his blood.⁴¹ *The Doctrine of the Hert* follows a similar model and says that to enter into one of these baths is 'noþing ellis but for to drenche þin affecioun and þi þoughtes in Cristes passioun, considering bothe þe shedyng of his blode and water, and also þe swetyng and þe wepyng of his body'.⁴² To 'drenche' or drown one's mind with thoughts of Christ's passion is to metaphorically 'drenche' oneself in his redemptive fluids, shed for Christians throughout his suffering in the Passion. In light of this network of bloody images, the line 'Adreynt al wyth shennesse' is used by Herebert to emphasise shame as a very proper response to God's actions on either a historical or metaphorical battlefield, but also to gesture towards the more productive contrition and redemption that such an emotional response can and should elicit. Herebert uses both blood and shame to embellish his source, and the addition of 'adreynt' effectively fuses the fluid and the emotion as the lyric draws to a close.

The changes Herebert makes to Isaiah 63: 1–7 in his lyric translation may be small but analysis suggests that they are all interconnected and work towards a similar end. A number of aspects of *Quis est iste qui uenit de Edom?* function to produce an array of emotions in the reader, which ultimately lead to shame and contrition. The depiction of Christ as a warrior-king creates fear and awe, whilst the allusions to his suffering body during the Passion elicit pity. The two spectacles that Herebert gestures towards in his version of the lyric – the historical battle at Edom and the metaphorical battle of the Passion, both of which cast the reader/listener as passive bystander – work to produce shame out of this awe and pity, which is then transformed into a more productive state of contrition. Gray suggests that the final couplet of the lyric may fall flat because Herebert followed his source too faithfully. However, I suggest that Herebert deliberately departs from his source in small but significant ways in order to make the final verses of Isaiah more relevant and dynamic in their new lyric context. Reader/listeners are prompted to feel shame. Crucially, however, they are also prompted by the final lines to pursue a proper outlet for this emotion, one that is scripted for them by the penitential Jews: mindfulness of Christ, his victories and his sufferings, followed by contrition and penitence.

---

41 B. Millett, ed., '*Ancrene Wisse*': *A Corrected Edition of the Text in Cambridge, Corpus Christi College, MS 402, with Variants from other Manuscripts*, 2 vols, EETS OS 325 and 326 (Oxford, 2005), I, 149.

42 C. Whitehead, D. Renevey and A. Mouron, eds, '*The Doctrine of the Hert*': *A Critical Edition with Introduction and Commentary* (Exeter, 2010), pp. 36–7.

7

Ihesus woundes so wide and the *fons vitae*: Text, Image and the Manuscript Context

Natalie Jones

Ihesus woundes so wide[1]

1   Ihesus woundes so wide,
      ben welles of lif to þe goode,
      Namely þe stronde of his syde,   *stream*
      Þat ran ful breme on þe rode.   *fiercely; cross*
5   3if þee liste to drinke,   *If you wish to drink*
      to fle fro þe fendes of helle,
      Bowe þu doun to þe brinke,   *Bow down; edge*
      & mekely taste of þe welle.

The single copy of *Ihesus woundes so wide* dates from the fifteenth century and survives in London, British Library, Arundel MS 286, on fol. 3. This short, mnemonic poem occupies a particularly interesting place within its manuscript, as rather than being recorded as a standalone lyric set out as verse, *Ihesus woundes so wide* is written out as prose and intercalated into a longer, devotional treatise that forms the first work in the manuscript. Although *Ihesus woundes so wide* has been included in a number of editions of Middle English lyrics, editors have tended to print the poem as an independent item of eight lines and have overlooked the fact that in its manuscript it is inserted in a longer, prose work. It is perhaps as a consequence of this editorial practice that those scholars who have commented on the lyric have frequently done so without a full appreciation of its manuscript context. Moreover, although critics have tended to refer to the lyric's imagery in relation to developments in late medieval piety and the

---

For another discussion of a lyric intercalated into a much longer text, see Chapter 12, Elizabeth Robertson, 'Lyric Interventions in *Troilus and Criseyde*'.

[1]   NIMEV 1787; DIMEV 2948. Reproduced from Brown *XV*, p. 149, with the addition of glosses. All subsequent references are to this edition, cited in the text by line number. For other editions see R. T. Davies, ed., *Medieval English Lyrics: A Critical Anthology* (London, 1964), p. 216; R. Oliver, ed., *Poems without Names: The English Lyric 1200–1500* (Berkeley, CA, 1970), p. 114; T. Silverstein, ed., *Medieval English Lyrics* (London, 1971), p. 120.

devotion to the Five Wounds of Christ, their treatment of the poem has also been decidedly brief. For instance, both Nigel Morgan and Eamon Duffy cite *Ihesus woundes so wide* as evidence of the cult of the Five Wounds, but neither engages critically with the poem's imagery or context.[2] Similarly, Alexandra Barratt refers to the poem only to point out that it demonstrates the 'extreme simplicity' of the devotion to Christ's wounds in the fifteenth century.[3] One scholar who has acknowledged the lyric's precise manuscript context is Douglas Gray who, in his study of the cult of the Five Wounds, refers to the poem and its place within the treatise.[4] Yet, as Gray's discussions are necessarily brief, there is still more work to be done on the relationship between the lyric and the treatise, and what this may tell us about the meaning and function of the poem and its imagery. Indeed, although *Ihesus woundes so wide* has typically been approached as a straightforward poem that draws on the terminology and imagery of the devotion to the Five Wounds, any assumptions we might harbour regarding its 'extreme simplicity' are belied by a consideration of the lyric in relation to its manuscript context.

While an examination of manuscript and textual context is key to a thorough understanding of any Middle English lyric, issues of context are especially pertinent when considering those poems such as *Ihesus woundes so wide*, which survive as part of larger prose works.[5] As noted, the single surviving copy of *Ihesus woundes so wide* is extant in BL, Arundel MS 286. This manuscript dates to the fifteenth century and can best be described as a religious anthology.[6] It contains a range of religious vernacular works such as the *Life of Soul*,[7] the *Book of Tribulacyon*,[8] and a treatise on virginity,[9] as well as more practical texts such

---

2   N. Morgan, 'An SS Collar in the Devotional Context of the Shield of the Five Wounds', *The Lancastrian Court: Proceedings of the 2001 Harlaxton Symposium*, ed. J. Stratford (Donington, 2003), pp. 147–62 (p. 160); E. Duffy, *The Stripping of the Altars: Traditional Religion in England, c.1400–1580* (New Haven and London, 1995), p. 245. See also the very brief comment on the poem in Oliver, ed., *Poems without Names*, p. 114.
3   A. Barratt, 'The Prymer and its Influence on Fifteenth-Century English Passion Lyrics', *Medium Ævum* 44 (1975), 264–79 (272).
4   D. Gray, 'The Five Wounds of Our Lord', *Notes and Queries* 208 (1963), 50–1, 82–9, 127–34, 163–8 (133–4); and see also Gray, *Selection*, pp. 35, 351.
5   On the importance of examining intercalated lyrics within their textual settings, see A. J. Fletcher, 'The Lyric in the Sermon', Duncan, *Companion*, pp. 189–209; S. Wenzel, *Verses in Sermons: 'Fasciculus Morum' and its Middle English Poems* (Cambridge, MA, 1978), and *Preachers, Poets, and the Early English Lyric* (Princeton, 1986).
6   For a full list of the works contained in the manuscript see J. Forshall, ed., *Catalogue of Manuscripts in the British Museum*, 3 vols (London, 1834–41), I, 84–5. Details of a number of the prose works preserved in the manuscript (but not including the Passion treatise) can also be found in P. S. Jolliffe, *A Check-List of Middle English Prose Writings of Spiritual Guidance* (Toronto, 1974).
7   H. M. Moon, ed., *Þe Life of Soule: An Edition with Commentary* (Salzburg, 1978).
8   A. Barratt, ed., *The Book of Tribulation* (Heidelberg, 1983).
9   This text (on fols 134r–148r) is referred to as *Of Maidenhode* in the entry for the manuscript in Forshall, ed., *Catalogue of Manuscripts*, pp. 84–5; see also Jolliffe, *Check-List*, p. 88, 142.

as a list of contemplations for the canonical hours. The manuscript also includes a number of texts based on Latin sources, such as translations of short works by Bonaventure, Anselm and Richard of St Victor.[10] The manuscript is the work of at least three scribes and although little is known about its exact provenance it has, on account of the scribal dialects, been located to the Midlands, most likely to Warwickshire.[11] While the content of the manuscript could be appropriate for both a lay or clerical audience, its portable size, as well as its simple and functional layout, may suggest that it was intended for personal use.[12] The treatise in which the lyric is intercalated is the first work in the manuscript and runs from fols 1r to 15v.[13] Although this work has been defined in simple terms as a 'treatise upon the passion of our Saviour',[14] its utilisation of a range of scriptural passages, as well as a number of themes concerning contemporary Christocentric devotion, make it a particularly interesting piece.

Running to a total of 876 lines, the treatise contains a number of thematic sections. It opens with a brief introduction (lines 1–17), which not only purports to explain how the work came to be written but, in so doing, affirms the text's role as a source of devotional instruction and comfort for the reader. The author states that he was instructed by a 'worschipful lady' to 'make som comfortable book of þe passioun of our saueour Ihesu Crist' so that 'she in hir honorable age of elde my3t haue some comfort in contemplatioun of þat blessed and profitable passioun þat is þe welle of lyf' (fol. 1r, lines 1–7).[15] The description of Christ's

[10] The works by Bonaventure and Anselm are falsely ascribed to Richard Rolle in the manuscript; see H. E. Allen, ed., *Writings Ascribed to Richard Rolle Hermit of Hampole and Materials for his Biography* (New York, 1927), pp. 355–6.

[11] On the suggestion that the manuscript has three scribes see R. Hanna, 'The Origins and Production of Westminster School MS.3', *Studies in Bibliography* 41 (1988), 197–218, especially 209–10. The spelling system adopted by the scribe who copied the opening treatise can be located to Warwickshire or Northamptonshire. It should be noted that a text from BL, Arundel MS 286 is included in the *LALME* survey, but this is by a different scribe from the one who copied the treatise; nevertheless, this hand has also been located to Warwickshire. See A. McIntosh, M. L. Samuels and M. Benskin, *A Linguistic Atlas of Late Medieval English*, 4 vols (Aberdeen, 1986), I, pp. 533–4.

[12] The manuscript is 220mm in height, 144mm in width. Commenting on the popularity of vernacular, religious prose works in the fifteenth century, N. R. Rice notes that the manuscript evidence suggests that such texts were used by both lay and clerical readers; see *Lay Piety and Religious Discipline in Middle English Literature* (Cambridge, 2008), pp. 135–7.

[13] Although the catalogue entry for the manuscript states that this treatise runs up to fol. 19v, this opening section (fols 1–19v), all written by the same scribe, contains two works. Following the devotional treatise, fols 15v–19v contain an extract from Book Seven of the *Revelation* of St Bridget; see D. Pezzini, '"How Resoun Schal Be Keper of þe Soule": Una Tradizione del Quattrocentro Inglese Dalle Rivelazioni (VII, 5) di S. Brigida di Svezia', *Aevum* 60 (1986), 253–81, and Jolliffe, *Check-List*, p. 75.

[14] Forshall, ed., *Catalogue of Manuscripts*, I, 84.

[15] 'Treatise on the Passion', beginning 'A worschipful lady hauynge a symple spirit', in BL, Arundel MS 286, fols 1r–15v. All transcriptions are my own; abbreviations and contractions have been silently expanded.

Passion as the 'welle of lyf' is a particularly significant thematic marker and directly leads into the first main section of the treatise, which explores the motif of the 'welle of þe passioun' (fol. 1r, line 18) and highlights the sacramental significance of Christ's death by drawing on the scriptural and iconographic tradition of the *fons vitae*, or fountain of life (lines 17–146). A sacramental emphasis also informs the second section of the treatise, as Christ's salvific blood is explored further through the Eucharistic image of Christ as the true vine and the image of the faithful drinking from the cup of the New Testament (lines 151–330). The remainder of the treatise explores man's debt to Christ more overtly: for example, the third part focuses on praise and considers the song that man should sing to God as an act of penance (lines 331–434). This is followed by an examination of man's trials on earth through the scriptural motif of the *miles Christi*, or knight of Christ (lines 513–63), as well as a lengthy discussion of the many allegorical and scriptural significations of Christ's cross (lines 564–747). Finally, the closing sections of the treatise explain why Christ's Passion should be praised above all other martyrdoms (lines 748–816) and why it is the most piteous (lines 817–76).

Ihesus woundes so wide is situated towards the beginning of the treatise on fol. 3r (lines 146–50), where it is written out as prose and indicated by a small, pointing manicule that is drawn in the right-hand margin. The inclusion of the lyric at this point is particularly noteworthy, as it is situated at the end of the treatise's opening section and thus functions as a form of conclusion to it. As a result of this careful positioning, the lyric comes to serve as a concise mnemonic aid, which encapsulates the themes and imagery of the treatise's opening movement. Indeed, through its depiction of Christ's wounds as 'welles', the lyric consciously echoes the treatise's opening focus on the 'welle of þe passioun' and thus further underlines the sacramental significance of Christ's death. As noted, the imagery of the treatise's opening section is directly informed by the tradition of the *fons vitae* and, when we read *Ihesus woundes so wide* in context, it becomes clear that we should also approach its imagery in accordance with this scriptural motif. The tradition of the *fons vitae* has a complex scriptural background and is informed by the vast array of water imagery that recurs throughout the Old and New Testaments. Although in the exegetical tradition the image of a fountain of life-giving water could often be understood allegorically,[16] from the patristic period the image was commonly invested with sacramental significance in line with the water symbolism of the Bible. It is this sacramental potentiality that is exploited most fully in the opening movement of the treatise, as it presents Christ as *fons vitae* and emphasises the redemptive power of his sacrifice by exploring the vivifying and salvific properties of water and blood in the sacraments.

From the early Christian period, the motif of the *fons vitae* was linked to the sacrament of baptism due to the long-standing scriptural emphasis on the

---

16 The image of the fountain of life was used as an allegory for Christ, the Virgin Mary, *Ecclesia* and the Holy Scriptures, particularly the four Gospels; see P. Underwood, 'The Fountain of Life in Manuscripts of the Gospels', *Dumbarton Oak Papers* 5 (1950), 41–138 (49).

life-giving properties of water.[17] The motif also increasingly came to be invested with Christological significance, however, as exegetes engaged in typological readings of scripture that led to some examples of water imagery in the Old Testament, such as the fountain of water in Paradise (Genesis 2: 6; 2: 10–14), being interpreted as types of Christ.[18] The depiction of Christ as *fons vitae* was further informed by the Christological reading of such favourite passages as Vulgate Psalm 35: 10 (36: 9), 'quoniam apud te est fons vitae',[19] and Isaiah 12: 3, 'haurietis aquas in gaudio de fontibus salvatoris'.[20] These words were deemed to be fulfilled in Christ's meeting with the Samaritan woman at the well in John 4: 13–14, where Christ identifies himself as the source of all living water:

> omnis qui bibit ex aqua hac sitiet iterum | qui autem biberit ex aqua quam ego dabo ei | non sitiet in aeternum | sed aqua quam dabo ei fiet in eo fons aquae salientis in vitam aeternam.[21]

Although this 'fons aquae' was understood in a sacramental context to refer to the waters of baptism, it was also invested with salvific import and was thought to foreshadow the 'aquae vivae' (John 7: 38) that flowed from the wound in Christ's side at the moment of his death.[22] As a consequence of this line of thought, the corpus of scripture that alludes to Christ as *fons vitae* was further employed by exegetes to interpret the *vulnus lateris*, or side wound of Christ, as a fountain of salvation from which the sacraments flowed.[23] For example, in his *Tractate on the Gospel of John*, Augustine explains that Christ's side was pierced so that 'uitae ostium panderetur, unde sacramenta ecclesiae manauerunt'.[24] Augustine further points out that as the stream that flowed from Christ's side comprised both water and blood, in accordance with John 19: 34, it should be understood as the source of both baptism and the Eucharist: 'Ille sanguis remissionem fusus

---

17 See the account of Moses smiting the rock to release water in Exodus 17: 5–7, as well as the description of the cleansing waters flowing out from the temple in Ezekiel 47. See also Exodus 15: 23–5, Exodus 40: 12–13, Isaiah 55: 10.
18 On the fountain in Paradise as a type of Christ see Ambrose, *Liber de paradiso* 3. 13, CSEL 32, p. 272.
19 'For with thee is the fountain of life'. All Bible quotations in English are taken from the Douay-Challoner translation of the Vulgate (available at http://www.catholicbible.online/); Bible quotations in Latin are taken from R. Weber et al., eds, *Biblia sacra iuxta vulgata versionem*, rev. R. Gryson, 5th edn (Stuttgart, 2007).
20 'You shall draw waters with joy out of the saviour's fountains'.
21 'Whosoever drinketh of this water, shall thirst again; but he that shall drink of the water that I will give him, shall not thirst for ever: But the water that I will give him, shall become in him a fountain of water, springing up into life everlasting.'
22 See also 1 Corinthians 10: 4 where the water struck from the rock by Moses is a prefiguration of the water that pours from Christ's side. Cf. H. Rahner, 'Flumina de ventre Christi: Die patristiche Auslegung von Joh. 7, 37.38', *Biblica* 22 (1941), 269–302, 362–403.
23 Cf. John Chrysostom, *Homiliae in Joannem* 85. 3, PG, 59: 463.
24 'the door of life was thrown open from which the mystical rites of the Church flowed'; *In Iohannis evangelium* 120. 2, CCSL 36: 661; J. W. Rettig, trans., *St Augustine: Tractates on the Gospel of John 112–24 and Tractates on the First Epistle of John*, Fathers of the Church 92 (Washington, DC, 1995), p. 50.

est peccatorum; aqua illa salutare temperat poculum; haec et lauacrum praestat, et potum.'[25]

In the later Middle Ages the sacramental import of the stream that flowed from Christ's side directly informed crucifixion iconography. As Gray has observed, the iconographic tradition of Christ as *fons vitae* was 'deeply influenced by the new types of "affective" devotion and especially by the cult of the Precious Blood', which had become increasingly popular in the fifteenth century.[26] In order to emphasise Christ's role as *fons vitae* more overtly, artists began to draw attention to the sacramental 'fountain' that issues from the *vulnus lateris* by depicting the crucified Christ in a basin filled with water and blood. An example of this mode of depiction is found in the central panel of the *Triptych of the Mystic Bath*, painted c.1525 by the Netherlandish artist Jean Bellegambe the Elder, and now housed in the Palais des Beaux Arts in Lille, France. This painting subtly evokes the sacraments of both baptism and the Eucharist, as it depicts a scene of spiritual cleansing in which the faithful joyfully wash themselves in a font, here reconfigured as a *lavacrum* or bath, filled with the stream from Christ's side.[27] Although this panel acknowledges the sacramental import of water and blood simultaneously, there also emerged a strand of iconography that depicts Christ as *fons vitae* in an exclusively Eucharistic context. This was informed by the belief that the stream from Christ's side could be regarded purely in Eucharistic terms due to the understanding that the comixture of water and wine in the chalice of the Mass became, on consecration, the sacrificial blood and water described in John 19: 34.[28] This idea informs an early sixteenth-century Flemish painting of the *fons vitae* in Porto (1520, Santa Casa de Misericórdia Museum, Porto).[29] In this image a fountain of blood issues from the wound in Christ's side and pours into a basin, which artfully resembles a Eucharistic chalice.

Although no English examples of this mode of iconography survive, the depiction of Christ as *fons vitae* would evidently have been familiar due to its

25 'That blood was shed for the remission of sins; that water provides the proper mix for the health-giving cup: it offers both bath and drink'; *In Iohannis evangelium* 120. 2, CCSL 36: 661; Rettig, trans., *St Augustine*, p. 50.
26 Gray, 'Five Wounds', p. 132. It should be noted that the *fons vitae* has a particularly complex iconographic background dating back to at least the fifth century. In the earliest images the *fons vitae* is depicted as a single fountain of water, in keeping with Genesis 2: 6. This fountain is typically conceived as a font surmounted by a dome and situated in the Garden of Eden. See Underwood, 'The Fountain of Life', pp. 41–138; E. Underhill, 'The Fountain of Life: An Iconographic Study', *Burlington Magazine* 17 (1910), 99–109; E. Mâle, *Religious Art in France, the Late Middle Ages: A Study of Medieval Iconography and its Sources*, ed. H. Bober, trans. M. Matthews (Princeton, 1984), p. 103.
27 See G. B. Krebber and G. Kotting, 'Jean Bellegambe en zijn Mystiek Bad voor Anchin', *Oud Holland* 104 (1990), 123–39.
28 Cf. Ambrose, *De sacramentis*, 5. 1. 4, CSEL 73: 60–1.
29 This painting is of uncertain origin but is deemed to be the work of a Brussels atelier, possibly the circle of Bernard van Orley: the work is catalogued by Pedro Dias as 'Oficina de Bruxelas. Van Orley?' in F. F. Paulino and R. Osório, eds, *Tesouros Artísticos da Misericórdia do Porto* (Porto, 1995), pp. 61–79, no. 1.

presence in the literary tradition: in addition to the treatise in BL, Arundel MS 286, we find allusions to Christ as *fons vitae* in a number of Latin hymns,[30] while some other vernacular works, such as *Pearl*, recall the motif by describing the faithful washing in the stream from Christ's side.[31] The opening section of the treatise in BL, Arundel MS 286 offers an extended discussion of Christ as *fons vitae* and, as we shall see, this motif also directly informs *Ihesus woundes so wide*. However, although *Ihesus woundes so wide* is a fitting conclusion to the treatise's opening section, an examination of its wider textual context reveals that it also has a structural purpose and functions as a bridge that links the first two movements of the longer work. Indeed, by exploiting the dual sacramental resonance invested in the stream that flows from Christ's side, the lyric's treatment of the 'stronde' (line 3) serves to unite the discussion of the 'welle of þe passioun' with the subsequent examination of Christ's salvific blood. As a result, in the wider context of the treatise the lyric serves as an important reminder that the sacramental grace available to man through baptism and the Eucharist is only made possible through Christ's sacrifice on the cross.

In its discussion of the 'welle of þe passioun' the treatise's opening section not only cites a number of scriptural passages integral to the *fons vitae* tradition, but also evokes the cleansing and vivifying qualities of water that are frequently alluded to in the Bible.[32] This focus on water imagery is evident from the section's opening, as it begins by stating that all men should have a 'grete desyr to drinke of þe welle of þe passioun' (fol. 1r, line 18) before quoting the words of Vulgate Psalm 41: 2 (42: 1): 'Quemadmodum desiderat cervus ad fontes aquarum | ita desiderat anima mea ad te Deus'.[33] In evoking this scriptural passage, the 'welle' of Christ's Passion is immediately figured as a source of *aqua vitae* that provides spiritual refreshment and cleansing. Although the depiction of the Passion as a 'welle' or 'fountain' of life is in keeping with the tradition of the *fons vitae*, the treatise is also informed by trends in contemporary devotion and exploits its use of the 'welle' motif by drawing on the popular conception of Christ's wounds as 'welles'.[34] Indeed, the treatise goes on to emphasise the sacramental import of *aqua vitae*, as it recalls the image of Christ as *fons vitae* by stating that this water finds its ultimate source in Christ's wounds: 'þese welles of watres bitokeneþ þe woundes þat our saueoure sufride on þe croys and þat welleþ ny3t and day grace and goodnesse to refreshe hise children' (fol. 1r, lines 22–5). The sacrament of baptism is clearly evoked at this point, as the treatise not only highlights the 'grace' invested in water, but notes that 'þe watres of welles seruen to

---

30 The hymn that begins *Ave, caput gloriosum / Cruentatum et spinosum* describes the stream from Christ's side as a 'flumen' or river; see AH, XXXI, 91.
31 See E. V. Gordon, ed., *Pearl* (Oxford, 1953), p. 24, lines 650–5, where it is stated that the water that flows from Christ's side serves to cleanse mankind, washing away the sins of Adam.
32 See note 17 above.
33 'As the hart panteth after the fountains of water; so my soul panteth after thee, O God.'
34 On the popularity of this motif in the fifteenth century see Gray, 'Five Wounds', pp. 129–31.

wasche ... [and] ȝeue drynke to men' (fol. 1r, lines 26–7). Although this section of the treatise frequently deploys water imagery, its depiction of Christ as *fons vitae* is also informed by an emphasis on the cleansing properties of blood. For instance, in keeping with the exegetical tradition, the treatise asserts that the river in Paradise that is divided 'in quattuor capita'[35] prefigures the four acts of bloodshed Christ suffered during the Passion: 'þese iiij. schedynges of blood beþ bitokened by þe well and flode þat was in paradyse þat moisted al paradyse and was departed in iiij hedes' (fol. 2r, lines 62–5).[36] In parallel to the treatise's depiction of cleansing water, this blood is also invested with sacramental grace as we are told that it 'refrescheþ and moisteþ by grace al holy chirche' (fol. 2r, lines 67–8). In spite of this emphasis on salvific blood, the treatise's depiction of the Edenic fountain as a type of Christ is explained most fully in relation to water and baptism:

> In tokene of þese holy watres of Cristes passioun cristen men ben baptised in water þat taken is spede and grace of þe principal font and welle of þe side of oure saueour þat schedde his blood and water in þe day of his martirdome. (fol. 2r, lines 69–73)

This description adheres to contemporary iconographic depictions of Christ as *fons vitae*, as the *vulnus lateris* is depicted as a 'font' or 'welle' from which the waters of baptism flow. Following this, and leading up to the intercalation of the lyric, the treatise turns to explore the motif of drinking from the 'welle of þe passioun' and asserts that all men, be they labourers, knights or pilgrims, 'nede to drinke drauȝtes of deuocioun of þe passioun of Ihesu Criste' (fol. 3r, lines 138–9). Although the treatise highlights the refreshment and comfort to be gained by drinking from this 'welle', it is ultimately presented as a spiritual act that demands man's contrition. Indeed, immediately before the intercalation of the lyric the treatise cites the words of Vulgate Psalm 35: 10 (36: 9) in order to emphasise that the drink of the sacraments is only made available to man through Christ as *fons vitae*: 'Lord at þee is þe welle of lif and in þi liȝt of grace of redempcioun we schul se lyȝt of euerlastinge blisse' (fol. 3r, lines 144–6).

The language and imagery deployed in *Ihesus woundes so wide* is directly shaped by its textual context, as the treatise's gradual unfolding of the 'welle' motif as a symbol of Christ's Passion, his wounds and, specifically, the *vulnus lateris*, is echoed in the lyric's depiction of the wounds as the 'welles of lif' (line 2). Although this description highlights the redemptive power of Christ's bodily suffering, the lyric singles out the *vulnus lateris* for special attention: 'Namely þe stronde of hys syde' (line 3). Here, the lyric affirms that the side wound is a conduit of everlasting life because of the sacramental significance of the stream that issues forth. Moreover, the lyric's use of concrete, visual images, such as the

---

35 Genesis 2: 10; 'into four heads'.
36 According to the treatise, the four occasions on which Christ shed his blood are the scourging, the crowning with thorns, the Crucifixion and the piercing of Christ's side after death (fols 1v–2r, lines 59–62).

descriptions of Christ's 'woundes so wide' (line 1) and the 'stronde' (*stream*) that 'ran ful breme on þe rode' (lines 3–4), clearly recalls the treatise's earlier presentation of Christ as *fons vitae* and the image of the *vulnus lateris* as a 'welle' from which the waters of baptism flow. Through its evocation of this earlier image, the lyric ensures that its depiction of the *vulnus lateris* and its 'stronde' is understood not only in relation to Eucharistic blood, but also to baptismal waters in accordance with the emphasis of the treatise's opening.

The discussion of drinking from the 'welle of þe passioun', which becomes increasingly prominent towards the end of the treatise's opening section, also finds fruition in the lyric's treatment of the *vulnus lateris* and the instruction to drink of the life-giving stream that pours from the wound: 'Bowe þu (*Bow down*) doun to þe brinke (*edge*) / & mekely taste of þe welle' (lines 7–8). This use of imagery resonates with a degree of literalism not found in the treatise, however, as it draws upon an established topos in Latin hymnody that transforms the *vulnus lateris* into a vessel or opening from which the faithful may drink.[37] Although the lyric's instruction to drink from the 'welle' coincides with the earlier emphasis on drinking the 'drauȝtes of deuocioun' (fol. 3r, line 138) made available to man through Christ's Passion, the lyric's final lines also resonate with an exclusively Eucharistic meaning. Indeed, having reconfigured the *vulnus lateris* as a mystical aperture, the stream that flows from Christ's side could now more firmly evoke the comixture in the Eucharistic chalice. This subtle change of direction is fitting in the broader context of the treatise, as it anticipates the extended discussion of Christ's sacramental blood that follows the lyric. This second section, which begins on line 151, examines the salvific import of Christ's blood through a range of established scriptural motifs. For instance, it begins by deploying the motif of Christ as the 'verray vine', whose blood is 'þe worþiest wyn and moost preciouse to drynke' (fol. 3v, lines 153–4),[38] before turning to examine the Isaiahan image of the Saviour trampling out the vintage in the winepress, 'Christ hym silf stamped out þe blood of þe grape wiþ hondes and fete' (fol. 3r, lines 170–1).[39] The lyric's closing instruction to 'taste of þe welle' (lines 7–8) neatly foreshadows the second section's central motif, as the depiction of Christ as the true vine reaches its fulfilment in the Eucharistic image of Christ offering this 'wine', his blood, to the faithful in a chalice: 'þe cuppe of þe newe testament in his blood' (fol. 3r, lines 179–80).[40] In spite of this subtle echo in imagery, the lyric's motif of drinking

---

37 See the hymn *Salutatio ad latus domini*, where the side wound is described as a 'mitis apertura' ('gentle opening') from which flows a life-giving spring; F-J. Mone, ed., *Lateinische Hymnen des Mittelalters*, 3 vols (Freiburg, 1853–5), I, 166–7.

38 The depiction of Christ as the vine originates in Isaiah 5: 1–7, but is also informed by the parable of the vineyard in Matthew 21 and the words of John 15: 1: 'ego sum vitis vera et Pater meus agricola est' ('I am the true vine and my Father is the husbandman'). For discussion of this motif see Hetta Elizabeth Howes, Chapter 6, this volume.

39 See Isaiah 63, and also Matthew 21: 33–43 and Revelation 14: 18–20. On the iconographic tradition of Christ in the winepress see Mâle, *Religious Art in France*, pp. 117–22.

40 See Luke 22: 20: 'Hic est calix novum testamentum in sanguine meo | qui pro vobis fundetur' ('This is the chalice, the new testament in my blood, which shall be shed for you').

directly from the *vulnus lateris* is perhaps the more powerful and visceral image and may thus remind the reader that while drinking from the 'cuppe of þe newe testament' is undoubtedly a spiritual act, it is grounded in the literal physicality of Christ's suffering and torment.

An examination of *Ihesus woundes so wide* in its manuscript context undoubtedly sheds new light on its imagery and meaning. Although the poem is in keeping with the popular devotion to Christ's wounds in the fifteenth century, its imagery can be traced back to a much earlier period and has its origins in the scriptural and iconographic tradition of the *fons vitae* and the sacramental significance of baptismal water and Eucharistic blood. A contextual reading of the poem also enables us to consider important issues of function and purpose. As we have seen, the lyric's careful use of imagery and language ensures that it not only provides an effective conclusion to the opening discussion of Christ as *fons vitae*, but also looks forward to the following section on Christ's blood. Consequently, the lyric's depiction of Christ crucified and the 'welles of lyf' (line 2) come to resonate with broad sacramental significance, as the poem is informed by images of Eucharistic sacrifice as well as the significance of water in a baptismal context. Indeed, the lyric's central image of the 'stronde' that flows from the *vulnus lateris* acts as a conduit that links the wider discussions of cleansing water and Eucharistic blood, reinforcing the belief that the sacraments take their course from Christ crucified.

To conclude, it is clear that *Ihesus woundes so wide* is directly informed by the imagery and themes of the treatise in which it is inserted. Although it has often been approached as a standalone poem, examining the lyric in relation to its textual context encourages us to rethink our understanding of its themes and imagery, and challenges the view that it is straightforward and rather simplistic. Indeed, the lyric's careful placement within the treatise reveals that it has an important structural function and is informed by a broad sacramental context that may otherwise be overlooked when considering the poem in isolation. As a consequence of the wealth of fresh insight that is borne out by a contextual reading of *Ihesus woundes so wide*, the poem serves as an important reminder of the need to be alert to the contexts in which lyrics survive. It also demonstrates that an analysis of a lyric's context, particularly with regards to those poems that are intercalated into longer prose works, is an especially fruitful area of study and one that is worthy of further exploration. Certainly, more work needs to be done on the status and role of lyrics integrated into prose works and on how this context may shape our understanding not only of a particular poem's imagery and meaning, but of the lyric form itself in the later Middle Ages.

8

'Written in gold upon a purple stain': Mariological Rhetoric and the Material Culture of Aureate Diction

Anne Marie D'Arcy

The infinite power essenciall[1]

1 The infinite power essenciall — *supremely divine*
   Me thoght I sawe, verrement, — *clearly*
   Procedyng from his trone celestiall — *throne*
   To a dere damsell that was gent. — *venerated lady, splendidly noble*
5 Songes melodious was in their tent — *were the intense purpose*
   Of Angells, synging with gret solemnite, — *great ceremonial reverence*
   Before a quene whiche was present.
   Ecce virgo, radix Jesse. — *Behold a virgin, root of Jesse.*

   Tota pulcra, to the lilly like. — *Wholly beautiful*
10 She was set withe saphures celestiall. — *adorned; sapphires*
   The odour of hir mowthe aromatike — *spiritual fragrance; sweet-smelling*
   Dyd coumford the world universall. — *alleviate*
   Moche clerer she was then the crystall. — *bright, transparent; than*
   She is the flowre of all formosite, — *beauty*
15 Devoide of actes criminall.
   Ecce virgo, radix Jesse.

   Oleum effusum, to languentes medsine, — *Oil outpoured; the languishing; spiritual remedy*

   A 'Maria' by denominacioun, — *designation*
   Fulgent as the beame celestine, — *incandescent; heavenly beam*

Religious lyrics are similarly considered in relation to visual images and artefacts in Chapter 2, A. S. Lazikani: 'Moving Lights: An Affective Reading of *On leome is in þis world ilist* and Church Wall Paintings', and Chapter 11, Katherine Zieman: 'Compiling the Lyric: Richard Rolle, Textual Dynamism and Devotional Song in British Library, Additional MS 37049', this volume.

1   NIMEV 3391; DIMEV 5343. Reproduced here from Brown *XV*, pp. 67–9, with added glosses (Brown's text is from London, British Library, Additional MS 20059). For other editions see R. T. Davies, ed., *Medieval English Lyrics: A Critical Anthology* (London, 1964), pp. 199–200 and K. Saupe, ed., *Middle English Marian Lyrics* (Kalamazoo, MI, 1998), pp. 113–15, 237–8.

20	Called unto hir coronacioun:	
	Phebus persplendent made his abdominacioun,	*Phoebus; all shining; abdication*
	Devoidyng all in tenebrosite,	*withdrawing himself; obscurity*
	For gret love of hir exaltacioun.	*zenith, elevation to high rank*
	Ecce virgo, radix Jesse.	
25	Ryght diligent were the minstrells divine,	
	Trones and dominaciones for to expresse,	*Thrones; Dominations; identify by name*
	Angells, Archangells, dubbit in doctrine,	*invested with dignity in doctrine*
	To ministre to that regall arrayed in richesse.	*royal person*
	The Prynce perpetuall spake to that Princesse,	
30	Smiling in his suavite,	*sweetness*
	'Columba mea, the cloystre of clandnesse,	*My dove; womb of purity*
	Ecce virgo, radix Jesse.	
	'Surge, true tabernacle of virginite,	*Rise*
	Bothe mother and maiden inculpable,	*sinless, blameless*
35	Cum furthe of thy consanguinite	*forth; earthly kinship*
	Unto glorye incomparable.'	
	Then kneled this orient and amiable	*lustrous pearl; worthy of admiration*
	Before the Pellicane of perpetuete,	*heavenly eternity*
	And he crowned that regient venerable.	*Lady ruler*
40	*Ecce virgo, radix Jesse.*	
	By the spectable splendure of hir fulgent face	*virtuous radiance; luminous*
	My sprete was raveshed and in my body sprent.	*spirit; leapt*
	Inflamed was my hert with gret solace	
	Of the luciant, corruscall resplendent.	*shining, sparkling radiant one*
45	Then this curious cumpany, incontinent,	*splendid; without delay*
	Withe the seraphinnes in their solemnite	*seraphim; veneration*
	Solemply sang this subsequent.	*Reverently; following in order*
	Ecce virgo, radix Jesse.	
	'O! Deifere delicate and doghter divine,	*Godbearer; glorious*
50	Mother of mercy and meyden mellefluous,	*sweet as honey*
	Devoide of disceite, dubbit in doctrine,	
	Trone of the Trinite, treite thow for us.	*Throne; mediate*
	Us defende from the dongeon dolorous,	*dungeon; desolate*
	And bring to abide in blisse withe thee,	
55	There to love our God most glorious.'	
	Ecce virgo, radix Jesse.	

When we turn to the complex, linguistic encrustations of many fifteenth-century lyrics, particularly those of John Lydgate and his contemporaries, aureate diction fulfils a similar function from an aesthetic perspective to late antique and medieval examples of the *liber aureus*, 'Written in gold upon a purple stain', as William

Butler Yeats describes it in 'The Gift of Harun Al-Rashid'.[2] In Lydgate's prologue to the *Troy Book* he uses the term 'lettris aureat' to describe chrysography in the manner of Chaucer's 'wordes al with gold ywriten' in the Second Nun's Tale, but the context also recalls the *litterae aureae* of classical Roman epigraphy: the monumental gilded bronze letters embedded in stone, which feature in literary sources since the Augustan age.[3] The reference in Lydgate's *Fall of Princes* to 'Writyng of old, with lettres aureat' is imbued with a clear sense of classical monumentality.[4] Moreover, the triumphal association of 'lettres aureat' with the *purpura* of martyrdom is explicitly evoked in his *Lives of Saints Edmund and Fremund*.[5] Similarly, in his *Testament*, the Holy Name is not only 'graven' on the purple-stained heart of another martyr, Ignatius of Antioch, 'With Aureat lettres / As gold that dyd shyne', in a manner strikingly reminiscent of chrysography, but he also wishes that his own heart be embellished 'With aureate letres'.[6] On several occasions Lydgate describes grace as a 'licour aureate', an 'aureat lycour', or a 'bawme aureate' that 'enlumynyth these rethoriciens', whether it springs from St Edmund or St Ambrose, or Calliope, Cleo and the other muses.[7] In *The Legend of Seynt Margarete*, he beseeches this 'gemme of gemmes' to 'shede of grace the aureat lycoure / In-to my penne', which once again recalls the act of writing in letters 'enlumyned with gold'.[8] However, as a bravura display of rhetorical aestheticism, stylistically analogous to the International Gothic style in the visual and decorative arts, aureate diction was particularly employed in encomia of the glorious mysteries of the Virgin, attained through Christ's victory over death. Here, it is the rhetorical counterpart of the burnished gilding and jewelled pigments lavished on these supernatural events by contemporary artists.

This is clearly demonstrated in the early fifteenth-century lyric, which begins 'The infinite power essenciall' (BL, Additional MS 20059, fols 99–100,

---

2   'Sailing to Byzantium' (1928) and 'The Gift of Harun Al-Rashid' (1924), in P. Allt and R. K. Alspach, eds, *The Variorum Edition of the Poems of W. B. Yeats*, 2nd edn (London, 1957), pp. 408, 461.

3   H. Bergen, ed., *Lydgate's Troy Book*, 4 vols, EETS ES 97, 103, 106, 126 (London, 1906–35), I, 6, line 211; Benson, p. 265, VIII. 210. On the *litterae aureae*, cf. G. Alföldy, 'Augustus und die Inschriften: Tradition und Innovation. Die Geburt der imperialen Epigraphik', *Gymnasium* 98 (2001), 289–324.

4   H. Bergen, ed., *Lydgate's Fall of Princes*, 4 vols, EETS ES 121, 122, 123, 124 (London, 1924–7), III, 476, line 106.

5   C. Horstmann, ed., *Altenglische Legenden: Neue Folge* (Heilbronn, 1881), p. 424, line 611.

6   *The Testament of Dan John Lydgate*, H. N. McCracken, ed., *The Minor Poems of John Lydgate*, 2 vols, EETS ES 107, OS 192 (London, 1911–34), I, 331, lines 37–8, and I, 348, line 508.

7   In addition to Horstmann, ed., *Altenglische Legenden*, p. 381, line 221, see MacCracken, ed., *Minor Poems*, for the following: 'Exposition of the Pater Noster', I, 70, lines 315–18; 'An Invocation to Seynte Anne', I, 131, line 14; 'Ballade at the Reverence of Our Lady', I, 255, lines 13–14; also 'A Mumming for the Mercers', II, 696, line 34. Cf. Bergen, ed., *Fall of Princes*, I, 13, line 461.

8   MacCracken, ed., *Minor Poems*, I, 175, lines 53–7. Cf. Bergen, ed., *Lydgate's Troy Book*, I, 2, lines 35–6: 'And of my penne the tracys to correcte, / Whyche bareyn is of aureate lycour'.

c.1425), also titled 'Mary, Queen of Heaven'. Here, a shining diptych of the Assumption, the Triumph of the Virgin, and the Coronation, unfolds in the narrator's mind. In this poetic vision, aureation is the literary correlative to what Lydgate describes as fretted work, deployed in the creation of such flamboyant *joyaux* ('objets of vertu') as *Das Goldene Rößl* (Paris, 1400–05: Altötting, Schatzkammer), presented as an *étrenne* ('new year's gift') by Isabella of Bavaria to Charles VI of France in 1405, or the Holy Thorn Reliquary of Jean, Duc de Berry (c.1400–10: London, British Museum).[9] Most *joyaux* are continental in origin, but some were produced in England, including possibly the Tableau of the Trinity sent by Joan of Navarre to her son John V, Duke of Brittany in 1412 (c.1390–1410: Paris, Louvre).[10] A notable feature of these *joyaux* is the use of specific enamelling techniques perfected in the fourteenth and fifteenth centuries, namely *basse-taille* and *en ronde bosse*.[11] *Basse-taille* involves chasing or engraving an intaglio pattern in metal, almost always silver, gold, or vermeil (silver gilt), then applying translucent blue, green, violet or, most rarely, *rouge clair* enamel so as to allow light to be reflected from the low relief of lustrous metal substrate.[12] This may be the technique the Auchinleck narrator describes in *Sir Orfeo*: the 'divers aumal' on the voussoirs of the 'rede gold' arches in the Fairy King's palace.[13] It is almost certainly familiar to the *Gawain* poet as 'grene aumayl', which 'on golde glowande bryȝter'.[14] It is equally likely the *basse-taille* technique influenced the description of tree trunks 'as blwe as ble of Ynde; / As bornyst syluer þe lef' in

---

9   Bergen, ed., *Fall of Princes*, I, 318, line 4231; and cf. *ibid.*, I, 161, line 161: 'A crowne of golde with ryche stones frette'; I, 174, lines 1022–3: 'many rube red / Fret enviroun'; I, 366, line 7747: 'fret with stonys riche'. Cf. also A. Erdmann and E. Ekwall, eds, *Lydgate's Siege of Thebes*, 2 vols, EETS ES 108 and 125 (London, 1911–30), I, 63, lines 1439–41: 'Tweyne mantels / vnto hem wer broght, frett with peerle / and riche stonys, wroght / Of cloth of golde / and veinyt cremysyil.' See R. Baumstark, ed., *Das Goldene Rössl: Ein Meisterwerk der Pariser Hofkunst um 1400* (Munich, 1995); J. Cherry, *The Holy Thorn Reliquary* (London, 2010).
10 See É. Kovâcs, 'Le Reliquaire de l'ordre du Saint-Esprit. La "dot" d' Anne de Bretagne', *Revue du Louvre* 31 (1981), 246–51, but cf. E. Taburet-Delahaye and F. Avril, eds, *Paris 1400: Les arts sous Charles VI* (Paris, 2004), pp. 166–7 (cat. 88).
11 Cf. J. Stratford, *Richard II and the English Royal Treasure* (Woodbridge, 2013), pp. 38–41.
12 M. Bimson and I. C. Freestone, '"Rouge Clair" and other late 14th Century Enamels on the Royal Gold Cup of the Kings of France and England', *Annales du 9e Congrès de l'Association Internationale pour l'histoire du Verre, Nancy 1983* (Liège, 1985), pp. 209–22. That *basse-taille* enamel was produced in England in the fourteenth century is evidenced by the Swinford pyx and the King's Lynn cup (c.1340); see M. Campbell, 'English *basse taille* enamels', *Annali della Scuola Normale Superiore di Pisa* 4 (1997), 37–46.
13 A. J. Bliss, ed., *Sir Orfeo*, 2nd edn (Oxford 1966), p. 32, lines 361–4. S. Lerer, 'Artifice and Artistry in *Sir Orfeo*', *Speculum* 60 (1985), 92–109 (100), does not recognise this as 'true enamel work', but rather *pictura translucida*, 'an artificial enamel made by painting on glass or foil'.
14 J. R. R. Tolkien and E. V. Gordon, eds, *Sir Gawain and the Green Knight*, 2nd edn, rev. N. Davis (Oxford, 1967), p. 7, line 236.

the orientalised, paradisal landscape of *Pearl*.[15] Encrusted or *ronde bosse* enamel is almost invariably on gold, built up with layers of colour in the round or in high relief, as in the Dunstable Swan Jewel (c.1400, London: British Museum).[16] In this context, we may note the description of the eagle of 'bournede golde' in *Sir Launfal*, embellished 'wyth ryche amall'.[17] Dunbar may well have either of these techniques in mind in the *Goldyn Targe*, when he praises Chaucer as a 'flour imperiall', whose 'fresch anamalit termes celicall' form the rhetorical seedbed for the stylised landscape that opens the poem, 'Anamalit was the felde wyth all colouris'.[18]

Certainly, Lydgate's description of Mary as a 'vinarye envermailyd' in his 'Ballade at the Reverence of Our Lady' suggests the transmutation of postlapsarian nature into something infinitely more precious in its artifice by the poet as *aurifaber*, or indeed, *jueler* as in *Pearl*.[19] Here, the patristic *topos* of Mary as the spiritual vineyard – as opposed to the *cella vinaria* of Song of Songs 2: 4 – who brought a vine out of Egypt as in Psalm 79 (80): 9 is transmuted into a vintage of metallised, vermilion grapes. Lydgate's viniculture, suggestive of red gold sifted with *rouge clair*, as in the seven horns of 'red golde cler' adorning the Lamb in *Pearl*, reminds us of Cellini's ascription of the discovery of this most prized enamelling technique to an alchemist, because of its difficulty.[20] In contrast to such poetic alchemists as Novalis, Baudelaire, Mallarmé, Von Hoffmansthal or Yeats, not all medievalists have been beguiled by metallised gardens, replete with enamelled, vermillion grapes, or silvered, azure boles, which bear witness to 'what is past, or passing, or to come'.[21] The disparagement of aureate diction became a well-established critical practice during the twentieth century, especially among critics of the Middle English lyric. Commenting on a version of Dunbar's 'Ane Ballat of Our Lady' preserved by William Forrest, Henry Noble MacCracken insists that 'When the poet with angelic mouth, aureate lips, and sugared tongue overgilt his rude Scots with mellifluate terms, his modern readers hasten to turn the page.'[22] Rosemary Woolf mistrusts the 'artificiality' of aureation, 'straining for effect that may be called stylistic insincerity'.[23] Yet, as Douglas Gray points out,

---

15   E. V. Gordon, ed., *Pearl* (Oxford, 1953), p. 3, lines 76–7.
16   Cf. J. Cherry, 'The Dunstable Swan Jewel', *Journal of the British Archaeological Association* 32 (1969), 38–53.
17   Thomas Chestre, *Sir Launfal*, ed. A. J. Bliss (London, 1960), p. 60, lines 269–70.
18   P. Bawcutt, ed., *The Poems of William Dunbar*, 2 vols (Glasgow, 1998), I, 184, line 13; I, 192, lines 257–8. Cf. A. C. Spearing, *The Medieval Poet as Voyeur: Looking and Listening in Medieval Love-Narratives* (Cambridge, 1993), pp. 247–8.
19   MacCracken, ed., *Minor Poems*, I, 256, line 45.
20   Benvenuto Cellini, *I Trattati dell'oreficeria e della scultura*, ed. C. Milanesi (Florence, 1857), p. 29. Cf. Gordon, ed., *Pearl*, p. 40, line 1111.
21   Yeats, 'Sailing to Byzantium', in Allt and Alspach, eds, *Variorum*, p. 408.
22   'New Stanzas by Dunbar', *Modern Language Notes* 24 (1909), 110–11 (110).
23   Woolf, p. 8.

there is 'usually some sense of decorum' involved in the use of aureation in the Middle English poetic tradition.[24]

Throughout the fourteenth and fifteenth centuries, poets strategically employ aureate terms, encrusted with the *colores rhetorici* or 'colours of rethoryk' as Chaucer puts it, to elevate their *prima materia* in the manner of the gilded and enamelled *joyaux* gracing the courts of Europe, so that their words might be wrought into precious, golden objects of virtu in themselves.[25] Many *joyaux* were specifically commissioned as *étrennes* and this tradition of a precious, highly wrought, novelty gift for the new year gave rise in turn to a lyrical *étrenne*.[26] During the course of the *étrennes* feast in the January calendar page of *Les Très Riches Heures du Duc de Berry* (c.1411/12–16; Chantilly, Musée Condé, MS 65, fol. 1v), the *chevalier d'honneur* issues an invitation to the gift givers in words that are literally gilded: 'aproche, aproche'. Similarly, the poetic *étrenne* was conceived as a form that makes a gift of golden words, metaphorically and, in some instances, in gilded letters on parchment, and although the form was only fixed by Clément Marot in the early sixteenth century, the conceit found favour with Deschamps, de Pisan and Dunbar, who wrote some verses for James IV in 'hansill of this guid New 3eir'.[27] Moreover, the predominantly sacred *matière* of the most prized *joyaux*, allied to the inherent sacredness of chrysography, informs the precise, rhetorical deployment of aureate diction. In the visual and decorative arts, the patron's insistence on gold and gilding in pure gold leaf, and lots of it, in envisioning the sacred has a sound exegetical and liturgical basis because the most precious of metals was particularly associated with those mysteries of the Christian faith that transcend nature. Similarly, in the Middle English lyric, aureation is employed to illuminate the supernatural glory of these mysteries, as in 'Mary, Queen of Heaven'.

In the opening stanza, Mary is borne up in triumph up through the circles of Heaven unto the 'trone celestiall' of the 'infinite power essenciall', which recalls Paul's title for the pre-existent Christ in 1 Corinthians 1: 24. Here, she is glorified by the ascending Orders of the Dionysian celestial hierarchy, upon reception by her son as the *Sponsa* of the Song of Songs. Although the Assumption and Queenship of Mary are distinct theological doctrines, they are inextricably linked by sacred tradition. This link is made manifest in the encyclicals *Fulgens Corona* (8 September 1953) and *Ad Caeli Reginam* (11 October 1954), which reaffirm the divinely revealed dogma of the Assumption *de fide credenda*, defined infallibly by the Apostolic Constitution *Munificentissimus Deus* (1 November 1950), in proclaiming Mary *Regina Caeli*. Mary's queenship is grounded in the

---

24 Gray, *Themes*, p. 65.
25 Benson, p. 178, V. 726.
26 Cf. B. Buettner, 'Past's Presents: New Year's Gifts at the Valois Courts ca. 1400', *Art Bulletin* 83 (2001), 598–625; J. Hirschbiegel, *Étrennes: Untersuchungen zum höfischen Geschenkverkehr im spätmittelalterlichen Frankreich zur Zeit König Karls VI (1380–1422)* (Munich, 2003).
27 'My Prince in God, Gif the Guid Grace'; Bawcutt, ed., *Poems of William Dunbar*, I, 129.

Judean regnal title, *Gĕbîrâ*, in the sense of 'mother of the king', adopted as a Marian epithet during the patristic period.[28] Scriptural authority was derived from Psalm 44 (45): 10, 'The queen stood on thy right hand, in gilded clothing; surrounded with variety', used in the Assumption liturgy, and the iconography of the Assumption and the Coronation of the Virgin are often conflated.[29] As an iconographic motif, the Coronation is generally regarded as having emerged in the Latin West during the twelfth century, whether of French, Italian or English provenance.[30] However, it is closely linked to the motif of *Maria Synthronos*, or Triumph of the Virgin, illustrating Psalm 44 (45): 10, which is ultimately of Byzantine origin, but most memorably depicted in the apse mosaic of Santa Maria in Trastevere (1100–43).[31] In the Triumph of the Virgin, the crowned Mary is depicted not as *Theotokos* or *Deipara*, but as *Sponsa*, bedecked in gold, which

---

28 See M. J. Donnelly, 'The Queenship of Mary During the Patristic Period', *Marian Studies* 4 (1953), 82–108; G. F. Kirwin, 'Queenship of Mary: Queen-Mother', *Marian Library Studies* 28 (2007), 37–320.

29 See 1 Kings 2: 19: 'and the king arose to meet her, and bowed to her, and sat down upon his throne: and a throne was set for the king's mother, and she sat on his right hand'. All Bible quotations in Latin are taken from R. Weber, ed., *Biblia sacra iuxta vulgata versionem*, 5th edn. rev. R. Gryson (Stuttgart, 2007). All Bible quotations in English are taken from the Douay-Rheims translation of the Vulgate, as revised by Richard Challoner.

30 E. Mâle, *L' Art religieux du XIIe siècle en France*, 4th edn (Paris, 1940), pp. 184–6, insisted it was originally French, created by Abbot Suger, subsequently inspiring the iconography of Innocent II's rebuilding of Santa Maria in Trastevere; cf. P. Verdier, 'Suger a-t-il été en France le créateur du thème iconographique du couronnement de la Vierge?', *Gesta* 15 (1976), 227–36, and *Le couronnement de la Vierge. Les origines et les premiers développements d'un thème iconographique* (Montreal and Paris, 1980). J. Vanuxem, 'Autour du triomphe de la Vierge du portail de la cathédrale de Senlis. Les portails détruits de la cathédrale de Cambrai et de Saint-Nicolas d'Amiens', *Bulletin monumental* 103 (1945), 89–102 (90), suggests an Italian provenance. On the English theory of origin, see G. Zarnecki, 'The Coronation of the Virgin on a Capital from Reading Abbey', *Journal of the Warburg and Courtauld Institutes* 13 (1950), 1–12; T. A. Heslop, 'The English Origins of the Coronation of the Virgin', *Burlington Magazine* 147 (2005), 790–7. The earliest English examples of a capital from Reading (c.1130–40) and the south doorway tympanum from St Swithin, Quedington, Gloucester (c.1140–50) actually depict an active coronation, rather than the Triumph of the Virgin.

31 In addition to A. Katzenellenbogen, *The Sculptural Programs of Chartres Cathedral: Christ, Mary, Ecclesia* (Baltimore, 1959), pp. 56–9, see G. A. Wellen, 'Sponsa Christi: Het absismozaiek van de Santa Maria In Trastevere te Rome en het Hooglied', *Feestbundel F. van der Meer*, ed. E. F. van der Grinten et al. (Amsterdam and Brussels, 1966), pp. 148–59; E. Kitzinger, 'A Virgin's Face: Antiquarianism in Twelfth-Century Art', *Art Bulletin* 62 (1980), 6–19; W. Tronzo, 'Apse Decoration, the Liturgy, and the Perception of Art in Medieval Rome. S. Maria in Trastevere and S. Maria Maggiore', *Italian Church Decoration of the Middle Ages and Early Renaissance: Functions, Form and Regional Tradition* (Baltimore, 1989), pp. 167–93; J. E. Barclay Lloyd, 'Das goldene Gewand der Muttergottes in der Bildersprache mittelalterlicher und frühchristlicher Mosaiken in Rom', *Römische Quartalschrift* 85 (1990), 66–85.

is the *ornamentum ecclesiae*, as reflected in this stanza.[32] However, the Triumph of the Virgin and the Coronation both refer to the *Sponsus* in loving union with the *Sponsa* in Song of Songs 4: 8, 'Come from Libanus, my spouse, come from Libanus, come: thou shalt be crowned.'

The first honorific title bestowed on Mary in this lyric is 'dere damsel', which consciously echoes the scriptural significance of *Gĕbîrâ* in the sense of 'Great Lady'. As *Desponia* or *Domina* she is 'exalted above the choirs of Angels', as in the antiphon from Alcuin's florilegium, *De laude Dei*, 'Exaltata es sancta dei genitrix super choros angelorum ad celestia regna', sung on the Feast of the Assumption (15 August) in both Sarum and York Uses.[33] It also reminds us of the iconographic shift in late medieval depictions of the Assumption, Triumph of the Virgin and the Coronation from scenes in which Mary is supported by angels, to those where she surpasses the entire celestial hierarchy.[34] Although Alcuin's antiphon 82 lauds the Virgin as *Mater et Sponsa*, it is her role as *Sponsa* enthroned as *Imperatrix angelorum*, not her divine motherhood, which is emphasised initially in this lyric, as in the greatest of Byzantine Marian hymns, the fifth- or sixth-century *Akathistos*.[35] The depiction of Mary as *Basilissa*, *Imperatrix*, or *Augusta* is found in Western Christendom as early as Alcuin's antiphon 84, but is more usually associated with the Byzantine influence of Empress Theophano on Ottonian Mariology.[36] In the Latin West, the motif of Mary as *Imperatrix angelorum* was specifically associated with her corporeal assumption, as it is here. This association had become an English devotional commonplace by the fifteenth century, due mainly to the influence of the sequence, 'Ave mundi spes Maria', generally

---

32   Cf. S. Riccioni, 'The Word in the Image: An Epiconographic Analysis of Mosaics of the Reform in Rome (Twelfth-century)', *Inscriptions in Liturgical Spaces*, ed. K. B. Aavitsland and T. K. Seim (Rome, 2011), pp. 85–137 (127–30).

33   In addition to M. Clayton, *The Cult of the Virgin Mary in Anglo-Saxon England* (Cambridge, 1990), p. 57, see R. Constantinescu, 'Alcuin et les "Libelli precum" de l'époque carolingienne', *Revue d'histoire de la spiritualité* 50 (1974), 17–56 (50).

34   See the stained glass window of Duccio di Buoninsegna, 'Assumption of the Virgin' (c.1287–90, Siena: Siena Cathedral), and Bernardo Daddi, 'The Assumption of the Virgin' (c.1337–39, New York: Metropolitan Museum of Art), where Mary is borne aloft in a mandorla by angels, in contrast to Bartolommeo Bulgarini, 'The Virgin of the Assumption with St Thomas Receiving the Girdle' (c.1365, Siena: Pinacoteca Nazionale), and Francesco Botticini, 'The Assumption of the Virgin' (c.1474–76, London: National Gallery).

35   See J. Osborne, 'Images of the Mother of God in Early Medieval Rome', *Icon and Word: The Power of Images in Byzantium. Studies presented to Robin Cormack*, ed. A. Eastmond and L. James (Aldershot, 2003), pp. 135–56.

36   Cf. Constantinescu, 'Alcuin', p. 50: 'Vere benedicta imperatrix et gloriosa castitatis regina' ('Truly blessed empress and glorious queen of chastity'); Bruno of Querfurt, *S. Adalberti Pragensis episcopi et martyris vita altera*, ed. J. Karwasińska (Warsaw, 1969), p. 4: 'bona angelorum imperatrix augusta' ('Noble empress of the angels, imperial majesty'). See A. Davids, ed., *The Empress Theophano: Byzantium and the West at the Turn of the First Millennium* (Cambridge, 1995); M. Vassilaki, ed., *Images of the Mother of God: Perceptions of the Theotokos in Byzantium* (Aldershot, 2005), p. xxii.

ascribed to Innocent III.³⁷ We may note the version in the Burnet Psalter, a Franco-Netherlandish manuscript for English use (Aberdeen, University Library, MS 25, fol. 100), also dating from the first quarter of the fifteenth century.³⁸ In keeping with the regnal theme, the refrain salutes Mary as *virga de radice Jesse*, which recalls her role as the *radix sancta* of Romans 11: 16. This epithet is not only invoked in one of the three principal Marian antiphons lauding the Virgin's exalted position in Heaven – the twelfth-century *Ave Regina Caelorum*, sung at None on the Feast of the Assumption – but is also given iconographic expression in the Tree of Jesse motif. As the holy root of salvation, Mary enabled the Incarnation and thus the Redemption, allowing patristic exegetes, particularly St Jerome, to apply to her the messianic prophecy of Isaiah 11: 1, 'And there shall come forth a rod out of the root of Jesse, and a flower shall rise up out of his root.'³⁹ We may also note the assonant wordplay on *virgo* ('virgin') and *virga* ('rod'), which echoes the Marian homilies of Bernard of Clairvaux.⁴⁰

The second stanza initiates a flamboyant *ekphrasis* of Mary; she is *tota pulchra*, like the *Sponsa* in Song of Songs 4: 7, 'Thou art all fair, O my love', and likened to a lily. Although the lily was interpreted in a number of senses by exegetes, the *lilium inter spinas* ('lily among thorns') of Song of Songs 2: 1–2 was usually deployed as a figure of Mary's virginity, yet paradoxical fecundity, as it is here.⁴¹ The poet envisions Mary adorned 'withe saphures celestiall', which denote her beauty, wisdom and purity in the petrified litanies composed in her honour, but the sapphire was particularly associated with the Assumption and the Coronation.⁴² In the *Purgatorio*, Dante describes the sky in terms of the 'Dolce color d'oriental zaffiro', which is explicitly linked to the Virgin in the *Paradiso*, where she is described as 'il bel zaffiro del quale il ciel più chiaro s'inzaffira'.⁴³ This recalls Bruno of Segni's exegesis of Exodus 24: 9–10, where the sapphire signifies the crystalline alterity of the empyrean.⁴⁴ The pungent, erotic imagery of the Song

---

37 In addition to 'Ave mundi spes Maria', PL 217: 917, see Godfrey of Admont, *Homilia* 67, PL 174: 974.
38 Cf. also the Bridgettine text from Syon Abbey, J. H. Blunt, ed., *The Myroure of Oure Ladye*, EETS ES 19 (London, 1873), p. 190.
39 Cf. *Commentariorum in Isaiam prophetam*, 4, CCSL 73: 147–9.
40 Cf. *Super 'Missus est'*, *Homilia* 2, PL 183: 63–4.
41 See E. Mâle, *Religious Art in France: The Thirteenth Century*, ed. H. Bober, trans. M. Mathews (Princeton, 1984), p. 36.
42 In addition to A. Salzer, *Die Sinnbilder und Beiworte Mariens in der deutschen Literatur und lateinischen Hymnenpoesie des Mittelalters* (Linz, 1898), pp. 254–62, see Pseudo-Ildefonsus of Toledo, *Libellus de Corona virginis*, PL 96: 296–7; Conrad of Haimburg, *Annulus Beatae Virginis Mariae*, AH 3, p. 26; Ulrich Stöcklin von Rottach, *Super Ave Maria*, AH 6, p. 45; *De Beata Maria Virgine*, AH 46, p. 157.
43 *Purgatorio*, I, 13: *The Divine Comedy of Dante Alighieri II: Purgatorio*, trans. J. D. Sinclair, rev. edn (Oxford, 1961), pp. 18–19: 'sweet hue of the oriental sapphire', and *Paradiso*, XXIII, 97–102, *The Divine Comedy of Dante Alighieri III: Paradiso*, trans. J. D. Sinclair, rev. edn (Oxford, 1961), pp. 344–5: 'the fair sapphire by which the sky is so brightly ensapphired'.
44 Bruno of Segni, *Expositio in Exodum* 24, PL 164: 304: 'totus tranquillus, totus serenus, coelo similis, terrae dissimilis, quatenus totus clarus et purus' ('wholly calm, wholly

of Songs, as used in the Office of the Assumption, pervades the entire stanza. 'The odour of hir mouthe aromatike' suggests a conflation of Song of Songs 3: 6, where the *Sponsa* is described as 'a pillar of smoke of aromatical spices, of myrrh, and frankincense, and of all the powders of the perfumer', and 4: 11, 'Thy lips, my spouse, are as a dropping honeycomb, honey and milk are under thy tongue; and the smell of thy garments, as the smell of frankincense'. That Mary is 'clerer then the crystall' recalls the *ekphrasis* of *Sapientia* in Wisdom 7: 26, which emphasises her brilliance as in the Assumption liturgy, 'For she is the brightness of eternal light, and the unspotted mirror of God's majesty'. At the close of the stanza, the Virgin is described as the uncorrupted 'flowre of all formosite', stemming ultimately from the encomiastic tradition that sprang up in the wake of Mary's proclamation as *Theotokos* by the Council of Ephesus (431). Similarly, the Virgin is hailed as a 'flower of incorruption' in the *Akathistos*.[45]

In the third stanza, the poet initially invokes the sweet scent of the Virgin's name, 'A "Maria" by denominacioun', which is traditionally identified with the name of the *Sponsus* as *oleum effusum*: the fragrant oil poured out in Song of Songs 1: 2, as in the Office of the Assumption.[46] The idea that Mary's name is an *oleum effusum*, acting as 'medsine' to 'languentes', is found in a highly influential thirteenth-century *Mariale*, formerly ascribed to Albertus Magnus, now thought to be the work of Richard of Saint-Laurent.[47] We are then reminded yet again of the incandescent brilliance associated with the Triumph of the Virgin. Phoebus has been invoked as a personification of sunlight, whereby he penetrates glass as a symbol of the divine paradox of Mary's virginity at the Incarnation, since at least the seventh century.[48] In John of Garland's *Epithalamium beate Marie virginis* (c.1230), Mary is hailed as Phoebe, who succeeds Phoebus in the celestial court.[49] By contrast, Phoebus withdraws into 'tenebrosite' in this lyric, albeit with stately, loving courtesy, having willingly abdicated his dominion in the face of Mary's 'exaltacioun'. We are reminded not only of Mary eclipsing Phoebus in Lydgate's *Life of Our Lady*, but also of Wisdom 7: 29, which formed the Little Chapter at Lauds for the Feast of the Assumption, according to several continental Uses:

---

serene, like the sky, unlike the earth, inasmuch as wholly brilliant and pure'). Cf. C. A. Cioffi, '"Dolce color d'oriental zaffiro": A Gloss on "Purgatorio" 1.13', *Modern Philology* 82 (1985), 355–64.

45 Cf. *Hymnus Acathistus*, PG 92: 1342: 'Ave, flos incorruptibilitatis.' Cf. also the homily ascribed to Basil of Seleucia, *Oratio 39, In Sanctissimae Deiparae Annuntiationem*, PG 85: 443–4.

46 Cf. Peter of Celle, *Sermo 6*, PL 202: 654; Alan of Lille, *Compendiosa in Cantica Canticorum ad laudem Deiparae Virginis Mariae elucidatio*, PL 210: 54.

47 Cf. *De Laudibus Beatae Mariae Virginis*, in A. Borgnet, ed., *Alberti Magni Opera Omnia*, 38 vols (Paris, 1890–99), XXXVI, 13–16.

48 Cf. Eugenius of Toledo, *Epitaphium* 31, PL 87: 392.

49 Cf. A. Saiani, ed. and trans., *Epithalamium beate Marie virginis* (Florence, 1995), p. 630, lines 175–6.

'For she is more beautiful than the sun, and above all the order of the stars: being compared with the light, she is found before it.'[50]

Mary is explicitly identified as *Maria Regina* in the fourth stanza, exalted above the celestial hierarchy, as 'dubbit in doctrine'. Initially, it is only the choirs of angels, archangels and denominations, surmounted by Thrones, that minister to this 'regall arrayed in richesse' in the presence of the 'Prince perpetuall', who greets his Mother and Daughter specifically as his Bride. Mary is hailed as *columba mea*, echoing Song of Songs 2: 14, 'My dove in the clefts of the rock, in the hollow places of the wall, shew me thy face, let thy voice sound in my ears: for thy voice is sweet, and thy face comely'.[51] The *Sponsa* as *columba mea* has been associated with the Assumption since at least the *Transitus Mariae* B2 of Pseudo-Melito (c.550), known in medieval England.[52] However, the description of Mary as a 'cloystre of clandnesse' reminds us that the predominantly Western motif of *Maria Regina*, which emerged in the late fifth century, emphasises the Virgin's role as mother, as in the revered icon of motherly mercy, the *Madonna della Clemenza* (c.705–7, Rome: Santa Maria in Trastevere).[53] This maternal imagery is reflected in the four great Marian antiphons celebrating her exalted position in Heaven, the *Alma Redemptoris Mater*, the *Ave Regina Caelorum*, the *Regina Caeli* and the *Salve Regina*.

In keeping with the maternal theme, Mary's role as a *tabernaculum gloriae*, also cited in the *Transitus Mariae* B2, is emphasised in the fifth stanza where she is described as the 'true tabernacle of virginite'.[54] This image of the virginal Mother of God as a sealed chamber is a patent evocation of the Incarnation; she is the vessel through which the New Dispensation is mediated to man, hence she is declared 'Bothe mother and maiden inculpable'. The lyric reaches its climax when the precious pearl of womanhood kneels before her Son, who crowns her *Regina Caeli*. Although it was more usual to describe Mary as the *concha margaritifera*, or nacreous shell that enfolded Christ as the pearl of great price (Matthew 13: 46), she was hailed as the *petra margaritae inaestimabilis* in her own right as early as the fifth-century Marian sermon of Chrysippus of Jerusalem, and most notably,

---

50   J. A. Lauritis, R. A. Klinefelter and V. Gallagher, eds, *A Critical Edition of John Lydgate's Life of Our Lady* (Pittsburgh, 1961), p. 229, lines 335–6: 'she fayrer was to see / Than outhir phebus, platly or lucyne.'

51   Cf. Song of Songs 5: 2: 'columba mea, immaculata mea' ('my dove, my undefiled'); 6: 8: 'una est columba mea perfecta mea' ('my dove, my perfect one').

52   See M. Hailbach-Reinisch, *Ein neuer 'Transitus Mariae' des Pseudo-Melito* (Rome, 1962), p. 85; Ambrose Autpert, *De Assumptione sanctae Mariae*, 1, CCCM 27B, 1027; Radbertus of Corbie, *De Assumptione sanctae Mariae virginis*, 9, 57, CCCM 56C, 134.

53   In addition to C. Bertelli, *La Madonna di Santa Maria in Trastevere* (Rome, 1961), see M. Lawrence, '*Maria Regina*', *Art Bulletin* 7 (1925), 150–61; U. Nilgen, '*Maria Regina*: Ein politischer Kultbildtypus?', *Römisches Jarbuch für Kunstgeschichte* 19 (1981), 1–33; M. Stroll, '*Maria Regina*: Papal Symbol', *Queens and Queenship in Medieval Europe*, ed. A. J. Duggan (Woodbridge, 1997), pp. 173–203.

54   Cf. *Hymnus Acathistus*, PG 92: 1346: 'Ave, tabernaculum Dei et Verbi' ('Hail, tabernacle of God and Word'); Joseph the Hymnographer, *Mariale*, 6, 5, PG 105: 1022: 'gaude, amplissimum Verbi tabernaculum' ('Rejoice, most abundant tabernacle of the Word').

in the *Transitus Mariae* B1 of Pseudo-Melito.⁵⁵ By the later Middle Ages, Mary was often lauded as the *margarita pretiosa* or *margarita caeli* by Latin Christian writers.⁵⁶ Although Mary's glorification in heaven requires her to transcend her 'consanguinite', the poet's use of the title 'Pellicane of perpetuete' redirects our thoughts to her earthly role in the plan of salvation; the vulning pelican is an allegory of the atoning Christ found frequently in the Middle English lyric.⁵⁷

In the sixth stanza we comprehend the spiritual and aesthetic effect the 'fulgent face' of *Maria Regina* has on the narrator. Once again the *claritas* of this 'spectable splendure' is stressed, which is in no way vitiated by the blinding *splendor* of this golden, 'luciant, corruscall resplendent', ornamented with rhetoric. We are reminded of yet another verse used in the Assumption liturgy, Song of Songs 6: 10, which is particularly associated with the iconography of the Coronation, 'Who is she that cometh forth as the morning rising, fair as the moon, bright as the sun, terrible as an army set in array?'⁵⁸ Mary's radiance outshines the rutilance of 'seraphinnes in their solemnite', now lauding their enthroned queen 'subsequent' to her accession as celestial protocol dictates, yet surpassing in fiery ardour the angelic choirs that heralded her elevation.

In the Dionysian celestial hierarchy, the Seraphim attend the divine throne directly, heading the Nine Orders; they overflow with the burning love of the Creator, which radiates down through the other Orders to the most wretched, earthly penitent. Thus it is fitting that the seventh and final stanza is a direct invocation to Mary, specifically in her maternal roles as 'Deifere', 'Mother of mercy', and 'Trone of the Trinite', to 'treite' on behalf of mankind as *Mediatrix* so that all the faithful might 'abide in blisse withe thee', sharing in the divine ministry ignited by the Seraphim, 'to love our God most glorious'. In medieval England, the image of Mary as *thronus trinitatis* is found in the Latin hymns of Adam of Dryburgh and Walter of Wimborne, and most memorably thereafter in the vernacular in the N-Town Play.⁵⁹ In the *Melos amoris*, Richard Rolle associates the motif with Mary as *Trinitatis triclinium*, or three-seater couch of

---

55 Cf. Chrysippus of Jerusalem, *Oratio in Sanctam Mariam Deiparam*, PO 19: 218–19; C. von Tischendorff, ed., *Apocalypses apocryphae* (Leipzig, 1866), p. 128: 'Veni preciosissima margarita, intra receptaculum vitae aeternae' ('Come, you most precious pearl, enter into the sanctuary of eternal life').
56 Cf. Salzer, *Die Sinnbilder*, pp. 243–8.
57 In addition to E. Mâle, *Religious Art in France: The Twelfth Century*, ed. H. Bober, trans. M. Mathews (Princeton, 1978), see V. E. Graham, 'The Pelican as Image and Symbol', *Revue de Littérature Comparée* 36 (1962), 233–43; C. Gerhardt, *Die Metamorphosen des Pelikans: Exempel und Auslegung in der mittelalterlichen Literatur* (Frankfurt am Main, 1979).
58 Cf. E. A. Matter, *The Voice of my Beloved: The Song of Songs in Western Medieval Christianity* (Philadelphia, 1990), p. 153.
59 Cf. Adam of Dryburgh, *Sermo 12, Sermones Fratris Adae, Ordinis Praemonstratensis*, ed. W. de Gray Birch (Edinburgh, 1901), p. 95; 'Ave Virgo Mater Christi', 19, in A. G. Rigg, ed., *The Poems of Walter of Wimborne* (Toronto, 1978), p. 150. Cf. also S. Spector, ed., *The N-Town Play: Cotton Vespasian D. 8*, 2 vols, EETS SS 11–12 (Oxford, 1991), I, 123, line 333: 'þou trone of þe Trinyté'; I, 135, line 138: 'þat are trone and tabernakyl of þe hyȝ Trinyté'.

the triune Godhead, imbued with the *thalamus* imagery of the Song of Songs.[60] Although this motif has been ascribed to Ildefonsus of Toledo, it would appear to have actually emerged in the twelfth century in a Victorine context.[61] It is specifically associated with the Coronation by such contemporary authors as Adam of St Victor, as it is in this lyric.[62]

Given its accomplished use of rhetorical decorum, mirroring the solemn progress of the Triumph of Mary and her Coronation as *Virgo Assumpta* with due propriety, as skilful in its depiction of these scenes as a consummate illuminator or *aurifaber*, this lyric has attracted a surprising amount of adverse criticism. It has been described by R. T. Davies as 'ridiculous in its self-conscious affectation', and by Douglas Gray as 'pedantic to the point of absurdity'.[63] According to Rosemary Woolf, the cumulative effect 'is that of an ugly, indiscriminate verbosity' that 'excludes the precision' to which the poet aspires.[64] However, as demonstrated above, there is nothing indiscriminate about the poet's *peritiae ostentatio*. Such a demonstration of expertise is eminently decorous in its application of amplification and ornamentation to the subject matter, and consistent in its doctrinal progression towards the final, glorious mystery of Mary's Queenship. But like the *joyaux* glinting in the *Schatzkammern* of Europe at the time of its making, the lyric's use of aureate diction stands testament to the timely, if not the timeless, nature of aesthetic sensibilities. As Erwin Panofsky remarked, the art (and at least some of the literature) of the later Middle Ages is a mixture of 'precocious naturalism' and 'extreme stylization'; of 'pseudoreality' and 'artificial glitter'.[65] Certainly, those who favoured the International Gothic style did not see the world, never mind the celestial spheres, as deceived by ornament, or the rhetorical technique of *ornatus*. To gild and enamel the *lilium inter spinas* with aureate diction is to transcend the transient beauty of the Virgin's earthly existence through the supernatural artifice of eternity, where she prevails in that realm, which is 'al of brende golde bry3t'.[66]

---

60 Cf. Richard Rolle, *Le Chant d'Amour: Melos Amoris I*, ed. F. Vandenbrouke, SC 168 (Paris, 1971), p. 226.

61 Cf. *Libellus de Corona Virginis*, 8 and 22, PL 96: 296, 314.

62 In addition to Adam of St Victor, 'Salve, Mater Salvationis', 11, *Quatorze proses du XIIe siècle à la louange de Marie*, ed. and trans. B. Jollès (Turnhout, 1994), p. 216, see Pseudo-Hugh of St Victor, *De bestiis et aliis rebus*, 4, 2, PL 177: 139. Cf. the fifteenth-century hymns in G. G. Meersseman, *Der Hymnos Akathistos im Abendland*, 2 vols (Freiburg, 1958-60), I, 201, 211; and P. Kern, *Trinität, Maria, Inkarnation: Studien zur Thematik der deutschen. Dichtung des späteren Mittelalters* (Berlin, 1972), p. 394. Cf. also D. Scaramuzzi, '"Totius Trinitatis Nobile Triclinium". Maria e la Trinità', *Rivista di Scienze Religiose* 1 (1987), 257-91.

63 R. T. Davies, ed., *Medieval English Lyrics: A Critical Anthology* (London, 1964), p. 26; Gray, *Themes*, p. 65.

64 Woolf, p. 301. For more positive accounts, see C. Whitehead, 'Middle English Religious Lyrics', Duncan, *Companion*, pp. 96-120 (117-19).

65 *Early Netherlandish Painting: Its Origins and Character*, 2 vols (Cambridge, MA, 1953), I, 69.

66 Gordon, ed., *Pearl*, p. 36, line 989.

9

Textual Lyricism in Lydgate's *Fifteen Joys and Sorrows of Mary*

Mary Wellesley

Extracts from *Fifteen Joys and Sorrows of Mary*[1]
Lines 1–35

	Atween mydnyht and the fressh morwe gray	
	Nat yore ago, in herte ful pensiff,	*long*
	Of thoughtful sihes my peyne to put away,	
	Caused by the trouble of this vnstabil liff,	
5	Vnclosyd a book, that was contemplatiff;	*opened; contained contemplative material*
	Of fortune turnyng the book, I fond	*by chance*
	A meditacioun which first cam to myn hond,	
	Tofor which was sett out in picture	
	Of Marie an ymage ful notable,	
10	Lyke a pyte depeynt was the figure	*pietà*
	With weepyng eyen, and cheer most lamentable:	
	Thouh the proporcioun by crafft was agreable,	*artistic skill*
	Hir look doun cast with teerys al bereyned, –	*entirely wet with tears*
	Of hertly sorwe so soore she was constreyned.	
15	Vpon the said meditacioun,	
	Of aventure, so as I took heed,	*chance*
	By diligent and cleer inspeccioun,	
	I sauh Rubrisshis, departyd blak and Reed,	*rubrics; divided*
	Of ech Chapitle a paraf in the heed,	*chapter, paragraph; paraph*
20	Remembryd first Fifteene of her gladynessys,	
	And next in ordre were set hyr hevynessys.	*sorrows*

For another essay focused on a Marian lyric, see chapter 8; for another essay discussing the authorial 'I' voice, see chapter 14.

[1] NIMEV 447; DIMEV 843. Reproduced by permission of the Council of the Early English Text Society, from *The Minor Poems of John Lydgate*, ed. H. N. MacCracken, 2 vols, EETS ES 107, OS 192 (London, 1911, 1934), I, pp. 260–79 (pp. 268–79), with the addition of glosses. All subsequent references are to this edition, cited in the text by line number. The poem in this edition is edited from BL, Harley MS 2255, fols 88r–93r.

Textual Lyricism in Lydgate's *Fifteen Joys and Sorrows of Mary*

Off ech of them the noumbre was Fifteene,
Bothe of hir Ioyes and her adversitees,
Ech after othir, and to that hevenlie queene
25 I sauh Oon kneele deuoutly on his knees;   *a certain person*
A Pater-noster and ten tyme Auees   *Lord's Prayer; Hail Marys*
In ordre he sayde [at thende] of ech ballade   *the end*
Cessyd nat, tyl he an eende made.

Folwyng the Ordre, as the picture stood,
30 By and by in that hooly place,
To beholde it did myn herte good;
Of affeccioun turnyd nat my face,
But of entent, leiseer cauht and space,   *intention; having found leisure*

Took a penne, and wroot in my maneere
The said balladys, as they stondyn heere.

Explicit prologus.

***

Lines 148–82
Ioyes fifteen remembrid heer to-forn   *before*
As the charg[e] was vpon me leyd,
150 In contemplacioun there be no tyme lorn,   *lost*
The Pater-nostres and the Aues dewly seyd,   *duly*
By interupcioun makyng noon abreyd,   *without a jarring interruption*
Tyl of our lady be sayd the ful Sawteer,   *decades of the rosary*
As heer-to-forn is shewyd the maneer.

155 As ye haue herd accomplisshid the gladnessis   *joys*
By a meditacioun toold in especial,   *in particular*
Folwyng in ordre were set his hevynessys
And remembryd his sorwys pryncipal,
Ful lamentable and somme ful mortal,   *deadly*
160 Of ech conservyd the observaunce,[2]
As heer-to-forn is put in remembraunce.

Off Paternostres and aues seid betweene
The same noumbre with good devocioun,
The hevenessys rehersyd ful ffifteene
165 At eende of everich, as maad is mencioun,   *each one*
By a maneer pitous compassioun   *adopting an attitude of*

---

[2] 'The custom of commemorating each is preserved'. The EETS edition of this poem reads 'acts' for 'ech' as a result of editorial intervention (see fn. 2 for full bibliographical details). London, British Library, Harley MS 2255, fol. 91r reads 'ech'; Cambridge, Trinity College, MS R. 3. 21, fol. 159r and fol. 240r, both have 'eche' and London, British Library, Cotton MS Appendix XXVII, fol. 2 also has 'eche'. I prefer this reading.

With our lady, hir sorwys to complayne,
Lik as the picture in ordre did ordeyne.   *In the same way; dictate*

Which to reherse, outhir to remembre,   *repeat; or*
170 Lyk as I fond I caste me to endite,   *set out to write down*
Of dreedful herte tremblyng in euery membre,   *fearful*
My penne quakyng whan I gan to write,
For to beholde the terys reed and white
In sondry placys from hir eyness reyne,   *eyes*
175 Which to considre it was to me gret peyne.

God graunt it be to hir no displesaunce,
That I was bold to writen, seyn, or reede
Hir heuynessis, list the remembraunce   *sorrows; lest*
Of sorwys passyd, which she felte in deede,
180 In any wise shuld trouble hir womanheede,
But of compassioun they may myn herte perce,   *pierce*
To that entent I do hem heere reherce.   *With that intention*

                ***

Lines 295–315
Lenvoye.

295 To alle that caste hem of devocioun   *apply themselves*
To been dilligent, by daily attendaunce,
To serve Mary, pryncesse of moost renoun,
And to his hihnesse for to do plesaunce,   *highness*
Lat hem empreente in her remembraunce   *imprint; their memory*
300 The ordre heer set, ffirst of hir gladnessys,   *order set out here*
And folwyng afftir hir gret heuynessys.

Which remembryd, as toold is the maneer,
In hir worship by humble affeccioun,
Of the heuenly pryncesse, to seyn an hool sawteer,   *entire rosary*
305 Lyk as to-forn is maad heer mencioun,
Therwith conceyvyng this compilacioun,
Thouh that it halte in meetre and elloquence,   *is lame, deficient*
It is heer write hir for to do reverence.

Goo litil tretys! and meekly me excuse,
310 To alle tho that shal the seen or reede;
Giff any man thy rudenesse list accuse   *wishes to*
Make no diffence, but with lowly heede   *defence*
Pray hym refourme, wher as he seeth neede;   *amend; whereever*
To that entent I do the forth directe   *with that intention*
315 Wher thu faylest, that men shal the correcte.   *fall short*

Textual Lyricism in Lydgate's *Fifteen Joys and Sorrows of Mary*

The Fifteen Joys and Sorrows of Mary by the Benedictine monk and poet John Lydgate (b. c.1370, d. c.1450) is a complex work. It is a poem that delights in its own textuality. The text is not simply a devotional catalogue of the Virgin's joys and sorrows, but also a poem about the act of reading itself, and one that collapses the boundaries between author and narrator, and narrator and reader. The text is highly self-referential and prescribes a specific kind of devotional use; in it verse and prayer are in a symbiotic relationship.[3] It is clearly intended to be used in a reader's personal, bookish devotions, and these expectations have a bearing on its modes of reception. The poem, like Lydgate's lyrics in general, has received limited critical attention.[4] It appears in six manuscripts (in one it appears twice),[5] and both this manuscript context and the poem's form have implications for our understanding of the way lyrics were transmitted, received and used in the fifteenth century.

* * *

Definitions of 'lyric' abound and rarely taxonomise the form adequately.[6] In fact the most appropriate definition may be a non-definition. Christiania Whitehead notes that religious lyrics in Middle English in themselves are 'a singularly heterogeneous brood'.[7] In Rosemary Woolf's seminal work on the genre, she offers a history of the term's use. She notes that 'lyric' was first used by Elizabethan critics: George Puttenham in *The Art of English Poesie* defines the lyric poet as one who writes 'songs or ballads of pleasure, to be song with the voice, and to the harpe'.[8] Today scholars recognise that an association between lyric and musicality is probably misplaced, yet the association, however vague, lingers.

---

[3] For a thought-provoking work that suggests that Middle English literature is an effect of the liturgy, see B. Holsinger, 'Liturgy', *Middle English*, ed. P. Strohm (Oxford, 2007), pp. 295–314.

[4] In 1984, A. S. G. Edwards noted that Lydgate's shorter religious poems have been understudied: 'Lydgate Scholarship: Progress and Prospects', *Fifteenth-Century Studies: Recent Essays*, ed. R. F. Yeager (Hamden, 1984), pp. 29–47. The situation has not changed hugely since then. Scholarly works that respond to this are cited, where relevant, below. There are several useful accounts of Lydgate's critical fortunes in general, which account for this and other lacunae in our knowledge of his work. See N. Mortimer, *John Lydgate's Fall of Princes: Narrative Tragedy in its Literary and Political Contexts* (Oxford, 2005), pp. 1–26; 'Introduction', *John Lydgate: Poetry, Culture and Lancastrian England*, ed. L. Scanlon and J. Simpson (Notre Dame, 2006), pp. 1–11.

[5] Oxford, Bodleian Library, MS Bodley 686, fols 204–08v; Cambridge, Jesus College, MS 56, fols 53–8; Trinity College, R. 3. 21, fols 157–61v, fols 238–42 Fitzwilliam Museum, Ms McLean 182, fol. 49; BL Cotton Appendix XXVII, fols 1–2v (defective at the start and finish, beginning at line 50 and ending at line 161); Harley 2255, fols 88–93v.

[6] R. Greentree, *Annotated Bibliographies of Old and Middle English Literature, VII: The Middle English Lyric and Short Poem* (Cambridge, 2001), pp. 5–37.

[7] C. Whitehead, 'Middle English Religious Lyrics', Duncan, *Companion*, pp. 96–119 (p. 96).

[8] Woolf, p. 1.

Lydgate's *Fifteen Joys and Sorrows* resists this association.[9] It is a text that relishes the devotional and imaginative possibilities offered by the act of reading words on a page. The poem is also unusual in other ways. Many Middle English lyrics survive in only one manuscript witness; as a genre they appear to be particularly ephemeral. Rosemary Greentree observes that 'the survival of many lyrics seems to owe much to chance'.[10] This poem, however, survives in seven versions (in six witnesses). Its presentation on the manuscript page is often carefully designed and visually appealing, its extra-textual apparatus apparently intended to heighten a specific reading experience. In this way, the poem feels neither ephemeral nor musical.

The scenario of the *Fifteen Joys and Sorrows* is, at times, confusing. The poem has a layered structure and, in these layers, it is sometimes unclear what is actually being described in the frame narrative, and where that frame narrative recedes and the central part of the poem begins. The poem is a catalogue of the Fifteen Joys and the Fifteen Sorrows of the Virgin, each bookended by returns to a frame narrative. The text begins with a description of a narrator reading what appears to be a Book of Hours (also known as a primer) containing the text of the *Fifteen Joys and Sorrows* (lines 5–21).[11] The poem explains how the Joys and Sorrows should be used devotionally, describing how after each joy and each sorrow 'A Pater-noster (*Lord's Prayer*) and ten tyme Auees (*Hail Marys*)' (line 26) should be said. What follows is a versification of the joys, with one stanza per joy (lines 36–147). This concludes with a return to the frame narrative, where the narrator's tone changes and he appears to address his readers more directly, instructing them that, '[i]n contemplacioun there be no tyme lorn / The Pater-nostres and the Aues dewly (*duly*) seyd ... Tyl of our lady be sayd the ful Sawter' (lines 150–1, 153).[12] The word 'sawter' here is probably used to mean much the same as 'the set of prayers recited upon a rosary, so called because the fifteen decades of Aves correspond to the hundred and fifty psalms of the psalter'.[13] After this, the poem catalogues the fifteen sorrows, again with one stanza allotted to each sorrow (lines 183–280), before concluding with a rhetorical envoy (lines 295–315).

---

9 I use the shortened form of *Fifteen Joys and Sorrows* to distinguish the text from Lydgate's *Fifteen Joys of Our Lady* (NIMEV 533; DIMEV 867), for which see Lydgate, *Minor Poems*, ed. MacCracken, I, pp. 260–7.
10 Greentree, *Middle English Lyric*, p. 14.
11 Eamon Duffy provides a helpful explanation of terminology: 'Books of Hours, [were] often known by their Latin name, "Horae" or the familiar English name "Primer"', *Marking the Hours: English People and Their Prayers 1240–1570* (New Haven, 2006), p. 3.
12 'lorn' here means 'lost', as the past participle of lēsen (v.)(4). MED.
13 MED.

From Artefact to Imagination

The poem opens with a prologue by the narrator that describes how, late at night 'atween mydnyght and the fresh morwe grey' (line 1), he '[u]nclosyd a book' (line 5). By 'fortune', the narrator comes across a 'meditacioun' (lines 6–7). At the beginning of this meditation there is an image of the Virgin: 'of Marie an ymage ful notable' (line 9). The appearance of this book is described. It has 'rubrisshis (*rubrics*), departyd (*divided*) blak and Reed' and 'a paraf (*paraph*)' at the start of each chapter (lines 18–19). It is striking that here the narrator is describing a sequence of extra-textual symbols that have non-lexical meaning. In some senses, the poem's opening premise bears a resemblance to the opening of a poem like Chaucer's *The Parliament of Fowls*. There the narrator describes how he 'happede me for to beholde / Upon a bok ... ', which 'Entitled was al ther ... Drem of Scipioun'.[14] As in the *Fifteen Joys and Sorrows*, night creeps up on the narrator of the *Parliament*, 'The day gan faylen, and the derke nyght, / That reveth bestes from her besynesse / Berafte me my bok for lak of lyght'.[15] After the appearance of night, the narrator of the *Parliament* falls asleep and dreams of the famous Valentine's Day convocation that follows. Yet the *Fifteen Joys and Sorrows* differs from the *Parliament* in that the 'Drem of Scipioun' is a disembodied work, a text whose content provides the inspiration for the narrator's dream. In the *Fifteen Joys and Sorrows*, the springboard into the action of the poem is both the text (accompanied by an image) and the physical book that contains it. The appearance of the manuscript page is described with specific details. The lyric is, at once, grounded in an inherently readerly and textual scenario. Crucially, the refashioning of the opening motif of the *Parliament* is one of several ways in which Lydgate reworks a familiar Chaucerian conceit for his own ends.[16] We shall see below how he also does this in his choice of form and in the poem's rhetorical envoy.

In some senses the opening premise of the *Fifteen Joys and Sorrows* also bears a resemblance to Lydgate's *Dolerous Pyte of Crystes Passioun*.[17] The *Dolerous Pyte* is designed to be used, in conjunction with an image of Christ, as a kind of instructional-devotional poem.[18] It instructs, 'Erly on morwe, and toward nyghte also / First and last, looke on this ffygure'.[19] The use of the demonstrative 'this'

---

14 Geoffrey Chaucer, *The Parliament of Fowls*, Benson, pp. 385–94, lines 18–19, 30–31.
15 Chaucer, *Parliament*, Benson, lines 85–7.
16 Elsewhere I have argued that we see Lydgate refashioning a Chaucerian conceit to strategic ends in another of his lyrics, the *Seying of the Nightingale* (NIMEV 1498; DIMEV 2525): M. Wellesley, 'Static "Menyng" and Transitory "Melodye" in Lydgate's *Seying of the Nightingale*', *Stasis in the Medieval West?: Questioning Change and Continuity*, ed. M. Bintley, M. Locker and V. Symons (New York, 2017), pp. 231–51.
17 NIMEV 702; DIMEV 1165, where it is titled *A tretys of Crystys Passyoun*. Lydgate, *Minor Poems*, ed. MacCracken, I, pp. 250–2.
18 On this poem and two other lyrics by Lydgate that use images for devotional purposes, see C. Cornell, '"Purtreture" and "Holsom Stories": John Lydgate's Accommodation of Image and Text in Three Religious Lyrics', *Florilegium* 10 (1988–91), 167–78.
19 Lydgate, *Minor Poems*, ed. MacCracken, I, p. 250, lines 1–2.

suggests that the poem was intended to accompany an image of the Passion. The poem informs readers that they must '[s]et this lyknesse in your remembraunce, / Enprenteth it in your Inward sight'.[20] Yet where it differs from the *Fifteen Joys and Sorrows* is that the *Dolerous Pyte* appears intended as a companion piece to an image, while in the *Fifteen Joys and Sorrows* the manuscript page itself is the facilitator for the central part of the poem. In some ways, the manuscript page is invoked in much the same way as the image of the Passion – its visual details acting as a devotional stimulus. Mary Carruthers notes that in the earlier medieval period 'letters used for writing were considered to be visual, as what we call "images" today; and that as a result the page as a whole, the complete parchment with its lettering and all its decoration, was considered a cognitively valuable "picture".[21] In the *Fifteen Joys and Sorrows*, the manuscript page is one such 'picture'.

In both lyrics – *Dolerous Pyte of Crystes Passioun* and *Fifteen Joys and Sorrows* – a particular object is used as a device that propels the reader into the imaginative realm of each poem's central section. Christiania Whitehead notes that Lydgate uses the 'movement from devotional artefact to the visualising imagination in several lyrics, suggesting that he regarded it [this movement] as a valuable route to meditation'.[22] The movement from object to imagination in the *Fifteen Joys and Sorrows* is not simply a linear route, however, but a two-way conduit. In the poem, Lydgate returns to the description of the manuscript page and its 'meditacioun' several times. At the end of the exposition of the joys of the Virgin, the narrator describes how the 'gladnessis' have appeared in the 'meditacioun' (lines 155–6) and how the 'picture in ordre did ordeyne (*dictate*)' (line 168) the recitation of the *Ave Maria* and the *Pater Noster*. Later, the narrator describes the image, detailing 'the terys reed and white', which in 'sondry places from hir eyness (*eyes*) reyne' (lines 173–4).

Yet what Whitehead calls 'the transition from artefact to vision' is at times confusing.[23] In the fourth stanza, the narrator explains how 'I sauh Oone kneele deuoutly on his knees; / A Pater-noster (*Lord's Prayer*) and ten tyme Auees (*Hail Marys*) / In ordre he sayde' (lines 25–6). At this point the scene described in the poem shifts. The narrator is no longer simply describing a past experience of reading the 'meditacioun' himself, but is now imagining the way in which the 'meditacioun' could be used devotionally. It is unclear who this 'Oone' is – a person also in the 'hooly place' (line 30) in which he (the narrator) finds himself? Or a figment of his imagination? Or perhaps even the reader of the poem?

---

20   *Ibid.*, I, p. 250, lines 9–10.
21   M. Carruthers, *The Craft of Thought: Meditation, Rhetoric and the Making of Images 400–1200* (Cambridge, 1998), p. 122.
22   Whitehead, 'Middle English Religious Lyrics', p. 110.
23   *Ibid.*, p. 110.

The Aural and the Visual

The *Fifteen Joys and Sorrows* is, in some senses, a homage to the activity of reading. Throughout the poem, Lydgate plays on the particular combination of the aural and the visual that makes the reading experience. We see this in various ways. In the stanza that describes the second of the Virgin's joys – the Annunciation – Lydgate describes how 'With this word Eva turnyd to Aue' (line 55). The Eva/Ave dichotomy is not an uncommon one, but here it works especially well as a visual and aural pun in a written text.[24] The palindromic inversion of the letters is best understood when seen on the page, but the rhythmic similarity between the two words (both disyllabic, with a stress on the first syllable) means that this is especially effective when read because, in reading the words, a reader of the poem experiences the pun both visually and aurally.

There are other instances in which Lydgate calls attention to the combination of visual and auditory experience. At the end of the catalogue of the joys, in a return to the frame narrative, the narrator describes how the joys have been 'heer-to-forn ... shewyd the maneer. / As ye haue herd accomplisshid the gladnessis' (lines 154–5). Albeit divided by a stanza break, here Lydgate uses the language of seeing ('shewyd') and hearing ('herd') side by side, encapsulating the particular sensation of reading. This conjunction also, perhaps, suggests that the poem was intended to be read both silently and aloud. The fact that this poem prescribes the recitation of the *Pater Noster* and the *Ave Maria* means that it repeatedly calls on the reader to respond both visually and performatively – reading the words of the poem (possibly aloud or possibly silently) and then saying the prayers aloud.

The Poem's Devotional Function

If the *Fifteen Joys and Sorrows* is in some ways a celebration of the readerly experience, it is also a homage to a bookish form of devotion. The poem needs to be placed against the backdrop of its historical circumstance. The fifteenth century was a period of expanding lay literacy.[25] This was an era in which ordinary layfolk had increasingly widespread access to books of devotion, and the poem is a product of this bookish culture. It is important to note that the Fifteen Joys of the Virgin and their French form, *Les Quinze Joies de la Vierge*, were particularly associated with Books of Hours in the period.[26] Vernacular prayers, on subjects such as the Fifteen Joys, were incorporated into prayer-books for a specific purpose. Eamon Duffy notes that the period 'saw a proliferation of prayers and meditations in English, paraphrasing or elaborating devotional themes

---

24   On the dichotomy generally, see J. Pelikan, *Mary Through the Centuries: Her Place in the History of Culture* (New Haven and London, 1996), pp. 39–54. For its presentation in Middle English lyrics, see A. Breeze, 'Two Bardic Themes: The Virgin and Child, and Ave-Eva', *Medium Aevum* 63 (1994), 17–33 (24–5).

25   A. Barratt, 'The Prymer and its Influence on Fifteenth-Century English Passion Lyrics', *Medium Aevum* 44 (1975), 264–79.

26   P. Rézeau, *Les prières aux saints en français à la fin du moyen age: introduction, les prières à plusiers saints* (Geneva, 1982), p. 14.

characteristic of the prayers of the primer'. These vernacular prayers were one 'of the ways in which "lewed" men and women could gain a working understanding of their Latin primers'.[27] Duffy also notes that verse translations of parts of the primer began to become more common and indeed were sometimes incorporated into the primers themselves. Books of Hours thus informed new kinds of literary creativity. Alexandra Barratt also comments upon the way in which the primer influenced certain kinds of Middle English lyric verse, especially Passion lyrics.[28] In turn, some of these lyrics exercised an influence upon Books of Hours: migrating into the books themselves and becoming a part of them.

Duffy's observation about the way vernacular prayers were incorporated into prayer-books holds true for some of the manuscripts containing Lydgate's lyrics. In some cases, the manuscripts of his lyrics suggest that the membrane between literary texts and prayer texts was permeable. One such manuscript deserves examination. London, British Library, Egerton MS 3883 is a fifteenth-century Book of Hours made in the southern Netherlands. In the second half of the fifteenth century the manuscript was modified, apparently after its arrival in England. It was adapted for use by a female patron and a series of devotional texts in Middle English were added (fols 36v, 59r–61r, 123r–177v). Amongst the vernacular texts added in this period is a copy of a lyric by Lydgate, the *Fifteen Joys of Our Lady*,[29] which is similar to the *Fifteen Joys and Sorrows*.[30] The appearance of the lyric in this Book of Hours suggests that not only did Lydgate intend for these kinds of poems to be read as a part of daily devotion, but that indeed they sometimes were.

The *Fifteen Joys of Our Lady* appears on fols 159r to 167r. It follows a Latin prayer to St John the Baptist and St Katherine on fol. 158v. The beginning of the vernacular poem on the facing page is almost imperceptible at first glance. The poem is written out as prose. Both texts are written in a *formata* hand, with gold initials on a mauve ground. Whoever made this book thought it unnecessary to make any kind of firm demarcation to alert the reader to the separate status of the Latin prose prayer and the vernacular verse text. The membrane between literary text and prayer is permeable here; both texts appear to have been used for an almost identical devotional purpose.

If the *Fifteen Joys and Sorrows* is a homage to bookish devotion, it also intersects with other kinds of devotional practice. The Fifteen Joys of the Virgin were especially associated with the rosary.[31] Lydgate's poem is, in some ways, a kind of textual rosary. Each stanza describes a different episode in the life of the

---

27 E. Duffy, *The Stripping of the Altars: Traditional Religion in England, c.1400–1500* (New Haven and London, 1992, repr. 2005), p. 223.
28 Barratt, 'The Prymer and its Influence', p. 264.
29 NIMEV 533.4; DIMEV 867.4 (*olim* Canterbury, Cathedral Library Law Society, Mendham Collection, MS 6).
30 A full description of Egerton 3883 can be found in the BL online manuscript catalogue.
31 J. M. Hand, *Women, Manuscripts and Identity in Northern Europe, 1350–1550* (Farnham, 2013), p. 134.

Virgin and each one is a focus of meditation, to be followed by ten *Ave Marias* and *Pater Nosters* (exactly as prescribed in the telling of the rosary). The text's form is, therefore, crucially important. The poem is written in rhyme royal – a form based on the Italian *ottava rima*, which was used by Chaucer for *Troilus and Criseyde* and for his hagiographies, the *Prioress's Tale* and the *Second Nun's Tale*. Lydgate's choice of form has two functions: first, in using a form associated with Chaucer, Lydgate signals his debt to Chaucer, but also his difference from him (we shall see the significance of this most clearly in the poem's rhetorical envoy, discussed below.) Second, the rhyme royal form has a specific purpose in enhancing prayer and contemplation.

Rhyme royal – a seven-line form – resembles a kind of mini-sonnet, or half-sonnet. As Peter Hyland notes, '[r]hyme royal echoes the structure of the sonnet': it requires three B rhymes, but contains a kind of *volta* or turn at the centre, in the fifth line, when the initial rhyme pattern of ABAB changes, and rather than the expected A rhyme, what follows forms a couplet of BB before a final couplet of CC.[32] The stanza, therefore, has a flow and pace that carries it over the first four lines, through the turn in the fifth, to the final couplet, with its rhyme change to CC. This final couplet has the effect of bringing the stanza to a more definite conclusion. As a consequence, the form achieves pace over long narratives (Lydgate uses it over some six thousand lines in the *Life of Our Lady*; Shakespeare deploys it in the *Rape of Lucrece*), but each stanza remains a solid entity in itself.[33] This is vital to the *Fifteen Joys and Sorrows*, where each joy and each sorrow are represented by a single stanza. The form resembles a verse rosary, in which each stanza stands as an individual unit to be ruminated upon – like a bead on a rosary – but is also linked to a larger whole. Theresa Krier argues that rhyme royal lends itself to the 'delineation of elusive temporal experiences: reverie, dream vision, thresholds between waking and sleeping, dawns and dusks'.[34] We might extend this and say that the form lends itself to prayer and reflection. So, although it is inherently grounded in bookish devotion, the *Fifteen Joys and Sorrows* – a sort of verse rosary – also links into a whole series of other kinds of devotional activity.

***

Thus far we have seen how the *Fifteen Joys and Sorrows* pays homage to the activity of reading by taking the manuscript page as a devotional springboard and calling attention to the peculiar combination of aural and visual that constitutes the reading experience. Given the repeated description of the manuscript

---

32 P. Hyland, *An Introduction to Shakespeare's Poems* (London, 2002), p. 189.
33 *A Critical Edition of John Lydgate's Life of Our Lady*, ed. J. A. Lauritis, R. A. Klinefelter and V. F. Gallagher, Duquesne Studies, Philological Series 2 (Pittsburgh, 1961); *Shakespeare's Poems: Venus and Adonis, the Rape of Lucrece and the Shorter Poems*, ed. K. Duncan-Jones and H. R. Woudhuysen (London, 2007).
34 T. Krier, 'Rhyme Royal', *Princeton Encyclopedia of Poetry and Poetics*, ed. R. Greene et al., 4th edn (Princeton, 2012), pp. 1193–4 (p. 1194).

containing the 'meditacioun', the reader's experience of the poem's text parallels the narrator's experience of the text in front of him. We have also seen how, in its form and content, the poem intersects with other forms of devotional activity, such that the poem becomes a *paean* to the imaginative and devotional possibilities that are offered by reading. In these ways, the poem is acutely self-referential – highlighting the very forms in which it reaches its readers. Yet, for all of its attention to the reading experience, the poem is also a celebration of the writerly act. Over forty-five stanzas, the narrator's voice frequently surfaces, as in: 'I fond / A meditacioun which first cam to myn hond' (lines 6–7), 'I sauh Rubrisshis (*rubrics*), departyd (*divided*) blak and Reed' (line 18), 'it did myn herte good' (line 31), 'Lyk as I fond I caste me to endite (*I set out to write down*)' (line 170), and 'To that entent (*with that intention*) I do the forth directe' (line 314). Crucially, however, this narrator's voice does not simply communicate the feelings of a disembodied, lyric 'I', but is used to present a partially delineated authorial persona. In this respect, Lydgate's poem contains a feature more commonly associated with verse of a later period. Rosemary Woolf writes that:

> The abnegation of individuality is one of the most important differences between the medieval and the seventeenth-century religious lyric. The writers of both draw upon the contemporary methods of meditation ... But, whereas the seventeenth-century poets show the poet meditating, the medieval writers provide versified meditations which others may use: in one the meditator is the poet, in the other the meditator is the reader.[35]

Whitehead concurs, noting that in thirteenth- and fourteenth-century lyrics, 'the meditator is generally encouraged to "see" directly, depending solely upon the visualising capacity of the written word'.[36] Yet Lydgate has gone one step further. He does not simply allow the reader the opportunity to see 'the poet meditating', but also to see the poet (or the narrator – it is unclear which) in the act of writing. We hear how he (narrator or poet), 'Took a penne, and wroot in my maneere / The said balladys, as they stondyn here' (lines 34–5).

At the end of the catalogue of the Virgin's Sorrows, this presentation of the authorial persona changes. There, Lydgate describes the anguish that he (or the narrator) experiences in writing the work. We hear how he was 'tremblyng in euery member / My penne quaking whan I gan to write' (lines 171–2). After this, he begs the Virgin to receive the verses without displeasure: 'God graunt it be to hir no displeaunce' (line 176). The final stanzas of the poem contain an anxious expression of authorial unworthiness. There the poet/narrator laments how the poem 'halte in meetre and elloquence' (line 307) and bids the work farewell, exclaiming, 'Goo litil tretys! And meekly me excuse' (line 309). This is a further debt to Chaucer, who ends *Troilus and Criseyde* with the famous injunction, 'Go, litel bok, go, litel myn tragedye'.[37] This use of the humility *topos* is a hallmark

---

35 Woolf, p. 6.
36 Whitehead, 'Middle English Religious Lyrics', p. 110.
37 Chaucer, *Troilus and Criseyde*, Benson, p. 586, line 1786.

Lydgatean manoeuvre. Meyer-Lee has noted Lydgate's 'obsessive deployment' of the motif,[38] while Pearsall calls his use of it an 'addiction'.[39] Although his use of the topos is not unusual, given that the poem makes clear that it should be used in a reader's personal devotions, Lydgate's decision to include the trope here is startling. He has inserted an authorial persona into a private, devotional experience. The topos performs a variety of functions, and it is important to register that it refers back to a biblical tradition of usage,[40] as well as conforming to more familiar models of strategic self-abnegation that we see in contemporary verse of the period.[41]

Writing about Lydgate's use of Chaucerian models more generally, Derek Pearsall notes that it is 'no accident that Lydgate will often proceed from his adulation of Chaucer and the acknowledgement that none can "counterfete / His gaye style" to the demonstration that he can not only do what Chaucer did, but do it better'.[42] In invoking both biblical and Chaucerian precedent in the use of the humility topos, Lydgate subtly positions himself as the 'spiritually correct successor of his lay predecessor', Chaucer.[43] The understated refashioning of Chaucerian motifs is visible in several places in the *Fifteen Joys and Sorrows*, and in each instance Lydgate 'outdoes' Chaucer by using Chaucerian models for a serious religious purpose. We see him using a Chaucerian motif at the poem's opening (namely, utilising a book as an imaginative stimulus, like the 'Drem of Scipioun' in *The Parliament of Fowls*), but surpassing it by using a devotional book as an imaginative and devotional stimulus. So too, in the rhetorical envoy, the narrator's anguished interjection has the feel of religious humility – a more solemn and proper use of the topos. In much the same way, in his choice of verse form – rhyme royal – a form popularised by Chaucer, Lydgate delicately attempts to outstrip his 'maister Chaucer', by turning it to purely devotional ends.[44]

---

38   R. Meyer-Lee, *Poets and Power from Chaucer to Wyatt* (Cambridge, 2007), p. 50.
39   D. Pearsall, 'Chaucer and Lydgate', *Chaucer Traditions: Studies in Honour of Derek Brewer*, ed. R. Morse and B. Windeatt (Cambridge, 1990), pp. 39–53 (p. 40).
40   See, for example, I Samuel 24: 15; Wisdom 9: 5.
41   For a history of the topos and an explanation of its biblical precedents, see E. R. Curtius, *European Literature and the Latin Middle Ages*, trans. W. R. Trask (London, 1953, repr. 1979), pp. 83–5. For an account of the more conventional fifteenth-century English uses, see D. Lawton, 'Dullness and the Fifteenth Century', *English Literary History* 54 (1987), 761–99 (esp. 762).
42   Pearsall, 'Chaucer and Lydgate', p. 45. Here Pearsall is quoting from *Floure of Curtesye*, lines 239–40, printed in Lydgate, *Minor Poems*, ed. MacCracken, II, pp. 410–20.
43   Meyer-Lee, *Poets and Power*, p. 55.
44   Lydgate, *Life of Our Lady*, ed. Lauritis, p. 426, bk 2, line 1628. Chaucer's hagiographies in rhyme royal, the *Prioress's Tale* and the *Second Nun's Tale*, could have been read as part of daily devotions, but the *Fifteen Joys and Sorrows* has an explicit devotional purpose.

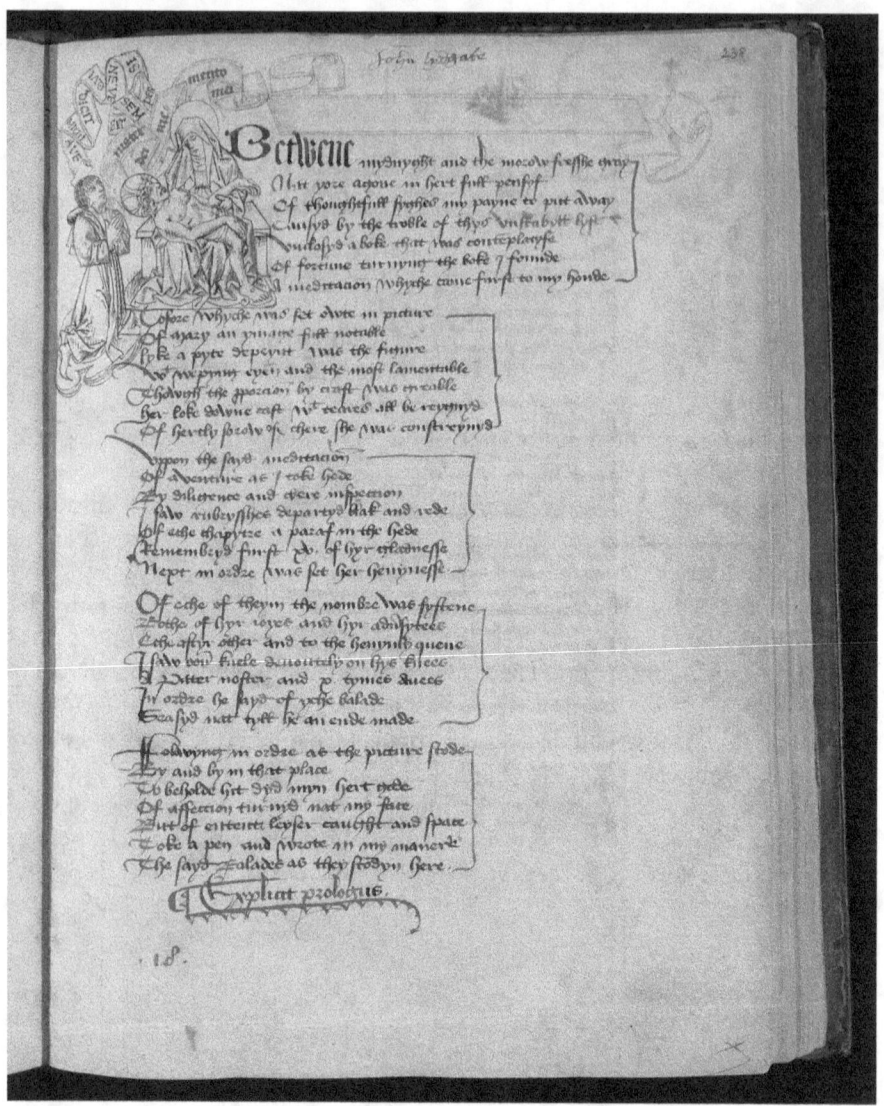

Fig. 1: Cambridge, Trinity College, MS R. 3. 21, fol. 238r. Reproduced by kind permission of the Master and Fellows of Trinity College, Cambridge

Manuscript Context

As noted earlier, the poem survives in six witnesses. In one the text is severely defective; in another: Cambridge, Fitzwilliam Museum, MS McClean 182, fol. 49, it is used as an envoy to Benedict Burgh and John Lydgate's translation of *Secreta secretorum*, the *Secrees of Old Philisoffres*.[45] In one manuscript, the poem appears twice.[46] Two of the witnesses deserve special attention, however: Trinity College R. 3. 21[47] and Harley 2255.[48]

Harley 2255 contains the arms of Bury St Edmunds (Lydgate's own abbey) on fol. 1. It is possible that Lydgate knew this copy, or that he may have even supervised its creation. As such, the text as it appears in this witness may possibly represent the *mise-en-page* that Lydgate envisaged for this most codicologically aware of poems. The manuscript is a carefully presented vellum codex. The pages containing the text (fols 88–93v) include a programme of attractive marginal decoration. The opening initial of the poem is in gold ink on a mauve and blue ground with green and gold flourishing extending into the margin. The first letter of each of the subsequent stanzas of the prologue is accompanied by paraphs in gold with mauve pen-flourishing, alternating with paraphs in blue with red pen-flourishing. Thereafter every initial letter of each stanza is in gold on a blue and mauve ground with white in-filling and green and gold leaf sprays extending into the margin. In the margin at the end of each stanza containing one of the joys or one of the sorrows, the words '*pater noster x ave*' are written in red ink. Just as the poem describes 'Rubrisshis, departyd blak and Reed', and 'a paraf in the heed' of each chapter (lines 18–19), so too Harley 2255 has a coloured paraph at the start of every stanza in the poem's prologue (lines 1–35; fols 88r-v). Additionally, the sequence of rubrics in red ink at the conclusion of each stanza echoes the poem's direction that 'Paternostres and aues [should be] seid betweene' (line 162). The mise-en-page of Harley 2255 serves to heighten the reader's experience of the text. It performs the very function the poem itself celebrates: opening up the devotional and imaginative possibilities offered by reading.

The second manuscript that deserves attention is Trinity College R. 3. 21 and, in particular, the second instance of the text in that manuscript. A reader opening fol. 238r (Figure 1) is greeted by a pen-and-ink image of the *pietà* in the top left-hand corner of the page, to the left of a rhyme royal stanza of Middle English

---

45 NIMEV 935; DIMEV 1544. This text, begun by Lydgate, was left unfinished at the point of his death and was completed by Burgh.
46 Trinity College R. 3. 21, fols 157–61v, fols 238–42.
47 On this manuscript, digitised at https://www.trin.cam.ac.uk/library/wren-digital-library/, see M. R. James, *The Western Manuscripts in the Library of Trinity College, Cambridge: A Descriptive Catalogue*, 4 vols (Cambridge, 1900–04), II, pp. 83–95. For a description of the scribes and booklets, see J. Boffey and J. J. Thompson, 'Anthologies and Miscellanies: Production and Choice of Texts', *Book Production and Publishing in Britain 1375–1475*, ed. J. Griffiths and D. Pearsall (Cambridge, 1989), pp. 279–316 (pp. 288–9). See also, L. Mooney, 'Scribes and Booklets of Trinity College, Cambridge, Manuscripts R. 3.19 and R. 3.21', *Middle English Poetry: Texts and Traditions*, ed. A. Minnis (York, 2001), pp. 241–66.
48 There has been some debate about whether this manuscript was made for William Curteys, Abbot of Bury St Edmunds, 1429–46. On this see S. R. Reimer and P. Farvolden, 'Of Arms and the Manuscript: The Date and Provenance of Harley 2255', *Journal of the Early Book Society for the Study of Manuscripts and Printing History* 8 (2005), 239–60.

verse.[49] In the image, a nimbed Virgin holds a haloed Christ, whose wounds are picked out in detail. To the left of the Virgin and Christ there is a kneeling male figure who wears monastic robes but lacks a tonsure. The identity of the figure is unclear: it may be a penitent or perhaps even a patron. Patron portraits were common in Books of Hours next to the Fifteen Joys of the Virgin.[50] This may be a visual representation of the narrator's description of how he 'sauh Oone kneele deuoutly on his knees; / A Pater-noster and ten tyme Auees / In ordre he sayde' (lines 25–6). Behind all three figures a looping scroll extends into the upper space of the page. It bears the words 'Mater Dei Memento Mei' ('Mother of God, remember me') in red ink, and 'Sint sem-per si-ne ve qui dicit michi ave' ('May they always be without woe who say Ave to me'), in brown ink. The image is not simply a decorative companion piece to the poem that it adjoins, but a sophisticated response to the text, visually realising the very scenario the poem envisages. Like Harley 2255, the poem in Trinity College R. 3. 21 also contains an extra-textual apparatus that prescribes the poem's devotional function. Each stanza is bracketed in red ink, highlighting its individual role in what I have termed a 'verse rosary'. Each of the stanzas containing one of the joys or sorrows is accompanied by the words 'Pater Aue', where the 'P' and the 'A' are in alternating blue or red ink. The use of the two colours acts as a reminder to the reader that they must say both the Pater Noster and then the Ave Maria, and it is these kinds of careful choices of layout and colour that heighten the reader's experience of the poem – the very heightening of experience described in the poem's own prologue. This witness makes a clearer distinction between the frame narrative and the central part of the poem by inserting Latin rubrics underlined in red ink, like that on fol. 241r, which reads 'Incipit prologus quindecim Dolorem beate Marie' ('Here begins the prologue of the Fifteen Sorrows of the blessed Mary'). Much like Harley 2255, this manuscript amplifies the reader's experience of the text, providing a series of visual prompts of a textual and extra-textual kind that stimulate both silent reading and spoken performance.

***

Lydgate's *Fifteen Joys and Sorrows* celebrates the act of reading text on a page. It pays homage to the complex range of sensory responses – visual and aural – that reading can engender, and is also a text in which the membrane between prayer and poetry remains permeable, asking its readers to recall a familiar pair of prayers and recite them between each stanza of its 'verse rosary'. The poem points to the complex ways in which lyrics made a play for reader's devotional attentions in the fifteenth century, a period of expanding lay literacy and book

---

[49] On the *pietà* and Lydgate's use of it in his lyrics, see S. Gayk, 'Images of Pity: The Regulatory Aesthetics of John Lydgate's Religious Lyrics', *Studies in the Age of Chaucer* 28 (2006), 175–203 (181–90).

[50] J. Naughton, 'A Minimally-Intrusive Presence: Portraits in Illustrations for Prayers to the Virgin', *Medieval Texts and Images: Studies of Manuscripts from the Middle Ages*, ed. M. Manion and B. J. Muir (Chur, 1991), pp. 111–26 (p. 111).

ownership. Indeed, readers encountering the poem in fifteenth-century manuscripts experienced a set of sensations akin to those described by the narrator in the poem itself. Yet, although the poem engages with a bookish form of devotion, it does so in a highly self-referential way. It quietly refashions a series of Chaucerian models for a solemn purpose and incorporates an ever-present authorial persona, effectively becoming an oblique homage to the writerly act as well.

PART III

MOUVANCE, TRANSFORMATION

10

Voice and Response: Lyric Rewriting of the Song of Songs

Anne Baden-Daintree

Undo thi dore[1]

Caput meum plenum est rore (Canticum 5). Ecce sto ad hostium et pulso (Apocalypsis 3)[2]

<table>
<tr><td>1</td><td>Vndo þi dore, my spuse dere,</td><td>Undo your door; spouse</td></tr>
<tr><td></td><td>Allas! Wy stond I loken out here?</td><td>why do I stand locked</td></tr>
<tr><td></td><td>Fre[3] am I thi make.</td><td>Noble / gracious; husband</td></tr>
<tr><td></td><td>Loke: mi lokkes and ek myn heued</td><td>Look; hair; also my head</td></tr>
<tr><td>5</td><td>And al my bodi with blod beweued</td><td>[is] covered with blood</td></tr>
<tr><td></td><td>For þi sake.</td><td></td></tr>
</table>

<table>
<tr><td></td><td>Responsio peccatoris:</td><td>The sinner's response:</td></tr>
<tr><td></td><td>Allas, allas! heuel haue I sped:</td><td>I have fared badly</td></tr>
<tr><td></td><td>For senne Iesu is fro me fled,</td><td>Because of [my] sin; Jesus; from</td></tr>
<tr><td></td><td>Mi trewe fere.</td><td>My faithful companion/ husband</td></tr>
<tr><td>10</td><td>Withouten my gate he stant alone;</td><td>outside; doorway; stands</td></tr>
<tr><td></td><td>Sorfuliche he maket his mone</td><td>sorrowfully; makes; complaint</td></tr>
<tr><td></td><td>On his manere.</td><td>In; manner</td></tr>
</table>

For a reading of another lyric repurposing Old Testament material to fit the crucifixion, see Hetta Howes (Chapter 6), '"Adreynt in shennesse": Blood, Shame and Contrition in *Quis est iste qui uenit de Edom?*'; for a further reading of a lyric attentive to its different manuscript versions and transformations, see Christiania Whitehead (Chapter 16), 'Musical and Poetic Form in *Stond wel, moder, under rode*'.

1   NIMEV 3825; DIMEV 6108. Transcribed from Edinburgh, National Library of Scotland, Advocates' MS 18. 7. 21, fol. 121v, with abbreviations expanded according to conventional practice and punctuation and glossary added.
2   'My head is full of dew (Canticles 5). Behold, I stand at the gate and knock. (Apocalypse 3).'
3   The manuscript is illegible at this point; I follow the reading of 'fre' in Brown *XIV*, p. 86. There are verbal similarities (as well as common theme) with a brief lyric at the foot of this column of the manuscript: 'Crist is offred for mannis sake / Of senne fre man to make. *Immolatus est Christus*'.

Ideo, þerfore:	*for that reason, therefore*
Lord, for senne I sike sore,	*sin; I sigh painfully*
Forȝef and I ne wil no more.	*Forgive; will no longer [sin]*
15 With al my mith senne I forsake,	*strength*
And opne myn herte þe in to take.	*open; to take thee in*
For thin herte is clouen oure loue to kecchen,	*cleaved; attain*
Þi loue is chosen vs alle to fecchen.	*seek / attain*
Myn herte it þerlede ȝef I wer kende,	*pierced; if, faithful*
20 Þi suete loue to hauen in mende.	*sweet; have; mind*
Perce myn herte with þi louengge,	*pierce my heart; loving*
Þat in þe I haue my duellingge. Amen.[4]	*dwelling*

The voice of Christ as bridegroom calling to Mankind, his beloved bride, drawing on the language, the figurative framework, the structural shape and the psychological landscape of the Song of Songs (hereafter also referred to as the Song) is clearly a fitting biblical source for affective religious lyric. It provides a recognised dialogue form, the possibilities of a commenting chorus, and an emotional and sensory framework that draws in the reader with an immediacy and instinctive point of engagement. While the language of the Song permeates much religious literature of the later Middle Ages, this is often fragmentary, drawing on individual words and phrases that function as verbal cues. Relatively few surviving lyrics provide extensive direct quotation. The Song is, however, frequently used as part of the descriptive framework in poems in praise of the Virgin Mary, particularly those that meditate on the names of the Virgin (as itemised by Helen Phillips),[5] and some of the aureate lyrics of the early fifteenth century. Three of the other most significant lyrics that allude to the Song of Songs are grouped together at the beginning of London, Lambeth Palace, MS 853: an Assumption lyric, '*Surge mea sponsa*', and the two poems with the refrain '*quia amore langueo*': one a Marian lyric beginning, *In a tabernacle of a tour*, and the other a Crucifixion poem voiced by Christ, *In a valey of þis restles mynde*.[6] Many other Middle English lyrics allude to the Song in a less direct manner with a vocabulary that draws on the material and sensory world of the biblical text, including fruit (apples, grapes, pomegranates), spices, honey, myrrh, flowers (particularly lilies), cypresses, turtle doves, gardens and fountains. The affectionate terms of address, together with the Song's imperative verbs of invitation (come, rise up, open) also signify the relationship of the bride and groom in

---

4   DIMEV suggests that the subsequent two lines complete this poem ('Womman Jon I take to þe / In stede of me þi sone to be. *Amen*'). Although the metre and rhyme scheme fit the final stanza of 'Undo thi dore', the subject matter is more appropriate to the subsequent lyric, and so I follow Karen Saupe in interpreting this couplet as an introduction to the Marian lament at the foot of the cross, which follows. See K. Saupe, ed., *Middle English Marian Lyrics* (Kalamazoo, MI, 1998), pp. 91, 219.

5   H. Phillips, '"Almighty and al merciable Queene": Marian Titles and Marian Lyrics', *Medieval Women: Texts and Contexts in Late Medieval Britain. Essays for Felicity Riddy*, ed. J. Wogan-Browne et al. (Turnhout, 2000), pp. 83–99.

6   NIMEV 3225 / DIMEV 5059; NIMEV 1460 / DIMEV 2461; NIMEV 1463 / DIMEV 2464. All these poems also appear in at least one other manuscript.

many other lyric texts. The use of the narrative framework of the Song, however, is much less common, and in surviving Middle English lyrics is employed only in the small group of related texts that form the basis of this chapter.

The poem that forms the epigraph to this chapter (referred to hereafter as *Undo thi dore*) draws on the narrative of the bride and groom from Song of Songs 5: 2. The earliest surviving version consists of two short stanzas, and is included in a thirteenth-century notebook containing mainly Latin preaching notes (London, Lambeth Palace, MS 557), although this seems to be, as most critics and editors suggest, imperfectly copied from a lost exemplar. It was also included in the preaching collection of the Norfolk Franciscan, John of Grimestone, assembled in 1372 (Advocates' MS 18. 7. 21), where it appears as a lyric intended for use during a Good Friday sermon, being placed alongside other Crucifixion lyrics.[7] Grimestone's text inverts the stanzas of the earlier poem, and adds a responding stanza that has received a less positive critical response. This chapter re-examines the relationship between the two versions of the poem alongside related texts in Latin and English, and the source narrative from the Song of Songs, in order to assess how the changes in presentation, textual detail and reading context might affect the reader's response. It also draws on a later witness to the poem, which again reorders the text, inviting a slightly different response in the reader. This final poem is part of a group of lyrics that fill the closing pages of an early fifteenth-century Franciscan manuscript containing William of Nassington's *Speculum Vitae*. The difference in reading context raises and revisits questions about the public/private nature of religious lyric, where the affective qualities of such lyrics imply an intimate spiritual engagement, but their use in sermons provides evidence of a clear didactic focus.

Reading the Song of Songs

In the allegorical reading employed in this lyric, the love between the bride and bridegroom of the Song represents the relationship between Christ and the individual soul:

> On my bed through the nights
> I sought him whom my soul loves
> I sought him and I did not find
> I will arise and go around the city
> through the streets and the courtyards
> I will seek him whom my soul loves
> I sought him and I did not find

---

7   As Edward Wilson comments, 'it is this preciseness in localization of date, place, and intellectual background which makes Grimestone's collection so valuable'. E. Wilson, *A Descriptive Index of the English Lyrics in John of Grimestone's Preaching Book* (Oxford, 1973), p. i.

> *in lectulo meo per noctes quaesivi quem diligit anima mea quaesivi illum et non inveni surgam et circuibo civitatem per vicos et plateas quaeram quem diligit anima mea quaesivi illum et non inveni.* (Song of Songs 3: 1–2)[8]

This passage expresses an absolute sense of absence: a searching for the object of desire that remains unfulfilled, unrewarded, representing the soul in its endless quest for union with God. But this mood does not last; the text of the Song is not static, but alternates between separation and intimacy, desire and satisfaction. Joy in the bridegroom's presence, and yearning in his absence, characterise the shifting moods of the Song, and also inform the mood of the associated Middle English lyrics. These alternations, the forward movement and retreat of both bride and groom, are the central narrative event of the *Undo thi dore* poems, which also draw on the following passage for their narrative framework:

> I sleep and my soul keeps watch
> the voice of my beloved knocking
> open to me, my sister my friend
> my dove, my spotless one
> for my head is full of dew
> and my hair of the drops of the nights
>
> *ego dormio et cor meum vigilat vox dilecti mei pulsantis aperi mihi soror mea amica mea columba mea immaculata mea quia caput meum plenum est rore et cincinni mei guttis noctium.* (Song of Songs 5: 2)

While direct citation is restricted to a single verse (5: 2), much of the subsequent narrative is also implicit in the lyric:

> 5: 4 my beloved put forth his hand through the hole
> and my belly trembled at his touch
> 5: 5 I rose to open to my beloved
> my hands dripped myrrh
> my fingers full of the finest myrrh
> 5: 6 I opened the bolt of the door to my love
> but he had turned away and gone over
> my soul melted as he spoke
> I sought him and I did not find him
> I called and he did not answer me

In this fuller exposition of the longing and searching for the beloved there is also a clearly expressed eroticism, mediated through the metaphor of 'opening'. The repetitions of 'open' refer to the beloved seeking admittance to the house, to the presence of his bride, but also to the female body opening to receive her lover.

---

[8] Latin Vulgate text and translation from E. A. Matter, *The Voice of My Beloved: The Song of Songs in Western Medieval Christianity* (Philadelphia, 1992), pp. xvi–xxxiii. This edition is employed throughout, as the minimal punctuation and closely literal English translation maintain and emphasise the 'song-like' qualities of the biblical text.

The Narrative of *Undo thi dore*

The Middle English poem begins with the scenario from the Song of Songs outlined above, where the bridegroom calls to his bride to let him in, but by the time she responds and unbolts the door to admit him he has already left, and she returns to searching the city for her lover. However, the lyric ends before the bride responds to her lover's call. In its allegorical reading of this text, the medieval lyric moves us from the present-tense appeal of Christ, locked out, on the other side of the door, through the immediate penitential response of the sinner, aware that Christ has fled from him, and finally to a later reflection by the sinner and a somewhat delayed impulse to spiritual action. As the superscript to Grimestone's text indicates, the poem also draws on the narrative and the language of Apocalypse 3: 20:

> *Ecce sto ad ostium, et pulso: si quis audierit vocem meam, et aperuerit mihi januam, intrabo ad illum, et cœnabo cum illo, et ipse mecum.*[9]

In the context of the final Judgement, this verse underlines the reciprocal nature of the relationship between God and man, and the parallels with the dramatic scene employed in the Song of Songs are clear. But the Song of Songs is the predominant influence in this lyric text, and it provides the emotional context, as well as the linguistic and narrative framework.

In *Undo thi dore*, Christ's call to Man at first directly reflects the language of the Song, in the appeal from the bridegroom: '*aperi mihi soror mea amica mea*' (open to me, my sister my friend), which becomes 'Undo þi dore, my spuse dere'. The Grimestone lyric echoes both tone and vocabulary, where the shift from '*amica mea*' to 'my spuse dere' reflects the bridegroom's intimate address elsewhere in the Song of Songs: the repeated '*soror mea sponsa*' (my sister, my spouse). But the words of the Song are then transformed by the application of Passion imagery; the dew of the night that soaks the lover's hair in the Song is replaced in the lyric by the blood of the Crucifixion. Christ's head and hair are 'beweued' with drops of blood. *Biweven* is related to covering or clothing, so in simple terms it means 'covered with blood', but it also carries associations of the related term 'weven', referring to weaving or interlacing, providing a strong visual image of strands of hair interwoven with rivulets of blood.[10] The groom is stuck or locked outside, the term *loken* suggesting that the bridegroom is unable to gain entry without the agency of the bride, that man's failure to repent prevents Christ's entry. This replaces the reading in the earlier version of the lyric (reproduced below, p. 147) of *stekyn*, also meaning locked or stuck. But the Crucifixion

---

9   'Behold I stand at the door and knock. If any man shall hear my voice and open to me the door, I will come in to him and will sup with him: and he with me'. S. Wenzel, *Preachers, Poets, and the Early English Lyric* (Princeton, NJ, 1986), pp. 108–11, comments on the repeated practice in this manuscript of employing brief Latin texts (not all of them biblical source material), followed by translation and expansion into Middle English lyric.

10 MED s.v. 'biweven' v. (1), 2 (b); 'weven' v. (1), 1.

imagery breaks through again, in the verb *stekyn*'s other meanings of 'to stab' or 'to pierce', together with its specific use in other texts of the period as referring to the nailing of Christ on the cross.[11] Yet Christ persists with his repeated call to undo the door, to open up to him. The insistent repetition of 'undo' in the Lambeth version indicates the patient repetition of Christ's presence. Rather than the erotic resonance of the repetitions of 'open' in the text of the Song of Songs, the repeated 'undo' indicates the way in which God persists in his suit to man outside of earthly temporality. Here, the bloodied body of Christ repeatedly and continuously suffers the Crucifixion on man's behalf, the verbal repetition underlining the perpetual nature of the exchange.

In Grimestone's second stanza, man's response, there is another shift of temporality. It begins with the soul's cry of despair at Christ's departure. But then, in an apparently simultaneous situation, Christ stands outside the door, calling for it to be opened, to be let in. The reader is presented with a collapsing of time in which Christ is both absent and present. Because of man's sin, Christ has fled from his presence, yet at the same time he waits patiently, calling to be admitted. In the final stanza the reciprocal 'opening up' and 'taking in' in this response alternates between images of comforting refuge and the violent action necessary to achieve this. From the symbolic gesture of the sinner opening his heart to take Christ in, the poem moves to a statement that Christ's heart has been 'cloven', that is, cleaved or split apart in order to receive mankind. This violent imagery is then turned upon the sinner, whose heart is 'thirlede' by the depth of Christ's love. *Thirled* is used here in a figurative sense, meaning a sudden sharp emotion (in this instance, compassion). But its literal meaning is 'stabbed' or 'pierced', as with a sword or spear.[12] This anchors the term to its Passion context: it is clearly intended to bring to mind the pierced side of the crucified Christ. The image of piercing is used once more in the closing lines of the poem. Man appeals to Christ to pierce his heart, so that it seems that both hearts, those of Christ and man, need to be violently opened up in order to achieve the mutual indwelling of the final line. The dwelling 'inside' Christ operates as a verbal cue to the literalisation of the metaphor as it is expressed in numerous literary and visual sources to depict the sinner climbing into a physical place of refuge inside the broken body of Christ, as, for example, in this extract from one of the *quia amore langueo* poems:

In my syde I haf made hyr nest –	*side; her*
Loke in me, how wyde a wound is here! –	*wide*
This is hyr chambre, here shall she rest,	*chamber*
That she and I may slepe in fere,	*together*
Here may she wasshe, if any filth were;	*be cleansed*
Here is socour for all hyr woo.	*support; suffering*
Cum if she will, she shall haf chere,	*have; comfort*
Quia amore langueo.[13]	*Because I languish for love*

11 MED, s.v. steken.
12 MED s.v. thirlen.
13 Cambridge, University Library, MS Hh. 4. 12, fol. 44v; Gray, *Selection*, pp. 41–3.

Voice and Response: Lyric Rewriting of the Song of Songs

As in many Crucifixion lyrics, the language of comfort and intimacy is juxtaposed with the visceral reality of Christ's wounds.

Reading and Listening: The Other Manuscript Witnesses

The earliest surviving witness of this poem is London, Lambeth Palace, MS 557, fol. 185v. As Douglas Gray confirms, this lyric 'occurs among some Latin notes on the Passion', in a late thirteenth-century manuscript.[14] This small manuscript appears to be a preacher's notebook, consisting largely of Latin notes, in various hands, to support sermon composition. The two Middle English texts within this manuscript are on consecutive pages, in the same hand, and conclude a section of notes with (unusually for this manuscript) a number of blank lines after the second poem. There is, elsewhere in the manuscript, at least one other text laid out in verse form, but this is in Latin. The presentation and subject matter of the two Middle English poems suggest that they were intended to be employed as companion pieces. The first of these presents a condensed version of the Grimestone lyric:

Allas, allas! wel yvel y sped:[15]	*I have fared very badly*
For synne Jesu fro me ys fled,	
That lyvely fere.	*lively/lovely*
At my dore he standes alone,	
And kallys 'Undo' with reuful mone,	*calls; pitiful*
On this manere:	
'Undo, my lef, my dowve dere,	*love; dear dove*
Undo! Wy stond y stekyn out here?	*locked*
Ik am thi make!	*I*
Lo, my heved and myne lockys	*head; hair*
Ar al bywevyd wyth blody dropys	*bloody drops*
For thine sake.'	

This is a simpler, and more dramatically focused, version of the poem in Grimestone's Book: there is no final 'responding' stanza (which survives uniquely in Advocates' MS 18. 7. 21 and may well have been added by Grimestone), and the two main stanzas are in the opposite order (beginning with man's cry of loss at Christ's departure, and then introducing his words as he petitions for admittance). Aside from the way in which this narrative ordering makes the dramatic scenario easier to understand (without altering or diminishing the temporal effects discussed above), there are a number of minor textual differences, some of which are discussed below. But although this earlier version of the poem is also intended for sermon use, its structural operation is less clear cut without the mediating glosses and directed response. Although we cannot know how the preacher might have followed the recital of the verse, the brevity, and the lack of

---

14 Gray, *Ibid.*, p. 124.
15 Transcribed from London, Lambeth Palace, MS 557, fol. 185v, with punctuation and glossary added.

conclusion to the narrative, is largely the point. The audience is presented with the image of the suffering Christ, petitioning in intimate and direct terms, and the openness of the ending encourages an individual emotional and spiritual response.

The second of the Middle English poems in this manuscript is also voiced by Christ on the cross, with the call to look at his broken body:

Alle þat gos and rydys, loket opon me:	*all who walk or ride; look*
If evere seye ye pynyn, man, also men pynen me.	*saw; suffering; torment*
Loke, man, to my back, hou yt ys ybetyn;	*look; how it is beaten*
Loke to my sydyn, wat blod it havyn iletyn;	*side; blood; has let flow*
Loke doune to myne fet, þat nayled been on rode;	*down; feet; nailed; cross*
Loke to myn hevyd, þat rennyn al on blode.	*head; runs; blood*
To clensyn þe of synne opon þe rode tre	*cleanse; cross*
I suffrede al þus pyne, man, for love of þe.	*suffered; this pain*
Gyf þou me þat soule, þat ys so dere ybouyhte,	*give; bought at such a price*
Of all þat I þole ne ys me þen nouyhte.[16]	*suffered; then; nothing*

Rosemary Woolf's analysis of this lyric demonstrates that it has an opening in the *O vos omnes* tradition, but with the descriptive detail of Christ's wounded body instead drawn from the *Respice in faciem Christi tui*.[17] This poem invites, even more explicitly than *Undo thi dore*, the imaginative contemplation of Christ's bleeding and broken body. Again, there is Christ's direct address to man, and the command to look as a means to understanding the process of exchange and reciprocity: 'I suffrede al þus pyne, man, for love of þe'. Further, this poem makes the required response equally explicit: 'Gyf þou me þat soule þat ys so dere yboughte'. In other words, 'I have suffered pain for you', says the crucified Christ, 'expecting to receive your soul in return'. The reciprocity is further emphasised by the repetitions of 'pynyn' in the second line, and the implications of man's responsibility in Christ's suffering, the reiteration of its purpose, and the necessity for response at the close of the poem. The visualisation of Christ's wounds – his damaged back, sides, feet and head – invites the engagement of the imagination, but also involves the process of recollection, triggering associations with prior experience of other written and visual images of the Crucifixion (perhaps even including the images within the church itself, such as stained glass, wall paintings or statuary).[18]

While it is likely that these poems were employed in Good Friday sermons (and probably composed for this purpose), the limited manuscript history that

---

16 Transcribed from London Lambeth Palace, MS 557, fol. 186r, with punctuation and glossary added. NIMEV 207; DIMEV 368.
17 Woolf, pp. 30–1, 43.
18 Recent publications on Middle English religious poetry draw attention to the way in which these aspects of visual culture inform and enhance understanding of poetry. See A. S. Lazikani, *Cultivating the Heart: Feeling and Emotion in Twelfth- and Thirteenth-Century Religious Texts* (Chicago, 2015); and E. K. Rentz, *Imagining the Parish in Late Medieval England* (Columbus, OH, 2015).

we have for *Undo thi dore* also indicates that it continued to have a life outside a sermon context. As Siegfried Wenzel has indicated, such verses employed in sermons are brief, rhymed and emotive, all factors that point to their memorial function. In other words, they are memorable precisely in order that they remain with their audience beyond and after their original delivery during a sermon – and so they continue to interact with the biblical and liturgical texts with which they are associated in a preaching context. Holly Johnson's description of the function and processes of the late medieval Good Friday sermon sheds light on the macaronic sermons she describes, but also on other texts associated with Good Friday, such as the lyric discussed here:

> The sermons appear designed to heighten and play a role within the larger liturgical experience. Their primary function is to make the events re-enacted on Good Friday a living reality, to draw audiences into that reality, and to evoke in them a number of affective responses, such as sorrow, pity, gratitude, and shame.[19]

The affective lyrics, such as those under discussion in this chapter, clearly play an important part in the experience of making the Passion a 'living reality', with their power to create and reinforce an emotional response with greater immediacy. Where written versions of sermons survive, it is not clear the extent to which embedded rhymed verse actually appeared in the spoken version, and how much such verse is an embellishment added as part of the 'artful conversation' of its 'fleshed out' written form.[20] With the *Undo thi dore* poems, however, we have a different process of recording: the poems survive in written form; the sermons themselves are, at best, a sketchy collection of Latin notes and a clustering of one or more other lyric poems of similarly appropriate theme. The verse elements are the only parts of a sermon that a preacher would need to memorise; extemporisation from notes (or in English from a Latin base text) is both likely and possible. The improvised re-creation of lyric form as part of sermon delivery, including the metre and rhyme that distinguish such elements as 'poetry', is not, however, being suggested here. It is rather that (as evidence from preaching notebooks confirms) relatively standardised poetic texts are associated with particular sermon contexts and a preacher would have a range of resources to draw from.

The final manuscript witness under discussion, however, takes this lyric out of its sermon context. This is New Haven, Yale University, Beinecke Library, Takamiya MS 15, fol. 84ra, which has not previously been taken into account in comparisons of the Lambeth and Grimestone poems.[21] This manuscript is largely

---

19 H. Johnson, *The Grammar of Good Friday: Macaronic Sermons of Late Medieval England* (Turnhout, 2012), p. xvii. Wenzel has demonstrated, however, that such embedded lyrics perform a structural function in the delivery of a sermon. Wenzel, *Preachers, Poets, and the Early English Lyric*, pp. 3–13.
20 Johnson, *The Grammar of Good Friday*, p. xviii.
21 See, for example, Woolf, pp. 51–2; Gray, *Selection*, p. 124. I am grateful to Professor Toshiyuki Takamiya, and the Beinecke Rare Books and Manuscripts Library at Yale

concerned with a copy of the Middle English verse *Speculum Vitae*, ascribed here to Richard Rolle (although since attributed to William of Nassington), but it concludes with a number of shorter pieces of devotional and didactic material. A date of c.1400 has been suggested by Ian Doyle, and a linguistic dialect analysis of the main text (the *Speculum Vitae*) by Ralph Hanna places its composition in 'a liminal area, the extreme north of the north Midlands'.[22] Hanna suggests, however, an East Anglian connection for two of the lyrics, as they both also appear in Grimestone's preaching book, and their language retains the dialects identified through the *Linguistic Atlas of Late Mediaeval English* as south-west Norfolk.[23] The context of this latest surviving witness places the poem alongside reading texts rather than sermon notes. The lengthy verse *Speculum Vitae* contains a number of scribal markings that indicate cues for reading aloud (even though the double-column presentation of the text is more indicative of private reading). But there should not be a straightforward assumption that the lyric is part of the same reading experience, whether for individual or group reading. The miscellaneous shorter texts and lyrics that fill up the closing pages of the manuscript are not connected in any simple manner. What we can see, however, is that the lyric has survived outside of its established sermon context, and was available for reading, at least in this one surviving example, without the mediation or explanatory context of a surrounding sermon. Some Latin marginal glosses provide, in the place of this, some orienting context.

A comparison of the two shorter versions of the poem reveals the degree to which subtle changes of detail influence the emotional range and import of the text. The Takamiya manuscript presents the poem as follows:

Exemplum[24]
Erat quidam bonus homine qui peccavit contra deus et sic dicit:[25]

University (where the MS is now held) for allowing access to the manuscript and providing digital reproductions. For a digital facsimile see https://brbl-dl.library.yale.edu/vufind/.

22   T. Takamiya, 'Richard and Robert as False Executors in Late Medieval England', *Anglistik* 8 (1997), 49–59 (51). See also T. Takamiya, '"On the Evils of Covetousness": An Unrecorded Middle English Poem', *New Science Out of Old Books: Studies in Manuscripts and Early Printed Books in Honour of A. I. Doyle*, ed. R. Beadle and A. J. Piper (Aldershot, 1995), pp. 189–206; R. Hanna, 'Takamiya MS 15: Some Liminal Observations', *The Medieval Book and a Modern Collector: Essays in Honour of Toshiyuki Takamiya*, ed. T. Matsuda, R. A. Linenthal and J. Scahill (Cambridge, 2004), pp. 125–34 (p. 126).

23   A. McIntosh, M. L. Samuels and M. Benskin, eds, *A Linguistic Atlas of Late Mediaeval English*, 4 vols (Aberdeen, 1986); Hanna, 'Takamiya MS 15', p. 133. Hanna also points out that all the Grimestone poems, or 'lyric scraps' have 'very narrow recorded circulations'.

24   Transcribed from New Haven, Yale University, Beinecke Library, Takamiya MS 15, fol. 84ra, with punctuation and glossary added.

25   'Indeed, there was a good man, and he sinned against God, and so he says ... ' I am grateful to my colleague, Gareth Griffith, for his help in transcribing and expanding the Latin abbreviations here.

Allas, allas, iuel haue I sped:	*badly; fared*
Ihesu for synne is fro me fled,	
That lufly fere.	*lovely companion*
Without my dore he standes alone,	*Outside*
He biddis undo with ruthful mone	*bids; pitiful*
On þis manere:	*In*
Et respondit Ihesu sic:	*And Jesus responds thus:*
'Behold, my body and my heued	*head*
With blody dropes is al beweued,	*covered*
For þi sake.	
I am þi spouse and þou my wife.	
Vndo þi dore, my leue lyfe:	*dearest love*[26]
Let in þi make.'	

Although some of the lines here are a little metrically awkward (and all three versions contain some metrical irregularities, as well as unsatisfactory 'fillers' to support the scansion), some of these differences resolve unsatisfactory readings of the earlier text. In line 3, for example, the 'lyvely' of Lambeth MS 557 is read by Woolf as scribal error for 'lufely' (lovely), and the Takamiya text appears to confirm this.[27] Furthermore, 'lufely' confirms the marital imagery of the Song of Songs (and shifts the tone into that domestic intimacy that is less apparent in the 'trewe fere' of the Grimestone lyric). Similarly, in line 5, the shift from 'calls' in Lambeth to 'bids' in Takamiya increases the sense of direct address, where a bid is a more focused request demanding a response.

The section referring to the drops of blood on the wounded Christ (lines 10–12 in Lambeth MS 557, lines 7–9 in Takamiya MS 15, and lines 4–6 in Grimestone) fails to provide a formally, logically and aesthetically 'best' version. Woolf, commenting on Lambeth, points out that it 'lacks a true rhyme', and of the Grimestone text she suggests that the detail is 'not original, as it is inconsistent with the source text in the Song of Songs' (where it is the bridegroom's head and hair, not his body, which is wet with the dew, or 'the drops of the night'). As we can see, the Takamiya manuscript repeats this substitution of the body for the more biblically correct 'locks' (*cincinni*). Woolf's conjectured original text of 'Lo mi lokkes and ek myn heved / Ar al wyt blody dropys bywevyd' is metrically and logically superior to the Takamiya version, retaining the head and hair of the Song, without the supplementary detail of blood flowing down onto his body.[28] As well as these minor differences, the Takamiya text inverts the two parts of

---

26   See MED s.v. lef, lif, and also n. 29, below. There are several possible readings for this phrase: 'leue' means either 'love' or 'beloved', and 'lyfe' could be read either as 'love' or 'life', giving a reading of 'dearest love', or 'my love, my life' (Christ is directly addressed in many other devotional texts as 'mi leof, mi lif').
27   Gray, *Selection*, p. 125, also comments on this, suggesting that 'the scribe's form probably represents *lefly/levely* "lovable, lovely, delightful", or (possibly) *luvely* "loving, lovable, beautiful"'.
28   Woolf, p. 51, n. 2.

Christ's speech in the second stanza. While the Lambeth text moves from a call to unlock the door towards a demonstration of his suffering on man's behalf, the later version moves in the opposite direction. It calls for the bleeding body to be taken as evidence for Christ's love, before moving to a reaffirmation of the marital relationship ('I am þi spouse'), with the request to undo the door embedded in between two further statements that confirm this relationship. The emphasis here is on duty, love and the associations of what that marriage implies. Having been defined as 'lovely (*dear*) companion' in the opening stanza, Christ demonstrates the mutual obligations of marriage: I am thy spouse, and thou [are] my wife. The final words of the poem 'let in thy make (*husband*)' leave little space for refusal. The Lambeth lyric, however, builds on the marital image of the Song of Songs through a more explicit use of its language of personal address: my love, my dear dove. In contrast the 'leue lyfe' of the Takamiya text has a familiar intimacy about it.[29] It works alongside the spousal relationship, where the 'dove' (*columba mea*) of the earliest version is replaced in the two later versions with 'spouse', recalling the *sponsa* of the Song of Songs.

The Lambeth text has no marginal glosses, as such: they are not necessary, as it is not a presentation copy for reading, but is preceded by sermon notes, and followed immediately in the manuscript by another lyric that also represents the sacrifice of the crucified Christ. The Grimestone lyric is preceded by the biblical texts to which the poem alludes, and simply introduces man's response with '*responsio peccatoris*', and the concluding stanza with '*ideo, perfore*'. The Takamiya text is presented with an expanded version of such orienting context. The poem as a whole is introduced as an *exemplum*, and the marginal notes delineate the different voices. The first stanza, then, is the voice of the good man who has sinned against God, and the second stanza is Christ's response. The presentation of the text suggests that these Latin glosses are integral to the reading of the poem. The poem itself is inset, with the rubricated glosses (which are in the same hand) aligned with the text of the preceding poem, giving them equal status with the poetic text. The *mise en page* of both the Lambeth and the Takamiya versions also makes clear the division between two voices, and is, again, a guide to interpretation; elsewhere in the Takamiya MS, poems are presented continuously with no stanza breaks, making the presentation of this poem particularly distinctive.

The orienting commentary that accompanies the texts works alongside the literary processes of the poems themselves, which operate to effect an emotional and spiritual response. In these poems, the erotic dynamic of the Song's relationships, the shifting sense of Christ's presence and absence, is shown to be

---

29 The phrase 'leue lyfe' also occurs in an *exemplum* verse in *Fasciculus morum*, in a story 'said to be about Aeneas', which shares the same biblical sources as *Undo thi dore*, and is discussed by Woolf, p. 50, in this context: 'Behold myne woundes how sore I am dyʒth, / Ffor all þe wele þat þu hast I wan hit in fyʒt. / I am sore wounded, behold on my skyn, / Leve lyf, for my love, let me comen in.' Oxford, Bodleian Library, MS Rawlinson C. 670, fol. 42v.

permanently entwined with the suffering of the Passion. The reader engages in this through a series of sensory metaphors: the imaginative sensation of piercing or stabbing, the visualisation of the bleeding, suffering Christ, and the recollection of the passage from the Song of Songs with its invitation to erotic touch. In its preaching context, during the Good Friday retelling of the Passion narrative, the listener is presented with the bloodied body of Christ appealing on the most personal and intimate level, demanding a response. There is also a significant role played by memory, imagination and intellectual engagement in such encounters, in the way in which language works to facilitate the experience of the sacred. How this operated in practice, however, is difficult to reconstruct. Grimestone's book is a valuable collection of source material, but provides little indication of how individual preachers may have used such texts in the contexts of their sermons. The poem is collected in Advocates' MS 18. 7. 21 with other Crucifixion lyrics, which, as in the sermon notes of Lambeth MS 557, indicates a Good Friday context, but the various surviving texts of vernacular Good Friday sermons such as those collected by Holly Johnson do not draw on this particular text (nor on other aspects of the Song of Songs), and this book of the Bible is not part of the liturgy for this day. Texts from the Song of Songs feature most prominently in the liturgy for the Feast of the Assumption, not Good Friday, although there is a limited tradition of Good Friday preaching where sermons draw on the *amore langueo* of the Song as a means of combining the recounting of the Gospel narrative with the scholastic processes of thematic development. Versions of a macaronic sermon exist in a number of manuscripts where seven aspects of love-longing (such as loss of strength, sighing, sweet speech) are each employed as a means of exploring related aspects of Christ's Passion (including the painful torments suffered, his words on the cross, his wounds).[30]

The Long and Wide Reach of the Text

This poem does not only engage intertextually with the Song of Songs, but also with a wider range of lyric texts in Latin and English. It is associated with the many poetic renderings of the scenario where Christ invites (or commands) the contemplation of his wounded body on the cross, typically beginning 'behold' or 'look'. When we begin to look at how these processes operate in the Middle English lyric, Woolf's 1968 analysis of the various categories of Passion lyrics is still pertinent. Within the many poems that feature a meditation on Christ's suffering on the cross where there is an injunction to look or behold, Woolf identifies three types of narratorial stance, each of which clearly produces distinctive emotional responses in the reader or listener. Such poems might be in the form of 'a sermon address': voiced by a preacher, exhorting his audience to gaze on the wounded body of Christ; others adopt the imaginative role of direct experience at the foot of the cross in a 'first person monologue'; the final group are voiced by

---

30 See Wenzel, *Preachers, Poets, and the Early English Lyric*, pp. 147–8, for a fuller description, including a listing of surviving manuscripts.

Christ himself, calling on man to observe his wounds.³¹ This poem engages with all these various forms of address: it is primarily voiced by Christ, it employs the first-person direct response and (in two of the manuscripts) it is mediated through the direction of a preacher.

The specific association between the contemplation of Christ's wounded body and the call to be admitted based on the language of the Song of Songs recurs in other lyric fragments, with no clear evidence of direct textual influence, although the Lambeth poem is the earliest surviving example. The poem with the closest textual similarity is in an early fifteenth-century sermon collection, containing Latin and macaronic sermons attributed to John Swetstock (including the *amore langueo* sermon mentioned above):

For þe I wax al blody open þe rode,	For thee I become all bloody upon the cross
to wasche in þi hert y scheedde mi blod.	cleanse; shed; blood
Amend þe betymes and seese of þi synne,	make amends; promptly; cease
Undo þe dore of þin hert and let me inne.³²	

Other poems that employ a similar framework are identified by both Gray and Woolf.³³ Woolf sets the text clearly within the tradition of Christ as 'lover-knight', while Wenzel considers it more specifically within the sermon tradition, confirming that the dramatic scenario is 'well known from an *exemplum* about Christ the Lover-Knight and its moralization in *Fasciculus morum*, from where it was appropriated for a fifteenth-century sermon'.³⁴ This sermon also, as Wenzel shows, delineates the soul's response in a similar manner to the final stanza of the Grimestone lyric. However, both biblical quotation and scenario are also combined in other, quite different contexts, such as the one of the many tales of deceitful wives in the Middle English version of *The Seven Sages of Rome*. Here, the unfaithful wife is locked out of the house by her older husband after being caught in an act of adultery. She then tricks her husband into thinking she has tried to drown herself in the well, and when he goes to save her, she locks him out and falsely accuses him. It is his unsuccessful attempt to re-enter his home that adopts these words.³⁵

This lyric rewriting of the Song of Songs has a much longer history, however, than just these late-medieval poems and their associated sermons. While the Middle English versions of this poem are clearly related, and derive ultimately

---

31 Woolf, p. 35.
32 BodL, MS Bodley 649, fol. 5v; Woolf, p. 51.
33 R. Woolf, 'The Theme of Christ the Lover-Knight in Medieval English Literature', *Review of English Studies* NS 13 (1962), 1–16; Gray, *Selection*, p. 125.
34 Wenzel, *Preachers, Poets, and the Early English Lyric*, p. 161.
35 'Dame, I ham here, / Thy spouse and thy trewe fere: / Arys uppe, and draw oute the pyne, / Goode lyf, and let me inne' (lines 1424–7). *The Seven Sages of Rome (Midland version)*, ed. J. Whitelock (Oxford, 2005). Cambridge, CUL, MS Dd. 1. 17; NIMEV 3187 / DIMEV 4986. This appears to be mediated through the language of the lyrics rather than directly derived from the biblical source.

from a (lost) single source, the adaptation of this specific passage from the Song of Songs into a Christological and Crucifixion-focused lyric has a history extending from the eleventh century through to the twentieth. The earliest example is a Latin poem, often attributed to Peter Damian, and discussed variously by Rosemary Woolf, Ann Astell, Peter Dronke and E. Ann Matter.[36] The poem begins:

> *Quis est hic qui pulsat ad ostium*
> *noctis rumpens somnium?*
> *me vocat: 'O virginum pulcherrima,*
> *soror, coniux, gemma splendidissima*
> *cito surgens aperi, dulcissima.*
>
> *Ego sum summi regis filius,*
> *primus, et novissimus,*
> *qui de caelis in has veni tenebras,*
> *liberare captivorum animas:*
> *passus mortem et multas iniurias.'*
>
> *Mox ego dereliqui lectulum,*
> *cucurri ad pessulum:*
> *ut dilecto tota domus pateat,*
> *et mens mea plenissime videat*
> *quem videre maxime desiderat.*

Who is this who knocks at the door, breaking the sleep of night? He calls to me: 'O fairest of virgins, sister, spouse, most splendid jewel! rise quickly to open, sweetest one. I am the son of the highest king, the first and the most new, I came here from heaven into this darkness to set free the souls of captives, suffering death and many injuries.' Presently I left my bed, I hurried to the bolt that the whole house might lie open to my love, and my mind might most fully see whom it longs greatly to see.[37]

This makes explicit the allegorical basis of the narrative, which has a less heavy-handed exposition in the Middle English lyric. A later version of this narrative is developed in a seventeenth-century Spanish sonnet by Lope de Vega, translated into English in the late nineteenth century by Longfellow, and more recently reworked in a free translation by Geoffrey Hill.[38] Hill's poem derives from the parallel text version of de Vega published by Penguin, a process that bears some similarity to the writing and rewriting of biblical texts through the interpretations of other poets during the Middle Ages. This most recent adaptation of the Song of Songs

---

36 See P. Dronke, *Medieval Latin and the Rise of the European Love-Lyric* (Oxford, 1965), pp. 269–71; Woolf, pp. 51–2; Matter, *The Voice of My Beloved*, pp. 188, 197–8; A. W. Astell, *The Song of Songs in the Middle Ages* (Ithaca and London, 1990), pp. 155–6.
37 Text and translation, Matter, *The Voice of My Beloved*, pp. 188, 197–8.
38 Lope de Vega Carpio, '¿Qué tengo yo que mi amistad procuras?', in *The Penguin Book of Spanish Verse*, ed. J. M. Cohen (Harmondsworth, 1956), p. 247; H. W. Longfellow, Translations from the Spanish, Sonnet II, 'To-Morrow', *The Complete Poetical Works of Henry Wadsworth Longfellow*, ed. H. E. Scudder (New York, 1902), p. 782; Geoffrey Hill, 'Lachrimae Amantis', *Tenebrae* (London, 1978), p. 21.

narrative does not directly employ the language of the Bible, but rather the image of the lover outside the door, seeking admittance:

> What is there in my heart that you should sue
> so fiercely for its love? What kind of care
> brings you as though a stranger to my door
> through the long night and in the icy dew
> seeking the heart that will not harbour you,
> that keeps itself religiously secure?
> At this dark solstice filled with frost and fire
> your passion's ancient wounds must bleed anew.

Only the night and the dew anchor this securely to the biblical text, but, as with the Latin poem, the perpetual repetition of the Crucifixion in these processes of petitioning and refusal is made explicit. Hill's sonnet continues with a less conclusive response to God's patient presence:

> So many nights the angel of my house
> has fed such urgent comfort through a dream,
> whispered 'your lord is coming, he is close'
> that I have drowsed half-faithful for a time
> bathed in pure tones of promise and remorse:
> 'tomorrow I shall wake to welcome him.'

The suggestion, of course, is that tomorrow never comes. The deferral of acceptance of God's presence becomes habitual, as the processes of God's repeated suit to man are dramatised through the perpetually fresh bleeding of Christ's wounds. The ambiguities of 'religiously secure', of 'urgent comfort', and the reluctant submission implied by 'drowsed half-faithful', could function as effectively through their indirectness in stirring a response as the more clearly directed and uncompromising terms of the Grimestone lyric.

Conclusion

Middle English lyric is not static, but dynamic, altering in transmission, in context, and in response to the aesthetic and theological choices of the scribe or compiler. But as these examples show, creative responses to specific biblical source material can be remarkably consistent over a period of several centuries. Each of these poems has a different range of sources; not all return to the biblical origins, but some build on or translate earlier texts. The smallest shifts in expression, in the ordering of material, in tone, affect the potential response of the poem's readers. The dramatic scenario of the biblical source plays a large part in ensuring a sense of intimacy in its lyric rewriting, and the use of direct speech enhances this. In a public reading context, the intimate address of Christ to man can open up a small private space for a listener to engage on both a spiritual and an emotional level. The Takamiya version of the poem provides the most coherent narrative of the medieval lyrics in terms of how it engages emotional affect in order to achieve a spiritual response. This is partly through its aesthetic qualities, but also through clarity of didactic purpose, and a coherent argument and narrative.

This is largely the point of such lyrics. Aesthetic judgement is only valid insofar as the literary qualities of the text enhance the spiritual process. These are functional texts, which harness the possibilities of condensed poetic language and metaphor as part of a range of preaching tools focused on salvation. In each of its Middle English written contexts, this poem is mediated through the explanations of the preacher and scribe. This is not simply a matter of identifying and visually demarcating the separate voices in the manuscripts, but also indicating the nature of the spiritual negotiations and exchange that it dramatises.

Furthermore, these poems contribute to the evidence of the porosity between the various textual aspects of worship: poetry, prayer, liturgy and Bible all work together in devotional practice and experience. The dividing lines between communal worship and private reading and prayer are not clear; the same material can be employed across these boundaries. The emotional impact of the Song of Songs alongside the depiction of the crucified Christ can operate both in the public context of sermon delivery and the more intimate setting of private reading. However, a comparison of different versions of a poem like this, tracing its development over time, and examining its manuscript and likely reading contexts, raises more questions than it answers. Ultimately, much about Middle English lyric is unknowable, despite the thorough work of earlier scholars, editors and cataloguers. This unknowability frustrates efforts to push scholarship further. We can analyse the verbal detail of each poem, itemise the differences between surviving versions and the implications for reception and interpretation, determine what the manuscript context tells us about likely audience and reading context, consider the intertextual and biblical allusions, and the relationship with other textual sources including the liturgy – and these processes are reflected in this chapter. But we cannot, in most cases, re-create the 'original' text, nor can we identify the author, the reason or occasion for composition, the lost manuscript witnesses, or the reading experience for the poem's medieval readers and listeners. What we can show, with lyrics such as this, is the way in which poetic ideas can be part of a dynamic process, stretching across time, and across languages.

11

Compiling the Lyric: Richard Rolle, Textual Dynamism and Devotional Song in London, British Library, Additional MS 37049

Katherine Zieman

London, British Library, Additional MS 37049, fols 36v–37r[1]

I

    Þe luf of God, whoso will lere,   *learn*   (cf. *Com* 217–20)[2]
    In his hert þe name of Jhesu he bere;
    For it puts oute þe fende & makes hym flee,   *vanquishes; devil*
    And fils a man with charyte.
5   Þerfore, to purche[s] þe ioy þat euer sal last,
    Deuoutly in Jhesu your hertes 3e kast.

    Jhesu, receyfe my hert & to þi luf me bryng;   (*ED* 196–7)
    Alle my desyre þou art; I couet þe, my Kyng.   *desire*
    To thynk is gret pyte, how demed þou art to ded,   *condemned* (*ED* 188–91)
10 And nayled on a tre, þe bright angels brede.   *food*
    Dryfen þou art to deole þat art our gastly gode,   *affliction; spiritual*
    And fowled as a fole, in heuen þe halows fode.   *defiled; saints'*

    Allas, my ioy & my swetyng is demed for to hyng! *darling* (*ED* 181–7)
    Nayled is his hende & nayled is his fete,
15 And þirled is his syde, so semely & so swete.   *pierced*
    Nakyd is his whyte breste, and rede his blody syde;

Lyrics are also explored in relation to adjacent visual materials in the essays by A. S. Lazikani (Chapter 2), 'Moving Lights: An Affective Reading of *On leome is in þis world ilist* and Church Wall Paintings', and Anne Marie D'Arcy (Chapter 8), '"Written in gold upon a purple stain": Mariological Rhetoric and the Material Culture of Aureate Diction'. The prose lineation of verse is also examined in Natalie Jones (Chapter 7), '*Ihesus woundes so wide* and the *fons vitae*: Text, Image and the Manuscript Context'.

1   NIMEV 3416.
2   Abbreviations in brackets indicate material derived from Rolle's Latin and English prose treatises, cited by text and line or chapter number. *Com* : *The Commandment*; *ED*: *Ego Dormio*; *FL*: *The Form of Living*; *IA*: *Incendium amoris*. For the three English prose treatises, see *Richard Rolle: Prose and Verse*, ed. S. J. Ogilvie-Thomson, EETS OS 293 (Oxford, 1988). For *Incendium amoris*, see *The Incendium amoris of Richard Rolle of Hampole*, ed. M. Deanesly (Manchester, 1915).

	Wan was his fayr hewe, his woundes depe & wyde.	*complexion*
	In fyfe stedes of his flesche þe blode gan downe glyde	*places*
	As streme dos of þe strande: þis payne is noght to hyde!	*torrent*
20	A wondyr it is to se, whoso vnderstode	(ED 192–5)
	How God of maieste was dying on þe rode.	*cross*
	Bot sothe þan is it sayd þat luf ledes þe ryng:	*truly; love leads the dance*
	Þat hym so lawe has layd, bot luf it was no thyng.	*low; without*
	Now Jhesu, þat with þi blode me boght,	(cf. ED 196–8)
25	Þat fro þi hert gon ryn,	
	Þow make me clere of al my syn,	*clean*
	And fest þi luf into my þoght,	*attach; thought/mind*
	So þat we neuer more twyn. Amen.	*separate*

II[3]

	I knaw no þinge þat so inwardly þi luf to God wyl brynge	(cf. Com 188–93)
30	As of Cristes Passion & deth deuoute þinkynge.	*devout thoughts*
	For fro þou be vsed þerin hawntyngly,[4]	*frequently*
	Þe wil þinke it more swete þan al erthly melody.	
	For erthly solace and myrth is bot noysum þinge	*annoying*
	Ta a mans hert þat in luf of God is brynynge.	*to; burning*
35	For he þat lufes God brynyngly euere mange	*passionately; mingling*
	Has myrth & melody in angelle sange	*song*
	Þerfore, þe luf of God, whoso wil lere,	(cf. Com 217–20)
	In hert þis name Jhesu he bere.	
	For it puttes oute þe fende & makes hym flee,	*vanquishes*
40	And fils a man with chariyte.	
	Þerfore, to purches þe ioy þat euer sal laste,	
	Deuoutely in Jhesu 30ur hertes 3e caste.	

III

	Whils I satte in a chapel in my prayere,	(cf. IA, ch. 15)
	A heuenly sounde to me drewe nere,	
45	For þe sange of sanges I felt in me	
	And my þought turned into luf dyte	*ditty/song*
	Of þe heuenly and sweetest armony,	
	Þe whilk I toke in mynde delitabylly;	*which, internalised delightfully*
50	Þerfore, I sytt and syng of luf langyng, þat in my breste is bred.	*generated* (ED 284–5)
	Ihesu, Ihesu, Ihesu, my kynge & my ioynge,	*joy*
	When wer I to þe ledde?	*will I be*
	Ihesu receyfe my hert and to þi luf me brynge.	(ED 196–7)

---

3   NIMEV 4076 ; DIMEV 2204.
4   'from the time that you become proficient in doing so frequently'.

Al my desyre þou ert; I couet þin cumynge.	are; yearn for
55 In luf þou wounde my þoght and lyft my hert to þe.	encircle (ED 203–5)
Þe saule þou has dere boght. Þi lufer make to bee.	lover
Bot þe I couet noght. Þis warld for þe I flee.	except for; nothing
When wil þou cum to comforth me, and brynge me oute of care,	(FL 598–601)
and gyf me, þat I may se, hafyng þe euermare.	having
60 Þi luf is ay swettest of al þat euer ware.	always
My hert when sal it bryst, þan langwys I na mare.	burst/break; languish
Ihesu, my saule þu mende, þi luf into me sende,	(ED 201–2)
Þat I may with þe lende in ioy withouten ende.	dwell
A wonder it is to se, whoso vnderstod,	(ED 192–5)
65 How God of mageste was dyinge on þe rode.	
Bot sothe þan is it sayd þat luf ledes þe rynge:	love leads the dance
Þat hym so lawe has layd, bot luf it was no þinge.	low; without
In fyfe stedes of his flesche his blode gan downe glyde	places (ED 186–9)
As streme dos of þe strande: þis payne is noght to hyde!	torrent
70 To þinke it is gret pyte, how demyd he is to dede,	
And nayled on a tre, þe bright angels brede.[5]	

Amongst the various devotional texts found in the well-known Carthusian miscellany, London, British Library, Additional MS 37049, are three that are relatively unusual in that their author is known. Grouped together in the same opening (fols 36v–37r), all three are drawn from the writings of Richard Rolle, the fourteenth-century Yorkshire hermit, whose image takes up most of the inner column of the page on the right of the opening (Figs. 1 and 2).[6]

---

5   These Rollean lyrics are authorial transcriptions from London, British Library, Additional MS 37049, fols 36v–37r (digitised at http://www.bl.uk/manuscripts/BriefDisplay.aspx), with expansions indicated by italics. As mentioned in this chapter, the poems are unlineated in the manuscripts. Rolle's metrical forms are variable and thus difficult to lineate consistently. Gestures towards lineation have been made by both the scribe and the corrector: the scribe has punctuated the texts with the use of *punctus* and majuscule letters to indicate metrical divisions ('lines'). Both are inconsistent in the first poem, shifting punctuation indicating six-stress long lines and shorter three-stress lines. While the scribe maintains the same inconsistency in the third poem, the corrector here has been more aggressive in marking the text as three-stress short lines. I have nonetheless maintained the more conventional form of long lines for the sake of consistency. On the long line form, see D. Sawyer, 'Codicological Evidence of Reading in Late Medieval England, with Particular Reference to Practical Pastoral Verse' (unpublished Ph.D. dissertation, University of Oxford, 2016), pp. 184–6; and E. Solopova, 'Layout, Punctuation, and Stanza Patterns in the English Verse', *Studies in the Harley Manuscript: The Scribes, Contents, and Social Contexts of British Library MS Harley 2253*, ed. S. Fein (Kalamazoo, MI, 2000), pp. 377–89.

6   Fol. 37r as well as other images of Rolle in the manuscript have been discussed by J. Brantley, *Reading in the Wilderness: Private Devotion and Public Performance in Late Medieval England* (Chicago, 2007), pp. 134–52.

Given that medieval lyrics, and especially religious lyrics, are so often anonymous, such an identification might seem to provide a stable footing from which to begin an analysis. Yet Rolle's presence ultimately raises questions about the relationship between the author and texts transmitted within a genre characterised by 'textual dynamism', as Ardis Butterfield has called it.[7] This dynamism is well-evidenced in the texts of these lyrics, creating problems of interpretation not only within each poem, but also across all three as they are juxtaposed with each other and with the two images in the opening. The various repetitions and seeming dislocations of lines suggest a different understanding of what constitutes the poetic object than is generally implied by the modern term 'lyric' and ultimately prompt a different understanding of authorship in relation to such texts. In this analysis, I hope to show that the Carthusian compilers of this opening articulated their understanding of these relationships through the concept of song. More specifically, they draw upon Rolle's spiritual experience of *canor*, or angelic song, as both inspiration for and authorisation of their own iterations of his vernacular lyrics in ways that allow us to understand both the form and the purpose of their compilation practices.

The hearing of angelic song was the most distinctive of Rolle's contemplative experiences as well as the one for which he was best known. Whilst it was linked to ideas of passion associated with medieval discussions of liturgical song, *canor* was heard with only the spiritual senses.[8] As angels rejoicing amongst themselves would have no need of human language, it did not involve words, let alone vernacular lyrics. Yet *canor* was remarkable amongst contemplative aspirations in that to hear angelic song was not to receive a particular vision or message, but rather to be attuned to a spiritual presence that revealed itself simultaneously with, and often in conflict with, mundane reality.[9] Associating this higher spiritual state with musicality – and specifically with song – left an indelible imprint on Rolle's writing. Marked by a flamboyant style often described as 'rhapsodic',[10] Rolle's prose emphasises extravagant emotion that at times seems to be prioritised over the construction of a linear argument. Formally, his prose is peppered with dramatic rhetorical gestures of *exclamatio* and *apostrophe*, which construct the speaker in relation to a divine presence. It is often structured by relentless alliteration, creating audible patterns of sound that focus as much attention on the embodied and affective experience of language as they do on the semantic

---

7   A. Butterfield, 'The Construction of Textual Form: Cross-lingual Citation in Some Medieval Lyrics', *Citation, Intertextuality and Memory in the Middle Ages and Renaissance*, ed. Y. Plumley, G. di Bacco and S. Jossa (Exeter, 2011), pp. 41–57 (p. 55).

8   See N. Zeeman, 'The Theory of Passionate Song', *Medieval Latin and Middle English Literature: Essays in Honour of Jill Mann*, ed. C. Cannon and M. Nolan (Cambridge, 2011), pp. 240–50.

9   K. Zieman, 'The Perils of *Canor*: Mystical Authority, Alliteration, and Extragrammatical Meaning in Rolle, the *Cloud-author*, and Hilton', *Yearbook of Langland Studies* 22 (2008), 138–45.

10 N. Watson, *Richard Rolle and the Invention of Authority* (Cambridge, 1991), pp. 20, 148, 172, *et passim*.

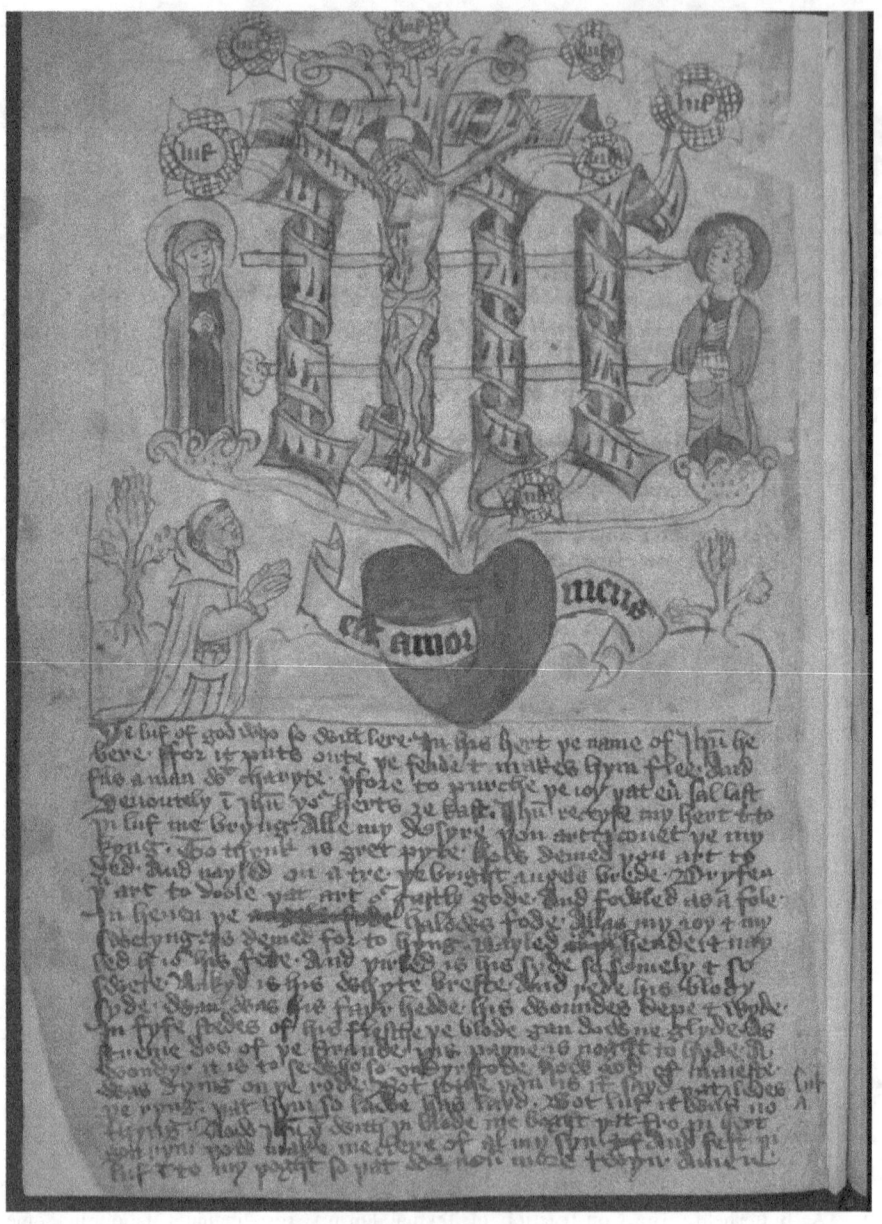

Fig 1: © The British Library Board. London, British Library, Additional MS 37049, fol. 36v

Compiling the Lyric: Richard Rolle and Devotional Song

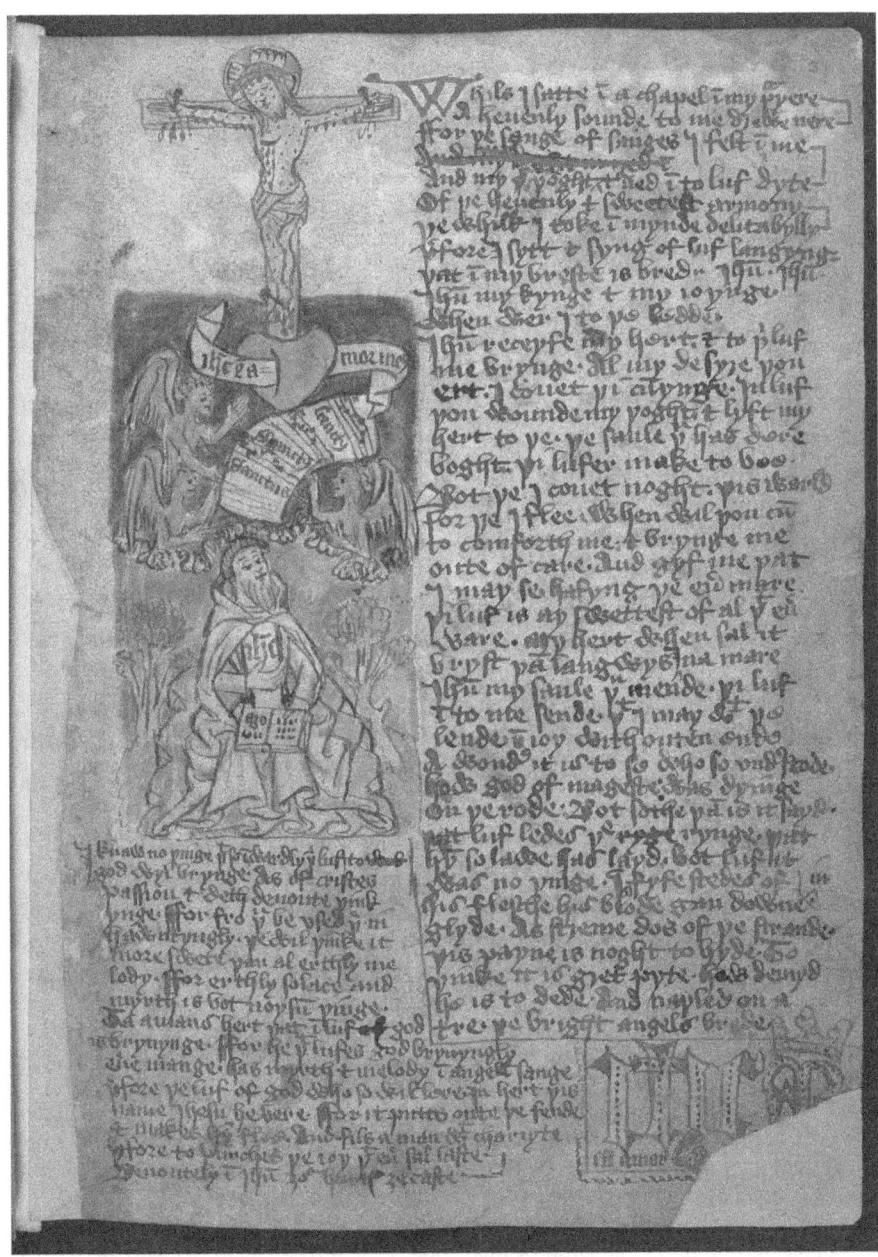

Fig 2: © The British Library Board. London, British Library, Additional MS 37049, fol. 37r

content of his words.¹¹ *Canor* thus comes to be associated with a style of writing and of engaging language – an emphasis on formal patterning, the construction of a sense of temporal presence – that modern theorists associate with the lyric.¹²

Yet if Rolle's prose could be described as 'lyrical', it was only in the context of his writing in English that he produced what we might consider 'lyrics', that is, discrete textual objects structured by these lyrical features.¹³ His *Form of Living* and *Ego Dormio*, texts written for his unlettered spiritual protégés, contain four poems, or 'songs', as he calls them, that are set apart from the rest of the prose text: 'Now I write a songe of loue þat þou shalt haue delite jn w[hen] þou art louynge Ihesu Criste', he states, to introduce the song with which he ends the *Ego Dormio*.¹⁴ As these treatises are designed as contemplative manuals, Rolle speaks less in the confessional mode that marks the works written for his latinate peers and more from the position of a spiritual mentor. Thus whilst his lyrical language in his Latin writings may have served to register the elevated spiritual state that resulted from his hearing of *canor*, his vernacular songs were designed to be used by others, provided as lyrical scripts to help aspiring contemplatives effect a disposition receptive to *canor*, as he makes clear in *The Form of Living*: 'amonge oþer affecciouns and songes þou may synge this in þyn herte to thy [lord] Ihesu, wh[en] þou coueiteste his comynge and [thy] goynge' (lines 595–7). These songs, Rolle suggests, serve both as a means of initiating communion with the divine presence and as a means of transport. Thus it is largely through the reconceptualisation of his relationship to his audience that Rolle's lyricism crystalised in discrete texts we would call 'lyrics'.

In this regard, the nature of Rolle's songs is illuminated by Butterfield's definition of poetry, as 'the creation of manuscript and authorial mediation of sound into sense for public consumption'.¹⁵ Though they cultivate the language of interiority, it is what David Lawton has called 'public interiority' – an interiority that is personal and deeply felt, yet one that can be inhabited by others with equal intensity.¹⁶ Whilst these devotional songs are offered to a 'public' as discrete

---

11 Zieman, 'The Perils of *Canor*', 144.
12 J. Culler, *Theory of the Lyric* (Cambridge, Mass., 2015), pp. 186–242, 172–85.
13 For a recent discussion of defining the lyric in medieval England, see I. Nelson, *Lyric Tactics: Poetry, Genre, and Practice in Later Medieval England* (Philadelphia, 2016). Whilst her theory of lyric appears to be consistent with much of this analysis, her book was published too recently for me to fully incorporate her ideas.
14 *Ego Dormio*, lines 265–6, in Ogilvie-Thomson, ed., *Rolle: Prose and Verse*. All further quotations from Rolle's English writings will refer to this edition and will be cited parenthetically by line number. These lyrics, or various recensions of them, appear to have circulated independently (though all extent independent versions survive in larger Rolle collections). The poems of Add. 37049 are, however, closest textually to the versions that are embedded in the prose treatises. For more on the independent lyrics, see Ogilvie-Thomson, ed., *Rolle: Prose and Verse*, pp. lxxxi–lxxxiii, and R. Hanna, ed., *Richard Rolle: Uncollected Prose and Verse*, EETS OS 329 (Oxford, 2007), pp. lxi–lxiv.
15 A. Butterfield, 'Why Medieval Lyric?' *English Literary History* 82 (2015), 319–43 (336).
16 D. Lawton, 'Voice After Arundel', *After Arundel: Religious Writing in Fifteenth-Century England*, ed. V. Gillespie and K. Ghosh (Turnhout, 2011), pp. 133–51, and discussed further

textual objects, it is not their specific, ossified forms that make them songs, as subsequent mediations involving both the text and *mise-en-page* will show. Their formal features define them as a different way of using language and communicating. One could argue that, for Rolle, this different way of communicating was ultimately more important than what was said.

Whether or not one could make such a claim about Rolle, it is clear that his Carthusian redactors either created or inherited a sense of 'Rollean' song that did not depend on maintaining the specific forms that were presented in his treatises.[17] The three poems that appear in fols 36v–37r of Add. 37049 are entirely made up of passages from Rolle's writings. As if following Rolle's instructions, the compilers present them as distinct scripts that, here juxtaposed with images, might be used to inspire devotion. Indeed the poems contain long passages drawn from the scripted songs embedded in the *Ego Dormio* and *Form of Living*, which contribute 75 per cent of poem I (lines 7–28) and 75 per cent of poem III (lines 50–71).[18] Yet the scripts are not followed verbatim. Rather, they are centonates, patchworks of passages variously arranged. This textual state of affairs is in many ways indicative of medieval lyrics in general. The poems demonstrate the kind of variation Paul Zumthor termed *mouvance* – variation that he believed derived from oral transmission and an understanding of textuality based more on the dynamics of performance than on the preservation of ossified works.[19] Julia Boffey has discussed a similar patchwork of courtly formulae in a lyric derived from John Lydgate's writings.[20] It is here that Butterfield's 'textual dynamism' comes into play. Her account describes the production of lyrics in terms based less on notions of vertical transmission from one copy to the next than on a set of horizontal relations involving 'cluster[s] of verbal and musical materials' on which creators draw.[21] Such an account makes sense not only of the lyrics as they have been mediated in Add. 37049, but also of Rolle's 'original' songs, insofar as one might reconstitute them, which themselves draw on prior materials, familiar tropes and conventional rhymes.[22] In fact, it is likely that Rolle himself created different recensions of his lyrics.

in 'Public Interiorities', *Handbook of Middle English Studies*, ed. M. Turner (West Sussex, 2013), pp. 93–107.

17 'Carthusian redactors' is used as a rhetorical expedient to refer to the indeterminable number of people (perhaps not all Carthusian) who had a hand in transmitting the poems in their various forms.

18 The precise line numbers are listed in detail in the edition of the poems at the head of this chapter. These identifications are based on those made by R. Hanna, *The English Manuscripts of Richard Rolle: A Descriptive Catalogue* (Exeter, 2010), pp. 78–9, and Brantley, *Reading in the Wilderness*, pp. 315–16, though with some revisions.

19 P. Zumthor, *La Poésie et la Voix dans la Civilisation Médiévale* (Paris, 1984), pp. 42–4, translated as *Towards a Medieval Poetics*, trans. P. Bennett (Minneapolis, 1992), pp. 41–9.

20 J. Boffey, 'Middle English Lyrics: Texts and Interpretation', *Medieval Literature: Texts and Interpretation*, ed. T. Machan (Binghamton, N.Y., 1991), pp. 128–9.

21 Butterfield, 'Why Medieval Lyric?', 330.

22 Hope Emily Allen notes, for example, echoes of *Jesu dulcis memoria*, as well as of several of Rolle's other works in one of the lyrics found in *The Form of Living*, in *Writings Ascribed*

But if the songs were not composed as ossified artefacts consisting of a linear succession of words, they are nonetheless made up of clusters of words perceived as formally patterned units. The differing arrangements of lines between Poem I and its closest extant version embedded in the *Ego Dormio* suggest a modular construction, wherein the integrity of rhymes is largely maintained and metrical patterns are salient:

Add. 37049
Jhesu, receyfe my hert & to þi luf me bryng;
Alle my desyre þou art; I couet þe, my Kyng.

To thynk is gret pyte, how demed þou art to ded,
And nayled on a tre, þe bright angels brede.
Dryfen þou art to deole þat art *our* gastly gode,
And fowled as a fole, in heuen þe halows fode.

Allas, my ioy & my swetyng is demed for to hyng!
Nayled is his hende & nayled is his fete,
And þirled is his syde, so semely & so swete.
Nakyd is his whyte breste, and rede his blody syde;
Wan was his fayr hewe, his woundes depe & wyde.
In fyfe stedes of his flesche þe blode gan downe glyde
As streme dos of þe strande: þis payne is noght to hyde!

A wondyr it is to se, whoso vnderstode
How God of maieste was dying on þe rode.
Bot sothe þan is it sayd þat luf ledes þe ryng:
Þat hym so lawe has layd, bot luf it was no thyng.

Ego Dormio, lines 181–97 (Longleat 29)[23]
Alas, my ioy and my swetynge is d[em]ed for to heng.
Naillet was his hende & naillet was his feet,
And þurlet is his side, so semly and so swete.
Naked his white breste, and rede his blody side;
Wan was his faire hewe, his woundes depe and wide.
In fyve stiddes of his fleisssche þe blode kan doun glide
As stremes done on þe strand[e]; þis peyn is nat to hide!

To þynke is gret pitte, how demed he is to deth,
And nailled on þe tre, þe bright angels brede.
Dryfen he is to dele þat is oure gostly good,
And fouled as a fole, in heuyn þe [halowes] food.

A wonder hit is to se, who-som vndrestood,
How God of mageste was deynge on þe roode.
Bot soth þan is hit said þat loue ledes þe rynge:
Þat hym so low hath leyd, bot loue hit was no thynge.

Ihesu, receyue my hert and to þi [loue] me brynge;
Al my desire þou art; I couait þi comynge.

The passage on the crucifixion might be said to have four modular elements: an address to Jesus ('Ihesu receyfe my hert') and two more distanced reflections ('To thynk is gret pyte', 'A wondyr it is to se') share the same metrical form with rhyme at the half-line, which distinguishes them from the more immediate exclamatory description ('Allas, my ioy'), which is itself structured by syntactic repetition rather than medial rhyme.[24] In the *Ego Dormio*'s version, the address to Jesus follows the experience of the Crucifixion, where it introduces another fourteen lines of prayer; in Add. 37049, by contrast, the address, extended by one of the reflective

to Richard Rolle, Hermit of Hampole, and Materials for His Biography (New York, 1927), pp. 289–90; passages from the *Candet nudatum pectus* (NIMEV 4088; DIMEV 6540.5) in one of the *Ego Dormio* songs are identified in NIMEV 2250; DIMEV 3617.

23 Warminster, Longleat, MS 29 was Ogilvie-Thomson's copy text for her edition. Whilst there are one or two variants in the section that do affect the lines and their order, they are less significant than the variants that occur in a lyric using the same material that appears independently of the *Ego Dormio*. See Ogilvie-Thomson, ed., *Rolle: Prose and Verse*, 'Lyrics (ii)', pp. 44–5, and Hanna, ed., *Rolle: Uncollected Prose*, pp. 24–5.

24 This more immediate passage has its source in the pseudo-Augustinian *Candet nudatum pectus*. See R. Hanna, 'Editing "Middle English Lyrics": The Case of *Candet Nudatum Pectus*', *Medium Aevum* 80 (2011), 189–200 (195).

passages recast in the second person, introduces the more vivid exclamation. Whilst there is little difference in the 'meaning' of the poem, there is a different choreography of affect and relation.[25] In the *Ego Dormio* version, one is moved to prayer by the vision of the Passion, whereas in Add. 37049 prayer initiates vision.

These differences are no doubt related to the framing of the passage. On either side of the verses are passages in four-stress couplets more reminiscent of pastoral verse than Rolle's canorous long lines. The first of these introduces the Passion meditation by referring to devotion to the Holy Name (lines 1–6), thus fusing this devotion with meditation on the Passion. This synthesis is most evident in the image, where the ascender of the 'h' in the trigrammaton 'ihc' becomes the upright of the cross on which Christ's suffering body hangs. It may at first appear an odd combination as it brings together detailed visceral description of the crucified body of Christ with a seemingly more abstract object of veneration. The prefatory lines seem to attribute almost talismanic power to the Holy Name: 'it puts oute þe fende & makes hym flee' (line 3). Yet the Holy Name functions not solely as an object, but also as a medium of relation. Whilst the trigrammaton 'ihc' dominates the image as a visual object, it also functions as a meaningful word, forming part of the declaration continued in the scroll that pierces the heart at the bottom of the image: 'ihc est amor meus'. Similarly, after the prefatory lines extolling the virtues of the Holy Name, the poem restates this declaration using it as a form of direct address: 'Jhesu, receyfe my hert' (line 7). The Holy Name becomes, for the supplicant who performs it, a point of entry. Whereas, as Sarah McNamer has argued,[26] meditation on the Passion was designed to elicit a connection to Christ through the cultivation of compassionate emotion, here it is also the act of address that initiates that connection.

Devotion to the Holy Name, furthermore, was a devotion specifically associated with Rolle.[27] Although his name appears nowhere in it, his presence governs the opening and signals that, even as the poems seem to participate in horizontal relationships, to be drawn from 'a cluster of verbal … materials that is (in part) common intellectual property',[28] the relationship of these words to Rolle in particular is important. There is, in other words, a vertical relationship implied by the distinctively 'Rollean' nature of the devotion represented. This relationship

---

25   The fact that the verses of the songs could be freely rearranged without obvious disruptions attests to the modularity of Rolle's verses as part of his style. H. E. Allen characterised Rolle's frequent metrical shifts as 'formlessness' and suggests that such formlessness 'may almost be called indicative of his authorship': *Writings Ascribed to Richard Rolle*, p. 288.
26   S. McNamer, *Affective Meditation and the Invention of Medieval Compassion* (Philadelphia, 2010).
27   On Rolle and devotion to the Holy Name, see D. Renevey, 'Name Above Names: The Devotion to the Name of Jesus from Richard Rolle to Walter Hilton's *Scale of Perfection* I', *The Medieval Mystical Tradition: England, Ireland and Wales: Exeter Symposium VI*, ed. M. Glasscoe (Cambridge, 1999), pp. 103–22, as well as Allen, *Writings Ascribed to Richard Rolle*, pp. 314–17, 349–51.
28   Butterfield, 'Why Medieval Lyric?', 330.

is underscored still further by the central image of him with a book in his lap – a book on which the visible word 'ego' declares the incipit of the textual source of much of the poems' language: *Ego Dormio*.[29] Yet whilst one might call the relationship of Rolle to his words one of authorship, that relationship is arguably secondary to the relationship of exemplarity that the opening encourages between Rolle and his readers. His words are uniquely authorised by his privileged position as exemplary contemplative, such that to reiterate them allows the reader to resonate with the sacred presence to which Rolle had access.

The repetition of poetic material across the opening underscores this sense of resonance and provides further insight into the complex nature of the relationship between contemplative and song. The beginning lines of Poem I (lines 1–6) reappear as the final six lines of Poem II (lines 37–42); the address to Jesus from one of the *Ego Dormio* songs occurs both in Poem I (lines 7–8) and in a similar position in Poem III (lines 53–4), as do several passages on the Passion, though in reverse order (lines 9–10, 18–19, 20–3 in Poem I recur in lines 70–1, 68–9, 64–7 of Poem III). Both poems on the right side of the opening are thus formal mirrors of the poem on the left. Though it is impossible from our vantage point to recover the precise series of mediations and mediators that produced these Rollean texts, the decision to place them on facing leaves creates a diptych in which these juxtaposed texts respond to each other. The images that accompany the texts function in a similarly recombinatory fashion, as the elements of the Crucifixion, the Holy Name, and the heart pierced with the scroll declaring love for Jesus are deconstructed and rearranged in each image, creating visual resonance between the two leaves.

More specifically, the left side depicts the devotional act of the contemplative inspired by Rolle, as modelled by the Carthusian monk in the lower left of the image, whose gaze travels upwards towards the image of the crucifix. In response, the right side seems to depict the divine response that the contemplative should hope for in the image of Rolle's hearing of the angelic choir. Poem II, in the inner column, makes this connection explicit. It begins by versifying part of a passage from *The Commandment* that was copied on the leaf prior to this one (fol. 35v):

> Werely I knawe no þinge þat so inwardly sal take þi hert to couet gods luf & to desyre þe ioy of heuen & to dispise þe vanytes of þis warld as stedfast þinkyng of þe disese & of þe woundes & of þe ded of Ihesu criste. It wil rayse þi þoght abowue erthly þinge & make þi hert to byrne in þe luf of god & purches þe suetnes & sauour of heuen into þi saule.[30]

Added to the passage, however, is the promise that once one has become accustomed to the discipline of such meditation ('fro þou be vsed þerin hawntyngly', line 30), it will not only become figuratively 'more swete þan al

---

29 Brantley, *Reading in the Wilderness*, p. 143.
30 cf. *The Commandment*, lines 188–93; Brantley, *Reading in the Wilderness*, pp. 146–7.

Compiling the Lyric: Richard Rolle and Devotional Song

erthly melody' (lines 31–2), but, still further, the 'suetnes & sauour of heuen' will be experienced as 'myrth & melody in angel sange' (line 36). The promise of heavenly melody in turn ('Þerfore' [line 37]) leads the compiler back to the Holy Name that on the facing page had been so closely connected to

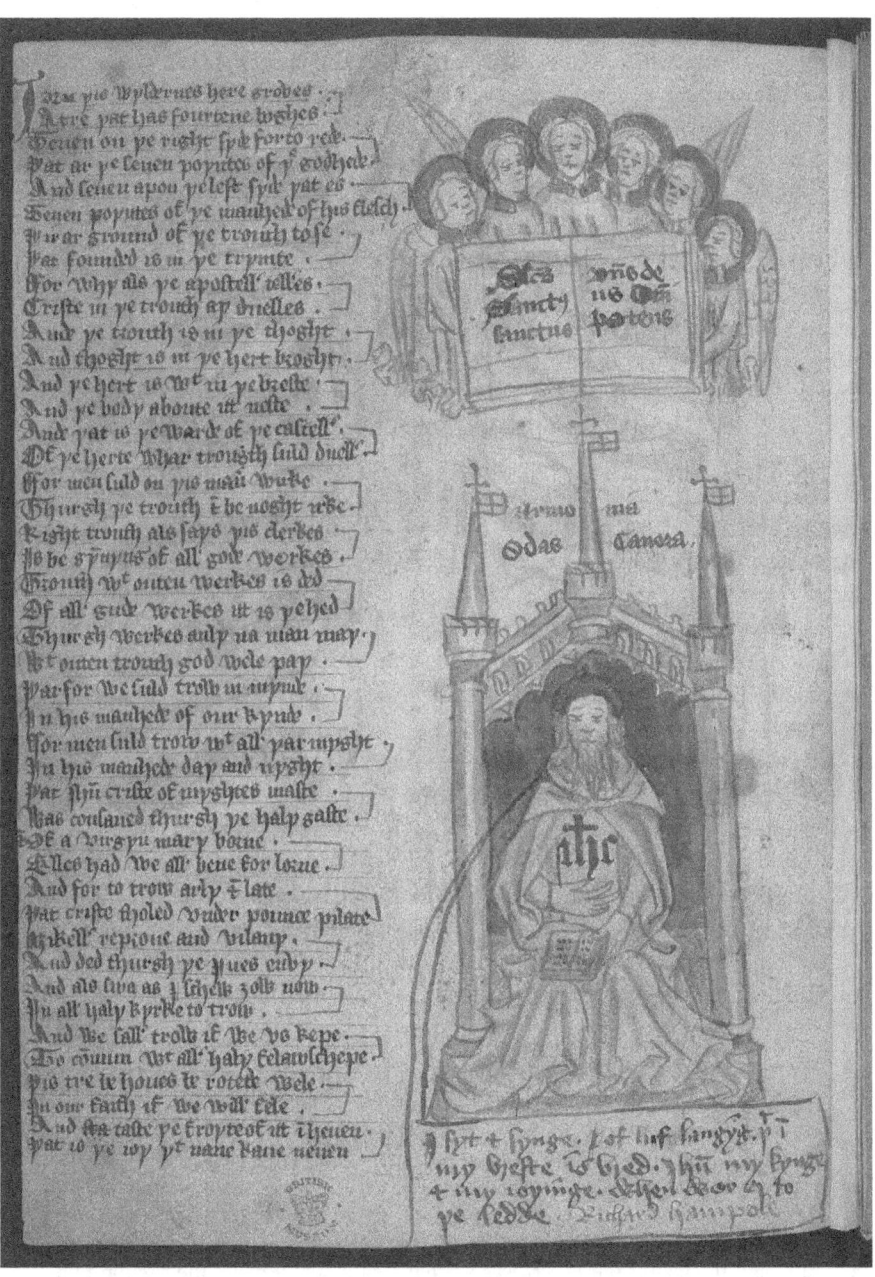

Fig. 3: © The British Library Board. London, British Library, Additional MS 37049, fol. 52v.

meditation on the Passion. The prefatory verses of the first poem are thus reinforced as a resonant refrain of the second.

The image on the right, depicting Rolle's hearing of *canor*, might at first seem to reinforce this pairing of call and response, cause and effect. Yet this image signifies within the same economy of repetition and recombinatory juxtaposition as do the words of the poem in ways that suggest a more complex relationship. Whilst the image contains many of the elements also seen in the image on the left, the composition of those elements has been appropriated from elsewhere: it is based on the image of Rolle that appears in connection with *The Desert of Religion* occurring later in this manuscript (fol. 52v) (Fig. 3), as well as in London, British Library, Cotton MS Faustina B VI, part II, fol. 8v.[31] There, the image is not directly related to the content of the text, but rather serves as one in a series of images of exemplary hermits that accompanies it. In Add. 37049's version of the *Desert*, however, Rolle's image also includes a couplet below it from one of Rolle's songs: 'I syt and synge of luf langy*ng* þat in my breste is bred / Ih*es*u my kynge *and* my ioynge, when wer I to þe ledde'. This couplet appears in one of the *Ego Dormio* songs as well as in a recension of the lyric that circulated independently.[32] Placed below the image, the couplet is followed by the name 'Richard Hampole' in red, identifying both the image and the trademark couplet that associated the hermit not solely with hearing angelic song, but with producing song as well.[33] Both the image and the page layout have been re-created in the opening on fol. 37r, with the space occupied by the *Desert* text here filled by Poem III. In this case, however, the poem is directly related to the image. Beginning with material translated and versified from Rolle's *Incendium amoris*, the poem relates the moment when Rolle first heard angelic song.[34] The prefatory verses serve as a gloss for the image and ultimately for the entire opening: Rolle's poetry is said to have been inspired by his hearing of *canor*, an experience that transformed his 'þought ... into luf dyte' (line 46), leading him to produce the trademark couplet attributed to him in the *Desert* image: 'Þerfore I sytt *and* syng of luf langyng, þat i*n* my breste is bred' (line 50). If the poem on the left of the opening suggests that Rollean song will allow one to hear *canor*, the poems on the right suggest that Rollean song is an effect of *canor*: Rolle 'sits and sings' *because* he has experienced angels' song.

The experience of *canor* conveyed in the opening is therefore not a matter of call and response but rather of simultaneous resonance with the eternal. Its effects

---

31   On the relationship between the extant manuscripts of the *Desert* and their illustrations, see A. McGovern-Mouron, 'The Desert of Religion in British Library Cotton Faustina B VI, Pars II', *The Mystical Tradition and the Carthusians*, ed. J. Hogg (Salzburg, 1997), pp. 149–62.

32   Hanna, *English Manuscripts of Richard Rolle*, p. 79; Ogilvie-Thomson, ed., *Rolle: Prose and Verse*, p. 45; Hanna, ed., *Rolle: Uncollected Prose*, p. 25.

33   Although the text of the *Desert* was written by a different hand, the caption under the image appears in the same hand as the poems on fols 36v–37r.

34   Deansley, ed., *Incendium amoris*, pp. 189–90 (ch. 15).

are meant to be internalised, perceived with the heart in ways that paradoxically obscure the agency of the singular will. The core of Poem III reinforces this idea by presenting a collection of passages that, after the fashion of a verbal concordance, all collocate the words 'love' and 'heart' (lines 53–4 [*ED*, lines 196–7]; lines 55–7 [*ED*, lines 203–5]; lines 58–61 [*FL*, lines 598–601]). Conventionally figured as the seat of passion and immediacy,[35] particularly in relation to the production of courtly song that the poem's language invokes, the heart is also the site of internalisation, as when one sings a song 'by heart'. This latter understanding of the heart was also relevant to liturgical song, on which the idea of the angelic choir is to some degree based.[36] To sing liturgical song from memory (by heart) was to perform one's internalisation and embodiment of sacred texts – to assimilate oneself to the text as a public interiority. Insofar as this assimilation was experienced viscerally, within one's body, it could be deeply personal and self-actualising, what Foucault called a 'technology of the self',[37] even if that self was a public interiority. The devotional expressions that issue from such an experience come both from the unmediated passions of the heart and from forces that act upon the heart: 'Ihesu receyfe my hert … and lyft my hert to þe' (lines 53, 55).

The recombinatory elements of the images reflect this complex sense of song. On the left, the heart is the pictorially explicit root of reflection on the Passion that grows upward to blossom in flowers containing 'luf'. On the right, that same heart is situated at the top of the image. The scroll that pierces the heart with its declaration of love for Jesus appears to be contiguous with the scroll containing the music and words of the angelic hymn 'Sanctus, sanctus, sanctus'. The music further serves as a visual conduit for the eye, creating a sense of movement from the scroll down towards the figure of the hermit who hears the song below. Just as the poem implies that the hearing of angelic song leads to the writing of devotional verse, the image depicts the hermit displaying the book of songs that he has been inspired to write.

The variation that arose from the transmission of those songs, I would argue, differs from *mouvance*. Zumthor describes *mouvance* as a variation that arises as the product of oral transmission, where orality is seen as opposed to the fixity of writing. In this opening, however, song is connected to writing. In addition to the depiction of the textual source, the angelic choir, despite the extralinguistic nature of *canor*, is shown singing from a sheet of music. The trigrammaton, the ritualised abbreviation of the name of Jesus central to the image on the left, is constructed from the vines that sprout from the heart, but is made legible by the scrolls that envelope those vines, marked as they are by the illegible 'writing' of Christ's blood. It is this abbreviated word, both impassioned address and non-phonemic visualisation, that has been internalised by the Rolle figure on the right. Reduced in size, it is nonetheless emblazoned on the

---

35 Zeeman, 'Theory of Passionate Song', p. 238.
36 For a discussion of the place of memorised song, see K. Zieman, *Singing the New Song: Literacy and Liturgy in Late Medieval England* (Philadelphia, 2008), pp. 43, 60–2, 69–71.
37 M. Foucault, *Technologies of the Self: A Seminar with Michel Foucault*, ed. L. H. Martin, H. Gutman, and P. H. Hutton (Amherst, 1988).

chest of the hermit – a figure of the way in which the Holy Name is now 'bred in his breast'. The imagery suggests that writing represents the sacred nature of contemplative song.

The most distinctively 'written' feature of these songs, however, is their prose lineation. Although the manuscript as a whole does not show signs of meticulous planning in terms of layout, poems are consistently lineated as verse throughout.[38] Indeed, the right side of the opening retains the double-column layout of its source that was intended for lineated verse. Jessica Brantley has suggested that prose lineation is meant to be suggestive of Rolle's effusive style, as exuberance that exceeds the boundaries of the poetic line.[39] A more mundane explanation, however, is that Rolle's verses were likely not lineated in the compiler's exemplar. It was in this period still common for verses embedded in prose texts to be written in prose lineation, and such is the case for the vast majorities of extant copies of both *Ego Dormio* and *The Form of Living*.[40] The redactors' choices, as well as the scribe's and corrector's punctuation, show an awareness of Rolle's rhyme and metre, but despite this awareness, and despite the fact that the lines have been extracted from their prose context and re-embedded in versified framework, they remain in prose lineation. Indeed, the notion that Rollean song should so appear has to some extent been generalised, such that some of the prefatory verses that have been added to Rolle's lines also appear in prose lineation, as have the lines added to Rolle's portrait on fol. 52r. This generalisation demonstrates an abstract yet decided visual element in the transmission of the poem, one that arguably attests to the 'serious', proseworthy nature of Rollean song as well as to the paradoxical combination of the embodied nature of song and the more abstract and ethereal state of hearing with the 'spiritual senses' that characterises Rollean devotion.[41]

Writing in this case was not meant to guarantee the fixity of the text in performance, nor to fix the intentions of an author. The *idea* of a written text, however, stands for a devotional resource that is stable. This stability could serve to guard against the excesses of the very passions it invites, aligning the source with which one resonates with the eternal. In producing such lyrics, Rolle likely hoped to provide his vernacular readers with material that they could internalise in the way that Latin literates could internalise the Psalms. True devotion, his

---

38 There are a very few instances where it is clear that the lack of verse lineation is a matter of space; verse is also written in prose lineation in the well-known *Charter of Christ*, which is laid out to look like a legal document rather than a poem (fol. 23r), but the Rolle poems provide no such aesthetic justification.
39 Brantley, *Reading in the Wilderness*, p. 145.
40 On the format of verse embedded in prose texts, see A. S. G. Edwards, 'Editing and Manuscript Form: Middle English Verse Written as Prose', *English Studies in Canada* 27 (2001), 15–28 (21–22); see also Sawyer, 'Codicological Evidence', p. 190 ff.
41 It is worth noting in this context that Rolle does not instruct his readers to vocalise his songs aloud. His instructions are carefully worded: 'And thynke of[t] þis of his passione' (*ED*, lines 173–4); 'synge this *in þyn herte* to thy [lord] Ihesu' (*FL*, lines 596–7). He makes a point of distinguishing the 'syngynge gostly to Ihesu and in Ihesu' that arises in the highest spiritual states from 'bodily cryinge with þe mouth' (*FL*, lines 574–5).

Carthusian readers seem to imply, involves the taking in of such holy words and allowing them to become part of one's own language, to be used at will rather than as the object of disengaged rehearsal. This inextricable relationship of text and performer, of production and reception, lies at the heart of Rollean song as they represented it.

12

Lyric Interventions in *Troilus and Criseyde*

Elizabeth Robertson

Antigone's Song (Chaucer, *Troilus and Criseyde*, II, 827–75)[1]

She seyde, 'O Love, to whom I have and shal
Ben humble subgit, trewe in myn entente,
As I best kan, to yow, lord, yeve ich al   *give*
830 For everemo myn hertes lust to rente;   *as tribute*
For nevere yet thi grace no wight sente   *person*
So blisful cause as me, my lif to lede
In alle joie and seurte, out of drede.   *security*

'Ye, blisful God, han me so wel byset
835 In love, iwys, that al that bereth lyf
Ymagynen ne kouthe how to be bet;
For, lord, withouten jalousie or strif,
I love oon which is moost ententif   *attentive*
To serven wel, unweri or unfeynd,
840 That evere was, and leest with harm desteyned. *stained*

'As he that is the welle of worthynesse,
Of trouthe grownd, mirour of goodlihed,   *excellence*
Of wit Apollo, stoon of sikernesse,   *Apollo: god of wisdom*
Of vertu roote, of lust fynder and hed,   *pleasure; originator; source*
845 Thorugh which is alle sorwe fro me ded –
Iwis, I love hym best, so doth he me;
Now good thrift have he, wherso that he be!

For another essay exploring the intercalation of a lyric into longer textual material, see Natalie Jones (Chapter 7), '*Ihesus woundes so wide* and the *fons vitae* : Text, Image and the Manuscript Context'; for an essay exploring allusions to Chaucer's romances of classical antiquity and Boethian mutability in a fifteenth-century short poem, see Julia Boffey (Chapter 13), 'Poems that Speak Volumes: Lydgate's *Thoroughfare of Woe*, and Lyric as Epitome'.

1 NIMEV 3327; DIMEV 5248. The extracts from Chaucer's *Troilus and Criseyde* are reproduced from Benson, with added glossary. All further quotations from the poem are from this edition, with line numbers provided in parentheses in the text.

'Whom shulde I thanken but yow, god of Love,
Of al this blisse, in which to bathe I gynne?   *begin*
850 And thanked be ye, lord, for that I love!
This is the righte lif that I am inne,
To flemen alle manere vice and synne: *banish*
This dooth me so to vertu for t'entende,
That day by day I in my wille amende.

855 'And whoso seith that for to love is vice,
Or thraldom, though he feele in it destresse,
He outher is envyous, or right nyce,   *either*
Or is unmyghty, for his shrewednesse,   *unable; wickedness*
To loven; for swich manere folk, I gesse,   *such*
860 Defamen Love, as nothing of hym knowe.
Thei speken, but thei benten nevere his bowe!   *never tried it*

'What is the sonne wers, of kynde right,   *how; in its proper nature*
Though that a man, for fieblesse of his yen,   *eyes*
May nought endure on it to see for bright?
865 Or love the wers, though wrecches on it crien?
No wele is worth, that may no sorwe dryen.   *prosperity; endure*
And forthi, who that hath an hed of verre,   *glass*
Fro cast of stones war hym in the werre!

'But I with al myn herte and al my myght,
870 As I have seyd, wol love unto my laste
My deere herte, and al myn owen knyght,
In which myn herte growen is so faste,
And his in me, that it shal evere laste.
Al dredde I first to love hym to bigynne,   *even though I was afraid*
875 Now woot I wel, ther is no peril inne.'

Dream of the Eagle (Chaucer, *Troilus and Criseyde*, II, 918–31)

A nyghtyngale, upon a cedre grene,
Under the chambre wal ther as she ley,   *next to*
920 Ful loude song ayein the moone shene,   *against, in the face of; bright*
Peraunter in his briddes wise a lay   *by chance, way*
Of love, that made hire herte fressh and gay.
That herkned she so longe in good entente,
Til at the laste the dede slep hir hente.   *dead; seized*

925 And as she slep, anonright tho hire mette   *dreamed*
How that an egle, fethered whit as bon,
Under hire brest his longe clawes sette,
And out hire herte he rente, and that anon,   *tore*
And dide his herte into hire brest to gon –   *put*
930 Of which she nought agroos, ne nothyng smerte –   *was frightened; felt no pain*
And forth he fleigh, with herte left for herte.

The most influential definition of the lyric and one that is applied to lyrics from a variety of periods is Hegel's. He explains that in the lyric the 'content is not the object but the subject, the inner world, the mind that considers and feels, that instead of proceeding to action, remains alone with itself as inwardness and that therefore can take as its sole form and final aim the self-expression of subjective life'.[2] Hegel's understanding of the lyric, as many recent medievalists have argued, can obscure an appreciation of medieval lyrics, which address many topics from the religious to the political, which are often embedded in various types of discourse ranging from literary works to sermons to historical documents, and which occur in a variety of lengths and poetic forms.[3]

Because of this range of topics and forms, medievalists have opted for more elemental definitions, especially when lyrics appear in longer narratives; Robert Payne, for example, designates such lyrics as *distillations* and Barry Windeatt describes them as *quintessences* linked to character.[4] These more fundamental definitions are helpful, especially when we analyse the lyrics in *Troilus and Criseyde*, but they fail to point us to the social and historical functions of many medieval lyrics. We can begin to appreciate these functions by bringing to bear on the lyrics Theodor Adorno's Marxist modification of the Hegelian lyric as a 'subjective expression of a social antagonism'.[5] While Adorno's definition was intended to describe nineteenth-century lyrics, it nonetheless illuminates the double valence of lyrics, even medieval ones, and even those found in narrative contexts, as turning at once inward into the self and outward into the social and historical.

Numerous lyrics appear in *Troilus and Criseyde*, ranging from Troilus's songs to the lovers' aubades, but in this chapter I focus my attention on those particularly

---

[2] G. W. F. Hegel, *Aesthetics: Lectures on Fine Art*, trans. T. M. Knox (Oxford, 1975), p. 1038; In the most recent extended study of the lyric, Jonathan Culler acknowledges that the lyric has a complex history, with roots in 'ancient conceptions of lyric as a form of epideictic discourse (the rhetoric of praise or blame, focused on what is to be valued)', but nonetheless finds Hegel's nineteenth-century definition most applicable to lyrics of all periods. See his *Theory of the Lyric* (Cambridge, Mass. and London, 2015), pp. 1–9; the quoted material is from p. 3; Culler cites the passage from Hegel on p. 92 and discusses it on pp. 92–105.

[3] For a definitive work on the literary history of the interpolation of lyrics in narrative in French and English medieval literature see A. Butterfield, 'Interpolated Lyric in Medieval Narrative', unpublished Ph.D. Dissertation, University of Cambridge, 1987; See also J. Jahner, 'The Poetry of the Second Barons' War: Some Manuscript Contexts', *English Manuscript Studies, 1100–1700* 17 (2013), 201–22; I. Nelson, *Lyric Tactics: Poetry, Genre, and Practice in Later Medieval England* (Philadelphia, 2017); and A. C. Spearing, *Textual Subjectivity: The Encoding of Subjectivity in Medieval Narratives and Lyrics* (Oxford, 2005).

[4] R. Payne, *The Key of Remembrance* (New Haven, 1963), p. 186. B. A. Windeatt, *Oxford Guides to Chaucer: Troilus and Criseyde* (Oxford, 1992) pp. 163–9, especially p. 164 and p.168.

[5] T. Adorno, 'On Lyric Poetry and Society', *Notes to Literature, Volume One*, trans. S. W. Nicholsen (New York, 1958), pp. 36–54 (45).

associated with the development of Criseyde's thought as she considers Troilus's suit, that is, the three lyrical interventions that appear in Book II of *Troilus and Criseyde*: Antigone's song, the lay of the nightingale and the dream of the eagle. That Chaucer adds these to his Boccaccian source reveals a shift in attention away from the Boccaccian admonitory story of female infidelity and towards a concern with probing the status of individual choice and desire within the matrix of war. The three lyric interventions of Book II, I demonstrate, not only distil the complexity of Criseyde's inner deliberations as she considers Troilus's suit, but also – by showing how Criseyde's choice to love is inflected by the condition of women subject to male desire within an economy of war – express the social antagonism between love and war that is the subject of the poem as a whole.

Antigone's song illustrates how Chaucer's poetic choices – especially his use of end rhyme, couplets, stress, diction, metaphors and proverbs – contribute to its expression of this social antagonism. Further, Chaucer's account of the lay of the nightingale, a song that he reports, but whose words he does not recount, distils the antagonisms expressed in Antigone's song. Not usually counted among the poem's lyrics, the third example, the dream of the eagle, fulfils many of the same Adornian expressive functions as the previous two.

The lyrics found in *Troilus and Criseyde* and indeed the poem as a whole emerge, as James Simpson has shown, from an Ovidian elegiac tradition, one that rests on an initial turning away from but then a powerful return to history and politics.[6] Book II of *Troilus and Criseyde* is particularly governed by Ovidian themes of seizure, rape and transformation, especially associated with Antigone herself, Philomel and above all Apollo. Rather than removing us from the history of war and its consequences for the individual in love that the larger narrative recounts, the lyrics of Book II take us to the war's essences. As lyric quintessences, the song and the lay and perhaps even Criseyde's dream express the desire for love as intertwined with the violence against women that is endemic to war. The conditions for women in love and in war in the world of this poem prove to be remarkably similar: in both arenas women are subject to seizure by men, and the realization of love and at times even survival under those conditions requires complex negotiations. These lyric interventions thus reveal the replications that Simpson identifies as characteristic of the whole poem: 'The poem as a whole cannot help exposing that its micro-world has replicated the macro-world of which it is a part; what looked like a digression from a war provoked by the capture of women turns out to converge with the same story'.[7]

Criseyde is well aware that violence against women is endemic to war. The poem records both her developing awareness of her subjection to seizure in the form of rape or abduction and her ultimate failed attempt to evade it. Scholars as different as the exegetical critic John Fleming, the historicist David Aers and the

---

[6] J. Simpson, 'The Elegiac', *Reform and Cultural Revolution: The Oxford English Literary History, Volume 2: 1350–1547* (Oxford, 2002), pp. 121–90. Simpson's chapter inspires much of this discussion.

[7] Simpson, *Reform*, p. 142.

feminist Carolyn Dinshaw have illuminated Chaucer's emphasis on Criseyde's subjection to rape, abduction and the traffic in women throughout the poem.[8] The first half of the poem narrates Troilus's and Pandarus's relentless pursuit of Criseyde who, through Pandarus's machinations, is eventually isolated in a room where she is told none of her ladies in waiting can hear her cries. Troilus's exultant statement in this scene clearly threatens rape: 'Now be ye kaught; now is ther but we tweyne! / Now yeldeth yow, for other bote is non!' (III, 1207-8). It is Criseyde's response along with Troilus's swoon, as Jill Mann so skillfully demonstrates, that rewrites the pursuit as a story of love rather than one of rape: 'Ne hadde I er now, my swete herte deere, / Ben yolde, ywis, I were now nought heere' (III, 1210-11).[9] Yet even the mutual love that Troilus and Criseyde realise cannot protect her from her subjection to the desires of other men in the war. Hector attempts to resist the ideology that underpins the war, arguing that 'We usen here no wommen for to selle' (IV, 182), and Troilus, too, refuses to 'ravish' Criseyde, 'syn thou woost this town hath al this werre / For ravysshyng of women, so by myght, / It sholde nought be suffred me to erre' (IV, 547-9). Despite these resistances, the perceived needs of Troy take precedence over the choices of either Troilus or Criseyde. Subjected to a hostage swap that typifies the status of women in war as objects of exchange, Criseyde is then prey to the relentless pursuit of her next suitor, Diomedes. Even her removal to a community Diomedes claims is more civilised than that of the doomed Troy does not allow her to evade her vulnerability in war; we last see her in that camp fearing rape: 'lo, this drede I moost of alle – / If in the hondes of som wrecche I falle' (V, 704-5). The pursuit of love in this version of the Troy legend is thus shaped by the fundamental status of women in war as subject to seizure by men, and the lyric moments of Book II articulate this condition.

Before turning to a detailed discussion of these lyric moments, I should note that *Troilus and Criseyde* in its entirety has a lyric disposition that troubles the idea that the lyric interventions are distinct shifts in literary mode. None of the lyrical interludes in the poem differ in verse form from that of the poem as a whole: rhyme royal, and as Windeatt points out, 'the associations of Chaucer's rhyme-royal stanza were probably still more with lyric than with narrative forms'.[10] Indeed the whole poem's lyrical status is indicated further 'through its proems, and through references to the narrative itself as song'.[11] Chaucer is interested, then, in importing song-like characteristics to the poem. The degree to which rhyme royal contributes to lyrical effects in the poem as a whole is

---

8 See J. Fleming, 'Deiphoebus Betrayed: Virgilian Decorum, Chaucerian Feminism', *Chaucer Review* 21 (1986), 182-99; D. Aers, 'Criseyde: woman in medieval society', *Critical Essays on Chaucer's Troilus and Criseyde and His Major Early Poems*, ed. C. D. Benson (Toronto, 1991), pp. 128-48; C. Dinshaw, 'Reading Like a Man: The Critics, the Narrator, Troilus, and Pandarus', *Chaucer's Sexual Poetics* (Madison, WI, 1989), pp. 38-64.
9 J. Mann, 'Troilus' swoon', Benson, ed., *Critical Essays*, pp. 149-64.
10 Windeatt, *Oxford Guides*, p. 165.
11 Ibid., p. 164.

well worth considering in a larger study, but in this chapter I focus much more narrowly only on those markedly lyrical moments in Book II that intervene in Criseyde's thinking.

Despite its consistent rhyme royal form, *Troilus and Criseyde* encompasses elements of a large variety of genres: epic, romance, history, tragedy, drama and lyric. What is most significant about the lyrics in Chaucer's poem, and one that Windeatt states is 'insufficiently recognized', is Chaucer's skill in placing lyrics within a narrative; indeed, he asserts that 'establishing a uniquely effective relation between lyric and narrative is one of Chaucer's achievements in this poem'.[12] Ardis Butterfield was one of the first to acknowledge both the importance of lyric interpolations in medieval narratives, including Chaucerian ones, and to trace the history of this mixed genre from Boethius and into the French tradition.[13] Through the juxtaposition of modes, Windeatt observes, Chaucer is able to present 'a mutual critique of the interpretations of life that they represent'.[14] Furthermore, as Butterfield argues, such juxtaposition lends itself to metadiscourse about the nature of poetry itself.[15] As I will show, even the lyrics themselves, at least those in Book II, contain within them unsettling juxtapositions.

It is at times difficult to recognise when we have entered a lyric domain in the poem. Critics have identified anywhere from ten to fifty-six lyrics embedded in *Troilus and Criseyde*, suggesting that for some readers singing is not the only measure of a lyric moment.[16] Windeatt's definition of what counts as lyric is capacious; he writes, 'lyric set-pieces become part of the accepted self-expression of his [Chaucer's] characters; not only performed songs but also the lovers' formal laments or "complaints", and so too by extension the courtly letters in which some of their entreaties and lamentations are expressed'.[17] If the letters the lovers exchange count as lyric effusions, we can extend the definition even further to include the dream of the eagle as such an expression, albeit an unconscious one.

That we are meant to recognise certain moments in the poem as distinctive shifts in mode is signalled, as Windeatt informs us, not by changes in form, but by rubrics or marginal notes in the manuscript (that may or may not be authorial), which indicate a *cantus* or *compleynt* to follow, or by references inside the text to the beginning and ending of lyric pieces.[18] Antigone's song is identified in all three ways; it is announced as a song in some manuscripts by a rubric, either

---

12 *Ibid.*, pp. 163, 164.
13 See Butterfield, 'Interpolated Lyric in Medieval Narrative Poetry'.
14 Windeatt, *Oxford Guides*, p. 169.
15 Butterfield carries this argument throughout her thesis.
16 Payne, *The Key of Remembrance*, p. 185, lists ten; Windeatt, *Oxford Guides*, pp. 166–7, lists sixteen complaints alone, and refers to many other kinds of lyric interventions including songs and letters; other critics broaden the definition even further. See Nelson, *Lyric Tactics*, p. 90.
17 Windeatt, *Oxford Guides*, p. 164.
18 *Ibid.*, p. 165.

'Cantus Antigone' or 'Cantus Antigone de Amore', or marginally as 'The Songe of Antigonee'.[19] Furthermore, within the narrative we are told that 'Antigone the shene / Gan on a Troian song to singen cleere' (II, 824–5). No such notations differentiate the dream of the eagle from the rest of the narrative, although it is preceded by a description of the performance of a song by a nightingale.

The few critics who have considered Antigone's song admire its tranquil beauty and overlook its darker undertones. Simpson calls it a 'beautiful lyric about the bliss and ease of love'.[20] Stephen Knight praises the song for its graceful verse and its balance and for offering Criseyde 'confidence and mental equilibrium'.[21] Offering a more complex reading, Clare Kinney argues that the song is a specifically 'female celebration of mutual bliss and security in love'.[22] Performed in an overdetermined feminine space, the enclosed garden, by a woman reciting a song made by another woman to an assembled group of women, Antigone's song, in Kinney's argument, presents a '"female" poetry of presence' in contrast to the masculine poetry articulated by Troilus, a 'Petrarchan lyric of privation'.[23] The song's presentation of an ideal of love offers a 'counter narrative' to the 'Boccaccian master plot', which, in tandem with the work's final prayer to God, offers a glimpse of a transcendent love that can undermine the poem's tragic ending.[24] While I agree that the song on one level celebrates an ideal form of love, the counter-narrative that Kinney delineates is, I suggest, present in the song itself, which undoes its affirmations at the very same time that it asserts them.

The first hint that the song is less soothing than it seems comes from the name of the singer, Antigone. Her name might evoke the violent history of Thebes with which she is associated, thus offering a glimmer of the Theban recursiveness that Lee Patterson argued governs the whole poem.[25] Her name might also evoke her troubling Ovidian metamorphosis into a bird for daring to compete with Juno.[26] Given that Chaucer provides us with nothing but her name, however, we are offered here only a suggestion of those dark histories.

Providing a pause in the narrative that interrupts Pandarus's relentless pursuit of Criseyde on Troilus's behalf, as well as our observation of her emotionally turbulent response, Antigone performs what seems to be a straightforward

---

19 See the note to line 827 of B. A. Windeatt's *Geoffrey Chaucer: Troilus and Criseyde: A New Edition of 'The Book of Troilus'* (London, 1984), p. 193. This edition lists the various manuscripts in which these annotations occur.
20 Simpson, *Reform*, p. 147.
21 S. Knight, *Rymyng craftil: Meaning in Chaucer's Poetry* (Sydney and London, 1973), p. 62.
22 C. R. Kinney, 'Who Made this Song?: The Engendering of Lyric Counterplots in *Troilus and Criseyde*', *Studies in Philology* 89 (1992), 272–92 (285).
23 Ibid., p. 279.
24 Ibid., p, 281.
25 L. Patterson, '*Troilus and Criseyde* and the Subject of History', *Chaucer and the Subject of History* (Madison, 1991), pp. 84–164.
26 M. M. Innes, trans., Ovid, *Metamorphoses* (London, 1955), p. 136, Book VI, lines 93–7.

song in praise of perfect love. The poem's opening stanza declares the speaker's confident affirmation of love:

> She seyde, 'O Love, to whom I have and shal
> Ben humble subgit, trewe in myn entente,
> As I best kan, to yow, lord, yeve ich al
> For evermo myn hertes lust to rente;
> For nevere yet thi grace no wight sente
> So blisful cause as me, my lif to lede
> In alle joie and seurte out of drede' (II, 827–33)

In exchange for her subjection to the power of Love, the speaker will be granted joy, security and freedom. The achievement of these virtues, however, comes only with some effort on her part, that is the amendment of her will; as the song says, 'day by day I in my wille amende' (II, 854).

Looking more closely at the lyric we find that its celebration of the permanence and stability of love is undercut by its poetic techniques. The vulnerable condition of women in both love and war is conveyed in part through verbal arrangement. The placement of the words in the lines, especially at the end of lines and in the couplets, undermines their confident avowals of the perfection of love. The end of the closing couplet of the first stanza, 'out of drede' (833), that is, 'doubtless', asserts certainty, yet the word 'dread', expressing the opposite idea, receives the final stress not only in the line but in the entire stanza.

The second stanza also comes to an unsettling close in its last words:

> Ye, blisful god, han me so wel byset
> In love, iwys, that al that bereth lif
> Ymagynen ne kouthe how to be bet;
> For, lord, withouten jalousie or strif,
> I love oon which is moost ententif
> To serven wel, unwery or unfeyned,
> That evere was, and leest with harm desteyned. (II, 834–40)

What might these stains of harm be: wounds, bloodstains? The lyric as a whole asserts the beloved's perfection, but this line disturbs the hyperbolic praise by suggesting the beloved is merely less stained than those around him. We have moved out of the realm of courtly love and into that of battle. This stanza, furthermore, using what Spearing has recently called a 'rhetoric of negation', asserts the beloved's positive qualities in a series of negations (without jealousy or strife, unweary, unfeigned) and negative diction (jealousy, strife, weariness, deception) that permeate the stanza.[27]

The lyric's movement into the metatextual in the third stanza contributes to a critique of the poem's presumed assurance and serenity. The speaker describes the beloved in terms of a list of metaphors that draw attention as much to the

---

27 A. C. Spearing, 'Middle English Lyrics, Lyrics in Narratives, and "Who made this song?"', p. 13. Professor Spearing has kindly shared this as yet unpublished essay with me.

mode of description used, metaphor, as to the qualities of the beloved that are celebrated:

> As he that is the welle of worthynesse
> Of trouthe grownd, mirour of goodlihed,
> Of wit Apollo, stoon of sikernesse,
> Of vertu roote, of lust fynder and hed,
> Thorugh which is alle sorwe fro me ded –
> Iwis, I love hym best, so doth he me;
> Now good thrift have he, wherso that he be! (II, 841–7)

The author here uses five metaphors of nature to describe the beloved: a well; ground; stone; root; and 'fynder', or source. In its assertion of the presence of the beloved in the fundamental elements of nature, the metaphors simultaneously alert us to his absence by substituting the metaphorical domain for the literal one. Furthermore, the presence of love in all of nature kills sorrow in the speaker, but the word that receives the stress at the end of the fifth line of the stanza (845) – dead – also suggests that love in its omnipresence in nature threatens to dissolve the boundary between the speaker and the natural world, either in an ecstatic dissolution or in death.

At the level of the metatextual, the paratactic list after a time draws the reader away from the qualities the metaphors point to and instead towards the nature of metaphoricity itself. The list, followed by an awkward syntactic inversion in the fifth line, requires what Nelson calls 'interpretive agility on the part of the audience'.[28] By inspiring cognitive activity rather than affective response, the stanza takes us out of the realm of individual desire and into one of thought and indeed into one of play, a realm that is pressed upon by the discourse of war that shapes it. Spearing attributes the power of the stanza to its syntactic variation:

> The beauty of these lines – hardly paralleled, I believe, in any earlier Middle English lyric – is not only a matter of alliteration, assonance, and the recurrence of liquid rs and ls, but of elegant syntactical patterning: the idea 'x of y' (as in 'welle of worthinesse') is varied to appear successively as 'x of y / of y x / x of y / of y x / x of y / of y x / of y x-and-z'.[29]

The diversity of patterns thus draws our attention to the nature of patterning itself. The syntactic variety and the very proliferation of metaphors underline the pleasure of the list of figures for its own sake and bring to the fore the poet's construction of reality in the midst of antagonism.

The poem then surprisingly shifts away from this description of a perfect lover to praise the god of love, thus drawing our attention in the poem to a triangulation between the speaker, the beloved and love. It is not clear if the stability of love described emerges from the god of love or from the beloved. Most importantly, the reciprocal love described at the beginning of the third stanza's closing couplet is undercut by the speaker's lack of knowledge of her

---

28 Nelson, *Lyric Tactics*, p. 100.
29 Spearing, 'Middle English Lyrics', unpublished paper, p. 12.

lover's whereabouts: 'Iwis, I love hym best, so doth he me; / Now good thrift have he, wherso that he be!' (846–7). This deictic moment, to draw on Spearing's illuminating use of the term, creates an epistemological uncertainty that casts doubt on the stability of the previous assertions.[30] Sister Borthwick argues that his mysterious whereabouts as well as his unimaginable qualities suggest that the beloved cannot be of this world; the qualities attributed to the beloved instead seem more suited to an absent divine figure.[31] That we are told later that the goodliest maid of Troy composed the lyric might indeed suggest that the original song was addressed by a virgin to an absent god. The primary effect of the line, however, is to make us aware that the seemingly perfect beloved is actually not there. This mysterious absence, furthermore, raises the question that Criseyde formulates at the end of the song – does such a love exist?

Although the speaker thanks the god of love in the fourth stanza for allowing her to experience a love that improves her own virtue and allows her 'to flemen alle manere vice and synne', the fifth stanza brings to the surface her defensiveness as she answers imagined attacks on the love she professes:

> 'And whoso seith that for to love is vice,
> Or thraldom, though he feele in it destresse,
> He outher is envyous, or right nyce,
> Or is unmyghty, for his shrewednesse,
> To loven; for swich manere folk, I gesse,
> Defamen Love, as nothing of hym knowe.
> Thei speken, but thei benten nevere his bowe!' (II, 855–61)

Furthering the 'rhetoric of negation' that we have already seen in the first stanza, negative words overwhelm this stanza: vice, servitude, distress, envy, fastidiousness, weakness, shrewdness, defamation – qualities of unsettled and dysfunctional social groups as well as qualities that contribute to war. The poem asserts that love negates an extensive list of deleterious qualities such as jealousy, strife, sorrow, vice, sin, but the very proliferation of these adverse attributes undermines their negation. As the poem progresses, the speaker's defensiveness and uncertainty destabilise the confident affirmations of its opening lines. The word that receives the most stress in the final position in the stanza, *bow*, in referring to a weapon of both love and war, reinforces how closely intertwined the two realms are.

The poem then broadens its rhetorical range by providing a list of proverbs to explain the ineffability of the beloved, another metatextual strategy that generalises and makes communal the experience of love at the same time that it emphasises the inadequacy of language to convey the individual's experience of it. The poem's various metatextual strategies ultimately draw attention to the

---

30 A. C. Spearing discusses deixis throughout his book *Textual Subjectivity: The Encoding of Subjectivity in Medieval Narratives and Lyrics* (Oxford, 2005).
31 Sister M. C. Borthwick, 'Antigone's Song as "Mirour" in Chaucer's *Troilus and Criseyde*', *Modern Language Quarterly* 22 (1961), 227–35.

inadequacy of meaning making in wartime, and indeed at any time.[32] The lyric continues:

> What is the sonne wers, of kynde right
> Though that a man, for fieblesse of his yen,
> May nought endure on it to see for bright?
> Or love the wers, though wrecches on it crien?
> No wele is worth, that may no sorwe dryen.
> And forthi, who that hath an hed of verre,
> Fro cast of stones war hym in the werre! (II, 862–8)

The proverbs themselves destabilise the poem's insistence on love's positive features, first by claiming that, just as there is no inherent harm to the sun because some are blinded by it, there is nothing wrong with love itself even though lovers suffer from it, and, second, by warning that those who criticise love are just as vulnerable to attack as those who live in glass houses. Through his volley of proverbs, the poet emphasises the ineffability and exclusivity of love. Furthermore, in the process of answering imagined objections to love, the poet admits what he has previously denied – that love itself involves pain – asserting that, 'No wele is worth, that may no sorwe dryen' (866).

The shift into the proverbial redirects attention away from the personal and towards the general. Sister Borthwick argues that the list of proverbs make sense only if we align them with the doubts about love that Criseyde had expressed earlier.[33] Nelson, however, argues that the poet's shifts from courtly love idiom to compressed metaphor to proverb 'speaks to the poem's larger political concerns'.[34] She proposes, 'By interrupting the elaboration of the stable feudal metaphors of courtly love with the rapid fire metaphors of exemplarity ... and the metaphorical proverbs, the song performs negotiation by means of rhetorical and formal tactics'.[35] The immersion into the proverbial again draws us into the textual and foregrounds rhetorical performativity even as it brings the reader fully into painful experiences – being blinded by the sun and feeling and lamenting necessary suffering.

The poem ends with an image of fertility and growth as the speaker expresses her devotion to a knight in whom her heart grows and whose heart grows in her – lines that foreshadow the dream of the eagle. The last couplet's assertion of love, however, begins and ends with words of fear and danger; love is framed by 'drede' and 'peril'. As Sister Borthwick writes:

> The ending – 'Al dredde I first to love hym to bigynne, / Now woot I wel, ther is no peril inne' (874–5) – although superficially it brushes away former fears,

[32] For a useful discussion of the ways in which proverbs both assert timelessness and contingency see K. Taylor, 'Proverbs and the Authentication of Convention in *Troilus and Criseyde*', *Chaucer's Troilus: Essays in Criticism*, ed. S. A. Barney (London, 1980), pp. 277–96.
[33] Borthwick, 'Antigone's Song', 227–35.
[34] Nelson, *Lyric Tactics*, p. 102.
[35] Ibid., p. 102.

startles us with the use of the words 'dredde' and 'peril' at the close of this lay of apparent lighthearted joy; and the final negative clause leaves us with the impression that the singer is not really so assured as she has seemed.[36]

Indeed, we can read the last two lines as a condensed version of the lyric as a whole. Both describe love as a perfect transformation of attitudes, but the negative words that enclose the couplet belie the perfect love it asserts and envelop us in the instability the larger context of war produces.

As if to register the metapoetic dimension of Antigone's song, Criseyde's responses to the song direct us to the poem's status as a textual construction rather than an emotional expression of the subject. Criseyde asks first, 'Who made this song now with so good entente?' (878). And then, 'Lord, is ther swych blisse among / Thise loveres, as they konne faire endite?' (885–6). Both questions draw attention to the song as a made object and to the poet who conceived it. Antigone answers that the poem was composed by 'the goodlieste mayde ... of Troye' (881–2) and then that love can hardly be described. We do not know the significance of the fact that the song is written by a maid (is this a song of a Virgin to a God? Is it Helen's song, as some have suggested – though she is hardly a maid?), nor does Antigone's response to Criseyde assure us that such a love is available for those who are alive. Criseyde is presented here as an astute critic, one who seeks to understand the contexts and conventions of the lyric and to probe its essential social antagonisms.

Whereas Adorno in the lyrics he considers reveals their expression of the contemporary conflicts produced primarily by capitalism, we, in these much earlier lyrics within a narrative, can find in them the social antagonisms of Chaucer's own society. We could find within these lyric moments and indeed the poem as a whole an expression of the conditions of Chaucer's life as one struggling to improve his class position as a knight *en service*, as one living in a dangerous courtly environment in which friends were executed or quickly became deadly enemies and as one well aware of the vicissitudes of a long-standing and ever shifting war with France, a condition Butterfield has so well explained to us.[37] Finally, and perhaps most significantly, the poem captures the social antagonism rife in late medieval aristocratic marriage practices concerning the uncertain status of female consent to marriage. However, as Adorno points out, it is not necessary to bring in material from outside specific lyrics to identify the contemporary antagonisms they engage. The lyrical interventions in *Troilus and Criseyde* bring to the surface the anxieties and tensions of the conflict between, on the one hand, communication, union through love and the making of community, and, on the other hand, the subjection of women to male sexual desires against their will as well as the destructiveness and dissolution of community caused by war – a dissolution resisted by the lyric's self-consciousness as a playful, made thing.

---

36 Borthwick, 'Antigone's Song', 228.
37 A. Butterfield, *The Familiar Enemy: Chaucer, Language and Nation in the Hundred Years War* (Oxford, 2009).

The lyric's expression of social antagonisms again emerges in the sequence that leads to the dream of the eagle as well as the description of the dream itself. The introduction to the dream refers to another performance of a lyric that influences Criseyde, the nightingale's lay of love, a lyric performance that again produces dissonances. The nightingale's song makes Criseyde's heart 'fressh and gay' (922), even though the bird sings the song of Philomel, a story of violence, rape and mutilation. The opening of Book II indicates that we should associate a nightingale with such a violent history when Pandarus is awakened by the swallow Procne, whose connection with the dark history of her sister's rape is made explicit in the poem:

> The swalowe Proigne, with a sorowful lay,
> Whan morwen com, gan make hire waymentynge
> Whi she forshapen was; and evere lay
> Pandare abedde, half in a slomberynge,
> Til she so neigh hym made hir cheterynge
> How Tereus gan forth hire suster take,
> That with the noyse of hire he gan awake (II, 64–70)

The nightingale here is male rather than female but the reader has already been conditioned to recall the more violent association of the bird's song with Philomel. Given that cedars are traditionally planted in cemeteries, it is ominous that the nightingale sings in the bough of a cedar tree. Furthermore, the last line of the nightingale's stanza introduces the idea of violent seizure that will be the subject of the dream: 'the dede slep hire hente' (924).

The dream itself, while drawing us deep into the psychic interior of the dreamer, also points outwards to the condition of war, seemingly shut out of Criseyde's house and garden walls:

> And as she slep, anonright tho hir mette
> How that an egle, fethered whit as bon,
> Under hire brest his longe clawes sette,
> And out hire herte he rente, and that anon,
> And dide his herte into hire brest to gon –
> Of which she nought agroos, ne nothyng smerte –
> And forth he fleigh, with herte left for herte. (II, 925–31)

We might describe the dream in Hegelian terms as a lyrical expression of Criseyde's innermost subjection to love. The dream is, of course, not presented as a first-person epideictic address of the same kind as Antigone's song. Nonetheless it shares lyric functions, or, to use Caroline Levine's recent term, 'affordances', allowing possibilities that the narrative precludes.[38] Like Antigone's song, it breaks off narrative time. Furthermore, it functions as a quintessence or distillation in that it crystallises and brings to a close our observation of Criseyde's thinking about Troilus's suit. Rather than expressing Criseyde's acceptance of that suit, as many critics have suggested, however, the dream, like Antigone's song and the

---

38 C. Levine, *Forms: Whole, Rhythm, Hierarchy, Network* (Princeton, 2015).

lay of the nightingale, presents a subjective response to her social condition as a woman subject to seizure in love and war; that is, it is a construction of the psyche's responses to experiences that intrude upon it from the outside.

The dream can be interpreted on one level as an expression of Criseyde's own desire. While it does capture the quintessential drama, if not violence, of such a dramatic change of heart, it also conveys darker messages about the violence inherent in a woman's subjection to male power, whether in love or war. While the eagle's white feathers evoke purity, in the comparison of the feathers' whiteness to bones, they also call to mind death. The event described is overtly violent: the eagle sets his long claws into her breast, and he tears out her heart. At the centre of this dream is an act that Criseyde fears in love and war: seizure.

An eagle, a bird associated with royal power, enacts the violence, underlying the power dynamics in the encounter. Indeed, its royal associations may reflect Criseyde's anxiety about being pursued by the son of a king, one she knows could 'have me in dispit' (II, 711), that is, seize her against her will at any moment. While the dreamer seems to accept the new heart she receives, the exchange is uneven – she does not participate in the exchange of hearts; only the eagle acts. Criseyde's passivity in the exchange anticipates not only her subjection to Troilus but also to Diomedes. Criseyde does not choose her lovers; they choose her. Such impositions of male power on women are common in love and war.

That Criseyde shows no fear or pain may signal her willing participation in the event. An exchange of hearts in the act of falling in love may be violently dramatic, but ultimately not painful. However, Criseyde's lack of fear or pain does not necessarily cancel out the violence of the eagle's act. Recall that many women who have been raped do not remember that they have been raped. We might understand these lines as Criseyde's wish for love to be free of pain at the same time that she acknowledges the inherent violence of subjecting oneself to another's desire. The dream thus epitomises the social antagonism of the place of female desire in both love and war.

The lyric interludes we have considered here are closely linked to Philomel, the violated nightingale remembered in the opening of Book II and whose violation echoes in the lay of the nightingale. Whether a male or female voice, the lyric voice of the nightingale can never escape its associations with a history of violence against women. Philomel is not the only figure in the poem to point us to the violence inherent in lyric form. While Book II is framed by the Ovidian story of the Philomel, the dominant Ovidian figure of the poem as a whole is the god of lyric poetry, Apollo. Jamie Fumo has persuasively demonstrated the ways in which Chaucer shapes his poem in an Apollonian frame: 'Apollo's reflexive association with erotic misfortune, medical insufficiency and counterproductive prophetic wisdom, all ... contribute to Chaucer's historical reshaping of his pagans' worldview'.[39] Apollo's failed pursuit of Daphne is perhaps even more significant for a discussion of the lyric interventions in *Troilus and Criseyde* since it is the body of Daphne in the form of laurel leaves that makes up the wreath granted to the winner of both poetic and military contests. The laurel wreath is of course an ambiguous sign of rape for it is made up of the body that escapes Apollo's desire. Apollo appears only obliquely in Antigone's song: Antigone's speaker's beloved has the wit of Apollo; perhaps he also has Apollo's right to seize at will. In the form of the sun, this Apollonian figure can shine dangerously bright. Apollo's meaning throughout the poem is obscure – associated with 'amphibologies' (IV, 1406) and 'ambages' (V, 897), his ambivalent prophecies require careful hermeneutic discernment.[40] Chaucer's use of the lyric and his evocation of the violent histories associated with its purported origins point us to some of the hidden meanings of the poem. If *Troilus and Criseyde* is fully an Ovidian elegy, it also carries within it a revelation of its violent origins in its lyric quintessences and in the character of Criseyde who listens to and interprets the social antagonisms of Ovidian lyrics so carefully.[41]

---

39 J. C. Fumo, *The Legacy of Apollo: Antiquity, Authority and Chaucerian Poetics* (Toronto, 2010), p. 125.
40 *Ibid.*, p. 132.
41 I would like to thank A. C. Spearing for a typically generous discussion of this argument, Mark Amsler, C. David Benson, Pamela King, Rachel Robinson and Georgina Wilde and the editors for helpful editorial comments, and Jeffrey C. Robinson for inspiring conversations about the nature of this lyric and lyric form more generally.

13

Poems that Speak Volumes: Lydgate's *Thoroughfare of Woe*, and Lyric as Epitome

Julia Boffey

John Lydgate, *Thoroughfare of Woe*[1]

1	Lyfte vp the eeys of yo*ur* aduertence	*eyes; consciousness*
	yee that be blyndede wi*th* <worldly> vanytee	
	Noo bettyr myrroure thene experyence	*than*
	ffor to declare ys mutabylyte	
5	Nowe wi*th* lord:[2] nowe wi*th* aduersyte	
	To yerthely pylgrymes passynge to & fro	*earthly*
	ffortune shewythe in hyghe & lowe degre	
	How this worlde ys a thorowefare fulle of woo	
	Boys in hys boke of consolacyone	*Boethius, in his* Consolation of Philosophy
10	Wrytys & reherses of fortune is varyaunce	*Fortune's changeableness*
	And there he makythe a playne discripcion	
	To truste in here <it> ys none assuraunce	*there is no security*
	Whoo mooste to here hathe <his> attendaunce	*pays attention*
	Shalle neuere be sykere whether she be frend or foo	*certain*
15	Nowe fayre now fowle showynge *in* resemblaunce	
	How thys wor<l>de ys a thorowfare fulle woo	

For further essays focused upon lyrics that shift in content, size and purpose in different manuscript versions, see Anne Baden-Daintree (Chapter 10), 'Voice and Response: Lyric Rewriting of the Song of Songs'; and Christiania Whitehead (Chapter 16), 'Musical and Poetic Form in *Stond wel, moder, under rode*'; for an essay on one of Lydgate's religious lyrics, also infused with Chaucerian references, see Mary Wellesley (Chapter 9), 'Textual Lyricism in Lydgate's *Fifteen Joys and Sorrows of Mary*'.

1   NIMEV 1872; DIMEV 3080. This version of the poem, transcribed from London, British Library, Additional MS 60577, fols 47–9 (digitised at http://www.bl.uk/manuscripts/BriefDisplay.aspx), is not taken account of in H. N. MacCracken, ed., *The Minor Poems of John Lydgate*, 2 vols, EETS ES 107, OS 192 (London, 1911–34), II, 822–8. In this transcription manuscript contractions have been expanded and italicised according to conventional practice. Angle brackets indicate inserted scribal corrections. Although the text at some points seems corrupt no efforts have been made here at emendation.

2   The manuscript reading 'lord' makes little sense. Other versions have 'ioye'.

In thys worlde ther ys noone abydynge place
but that hit ys by processe remeveable   *mutable over time*
Late see who hathe in erthe nowe suche a grace   *Look*
20 To make fortune with hym abyde stable
Heere dowble vysage ys soo varyable
Olde folke cane telle the trouthe yf hit be soo
There experyence & ymages fulle notable
Howe thys world ys a thorowe fare fulle of woo

25 Adam oure fader be ganne with grete travayle   *labour*
Whan he was putt furste ought of paradyse
Whate myght thenne gentylnes hym avayle   47v   *nobility of birth*
                                                              or manners
Whane the furste stocke of labour toke his price   *source; work*
Adam in tylthe was holden wonder wyse   *labour*
30 Eve in spynnynge what cowde she els doo
Thus to declare as by myne advyse
Thys world ys but a thorowefare ful of woo

ffor to telle you playnly and nott spare
Whiche haue be surmountynge in noblesse   *Those who have been most noble*
35 And hathe be tymes passyde this thorowefare
& cowde ther inne fynde noo sykernes   *certainty*
In theire abydynge chaunge & dowblenes
what was þer syne whan they shuld hens goo   *How had they sinned*
Rede the cronycles & trouthe shal expresse
40 How thys worlde ys a thorowefare ful of woo

Who was more goodly than was Iosuye   *Joshua*
Whiche honged vij kynges vp at gabaone
Or more goodly than Iudas Machabye   *Judas Maccabeus*
Meekere then dauid: wyser thanne Salamone   *David; Solomon*
45 Or fayrer founden: thene was Absolone   *Absolom*
Reken ther paradye & take good heede ther to   *death*
Aryue by exsample of Arcules & Sampson   *Deduce; Hercules; Samson*
How thys world ys a thorowfare fulle of woo

Ector was slayne by cruell Achylles   *Hector*
50 As he mett vnwarned in Batayle
Cesar Iulius murdrede was in the prese   *Julius Caesar; crowd*
Senatours of Rome hym dyde assayle
Whate myght the conqueste of Alysaunder avayle   48r   *Alexander*
A gaynste the poyson that was hys foo
55 Pompay or porras[3] for alle ther plate or mayle   *Pompey the Great*
Were slayne in thys thorowe<fare soo> fulle of woo

---

3   The identity of 'porras' is obscure. No figure of this name is mentioned in the other versions of the poem.

Remembre alsoo of many ryche realme
That hathe be to fore caste down & ouer throwe
Prynces of prouynce whylome of Iherusalem
60 ffor synne be Tytus were brought fulle lowe   *Titus*
Sede of discorde that was sowene in Troye
Emonges them self whene the Grekes were agoo *Among them; had gone*
The beste evidence to make mene to knowe   *men*
How this world ys a thorowefare fulle of woo

65 Remembre of Tyrauntes that hathe be to fore
the sturdy hunter Nembrolle by hys name   *Nimrod?*
ffor gete we nott Nabugodonosor   *Nechadnezzar*
thar fforester of Alix Delira[4] was hys name
And Nabuzardan was for hys Boste to blame *Nebuzaradan*
70 And Judithe that was frowarde with ffarowe *Pharoah*
Alle theis dyede at myschef and at shame
Here within thys thorowfare that ys soo ful of woo

And of Babylon the grete Baltazare   *Belshazzar*
Syttynge hygheste in hys astate royalle   *state*
75 All sodeynly for hym lyste nott be ware   *because he took no heed*
ffrom hys Empyre he hadde a dredfull falle
Mane . Techel. Phares was wrytene on the walle *'Mane, thekel, phares'*
God was hys lord he toke noo heede ther too
An example full ryght in especyalle
80 How this world ys a thorowfare fulle of wo

To the grete stryffe and devi[ ]cioun   48v *division*
Of Pompay and Cezar Julius
Rote & ground why that realme to forne
Destroyed was Croncyles tellys thus
85 Cezar was slayne by Brutus Casius
ffaute of fortune causyde hit to be soo   *fault*
A playne exemplicer nowe shewyd vn to vs *exemplar*
How thys world ys a thorowefare fulle of woo

ffloure of knyghthod in Brytayne was Arthure
90 Manly hys fader vter pendragoun   *Uther Pendragon*
And of late date wylliam Conqueroure
Put owte harowlde not fulle yore agoun   *Harold; not long ago*
Marchal Richard may be sette for oone   *warlike Richard*
Called Cure de lyoun in what he hadde to doo *'lionheart'*
95 worthy edwarde reynynge in the ordre Celyoun[5]
they be passyde by thys thorowfare fulle of woo

4 An obscure phrase, possibly a scribal corruption, that does not appear in the other versions.
5 Obscure, and not in the other versions.

Rychard in Order callede the seconde was	
ffulle plenteuous of tresoure & of rychesse	
the fourthe Henry a manly knyght was	
100 worthely exilede Cronycles can expresse	
He resortede a gayn by manly hyghe prowesse	returned
by grete experyence he was taught also	
Bothe by rebellyon & constreyned with sekenesse	
How this world ys a thorowefare fulle of woo	
105 Henry the v^(the) a manly warryoure	
to seke reste be twyx Englonde & Fraunce	
whiche dyde hys payne & dylygent laboure	
As hit knowe by knyghtely gouernaunce	
But oo alas of fortunes varyaunce	
110 To the grete damage of these realmes too	two
Toke hym awaye to showe vs in substaunce	49r
How thys worlde ys a thorowfare fulle of woo	
Clarence hys brother example of gentylnes	Thomas of Clarence
& of knyghthode the verray loode sterre	loadstar
115 the duke of Exeter fulle famouse of prowes	Thomas Beaufort, Duke of Clarence
whiche was bothe knyghtly and debonorye	gracious
to suffre them lyve deth was contrarye	allow
To salesbury Callyde Mountegewe alsoo	Thomas Montagu, earl of Salisbury
A playne myrrour how thys world cane varye	
120 And ys appelyde a thorowefare fulle of woo	called
Dan Johan lyddegate Monke of Bury	Master John Lydgate

There is wide agreement that the poems usually now termed 'Middle English lyrics' have few characteristics in common. Their forms, their voices, their subjects, the situations they evoke, are strikingly diverse, to the extent that discussion has struggled to determine whether these poems constitute a genre at all. A recent essay by Ardis Butterfield has indeed advanced the suggestion that we think of them collectively as 'formless, as an ungenre'.[6] One of the very few distinguishing characteristics that can be isolated in regard to these poems is that they are short, or at least shortish – a feature that may have recommended itself to twentieth-century New Critics but has apparently in more recent years come to seem off-putting. A short poem may all too readily seem a nugatory one, unlikely to repay closer study. As Michael Kuczynski has noted of one particular category of Middle English lyrics, 'the chasm between amplified didactic and narrative texts and the abbreviated forms of many Middle English religious lyrics seems vast', constituting a gap that contributes to the 'almost total neglect' of these short pieces.[7]

---

[6] A. Butterfield, 'Why Medieval Lyric?' *English Literary History* 82 (2015), 319–43 (327).
[7] M. P. Kuczynski, 'Theological Sophistication and the Middle English Religious Lyric: A Polemic', *Chaucer Review* 45 (2011), 321–39 (329).

Words like 'abbreviated', 'short' and 'shortish' are not always easy to define in relation to items of verse. Poe's discussion of poetic composition, highlighting the virtues of unity of effect, famously suggested that anything much over a hundred lines becomes a long poem (his own *The Raven* squeaks into the short poem category at 108 lines).[8] Many of the Middle English poems conventionally categorised as lyrics are very much shorter than this, with line numbers often only in single figures. But a substantial body considerably exceeds the hundred-line limit: the well-known 'lyrics' from the Vernon and Digby manuscripts, for example (Oxford, Bodleian Library, MSS Eng. poet. a.1, and Digby 102) include many that are approximately this length and in some cases even longer.[9] It is probably fair to say that the catch-all term 'Middle English lyric' has come in general usage to comprehend most verse items of a short or shortish nature; and that 'shortness' mostly, but not always, is understood to have an upper limit somewhere between one hundred and two hundred lines.

Whether because it made them easily memorable or readily fitted to social or manuscript contexts where a short rather than a long item was appropriate, the brevity of these poems seems likely to have been one of their attractions. In practical terms these attractions may have seemed all the greater in cases where a short poem summarised or memorably invoked a larger body of useful argument or instruction. In their own different ways, many of these poems of few words successfully manage to allude to multitudes even if they do not literally contain them. In some instances this effect is contrived situationally, as often in post-medieval lyrics, by the implying of a larger context in which the lyric voice functions as one small interjection, inviting a reader or listener to supply an imagined context (such situations are often dramatic or quasi-dramatic, involving short conversations or exchanges, perhaps between Christ and man, or between a lover and a mistress). In other cases the effect of *multum in parvo* is achieved by compressing, into an ostensibly simple arrangement of a few words, allusion to a substantial body of doctrine or argument. Douglas Gray explored these effects in his discussion of 'themes and images' in religious lyrics such as the following:[10]

> Byhalde merveylis: a mayde ys moder,
> Her sone her fader ys and broder;
> Lyfe faught with dethe and dethe is slayne;
> Most high was lowe – he styghe agayne.   *ascended*

Bodies of secular teaching were in some cases similarly encapsulated in miniature form. Versions of the widely circulated so-called *ABC of Aristotle*, for example,

---

8   Edgar Allen Poe, 'The Philosophy of Composition', first published in *Graham's Magazine* 28.4 (April, 1846), 163–7; see J. E. Harrison, ed., *The Complete Works of Edgar Allan Poe*, 17 vols (New York, 1979), XIV, pp. 193–8. I am grateful to Professor Beth Robertson for discussing this issue with me.
9   H. Barr, ed., *The Digby Poems: A New Edition of the Lyrics* (Exeter, 2009): poems 1, 3, 7–21, 23–24 (i.e. 19 out of 24 poems) exceed 100 lines.
10 Gray, *Themes*, p. 77.

compress instruction on the doctrine of the golden mean from the *Nichomachean Ethics* into twenty-one alphabetically organized lines.[11] The poem does not name Aristotle, and it is only the reference in its final line to 'a mesurable meene', and the title by which it is introduced in some copies, that affords any clue to its Aristotelian import. Although for many it must have been simply an effective and anonymous mnemonic that packaged up stray bits of wisdom, an alert and educated reader would presumably have made a connection between moderation and Aristotle's advice.

In some lyrics and short poems the references to longer works are more specific, directing readers and listeners to recall or to search out more extensive bodies of material, and to allow consideration of their significance to grow out of a miniature summary of their contents. This is the strategy of John Lydgate's *A Thoroughfare of Woe*, a poem of 192 lines in the standard edition of Lydgate's shorter works, where its editor, H. N. MacCracken, categorised it as one of Lydgate's 'Little homilies with proverbial refrains'.[12] In its longest version (London, British Library, Harley MS 2251, MacCracken's base text) *Thoroughfare of Woe* consists of 24 eight-line *ballade* or 'Monk's Tale' stanzas. It starts with an injunction to people blinded with worldly vanity: 'Lyft up the ieen of your aduertence' ('lift up the eyes of your consciousness or spirit', in other words 'direct your attention'), and look to your daily experience to see that 'this world is a thurghfare ful of woo', an apothegm that will function as a refrain line throughout the poem. Moving from some statements about the nature of worldly Fortune through a series of examples, from both history and the contemporary world, it demonstrates that 'Stabilnesse is founde in nothyng' (line 128), concluding with a Christian message to take adversity in good part, to thank God and to suffer patiently.

Clearly at one level this poem can be read as an extended meditation on a proverbial saying, one for which there were both biblical and classical precedents, and that survives in a variety of Middle English formulations.[13] One

---

11 NIMEV 471, 3793; DIMEV 6054; NIMEV 4155; DIMEV 6654. For a recent edition, see M. D. Rust, 'The ABC of Aristotle', *Medieval Literature for Children*, ed. D. T. Kline (London, 2003), pp. 63–7, and further discussion in M. D. Rust, *Imaginary Worlds in Medieval Books: Exploring the Manuscript Matrix* (New York, 2007), pp. 69–72.

12 MacCracken, ed., *Minor Poems*, II, pp. 822–8; MacCracken numbers 191 lines, omitting to number a line omitted in BL, Harley MS 2251 and supplied in his edition from BL, Additional MS 29729. All quotations and line references on pp. 194–200 are to the long version of the poem edited by MacCracken, rather than to the abbreviated text of BL, Additional MS 60577 transcribed at the start of this chapter and discussed below.

13 Douglas Gray's chapter on 'Death and the Last Things' (Gray, *Themes*, pp. 176–220), includes several references to lyrics based on the notion of life as a journey towards death and thus as a form of pilgrimage. For discussion of biblical and classical precedents, see R. M. Smith, 'Three Obscure English Proverbs', *Modern Language Notes* 65 (1950), 441–7 (443–7). B. J. Whiting, *Proverbs, Sentences and Proverbial Phrases From English Writings Mainly Before 1500* (Cambridge, MA, 1968) lists a number of references to Middle English variations on 'We are pilgrims in the world' and 'the pilgrimage of this life', under P200 and P201.

way of understanding the poem is as a typically Lydgatian amplification of a short commonplace. But it can also be understood the other way around, as a summary or epitome of more extended kinds of discourse. Longer works are invoked in the poem at a variety of points. The first to be mentioned is Boethius's *Consolation of Philosophy*:

> Boys in his booke of Consolacioun   *Boethius*
> Writeth and rehersith fortunes variaunce, *Fortune's changeableness*
> And makith there a playne discripcioun
> To trust on hir ther is none assuraunce;   *there is no security*
> For who til hir, lo! hath attendaunce,   *pays attention*
> Is liche a pilgryme passyng to and froo,
> To shewe to vs with sugred false plesaunce,
> How this world is a thurghfare of wo. (lines 9–16)

The poem makes no attempt at an extended summary of the *Consolation*, and indeed its content has been signalled as evidence that Lydgate may not have read Boethius at first hand;[14] but it certainly makes sufficient gestures towards the contents of the *Consolation* to suggest some knowledge on Lydgate's part. It would probably be fair to say that the parts of the *Consolation* based on Boethius's questions and complaints inform *Thoroughfare of Woe*, even if Lydgate collapses Philosophy's extended investigation of 'consolation' into a more streamlined Christian message.

Inevitably, Lydgate's Boethius is projected in this poem through the lens of Chaucer. Memories of Chaucer's own short poem *Fortune* seem to hover around the edges of Lydgate's poem (especially at lines 19–28); and there are echoes of Chaucer's *Truth* and *Gentilesse*.[15] Most strikingly of all, the Boethian message is diffused into Lydgate's poem through recollection of the *Knight's Tale*, with Lydgate's refrain, 'this world is a thurghfare of wo', echoing the words of old Egeus, as he comments on the unhappy outcome of the tournament held to settle the love rivalry between Palamon and Arcite: 'This world nys but a thurghfare ful of wo, / And we been pilgrymes, passynge to and fro'.[16] In his final stanza Lydgate refers to Chaucer quite explicitly:

> O, ye maysters, that cast shal yowre looke *masters*
> Vpon this dyte made in wordis playne,   *poem*
> Remembre sothly that I the refreyd tooke *truly; refrain*
> Of hym that was in makyng souerayne,   *sovereign poet*
> My mayster Chaucier, chief poete of Bretayne,
> Whiche in his tragedyes made ful yore agoo, *a long time ago*

---

14 E. Gattinger, *Die Lyrik Lydgates*, Wiener Beiträge zur Englischen Philologie, 4 (Vienna, 1896), p. 49.
15 For *Fortune*, see Benson, pp. 652–3; for *Truth*, Benson, p. 653 (Chaucer's lines 'Her is non hoom, her nis but wildernesse: / Forth, pilgrim, forth! Forth, beste, out of thy stal!', lines 17-18, seem to be echoed in Lydgate's 'In this world here is none abidyng place ... Seeth by these pilgrymes that passen to and fro', lines 17–22); for *Gentilesse*, Benson, p. 654 (Chaucer's 'The firste stok, fader of gentilesse', line 1, is echoed in Lydgate's 'Oure fader Adam ... The firste stokke of labour toke his price', lines 33–6).
16 Benson, p. 63, I, lines 2847–8.

> Declared triewly and list nat for to feyne,   *had no wish to lie*
> How this world is a thurghfare ful of woo. (lines 184–91)

It is possible to feel that Lydgate's reading of the *Knight's Tale* is a partial one, privileging Egeus's downbeat view of earthly life over Theseus's philosophical rationalisation of change. But whatever its tenor, it stands out as an invitation to readers and listeners to draw into their reception of Lydgate's poem their knowledge and memories of other, longer works.[17]

The two works discussed thus far, Boethius's *Consolation* and Chaucer's *Knight's Tale*, are invoked respectively at the start and end of Lydgate's poem, rather effectively, and literally, book-ending it. There is yet another invitation in the main body of the poem to think of longer works, too, as Lydgate exhorts his audience: 'redith the cronycles' (line 55), in order to call to mind a long sequence of worthies whose earthly prosperity has come to nothing:

> For deth ne sparith emperour ne kyng,
> Though they be armed in plates made of stele:
> He castith downe princes from Fortunes wheele,
> As hir spokes rounde aboute goo … (lines 130–3)

In the somewhat unspecific reference to 'the cronycles' it is tempting to see a pointer to what might have been Lydgate's preoccupation with the narratives to be included in the *Fall of Princes*. The respective dates of the long and the short poem do not rule this out, since Lydgate records that the *Fall* was commissioned by Duke Humphrey of Gloucester in 1431, and internal evidence in *Thoroughfare of Woe* indicates that its composition cannot be dated earlier than November 1428.[18] For readers in the later fifteenth century and beyond, memories of Lydgate's longer engagement with the falls of the famous could certainly have hovered around the edges of this section in *Thoroughfare of Woe*.

MacCracken's edition of *Thoroughfare of Woe* was based on the text in London, British Library, Harley MS 2251, a major repository of Lydgate's shorter works made by a London copyist with access to the anthologies of John Shirley, an earlier scribe who may have had some hot line directly to Lydgate.[19] Textually this is very close to John Shirley's own copy in Cambridge,

---

17 In similar vein Lydgate's short poem *Amor vincit omnia*, lines 17–24, offers a short synopsis of *Troilus and Criseyde*. See MacCracken, ed., *Minor Poems*, II, p. 745.
18 On the dating of *Fall of Princes*, see D. Pearsall, *John Lydgate* (London, 1970), p. 223; and on that of *Thoroughfare of Woe*, see W. F. Schirmer, trans. A. E. Keep, *John Lydgate: A Study in the Culture of the XVth Century* (Westport, CT, 1961), pp. 202–3.
19 On Harley 2251, see E. P. Hammond, 'Two British Museum Manuscripts: A Contribution to the Bibliography of John Lydgate', *Anglia* 28 (1905), 1–28, and on its relationships to Shirley's manuscripts, M. Connolly, *John Shirley: Book Production and the Noble Household in Fifteenth-Century England* (Aldershot, 1998), pp. 178–82. John Shirley's possible relationship with Lydgate is discussed by A. S. G. Edwards, 'Lydgate Manuscripts: Some Directions for Future Research', *Manuscripts and Readers in Fifteenth-Century England*, ed. D. Pearsall (Cambridge, 1983), pp. 15–26, and 'John Shirley, John Lydgate, and the Motives of Compilation', *Studies in the Age of Chaucer* 38 (2016), 245–54.

Trinity College, MS R. 3. 20, which MacCracken seems not to have consulted in establishing his text. One of the other extant copies, in London, British Library, Additional MS 29729, made in the sixteenth century by John Stow, who owned some of Shirley's manuscripts and was able to see others based on them, is textually very close to the copies in Harley 2251 and Trinity College, R. 3. 20.[20]

The remaining witness to *Thoroughfare of Woe*, however, preserves a rather different text. This copy, transcribed at the start of this chapter, is in London, British Library, Additional MS 60577, the so-called 'Winchester anthology', evidently copied in the very late fifteenth century at the Benedictine priory of St Swithun at Winchester.[21] It differs from the three other texts (those forming the Shirley tradition) in a number of respects. For a start, and significantly for this discussion of lyric brevity, it is shorter, a telescoped fifteen-stanza version of what in the other copies is a poem of twenty-four stanzas.[22] Although the reference to Boethius remains at the start, the reference to Chaucer, made at the end of the poem in the other versions as a concluding prod to remember the *Knight's Tale*, is absent. The list of famous unfortunates remains; but here it is in somewhat confused form, with the names of both Julius Caesar and Pompey repeated, and with the addition of some names that do not feature in the Shirley-related copies.[23] What happens next is curious. Following the list of unfortunates are four stanzas that open with a reference to King Arthur and then move into a condensed list of kings of England from William the Conqueror to Henry V, rounding off the list of the noble dead with short references to Henry's brothers Exeter and Clarence, and to 'salesbury Callyde Mountegewe' (line 118). The effect is rather as if the redactor of this version (probably a later reader or scribe, rather than Lydgate himself; and possibly even someone working from a memory of the poem rather than a written copy) has moved into a riff based on Lydgate's own widely circulating *Verses on the Kings of England*.[24] Such reconfiguration makes this version of *Thoroughfare of Woe* into a much more history-focused poem than in its other witnesses, with the injunction to 'read the chronicles' (line 39) at the front of the redactor's mind rather than any obligation to remember Chaucer and his writings.

20   The ascription to Lydgate is present in Trinity College, R. 3. 20 (on which see Connolly, *John Shirley*, pp. 69–101), and in Add. 29729, but absent from Harley 2251 (here a later, probably sixteenth-century hand has written next to the start of the poem 'Reade this agayne').
21   E. Wilson, intro., *The Winchester Anthology: A Facsimile of British Library Additional Manuscript 60577* (Cambridge, 1981); Wilson suggests (pp. 4, 13) that the principal scribe was a monk of the priory.
22   Copied on fols 47–9 of the manuscript, *Thoroughfare of Woe* here occupies the last leaf of quire 5 and ends at the start of the top recto of the second leaf of quire 6 (see the collation in Wilson, *The Winchester Anthology*, p. 3). It continues without any apparent break across the two gatherings, and its abbreviated text does not seem related to any physical losses from the manuscript.
23   See the transcription above, lines 66–70: 'Nembrolle', 'Alix Delira', 'Nabuzardan', 'Judith'.
24   NIMEV 3632; DIMEV 5731, ending most frequently with King Henry VI.

Both the content of *Thoroughfare of Woe* and the processes to which it was apparently subject in transmission offer pointers for understanding and assessing Middle English lyrics. To take content first: although it is indeed, in MacCracken's words, a little homily with a proverbial refrain, its terse homiletic message is given weight by association with larger discourses invoked by allusion to other writings: Boethius's *Consolation*, Chaucer's *Knight's Tale*, *de casibus* narratives of kinds prominent in Chaucer's *Monk's Tale* and to be multiplied in Lydgate's own *Fall of Princes*, and the examples from English history encapsulated in Lydgate's *Verses on the Kings of England*. In transmission, some of these associations appear to have been jettisoned or lost, others newly incorporated, in a sequence whose chronology resists analysis (the most that can be said is that the poem survives in the texts known to MacCracken as a 'little homily', and in the copy in the Winchester anthology as a still smaller one). The proverbial statement of the poem's refrain, 'this world is but a thoroughfare of woe', was both its irreducible core and a peg on which to hang various kinds of elaboration invoking longer works.

Lydgate's shorter poems seem to have offered themselves up very readily to processes involving the kinds of shrinkage or expansion evident here.[25] Their comparatively extensive circulation may have given them a prominence that attracted forms of scribal or readerly *remaniement*. The *Pageant of Knowledge*, *Tied with a lyne* and the *Treatise for Laundresses* all survive in both longer and more condensed versions, while the textual history of the *Verses on the Kings of England* illustrates examples of different forms of adaptation, condensation and expansion.[26] The *Doctrine for pestilence* distils the advice of the *Dietary*, and the seven-stanza poem known as *The sodein fal of princes in oure dayes* seems to have some kind of relationship to the *Fall of Princes*, maybe that of a sample or advertisement.[27] Outside Lydgate's writings, examples of the phenomenon of epitomes of longer works could include Chaucer's short poem *Fortune* in relation to Boethius's *De consolatione Philosophiae* and to Chaucer's own *Boece*. While evidence of processes of expansion and contraction can be found in many kinds of Middle English, the phenomenon seems especially worth exploring in relation to lyrics and shorter poems.

---

25 For some discussion of these processes, see H. Hargreaves, 'Lydgate's *A Rams' Horn*', *Chaucer Review* 10 (1976), 255–9.

26 For the *Pageant* (NIMEV 3651, 576; DIMEV 5788, 939) and *Tied with a lyne* (NIMEV 3503, 3504; DIMEV 5533, 5534), see MacCracken, ed., *Minor Poems*, II, pp. 724–38; for the *Treatise* (NIMEV 4254, 2668; DIMEV 6830, 4240), see MacCracken, ed., *Minor Poems*, II, pp. 723–4; and for the *Verses* (NIMEV 3632, 882; DIMEV 5731, 1472), see MacCracken, ed., *Minor Poems*, II, pp. 710–22, and also Schirmer, *John Lydgate*, pp. 236–7, and L. R. Mooney, 'Lydgate's "Kings of England" and Another Verse Chronicle of the Kings', *Viator* 20 (1989), 255–89.

27 For the *Dietary* and the *Doctrine* (NIMEV 824 and 4112; DIMEV 1356 and 6586), see MacCracken, ed., *Minor Poems*, II, pp. 702–7; and for *The sodein fal* (NIMEV 500; DIMEV 813), see MacCracken, ed., *Minor Poems*, II, pp. 660–1, and also E. P. Hammond, 'Two Tapestry Poems by Lydgate', *Englische Studien* 43 (1910–11), 10–26 (23–6).

The explicit invocation and summary of other, longer works that is a notable feature of *Thoroughfare of Woe* is identifiable in other short Middle English verse texts such as this example from the Vernon lyrics:

In a pistel þat Poul wrou3t	*In a letter that Paul made*
I fond hit writen & seide right this:	
Vche cristne creature knowen himself ou3t	*Each; ought*
His oune vessel; and soþ hit is.²⁸	*body*

The message of this poem, encapsulated in the refrain 'vche mon oughte him-selfe to knowe', is developed from the writings of St Paul, specifically from verses in the first epistle to the Thessalonians.²⁹ Although its stanzas develop nuggets of advice not specifically related to the Pauline epistle, the refrain line has the effect of keeping the biblical authority prominent in the mind of the poem's reader or listener. In just a few instances, when short poem and longer referent are brought together in the context of a single manuscript, this relationship takes material form, becoming one of contiguity as well as of allusion. Such is the case with some copies of the tiny poem *On the evils of the times*, a gnomic comment on difficult years in the reign of Richard II, which accompany longer chronicle accounts giving more detail on precisely those difficulties:

Man be ware and be no fool:	
þenke apon þe ax, and of þe stool!	*Think about; execution block*
þe stool was hard, þe ax was scharp,	
þe iiij 3ere of kyng Richard.³⁰	*fourth year*

The terse lines of the short poem release their meaning in relation to the events recounted in the longer chronicle accounts. At the same time they summarise the longer works for the reader, perhaps even standing in for the labour of reading them. These lines, like those of many lyrics and short poems, have a practically useful as well as an imaginatively striking role in compressing and making memorable a larger body of material. Words such as 'summary' and

---

28 Brown *XIV*, p. 139.
29 The advice proffered in I Thessalonians 4: 3–5 advocates the avoidance of fornication as a particular form of respect for one's body (in the Douay-Rheims translation: 'For this is the will of God, your sanctification: That you should abstain from fornication: That every one of you should know how to possess his vessel in sanctification and honour, Not in the passion of lust, like the Gentiles that know not God').
30 NIMEV 3306; DIMEV 5198; for this version of four lines, see Robbins *Hist.*, p. 54. It occurs on fol. 312 of Cambridge, University Library, MS Dd. 14. 2, which also contains an English metrical chronicle including details of Richard II's reign; see U. O'Farrell-Tate, ed., *The Abridged English Metrical Brut*, Middle English Texts (Heidelberg, 2002), p. 19. A two-line version, without the introductory couplet, occurs on fol. 57 of Oxford, St John's College, MS 209, accompanying Latin annals from William the Conqueror to Henry VI: see R. Hanna, *A Descriptive Catalogue of the Western Manuscripts of St John's College, Oxford* (Oxford, 2002), p. 310.

'epitome' have an off-puttingly functional ring,[31] but they may nonetheless point to instructive ways of understanding both the form and content of such works.

---

[31] The OED definitions of *epitome*, 'A summary of a written work, an abstract', and 'A thing representing something else in miniature', are appropriate to this context, although the earliest attestation is 1529, occurring in John Frith's *Pistle to the reader*, which offers a concluding *epitome* 'of all things that are examined more diligently in the aforesaid book'. The earliest attestation of *summary* is from 1509, in a specifically legal context. *Reduction* is not current until the mid sixteenth century and *precis* not in use before the eighteenth century. *Abreggement* and *abstract* were in use in the fifteenth century.

14

'Short song is good in ale': Charles d'Orléans and Authorial Intentions in the Middle English *Ballade 84*

Denis Renevey

Ballade 84[1]

3110 But for bi cause that deynte lo is leef	*delicacy; pleasing*
Which doth oft tyme the grose mete sett aside	*plain*
That is the cause that motoun veel or beef	
Nor pigge nor goos y cast yow noon provide	
But and ye lust so poore a fare abide	
3115 In stede of mete y fede yow shalle with song	
And for mysvse though that my wordis glide	
Take them aworth y pray yow alle among	*kindly; together*

And for folk say short song is good in alle
That is the cause in rundelle y hem write

I would like to dedicate this essay to my colleague Jean-Claude Mühlethaler, Emeritus Professor at the University of Lausanne (February 2017), to whom I owe my growing interest in Charles d'Orléans. The two classes we taught jointly in the last few years were among the most stimulating ones I experienced during my teaching career.

For a further essay focused on a lyric that scrutinises authorial practice and the authorial 'I', see Mary Wellesley (Chapter 9), 'Textual Lyricism in Lydgate's *Fifteen Joys and Sorrows of Mary*'.

1 NIMEV 553; DIMEV 902. Reproduced by permission of the Council of the Early English Text Society here with the addition of glosses, from R. Steele and M. Day, eds, *The English Poems of Charles d'Orléans*, EETS 215 and 220, revised edn in one volume (London, 1970), p. 104. Apart from *Ballade 84*, which is quoted by line numbers from Steele and Day, all other quotations (by line number) from Charles's English writings are from M.-J. Arn, ed., *Fortunes Stabilnes: Charles of Orléans's English Book of Love: A Critical Edition* (New York, 1994). For his French poetry, with facing Modern English translations, see J. Fox and M.-J. Arn, ed., *Poetry of Charles d'Orléans and His Circle: A Critical Edition of BnF MS. Fr. 25458, Charles d'Orléans's Personal Manuscript* (Tempe, 2010). All quotations from the French are from this edition; see also Charles d'Orléans, *Ballades et Rondeaux. Edition du manuscript 25458 du fonds français de la Bibliothèque nationale de Paris*, ed. J.-C. Mühlethaler (Paris, 1992). For historical, codicological and textual investigations linked to the period of Charles's English captivity, from 1415 to 1440, see the chapters in M.-J. Arn, ed., *Charles d'Orléans in England 1415–1440* (Cambridge, 2000).

3120 The swettist mete als is of birdis smale
    As quaylis rounde and eek the larkis lyte
    But what alle this y putt hit in respite
    For fowlis alle reherse here were to long
    But loke wherto ye haue yowre appetit
3125 And seke hem in this disshis for among

    Parde folk sayne that lovers lyue by lokis
    And bi wisshis and other wanton thought   *lusty*
    Wherfore sum thing y trust in this bok is
    To fede them on if hit be welle out sought
3130 And if so that hit him prevaylen ought   *of any use to them*
    Without they konne me thonk thei don me wrong
    For with laboure y haue it for hem bought
    As them to plese and fede them with among

    Wherfore as this vnto yow louers alle
3135 Here is my fest if hit plese yow to fong   *accept*
    But pardon me that hit is lo so smalle
    At sum tyme if y mende hit shalle among.

The English poetry of Charles d'Orléans is receiving considerable attention at present, with an interest in the interface between his French and English productions, more especially those in his personal manuscript, Paris, Bibliothèque Nationale de France, MS fr. 25458, and in London, British Library, Harley MS 682 (his *English Book*, given the title *Fortunes Stabilnes* by Mary-Jo Arn, its modern editor). Fruitful discussions on subjectivity and persona, self-presentation as well as translating practices, have given rise to a re-evaluation of both the poetic and political achievements of Charles d'Orléans, as well as offering a more complex comparison of the different ways in which autobiography and self-presentation are implicated in his French and English compositions.[2] The understanding of the encoding of subjectivity, and the representations of selves in his corpus, needs to take into consideration the way by which love convention and autobiography blend in complicated ways in the compositions in both languages.[3] Another issue that invites attention is the extent to which the confessional mode, so characteristic of much Middle English poetry, impacts on Charles's shaping of subjectivity

---

[2] R. Critten, 'The Political Valence of Charles d'Orléans's English Poetry', *Modern Philology* 111 (2014), 339–64, offers a good summary; see also: A. C. Spearing, 'Prison, Writing, Absence: Representing the Subject in the English Poems of Charles d'Orléans', *Modern Language Quarterly* 53 (1992), 83–99; J. Summers, *Late-Medieval Prison Writing and the Politics of Autobiography* (Oxford, 2004), pp. 90–107; S. Crane, 'Charles d'Orléans: Self-Translation', *The Medieval Translator* 8, ed. R. Voaden (Turnhout, 2003), pp. 169–77; M.-J. Arn, 'Charles of Orleans: Translator?', *The Medieval Translator* 4, ed. R. Ellis and R. Evans (Exeter, 1994), pp. 125–35.

[3] See A. C. Spearing, *Textual Subjectivity: The Encoding of Subjectivity in Medieval Narratives and Lyrics* (Oxford, 2005), pp. 225–47. For a more general consideration of the lyric in relation to subjectivity, see also pp. 174–81; for a more extensive and theoretical investigation, see J. Culler, *Theory of the Lyric* (Cambridge, 2015).

across his French and English writings. The popularity of confessional literature in medieval England is evident in the number of extant manuscripts whose content served priests and penitents in the exercise of self-examination based on the seven deadly sins. Its influence can also be traced in the penitential aspect of some major late fourteenth-century writings, such as *Sir Gawain and the Green Knight*, *Piers Plowman*, several of Chaucer's *Canterbury Tales* and, of course, Gower's *Confessio Amantis*.[4] According to Raskolnikov, the penitential texts offer an alternative to Aristotelian/philosophical or Galenic/medical modes of thinking about the self, which she labels as vernacular psychology.[5] Indeed, the preponderance of this catechetical literature, and its practical and regular use in processes of introspection by medieval subjects, played a role in the creation of 'confessional literature' and 'confessional narratives' that integrated the introspective methodologies of the former, based on the seven deadly sins, into confessional narratives that moved beyond the strict confines of the genre. Gower's *Confessio Amantis* is a good case in point. As argued by Raskolnikov, it integrates in a very interesting way the confessional narrative mode with courtly models influenced by the 'Ditz amoureux' of the French tradition.[6]

Charles d'Orléans must have been familiar with some of the Ricardian masterpieces that presented themselves as confessional narratives.[7] In addition, he was directly familiar with this tradition as the owner of several devotional texts and the author of a mystical poem, the *Canticum amoris*, a 624-line paraphrase of the Anglo-Norman *Philomela* by John of Howden.[8] As argued by Rory Critten, Charles d'Orléans constructs different personae between his French and English compositions and it may very well be that further comparative investigations between the two will demonstrate the impact of the English confessional

---

[4] See M. Raskolnikov, 'Confessional Literature, Vernacular Psychology, and the History of the Self in Middle English', *Literature Compass* 2 (2005), 1–20; *The Prick of Conscience*, written in the mid-fourteenth century in Yorkshire, but circulating very broadly in the rest of England, is a good example of the kind of vernacular psychology Raskolnikov has in mind; see R. Hanna and S. Wood, eds, *Richard Morris's Prick of Conscience*, EETS OS 342 (Oxford, 2013).

[5] See Raskolnikov, 'Confessional Literature, Vernacular Psychology', p. 1.

[6] Ibid., p. 6; see also D. Poirion, *Le poète et le prince. L'évolution du lyrisme courtois de Guillaume de Machaut à Charles d'Orléans* (Paris, 1965).

[7] See J. Boffey, 'Charles of Orleans Reading Chaucer's Dream Visions', *Medievalitas: Reading the Middle Ages: The J. A. W. Bennett Memorial Lectures, Ninth Series, Perugia*, ed. A. Torti (Cambridge, 1996), pp. 43–62; A. C. Spearing, 'Dreams in *The Kingis Quair* and the Duke's Book', Arn, ed., *Charles d'Orléans in England*, pp. 123–44; and A. Petrina, 'Creative *ymagynacioun* and Canon Constraints in the Fifteenth Century: James I and Charles d'Orléans', *Inspiration and Technique: Ancient to Modern Views on Beauty and Art*, ed. J. Roe and M. Stanco (Bern, 2007), pp. 107–25.

[8] See G. Ouy, 'Un poème mystique de Charles d'Orléans: le *Canticum amoris*', *Studi francesi* 7 (1959), 64–84; see also G. Ouy, 'Charles d'Orléans and his Brother Jean d'Angoulême in England: What their Manuscripts Have to Tell', Arn, ed., *Charles d'Orléans in England*, pp. 47–60 ; and G. Ouy, *La librairie des frères captifs: les manuscrits de Charles d'Orléans et Jean d'Angoulême*, Texte, codex et contexte, 4 (Turnhout, 2007).

tradition on his English text.⁹ This chapter investigates the representation of one particular self, the authorial self, in a single English ballade, *Ballade 84*, looking at the ways in which the narrator extricates himself from a situation of crisis marked by lack of poetic inspiration, where he considers giving up the composition process, to create a vision for a new project based on the use of the roundel. The example of *Ballade 84* demonstrates the potential for short poetry to offer a space where authorial intentions can be asserted and discussed.¹⁰

Both Charles's French and English compositions are replete with references to the writerly process. Indeed, as argued by Spearing, Charles's ballades are presented as 'written fictions of writing' rather than as the reproduction of a speech act conveyed in writing, such as in the tales offered by the Canterbury pilgrims in Chaucer's *Canterbury Tales*.¹¹ As a result, the writerly dimension often serves to highlight the absence of what the poem refers to and compels the narrator to consider the lonely situation in which he finds himself. As pointed out by Spearing, when talking about the lady, the French composition uses 'loingtain' (*far away*) where the English ballades have 'absent', showing the way in which a specific locale invites a different representation of the writing self on the part of the author. In other instances, the narrator makes more formal but brief references to the ballade genre in which writerly activity is taking place. The refrain of *Ballade 40* begins with the verb 'to balade' (line 1440), that is to compose a balade, which alludes to this process as a poor substitute for the presence of and possible physical contact with the lady. Further, the refrain of *Ballade 52* reinforces the inadequacy of writing as the 'medium of love' by making reference to 'this poore balade' (line 1506), which in my view does not refer to its literary quality, but to its disappointing function as an alternative to a real love encounter.¹²

If references to literary activities are present in both the French and English books, *Ballade 83* and *Ballade 84* (the latter having no French equivalent) are central to our understanding of the authorial intentions of Charles d'Orléans in the *English Book*. Indeed, this two-ballade sequence shapes the succeeding roundel sequence in the second part of the *English Book* in a way that the French does not. Before focusing on *Ballade 84* in the remaining part of this chapter, a few words on the authorial move in the preceding ballade should help in assessing the significance of this moment in the English text. If taken at face value, *Ballade 83* announces the end of the composition process by the narrator, who acknowledges he has fallen out of touch with 'baladis, songis, and complayntis' (line

---

9   See Critten, 'Political Valence', pp. 345–6.
10 See Arn, 'Charles of Orleans: Translator?', p. 127, on Orléans and the way in which he could negotiate questions of *auctoritas* more flexibly than other medieval authors and translators, due to the fact he was dealing with his own writings when translating from French into English.
11 See Spearing, *Textual Subjectivity*, p. 231.
12 Ibid., p. 246. For further references to the process of composition, with reference to ballades and roundels, see lines 764, 4652–9 and 5601.

3071) as he is now out of Love's service and in the hands of Indifference, a useless substitute for Love in triggering quality literary activity. Although the narrator has not yet given up the writing process, he acknowledges that he is unable to compose properly since his tongue twists words inappropriately. The representation of the writing self is anything but confident here, and is followed in the French book with a ballade that measures the loss of poetic invention against the relief of being released from the ties associated with the malady of love. *Ballade 72* in the French book (English 83) is preceded by the *Songe en complainte* (lines 1–274) and *La Departie d'Amours en balades* (lines 275–550) and posits a writing self that has negotiated its release from servitude to the Love of God using legally charged vocabulary. The *Departie d'Amours* ends in a formal and legalistic way:

Escript ce jour troisiesme, vers le soir,	Written on the third day, toward evening,
En novembre, oiu lieu de Nonchaloir.	Of November in the dwelling of Indifference.
Le vien vostre, Charles, duc d'Orlians,	Yours truly, Charles, duke of Orleans,
Qui jadis fut l'un de voz vrais srvans.	Who was formerly one of your true servants.
(lines 547–50)	

The English passage leading to *Ballade 83* follows the French closely, but its dating is different:

Wrete in No Care, the date yove to remembre	Written at No Care, the date given as a reminder,
As on the thrittenthe day of Novembre,	The thirteenth day of November,
Bi the trewe Charlis, Duk of Orlyaunce,	By the faithful Charles, Duke of Orleans,
That sumtyme was oon of yowre pore servaunce.	Who at some point was one of your true servants.
(lines 3042–5)	

Although making reference to a slightly different date, which could be due either to a scribal error, or an indication of a move away from the French material in *Ballade 83*, both versions display an 'I-voice' engaging seriously with issues linked to authorial intentions.

English *Ballade 84* has no French equivalent. In my view it offers one of the most significant indications about the ways in which the English book will be structured independently of the French text from this point on. The latter continues with a sequence of thematically loose ballades, including *Ballade 76* written in 1453 on the occasion of the liberation of the provinces of Guienne and Normandy from the English. This ballade is harsh towards Charles d'Orléans's former jailors who betrayed their own king, speak ill of him and are hated by God himself![13] From this moment onwards, and although several roundels or chansons are still shared between BnF, MS fr. 25458 and BL, Harley MS 682, the rationale behind the structuring of the books diverges irremediably.

---

13   See Mühlethaler, ed., *Ballades et Rondeaux*, p. 11.

The French book claims the end of Love's ascendancy over the narrator in *Ballade 73*. However, that confident tone then gives way to a pleading request to Love in a sequence of two complaints of twelve stanzas each.[14] From an initial appeal for Love's recognition of the narrator's past service, the main theme of the second complaint is the absence of the lady and the misery this causes the narrator.[15] *Ballade 75*, which begins with 'Je meurs de soif en couste fontaine' (*I die of thirst beside the fountain*) (line 1), plays on the narrator's feelings using a chain of oxymorons that emphasise confusion, despair and dissatisfaction. It is significant that the theme of dying of thirst beside the fountain will be the one chosen for the *concours de Blois*, a poetry competition at the Court of Blois in 1458, presided over by Charles d'Orléans, which was transcribed into his personal manuscript. Together with *Ballade 76*, this ballade marks the end of the structural similarity between the French and the English books.[16]

This structural difference is confidently negotiated in the English *Ballade 84*. I would like to contend that behind the bawdy humour associated with food and ale imagery, the narrator presents a self whose authorial intentions are precisely defined according to a set of literary tools that circulated, among other texts, in Anglo-Norman and Middle English prologues in late medieval England.[17] Although the food imagery will shortly be used as a vehicle for contrasting the poetic forms of the ballade and roundel, it is initially evoked to think about and contrast carnal/linguistic ingestion, in a way possibly influenced by the monastic tradition of *ruminatio*.[18] Readers are informed that 'Instede of mete, y fede yow shall with song' (line 3115), idealising the state of the lover, and relying upon the stereotype of word as nourishment found in the hermeneutics of both the Bible and the courtly love tradition.[19] True to his statement in the previous ballade, announcing that he is giving up Love's service (English *Ballade 83*), the narrator creates an authorial self who invites his audience to participate in a dialogic relationship: gone are the gestures of self-introspection that represented a self wounded by love, and by the absence of a lady, or by that lady's lack of response. The shift is striking from the incapacitated mood of hopeless literary production under the yoke of Indifference in *Ballade 83* to such a confident affirmation of authorial intentions.

---

14   See Arn and Fox, eds, *Poetry of Charles d'Orléans*, pp. 174–85.
15   Ibid., pp. 180–5.
16   See Mühlethaler, ed., *Ballades et Rondeaux*, p. 267. The theme recurs in *Ballades 97, 102–5, 107–13*.
17   See J. Wogan-Browne, N. Watson, A. Taylor and R. Evans, eds, *The Idea of the Vernacular: An Anthology of Middle English Literary Theory 1280–1520* (Exeter, 1999); especially the prologues to Thomas Usk's *Testament of Love*, and to John Walton's translation of Boethius, pp. 28–38. For an exploration of literary theory in Anglo-Norman texts, see J. Wogan-Browne, T. Fenster and D. Russell, eds, *Vernacular Literary Theory from the French of Medieval England: Texts and Translations, c.1120–c.1450* (Cambridge, 2016).
18   For a study of monastic culture and the role of *ruminatio*, see J. Leclercq, *The Love of Learning and the Desire for God*, 3rd edn (New York, 1982).
19   See D. Kelly, *Medieval Imagination: Rhetoric and the Poetry of Courtly Love* (London, 1978).

This authorial move finds expression via the use of an extensive metaphor based on food consumption. However, beneath this amusing and entertaining veneer the narrator proposes a set of authorial decisions that are configured in a way similar to fifteenth-century vernacular prologues borrowing from the scholastic tradition.[20] As such, the use of 'cause' in the first and third line (lines 3110 and 3112) needs to be read with the context of the Aristotelian four causes (*efficiens, materialis, formalis* and *finalis*) held in mind. It is indeed most likely that Charles d'Orléans was familiar with the four causes of composition discussed in Latin and vernacular prologues.[21] Absorption of these ideas gives the ballade something of the feel of a vernacular prologue, appropriate to the significant change that takes place at this specific point in the English sequence:

> But for bi cause that deynte lo is leef
> Which doth oft tyme the grose mete sett aside
> That is the cause that motoun veel or beef
> Nor pigge nor goos y cast yow noon provide. (lines 3110–13)

The food imagery represents in a remarkably light but effective way the change that the narrator wishes to bring to the content of his sequence. Even if this change is temporary, since a final sequence of ballades will follow the roundel sequence, nonetheless Charles represents the roundel as a poetic form articulated by a self disentangled from the bonds of love, which aims to support lovers looking to channel their amorous feelings via a textual conduit. The way in which this writerly self situates himself with regard to this new authorial role is completely new in the English sequence *Fortunes Stabilnes* and has no counterpart in the French book. In the context of the new authorial role the 'I-voice' confers upon itself, the warnings about the slipperiness of his language at the end of the first stanza have a ring of immediacy and actuality. It fits well with the 'I-voice' in its attention to the processes of writing and reading that he should demonstrate such concern for misreadings of language.

The case for deliberate reference to the Aristotelian four causes, in particular, the *causa finalis*, is strengthened by the announcement made in the first two lines of the second stanza: 'And for folk say "short song is good in ale" / That is the cause in rundell y hem write' (lines 3119–20).

Fortunes Stabilnes, composed of mixed forms, begins with an allegorical opening, followed by a first sequence of eighty-four ballades. It is followed by a vision of Age, and what one could term the 'withdrawal from Love's service', which is expressed in the form of the roundel (one hundred of these in total). A new allegorical section follows, which depicts an encounter with Venus, Fortune

---

20 See A. J. Minnis, *Medieval Theory of Authorship: Scholastic Literary Attitudes in the Late Middle Ages*, 2nd edn (Aldershot, 1988), pp. 28–39.
21 For instance, Osbern Bokenham's prologue to the *Legendys of Hooly Wummen* offers a substantial account of the Aristotelian causes, translated as 'effycient' (line 10), 'materyal' (line 11), 'formal' (line 12) and 'fynal' (line 12); see Wogan-Browne et al., eds, *The Idea of the Vernacular*, pp. 64–72.

and a second lady. The English book concludes with the second sequence of ballades (thirty-seven of these).

Ballade 84 therefore concludes the first sequence of ballades and offers justification for the shift in poetic form by means of a proverb, 'short song is good in ale', which assists the narrator in negotiating this significant move. What the proverb means is that the shorter a song, the more time it will allow one to consume ale, thus suggesting an (imaginary) context of literary and alcoholic consumption far removed from a noble setting.[22] It initially points to the form of the roundel as an inferior form to the one in which that aesthetic judgement is embedded, that is, the ballade. That position, however, does not seem to be given such prominence in the remaining lines of the ballade. The *causa finalis* of the collection, 'the cause in rundell y hem write', seems to make reference to an audience expectation that love poems will be short, rather than upon the personal need to couch personal experience in a pseudo-autobiographical mode.[23]

Moving back to the food imagery that associated the ballade with delicate meat, such as 'motoun', 'veel', 'beef', 'pig' or 'goos', the roundel itself is categorised within that frame as being the 'swetist' meat made up of the flesh of small birds, such as the round quail or the small lark.[24] Although medieval food practices, and more particularly medieval taste, cannot be assessed in any objective way, the comparison of these different courtly foodstuffs seems to indicate that the difference between the two poetic forms is based primarily upon their comparative delicacy and size, with the roundel emerging as the less 'dainty', but more miniature of the two. The narrator of *Ballade 84* therefore offers an apology for lyrical forms such as the ballade and the roundel. He even suggests a mode of consumption for a lyric sequence to his readership, by inviting them to select from the several dishes on display, and to pick and choose according to their own special wishes and needs.[25]

Ballade 84 not only offers a justification for short poetry, it also suggests a selective way of reading collections of short poetry in accordance with the aspirations and needs of readers. By outlining this mode of reading, it bears importantly upon *Fortune Stabilnes* as a whole, as well as, more particularly,

---

22 See the notes in Arn, ed., *Fortunes Stabilnes*, p. 487.
23 'The final cause was the ultimate justification for the existence of a work, the end or objective (*finis*) aimed at by the writer'; see Minnis, *Medieval Theory*, p. 29. On autobiography in Charles d'Orléans's English poems, see Summer, *Late-Medieval Prison Writing*, pp. 1–23, 90–107.
24 The first two lines of *Ballade 84* are ambiguous. My understanding is that the 'I-voice' considers 'motoun', 'veel' and so on as delicacies. He will therefore refrain from offering them so that the plain food will be consumed. Transposed in terms of literary forms, it means that the 'I-voice' gives up (for the time being) the form of the ballade, and offers the roundel instead.
25 This suggestion of ad hoc, selective reading, echoes scholastic and devotional practices that had already emerged in vernacular religious texts of the thirteenth century; see M. Parkes, 'The Influence of the Concepts of *Ordinatio* and *Compilatio* on the Development of the Book', *Medieval Learning and the Book: Essays Presented to Richard William Hunt* (Oxford, 1976), pp. 115–41.

guiding our reception of the roundel sequence that follows.[26] *Ballade 84* stands, then, as the locus for the expression of significant authorial decisions explicating the change from the ballade to the roundel as a poetic medium, and deserves far greater attention than it has had as a unique defence of poesy expressed in poetic form in support of short verse. The ballade, with its decasyllabic lines, and its eight-line stanzas followed by a four-line envoy, provides the space necessary to express a sophisticated literary theory about the role and ways of reading short poetry. Both ballade and roundel fulfil different roles in the eyes of Charles d'Orléans. The *causa finalis*, or ultimate purpose, of each is quite distinct.

New eating fashions of the nobility in the early modern period in England aimed to present lighter dishes in more modest presentations.[27] Small birds may have figured largely in these dishes, as substitutes for the fatter dishes composed of beef, lamb or mutton. It seems likely that Charles d'Orléans's extension of food imagery in the third stanza makes reference to new ways of consuming food in the late medieval/early modern period. If that is the case, it suits very well what Charles has in mind with regard to the way in which his collection of roundels should be consumed. Lovers governed by desire and lusty thoughts will be able to select what they need in the collection that the narrator has prepared for their attention. The 'I-voice' of *Ballade 84* has a strong sense of the importance of the significant task given to the human *auctor* and has no qualms in insisting on the difficulties it entails for him. The wish of the 'I-voice' to be recognised as the *causa efficiens* for this particular part of the collection implies a confident authorial self who, although willing to accept potential criticism for the inadequacies of some of its verse, would also like his readership to credit him if his food has been of any use to them. Indeed, he insists that not to do so would be to 'do him wrong':

> And if so that hit him prevaylen ought
> Without they konne me thonk thei don me wrong
> For with laboure y haue it for hem bought
> As them to plese and fede them with among. (lines 3130–3)

The envoy further confirms the idea of *Ballade 84* standing as a proto-prologue to the sequence of one hundred roundels that follows. 'Here is my fest', says the 'I-voice', continuing the analogy of the roundel sequence with the display of

---

26   My point here, that scattered reading of the contents of *Fortunes Stabilnes* was an option, complements rather than contradicts Arn's view of *Fortunes Stabilnes* as a work to be read as a whole; see M.-J. Arn, 'Two Manuscripts, One Mind: Charles d'Orléans and the Production of Manuscripts in Two Languages (Paris, BN, MS fr. 25458 and London, BL MS Harley 682)', Arn, ed., *Charles d'Orléans in England*, pp. 61–78.

27   It may be that Charles d'Orléans is making reference to new culinary practices that, according to Alison Findlay (private communication), were in vogue in early modern England. For an investigation of table manners and food consumption in late medieval England, see A. Petrina, 'One Bowl, Two Eaters: Medieval Eating Habits in the "Babees' Books"', *A Garland of True Plain Words: saggi in onore di Paola Bottalla*, ed. A. Oboe and A. Scacchi (Padua, 2012), pp. 231–47.

small and lighter dishes that may have become fashionable in the later medieval period. It invites its audience to select from a choice, according to personal taste and needs. It also requests tolerance, since the narrator is aware that the selection may be both limited and also in a state of *mouvance*, for which the 'I-voice' takes responsibility as it announces further additions, emendations and corrections.

This chapter examines *Ballade 84* as a central cog in the machinery that structurally strengthens Charles d'Orléans's *English Book*.[28] It identifies an English authorial voice that confidently cuts and pastes scholastic Aristotelian prologue practices to fit a pattern for which they were not initially intended. The food imagery that pervades the entire poem should not distract us from detecting a well-thought-out argument explicating the short poem as an appropriate locus for transmitting sophisticated reflections about authorial persona and intentions. On the contrary, if read perspicaciously, the reference to new ways of selecting and consuming lighter dishes demonstrates further the innovative authorial move of the 'I-voice' of *Ballade 84*. The invitation to undertake a scattered reading of the roundel sequence following *Ballade 84* is argued with great subtlety.

As mentioned before, the fact that *Ballade 84* has no French equivalent makes the suggestion that it stands as a new beginning for the English book even more enticing. In my view it fulfils the role usually attributed to vernacular prologues, positioning itself as a threshold from which one is presented with a view of new dishes that must be tasted and ruminated on in order to appease one's appetite. Considered within the larger context of poetic practice, *Ballade 84* offers one of the best defences of English short poetry in the late medieval period, and it is time that we regarded it as a significant contribution informed by widespread love conventions and an intimate knowledge of English poetic practice.

---

28   Boffey, 'Charles of Orleans Reading Chaucer's Dream Visions', p. 45, makes reference to the content of *Ballade 83* to discuss the change from the ballade to the roundel genre; see also M.-J. Arn, 'Poetic Form as Mirror of Meaning in the English Poems of Charles of Orleans', *Philological Quarterly* 69 (1990), 13–29 (esp. 16), where Arn makes a brief reference to *Ballade 84* as part of a transitional passage that 'prepares us for the shift in tone and in purpose of the roundel series which follows'.

Part IV

WORDS, MUSIC, SPEECH

15

All Adam's Children: The Early Middle English Lyric Sequence in Oxford, Jesus College, MS 29 (II)

Susanna Fein

An Orison to Our Lord[1]

(Oxford, Jesus College, MS 29 (II), fols 192r–93r)

    Louerd Crist, ich þe grete –
    Þu art so mylde and swete.
    From heouene, Louerd, þu hider come,   *hither came*
    And of þe swete mayde þu fleys nome;   *flesh took*
5   And hw hit ferde mon may esche: *how; happened; witness* (isen)
    Þi goddede wes ihud in fleysse;   *godhead; hidden*
    Of þe mayde þu were ibore
    God and mon, so wel icore;   *chosen*
    Þo þu hire to come, heo mayde wes,   *When; she was a virgin*
10   And mayde heo wes after, wemmeles.   *unblemished*

    Ihesu, ich þe grete, as ich er seyde.   *earlier*
    Þu were ibore, Louerd, of þe swete mayde;
    Þu vndervenge al vre wowe   *took on; woe*
    Wiþvte sunne, þat riht wule knowe.   *sin; as can be affirmed*
15   As oþer childre, þu eodest and speke;   *walked*
    Hunger and þurst þu þoledest eke.   *suffered too*
    Buhsum and poure þu were iwis;   *Humble; poor; indeed*
    Forbysne þu vs yeue and nouht amys.   *Example; gave; nothing amiss*

    Ihesu, ich þe grete, Cryst, Louerd min,

For additional essays that offer a lyric in a new edition, and pay extended attention to manuscript context, see Michael P. Kuczynski (Chapter 4), 'Textual and Affective Stability in *All Other Love is Like the Moon*', and Julia Boffey (Chapter 13), 'Poems that Speak Volumes: Lydgate's *Thoroughfare of Woe*, and Lyric as Epitome'. For another essay concerned with a lyric sequence, see Denis Renevey (Chapter 14), '"Short song is good in ale": Charles d'Orléans and Authorial Intentions in the Middle English *Ballade 84*', all in this volume.

1   NIMEV 1948; DIMEV 3190; newly edited and glossed here, with modern punctuation added and abbreviations expanded. The only previous edition is R. Morris, ed., *An Old English Miscellany*, EETS OS 49 (London, 1872), pp. 139–41.

20	Þat for vs þoledest so swi þe muchel pyn.	*suffered such intense pain*
	Wunderliche, þurh wacche and fast,	*watching; fasting*
	Þi swete lychome þu teonedest	*body; mortified*
	God to doune and vuel to byleue;	*Good; do; evil; forsake*
	Ful gode vorbysne þu vs yeue!	
25	No more luue ne may mon cheosen	*greater*
	Þane deþ to þolyen for oþer to alesen.	*suffer to redeem another*
	Ihesu, ich þe grete, þat were þar harde ibunde;	*tightly bound*
	Wiþ scurges þu þoledest mony blodi wunde.	
	Bivore þe he þene men þu stode,	*heathen*
30	Naked and bylaued² myd blode.	*streaming*
	Buffetes þu þoledest inowe;	*extremely*
	Bispat þu were and al myd wowe.	*Spat upon; engulfed in*
	Mid on red mantel þu were byweued;	*clothed*
	Crune of þornes þu heuedest on heued.	*Crown; had; head*
35	Ne myhte þe mixes³ þo wurse þe don	*couldn't then do worse to you*
	Bute among þeoues on rode anhon.	*Than; thieves; cross; hang (you)*
	Al þu þoldest for vre sake –	
	Al þe seorewe þat heo þe myhte make!	
	Ihesu Crist þat so luuedest mon,	
40	Ich þe grete al so ich best can,	*as best as*
	Þat þoledest þat þi swete lich	*body*
	Of heþene todreued wes sullych:	*tormented; horribly*
	Iþurled weren myd nayles þreo	*Pierced; three*
	Honden and fet faste to þe treo;	
45	Þat cold iren þu þoledest in þi syde,	
	Of þe spere kene, to þin heorte glyde.	*sharp; cut*
	As þu þoledest þeos fyf wunde	*Just as*
	Of seorewe and sunne, wite us myd isunde.	*keep us sound of body* (witien v.(1))
	Ihesu, ich þe grete, and þat is wel ryht,	*very fitting*
50	And þarto to don bo þe mayn and myht.	*to that end exert; strength; power*
	For þe muchel þoleburne[sse]⁴	*profound submissiveness*
	Þer⁵ þu schawedest monkunne þo þu þoledest deþ,	*showed; when*
	After alle þe pyne þat þe runnen a blode,	*streaked you with blood*
	Þoledest, Louerd Crist, þat me þe dude on rode.	*when men placed*

---

2   According to the MED, s.v. 'bilaved' (ppl.), this word is not recorded elsewhere.
3   The word *mix* denotes 'filth, dung'; hence, the torturers are here called 'dirt' or 'befoulers' (MED, s.v. 'mix' (n.)).
4   MS reads: 'For þe muchel þoleburne, and þarto don boþe mayn & myht'. The MED notes that 'þoleburne' is an error for 'þoleburnesse' (s.v. 'thole-burdnesse' (n.)). The repetition of line 50 is also an error, so it is deleted here. I have not attempted to emend the faulty rhyme of lines 51–2. 'Schawedest' may have rhymed with 'þoledest' in the original verses.
5   Morris prints 'þat', but the MS reads: 'þer' (*er* abbreviated).

55	Hwoso hit ileueþ myd gode wille,	*believes it; intent*
	Ne may nouht þe feond his saule aspille!	*destroy*

	Ihesu, ich þe grete so wysslych	*as faithfully*
	As þu deþ þoledest myldelich.	
	Ich þe bidde, Louerd, þurh þe ilke rode	*pray to; very*
60	Þar þu myd blodie wunde stode,	*Where; endured*
	On þine werkes, so my lif leade,	
	And so do by þine rede,	*counsel*
	Þat my saule habbe lysse,	*comfort*
	Þat myn ende come to eche blysse. Amen.	

A Little Sooth Sermon[6]

(Oxford, Jesus College, MS 29 (II), fol. 185r–v)

	Herkneþ alle gode men and stylle sitteþ adun,	
	And ich ou wile tellen a lutel soþ sermun.[7]	
	Wel we wuten alle, þey ich ou nouht ne telle,	*know; though I didn't tell you*
	Hw Adam vre vormefader adun feol into helle.	*forefather*
5	Schomeliche he forles þe blisse þat he hedde	*Shamefully; forfeited*
	To yuernesse and prude – none neode he nedde!	*avarice; pride; no need had he!*
	He nom þan appel of þe treo þat him forbode was,	*took; forbidden to him*
	So reuþful dede idon neuer non nas!	*So pitiful a deed was never done!*
	He made him into helle falle,	
10	And, after him, his children alle.	
	Þer he wes, fort vre Drihte	*until; Lord*
	Hyne bouhte myd his myhte.	
	He hine alesede myd his blode	*redeemed*
	Þat he schedde vpon þe rode.	*cross*
15	To deþe he yef him for vs alle	*gave himself*
	Þo we weren so strong atfalle.	*When; utterly fallen*
	Alle bakbytare, heo wendeþ to helle,	*backbiters; shall go*
	Robbares and reuares and þe monquelle,	*thieves; murderers*
	Lechurs and horlyngs, þider schulleþ wende,	*whoremongers; thither*
20	And þer heo schulle wunye euer buten ende.	*dwell forever without end*
	Alle þeos false chapmen, þe feond heom wule habbe,	*merchants*

---

6   NIMEV 1091; DIMEV 1773; newly edited and glossed here, with modern punctuation added and abbreviations expanded. Another copy appears in London, British Library, Cotton MS Caligula A IX, fols 248v–49r. Previous editions are R. Morris, ed., *An Old English Miscellany*, EETS OS 49 (London, 1872), pp. 186–91, and T. Wright, ed., *The Owl and the Nightingale: An Early English Poem attributed to Nicholas of Guildford, with Some Shorter Poems from the Same Manuscript*, Percy Society 11 (London, 1843), pp. 1–84 (pp. 80–4).

7   Cotton MS reads: 'a lutel sermun'.

	Bakares and breowares, for alle men heo gabbe.	*they deceive*
	Lowe heo holdeþ heore galun;⁸ mid beorme heo hine fullþ,	*gallon measure; ale-froth; fill it*
	And euer of þe purse þat seoluer heo tulleþ.	*always they charge silver from the purse*
25	Bo þe heo makeþ feble heore bred and heore ale –	*Both of them; weak*
	Habbe heo þat seoluer, ne telleþ heo neuer tale!	*Once they have; they don't care*
	Gode men, for Godes luue, bileueþ sucche sunne,	*abandon; sin*
	For at þen ende hit binymeþ heueriche wunne.	*forfeits heavenly joy*
	Alle preostes wives, ich wot, heo beoþ forlore;	*know; they'll be lost*
30	Þes persones, ich wene, ne beoþ heo nouht forbore,	*parsons; think; they'll not be spared*
	Ne þeos prude yonge men þat luuyeþ Malekyn,	
	And þeos prude maydenes þat luuyeþ Ianekyn.	
	At chireche and at chepyng, hwanne heo togadere come,	*church; market*
	Heo runeþ togaderes and spekeþ of derne luue.	*They whisper; private love*
35	Hwenne heo to chirche cumeþ to þon holy daye,	
	Euerych wile his leof iseo þer yef he may.	*Each; see his sweetheart; if*
	Heo biholdeþ Watekin mid swiþe gled eye;	*She; very flirty*
	At hom is hire Paternoster, biloken in hire teye.	*home; locked up; box*
	Masses and matynes ne kepeþ heo nouht,	*pays no attention to*
40	For Wilekyn and Watekyn beoþ in hire þouht.⁹	*are*
	Robyn wule Gilothe leden to þan ale,	*alehouse*
	And sitten þer togederes and tellen heore tale.	*(they) sit; spin their tales*
	He may quyten hire ale and seoþ þe don þat gome;	*pay for; later play that game*
	An eue to go myd him ne þincheþ hire no schome.	*At night; she thinks it no shame*
45	Hire syre and hire dame þreteþ hire to bete;	*father; mother; threaten*
	Nule heo furgo Robyn for al heore þrete.	*She won't give up*
	Euer heo wule hire skere ne com hire no mon neyh,	*she'll claim no man came near her*
	Forte þat hire wombe vp aryse an heyh.	*Until; high [in pregnancy]*
	Gode men, for Godes luue, bileueþ oure sunne,	*abandon your sin*
50	For at þon ende hit binymeþ heoueryche wunne.	*forfeits heavenly joy*
	Bidde we Seynte Marie for hire milde mode,	*Let us pray to*
	For þe theres þat heo weop for hire Sune blode.	*tears; weeps; Son's blood*

---

8   The earliest citation of this word; see MED, s.v. 'galoun' (n.). The brewer cheats customers by filling the measure with froth.

9   The Cotton MS lacks this line.

Al so wis so he god is, for hire erendynge,	*good; intercession*
To þe blysse of heouene he vs alle brynge. Amen.	*may he bring us all*

Instead of looking at a single lyric, I focus here on two from the same manuscript: *An Orison to Our Lord* and *A Little Sooth Sermon*. Neither has ever been included in a modern anthology of Middle English lyrics. Both survive in an extraordinary thirteenth-century literary sequence of moral and didactic poems compiled and disseminated in the West Midlands of England. Looking at these neglected lyrics helps to demonstrate the aesthetic range of this series, which, through them, can be shown to extend beyond familiar modes seen in its better-known items: wise sayings in the *Proverbs of Alfred*, advice on a good life in *A Moral Ode*, strains of mystic love-longing in Thomas of Hales's *Love Rune*. To date, little has been written about the full sequence's nature, qualities or purpose. For most individual items, scant has been said beyond brief mentions.[10] Scholars who have heeded the cluster in its fullest witness, Oxford, Jesus College, MS 29 (II), have tended mainly to consult that manuscript on account of its best-known member, the early Middle English *Owl and the Nightingale*. The remarkable existence of that learned, spritely, vernacular poem has almost wholly eclipsed our taking notice of its place beside an authentic medieval anthology of English religious verse, another rare and remarkable literary phenomenon for its time.

The lyric sequence survives nearly intact in Jesus, and a portion of it (including *Sermon* but not *Orison*) survives in the second *Owl* manuscript, BL, Cotton MS Caligula A IX, which evidently shared an exemplar with Jesus.[11] Six lyrics are copied in Cotton in the same order, and one more, *Will and Wit*, appears where a leaf is gone in Jesus, so it is reasonable to think that this brief lyric also belonged to the original set (which I will hereafter term the 'CJ Lyrics').[12] Jesus and Cotton are among the more important manuscripts from the era of trilingual book making, and for most of these lyrics,

---

[10] The fullest account to date is N. Cartlidge, 'The Composition and Social Context of Oxford, Jesus College, MS 29(II) and London, British Library, MS Cotton Caligula A.ix', *Medium Aevum* 66 (1997), 250-69. See also N. R. Ker, intro., *The Owl and the Nightingale Reproduced in Facsimile from the Surviving Manuscripts Jesus College Oxford 29 and British Museum Cotton Caligula A.ix*, EETS OS 251 (London, 1963), pp. ix-xxi; B. Hill, 'The History of Jesus College, Oxford MS. 29', *Medium Aevum* 32 (1963), 203-13; N. Cartlidge, *Medieval Marriage: Literary Approaches, 1100-1300* (Cambridge, 1997), pp. 163-6; N. Cartlidge, ed. and trans., *The Owl and the Nightingale: Text and Translation*, Exeter Medieval Texts and Studies (Exeter, 2001), pp. 27, 30, 38; and B. Hill, 'Oxford, Jesus College MS 29, Part II: Contents, Technical Matters, Compilation, and Its History to c.1695', *Notes and Queries* 50 (2003), 268-76.

[11] On the shared exemplar, see especially N. Cartlidge, 'Imagining X: A Lost Early Vernacular Miscellany', *Imagining the Book*, ed. S. Kelly and J. J. Thompson (Turnhout, 2005), pp. 31-44.

[12] Three leaves are missing from Jesus 29, and the one lost after fol. 180 affects the English lyrics. See C. Sisam, 'The Broken Leaf in MS. Jesus College, Oxford, 29', *Review of English Studies*, NS 5 (1954), 337-43.

they are the only witnesses.[13] The coincident poems indicate the existence of a kind of 'literary canon' of moral verse in Middle English circulating in the West Midlands from about 1250 to 1340.[14] The following table lists the contents of both manuscripts, demarcating the section of CJ Lyrics and providing their metrical profile.

Oxford, Jesus College, MS 29 (II)	BL, Cotton MS Caligula A IX
The Passion of Jesus Christ (NIMEV 1441) *The Owl and the Nightingale* (NIMEV 1384)	Layamon, *Brut* (NIMEV 295) Chardri, *The Life of St Josaphaz*[15] Chardri, *The Life of the Seven Sleepers* English Prose *Chronicle* *The Owl and the Nightingale* (NIMEV 1384)
The CJ Lyrics	The CJ Lyrics

A Moral Ode (NIMEV 1272)
   378 septenary lines, couplets
Sinners Beware (NIMEV 3607)
   354 lines, 6-line stanzas, aabaab$_3$
Woman of Samaria (NIMEV 3704)
   77 septenary lines, couplets
Weal (NIMEV 3873)
   4 septenary lines, aaaa$_7$
Death's Wither-Clench (NIMEV 2070)
   50 lines, 10-line stanzas, ababbaabbb$_4$
An Orison to Our Lady (NIMEV 2687)
   50 lines, 10-line stanzas, ababaababa$_4$
Annunciation (NIMEV 877)[16]
   7 lines, aaabbbb$_{5-7}$ (a fragment)
Seven Joys of Our Lady Saint Mary (NIMEV 1833)
   48 lines, 8-line stanzas, abababab$_{3-4}$
When Holy Church Is Overcome (NIMEV 4085)
   36 septenary lines, rhyming aa$_7$, aaa$_7$, or aaaa$_7$
	Death's Wither-Clench (NIMEV 2070)
	
	An Orison to Our Lady (NIMEV 2687)
	
	Will and Wit (NIMEV 4016)
	   8 lines, abababab$_4$

13   Other thirteenth-century witnesses with the most overlapping lyrics are: BodL, MS Digby 86 (three lyrics, two analogues); Cambridge, Trinity College, MS B. 14. 39 (four lyrics); and Maidstone Museum, MS A.13 (three lyrics).

14   S. Fein, 'The Fillers of the Auchinleck Manuscript and the Literary Culture of the West Midlands', *Makers and Users of Medieval Books: Essays in Honour of A. S. G. Edwards*, ed. C. M. Meale and D. Pearsall (Cambridge, 2014), pp. 60–77 (pp. 62–3). Compare Cartlidge, 'The Composition', pp. 259–60.

15   The Anglo-French author Chardri, present in both manuscripts, is likely 'Richard' in anagram. N. Cartlidge, trans., *The Works of Chardri: Three Poems in the French of Thirteenth-Century England: 'The Life of Seven Sleepers', 'The Life of St. Josaphaz', and 'The Little Debate'*, French of England Translation Series 9 (Tempe AR, 2015).

16   This fragment is probably a portion of the lyric that follows *Love Rune* in Jesus.

Doomsday (NIMEV 3967) *Doomsday* (NIMEV 3967)
    44 septenary lines, 4-line stanzas, aaaa₇
Death (NIMEV 3517) *Death* (NIMEV 3517)
    132 septenary lines, 4-line stanzas, aaaa₇
Ten Abuses (NIMEV 4051) *Ten Abuses* (NIMEV 4051)
    14 lines (2–3 stresses), irregular rhyme
A Little Sooth Sermon (NIMEV 1091) *A Little Sooth Sermon* (NIMEV 1091)
    54 lines, mostly septenary, couplets
Antiphon of St Thomas the Martyr (*NIMEV* 1233)
    10 lines, aabccddee₄
On Serving Christ (NIMEV 4163)
    78 septenary lines, couplets
Thomas of Hales, Love Rune (NIMEV 66)
    105 septenary lines with internal rhymes, aaaa$_{7-8}$
Annunciation of the Virgin Mary (NIMEV 877)
    11 lines, irregular rhyme (a fragment)
Fragment on Doomsday (NIMEV *2284.3)
    4 septenary lines, some internal rhyme, aaaa$_{7-8}$
Signs of Death (NIMEV 4047)
    12 lines, aabbccddeeff$_{3-4}$
Three Sorrowful Things (NIMEV 695)
    6 lines, aabbcc₄
Proverbs of Alfred (NIMEV 433)
    455 lines, irregular rhyme
An Orison to Our Lord (NIMEV 1948)
    64 lines, couplets, stanzas of irregular length
Duty of Christians (NIMEV 3474)
    60 septenary lines with internal rhymes, aaaa$_{7-8}$

The Shires of England Chardri, *The Little Debate*
Assisa panis Anglie
Extract from *Tobie*
The Eleven Pains of Hell (NIMEV 3828)
Le Doctrinal Sauvage[17]
Chardri, *The Life of the Seven Sleepers*
Chardri, *The Life of St Josaphaz*
Chardri, *The Little Debate*

Overall, Jesus contains more items than does Cotton: thirty-three versus thirteen. The lyric sequence in Jesus numbers twenty-three items versus seven in Cotton. Nearly all of Cotton's texts appear in Jesus, the only exceptions being an important copy of Layamon's *Brut*, another chronicle, and the aphoristic *Will and Wit*. The fact that the Cotton lyrics appear in the order found in Jesus is evidence that both manuscripts descend from a model in which the CJ Lyrics appeared as in Jesus. Carleton Brown notes that Jesus and Cotton's sequential

---

17 A. Sakari, ed., *Doctrinal Sauvage, publié d'après tous les manuscrits*, Studia Philologica Jyväskyläensia 3 (Jyväskylä, 1967).

repetition 'is a situation ... not paralleled in any of the other collections of thirteenth-century lyrics'.[18] Moreover, in comparing the Cotton and Jesus copies of *Owl*, one sees much similarity in their layouts.[19] Both seem to preserve the page-by-page appearance of an exemplar.

Given the presence of three additional items of English verse in Jesus (*Passion of Jesus Christ*, *Owl* and *Eleven Pains of Hell*), how does one know where to demarcate the CJ Lyrics? Hypothetically, they might be viewed as beginning devotionally with the 706-line *Passion* and ending eschatologically with the *Eleven Pains* (a version of the Vision of Saint Paul). By this view, the long debate-poem *Owl* would be its second, least lyric-like member. The sheer length of the first two poems argues, however, against their inclusion: the combination of *Owl* with *Passion* (the second-longest item) roughly numbers as many lines as are found in the book's remaining English verse (about 2,500 lines for each portion). Meanwhile, anomalies at the end argue against extending the sequence to *Eleven Pains*. Between the *Duty of Christians* and *Eleven Pains*, oddities crop up: a prose account of England's shires, a Latin assise for bread prices and an extract from the French *Life of Tobie*.[20] Amid these disparities, it seems best to view the series as beginning and ending where it is visibly unified and consistent in its nature as English moral verse, that is, the items running from *A Moral Ode* to the *Duty of Christians*. In both manuscripts, the sequence directly follows *Owl*.

In Jesus especially, this long sequence of 'decidedly austere' English poems indelibly marks the book's character.[21] Noting the tenor of this verse, Celia Sisam calls the Jesus volume 'a serious and edifying collection',[22] while Annette Kehnel, influenced by the presence of *Owl*, defines it more fulsomely as 'a poetic anthology'.[23] Combining both views, John Frankis terms Jesus 'a neat anthology for churchmen' that is 'strikingly literary', while also noting distinct tonal differences between the book's English and French portions: the English lyrics brandish a fiery 'evangelical puritanism', while the French texts adhere more circumspectly to 'religious sobriety and conformity'.[24] The presence of *Owl* adds diversity and

---

18 Brown *XIII*, p. xxv.
19 They can be viewed side by side in Ker, intro., *The Owl and the Nightingale*.
20 On the prose texts, see Hill, 'The History', pp. 204–7; and Cartlidge, 'The Composition', pp. 259–60. On *Tobie*, see R. Reinsch, ed., 'La vie de Tobie de Guillaume le Clerc de Normandie', *Archiv für das Studium der Neueren Sprachen und Literaturen* 62 (1879), 375–96.
21 Cartlidge, *The Works of Chardri*, p. 4.
22 Sisam, 'The Broken Leaf', p. 343. Compare D. Pearsall, *Old English and Middle English Poetry* (London, 1977), p. 96.
23 A. Kehnel, 'Poets, Preachers and Friars Revisited: Fourteenth-Century Multilingual Franciscan Manuscripts', *The Beginnings of Standardization: Language and Culture in Fourteenth-Century England*, ed. U. Schaefer (Frankfurt am Main, 2006), pp. 91–114 (p. 96). Compare S. Wenzel, *Preachers, Poets, and the Early English Lyric* (Princeton, 1986), p. 8.
24 J. Frankis, 'The Social Context of Vernacular Writing in Thirteenth Century England: The Evidence of the Manuscripts', *Thirteenth Century England I: Proceedings of the Newcastle upon Tyne Conference 1985*, ed. P. R. Coss and S. D. Lloyd (Woodbridge, 1986), pp. 175–84

literary flair to the book's English side, tempering its prevalent salvific fervour with an enjoyably worldly wrangling and wit. At the same time, the CJ Lyrics are not themselves wholly devoid of diverse modes and artful impacts.[25] The two highlighted here – *An Orison to Our Lord* and *A Little Sooth Sermon* – provide intimate glimpses into patterns of thought that informed thirteenth-century religious sensibilities. In them, practices of devotion and penance, as were counselled to laity by priests and confessors (no doubt the authors), are aesthetically amplified and made vivid.

The CJ Lyrics' obscurity as a group stems, in part, from how surviving specimens of medieval English lyrics have tended to be disseminated to readers and scholars – across the modern era of literary criticism and editorial activity, from the mid-1800s until now – via anthologies that alter and consequently blur their historical contexts. Until recently, for example, the robust record of poetic entertainments found in BL, Harley MS 2253, c.1340, was largely unavailable to readers drawn to the manuscript for its fine set of English poems. The well-known Harley Lyrics had been selectively extracted, while other texts in Harley were left opaque, untouched by editors, unread by literary scholars.[26] Meanwhile, other late thirteenth- and early fourteenth-century literary manuscripts from England still await full attention to the entirety of their contents. Many have been classed broadly by modern scholars as 'trilingual miscellanies', a blanket term by which we often concede ignorance of their original purposes, manners of construction and possible rationales for inclusion of matter.[27]

Moreover, in the case of the lyrics in Jesus, Cotton, and their exemplar, a debate over original milieux has regrettably drawn more scholarly notice than has the sequence itself. The idea that friars – usually named as the Franciscans, who came to England in 1224 – produced the bulk of surviving early Middle English lyrics and constructed the books that preserve them was once a staple theory enveloping Jesus and other early miscellanies holding lyrics.[28] The notion

---

(p. 181). The French matter that fills the end of Jesus occupies as much space as the mostly English matter that fills the first half (fifty-seven folios each). Cartlidge disputes the 'neat anthology' idea, arguing that it 'suggests a tidiness and clarity of purpose which the collection certainly does not possess' ('The Composition', p. 262).

25 The most celebrated among them is Thomas of Hales's *Love Rune*. See S. G. Fein, ed., *Moral Love Songs and Laments* (Kalamazoo MI, 1998), pp. 11–56 (esp. pp. 15–24).

26 For example, Brook. BL, Harley MS 2253 has now been fully edited: S. Fein, ed. and trans., with D. Raybin and J. Ziolkowski, *The Complete Harley 2253 Manuscript, Volumes 1–3* (Kalamazoo, MI, 2014–15).

27 T. Hunt, 'Insular Trilingual Compilations', *Codices Miscellanearum*, ed. R. Jansen-Sieben and H. van Dijk, Archives et Bibliothèques de Belgique 60 (Brussels, 1999), pp. 51–70. See also J. Boffey and A. S. G. Edwards, 'Towards a Taxonomy of Middle English Manuscript Assemblages', *Insular Books: Vernacular Manuscript Miscellanies in Late Medieval Britain*, ed. M. Connolly and R. Radulescu (Oxford, 2015), pp. 263–79; and A. Bahr, 'Miscellaneity and Variance in the Medieval Book', *The Medieval Manuscript Book: Cultural Approaches*, ed. M. Johnston and M. Van Dussen (Cambridge, 2016), pp. 181–98.

28 For a summary and refutation of the theory, see esp. Frankis, 'The Social Context', pp. 179–82; Cartlidge, 'The Composition', pp. 258–62; S. Wenzel, *Verses in Sermons: 'Fasciculus*

attached particularly to Jesus because of *Love Rune*'s ascription to Brother Thomas of Hales. By association, Cotton was tightly drawn into the same circle. Now, however, assertions of predominantly fraternal authorship have been retired because, as Cartlidge has noted, many other types of ascription exist in Jesus, showing that monks, canons and secular clergy numbered among the authors. Jesus, Cotton, Harley and books like them, represent a healthy amount of social and cultural 'fluidity' among authors of different sorts, and among audiences too.[29]

However these texts were used – by friars, secular clerks, lay patrons or others, as literature read aloud or in private – they form the matter of vernacular religion in the West Midlands of the thirteenth century. Several recurrent threads are clear: for example, exclamations of *ubi sunt*, conflicts of body and soul, signs of death and doomsday, and vivid imaginings of the pains of hell. Many CJ Lyrics, austere indeed, enact a kind of terror campaign in the name of reforming souls. Medieval verse dictums on moral conduct, on the transience of life and the certainty of death, whether aimed at a lay or fraternal audience, may strike today's readers as fraught with repetition and convention; numerous lines exhort listeners to repent now or face eternal pain and torment. But, in embracing the whole sequence, a medieval audience would have heard, too, pastoral assurances of God's ready love.

The collection of lyrics in Jesus and Cotton possesses illuminating moments of verbal and aesthetic excellence, moments that approach the exuberant sociability of *Owl* and the mystic seductiveness of *Love Rune*. There are further lyric gems in Jesus – garnets if not pearls – that reward close attention. To show off some sparkles, I here display two CJ Lyrics: first, *An Orison to Our Lord*, a meditative prayer that asks for an intensely affective, devout response to Christ's incarnation; next, *A Little Sooth Sermon*, a preacher's lesson that paints a colourful, satiric vignette of English village life in order to drive home the doctrine of original sin.

An Orison to Our Lord

The prayer-lyric *An Orison to Our Lord* consists of seven stanzas of variable length. Stanza divisions can be discerned by the scribe's placement of red capitals and by the anaphoric 'Ihesu, ich þe grete', which opens five stanzas, while two others open with similar variants (lines 1, 39) that maintain a mode of direct address to Jesus by name. The lengths of stanzas that rhyme in couplets are 10, 8, 8, 12, 10, 8 and 8 lines. Most of its sixty-four lines occupy a single manuscript line, but sometimes couplets are copied continuously (lines 1–2, 7–8, 31–2, 61–2), which may indicate that the Jesus scribe has altered a 32-line layout found in

---

Morum' and Its Middle English Poems (Cambridge MA, 1978), pp. 90–3; and Wenzel, *Preachers*, pp. 7–8.

29 Cartlidge, 'The Composition', p. 262; and J. Boffey, 'Middle English Lyrics and Manuscripts', Duncan, *Companion*, pp. 1–18 (p. 8).

his exemplar. To judge by script and page size, he would not have had room to always copy one couplet per line – a consideration that must have informed the present layout. He makes an error by repeating line 50 at the end of line 51. This mistake loses the rhyme, which cannot be restored, but the sense is still good once the duplicate line is removed.

The internal, aesthetic flow of this intimate prayer-poem is fascinating. The first stanza depicts Christ's incarnation in 'wemmeles' Mary (line 10). The meditational emphasis is on the Godhead wrapped in human flesh, and on how this was accomplished without physical blemish. Then (in the second stanza) there appears Christ as a child who walked and spoke like other children, and who also suffered hunger and thirst, and was obedient and poor. These details call for an affective response, asking an audience to empathise and feel protective towards a virtuous, vulnerable child suffering human wants. In this way, we are told, Christ gave us a good 'forbysne' (*example*; line 18).

Gradually the poet focuses on how this 'swete lychome' (*sweet, tender body*; line 22) came to suffer torture, mortal piercing and bloody death. In the long central stanza the prayerful reader visualises the Passion unwaveringly, witnessing how Christ suffered (lines 27–38). Here, at the lyric's midpoint, Christ's tortured body emblazons a paradoxical vision of royal sovereignty, as he is said to be 'byweued' in a red mantle – that is, the streaming blood weaves a royal cloak – and he is crowned with thorns. On either side of these lines the poet portrays the torturers who spit at him, calling them vile 'mixes', that is, wretches (or, literally, persons made of filth or dung). The cold inanimate iron of nails and a spear are driven in his body in the fifth stanza, where the poet prays, 'As þu þoledest þeos fyf wunde / Of seorewe and sunne, wite us myd isunde' (*Just as you suffered these five wounds / For sorrow and sin, keep us sound of body*; lines 47–8). Christ's bodily pain becomes the audience's means to escape everyday pain. By line 56 it is clear that the torture most to be feared is what the devil will inflict in hell, yet *Orison*'s emphasis on Christ's willed submission to present suffering may suggest an audience wishing to alleviate daily hardships by regular thinking on the Passion. At line 51 it is Christ's amazingly *patient* endurance of pain (his 'þoleburne[sse]') that serves as example for mankind.

As *Orison* ends, it is Christ's capacity to withstand suffering with mild acceptance that promises the petitioner's path to bliss. The argument is based in human corporeality and affective identification with Jesus's flesh. Christ, born whole and tender from Mary's spotless body, is torn, punctured and desecrated, all so that our own vulnerable bodies can avoid that fate in hell and remain 'isunde'. The petitioner's address to Jesus grows in intimacy and conviction, so that by the last stanza he strives to match his level of belief to Christ's inexplicable patience: 'Ihesu, ich þe grete so wysslych / As þu deþ þoledest myldelich' (*Jesus, I greet you as faithfully as you suffered death mildly*; lines 57–8). Christ's transcendent forbearance of body inspires the keen meditative focus expressed in this vernacular song of devotion.

A Little Sooth Sermon

My second example is slightly better known, but its aesthetic sophistication has not received sustained attention. Critics have mentioned it only in passing, noting its standard message of damnation as the consequence for sin. Derek Pearsall comments that *A Little Sooth Sermon* 'develops its theme of penitence on a frankly popular level' and he suspects the crowd would have cheered when the poet consigned priests' wives, then their husbands, to hell (lines 29–30).[30] Thomas Heffernan comments rather too seriously that 'it may speak to a genuine problem in the ranks of the rural clergy. Indeed there would hardly be a need for such an admonition if the clergy were not cohabiting.'[31] Cartlidge sums up the piece as 'a lively and unsubtle essay in social satire'.[32]

My edition sets this poem as fifty-four lines, as in the manuscript. Richard Morris's edition looks entirely different because he gives it short lines, ignoring that there are virtually no internal rhymes in its septenaries. The final four lines turn to Mary as intercessor, and then to her son. The argument falls into four-line patterns, so I present *Sermon* according to these stanza-like groupings, although the scribe does not indicate stanza divisions. Interestingly, the metre changes to shorter lines of three or four stresses in the third 'stanza' (lines 9–16). These lines encapsulate the fall of mankind resulting from Adam's deed and the fortunate redemption Christ bought with his blood, that is, the poet's theological message in a nutshell. In addition, the preacher punctuates his sermon by a formal three-part structure, calling out to an audience of 'good men', exhorting them at beginning, middle and end (lines 1, 27, 49). The second and third addresses repeat each other in the manner of a refrain: 'Gode men, for Godes luue, bileueþ sucche sunne / For at þen ende hit binymeþ heueriche wunne' (*Good men, for God's love, abandon such sin, / For in the end it forfeits heavenly joy*; lines 27–8).

Sermon is a miniature masterpiece of moral-social observation, drawn with biting vernacular precision. It belongs to a rare, highly prized class of wittily sharp, comic lyrics that revel in the linguistic flavouring of English, poems such as Harley 2253's *Man in the Moon* and *Satire on the Retinues of the Great*.[33] What distinguishes *Sermon* most of all is its infectiously imagined English provincial town, with parish church, ale house and market – a setting inhabited by bakers, brewers, parsons with wives, vigilant parents and hormonally active teenagers.

---

30 Pearsall, *Old English and Middle English Poetry*, p. 97.
31 T. Heffernan, 'Early Middle English Sermons and Homilies', *A Manual of the Writings in Middle English 1050–1500*, Vol. 11, ed. P. G. Beidler (New Haven, 2005), pp. 3996–4056 (p. 4046).
32 Cartlidge, 'The Composition', p. 258.
33 NIMEV 2066, 2649; Fein, ed., *The Complete Harley 2253 Manuscript*, III, 148–51, 218–21. The lyric also provides a rare early glimpse into the subculture of unmarried young girls; compare F. Riddy, 'Mother Knows Best: Reading Social Change in a Courtesy Text', *Speculum* 71 (1996), 66–86 (86); and N. Cartlidge, '"Alas I Go with Chylde": Representations of Extra-Marital Pregnancy in the Middle English Lyric', *English Studies* 79 (1995), 395–414 (409–11).

These young people gather at church and market to seek opportunities to flirt and whisper (lines 33–40). Each action is charming and expressive. Our characters have the generic names of common folk: Malekyn, Janekyn, Watekin, Willikyn, Robyn, Gilothe. Robyn and Gilothe spend too much time at the tavern, and she is easily seduced: 'An eve to go myd him ne þincheþ hire no schome' (*At night she thinks it no shame to go with him*; line 44). Her parents are angry and threaten to beat her, but to no avail; she makes excuses and says no man has come near her, until her expanding waist tells another story.

There is an artistic elegance about this sermon-lyric that reveals, alongside a preacher's rhetorical skills, the craft of a poet. First of all, the theme of the fall is deftly handled, from the story of Adam to the animated coming-to-life of the foibles enacted here and now by Adam's own sinful children: 'Just look around! Our vice-ridden neighbours illustrate well enough the lesson to be learned here'. But more than this is the artful modulation of the theme of generations stemming from Adam, who is called our 'vormefader' (*forefather*; line 4). The sinners listed first are generic and all seemingly male: backbiters, robbers, thieves, murderers, lechers, whoremongers and, finally, the false 'chapmen' (*merchants*), who quickly become the more vivid bakers and brewers who cheat us in our own community.

After the central exhortation to 'gode men', the sinners seem to grow more familiar to us with their homespun names and, after the shocking priests' wives, the genders now intermingle (lines 31–2). Men sin with women; women sin with men. The liveliness of idiom and sketched characters suggests a surprising degree of bemused observation from a moralising author; he seems well aware of how such narrative captures the attention and entertains. Eventually we learn of the inner intentions of women: first, one whose mind strays from her Paternoster to Willekyn and Watekyn; and second, poor Gilothe, who disobeys her parents, dallies with Robyn, and finds herself pregnant. Adam's fall is traced inexorably from men sinning in generic categories, to men and women toying with each other, to the subjective thought processes of weak-minded women and, finally, to the physically altered body of an unwed girl.

At the same time we may trace a paternity theme from Adam our forefather, from whom all sinners descend as children, to the Paternoster (the '*Our Father*') neglected by the infatuated girl, then to the angry parents – 'syre' and 'dame' – who try vainly to impose Gilothe's curfew, and finally to the non-immaculate paternity of Gilothe's conceived foetus. All is fallen after Adam, and what is risen is the womb in which more sinners are bred (line 48). The poem tumbles forwards with its sense of fallenness.[34] Counterpointing this impetus are the preacher's calls to understand sin and gain heavenly joys and, most conclusively, the quiet petition to 'Seynt Marie' (line 51), our blessed *Mother*, who displaces father Adam with her immaculately conceived son.

---

34   The theme begins cleverly in the first line when the speaker tells 'alle gode men … sitteþ adun'.

This vivacious lyric might even be constructed by sacred number in a manner similar to Thomas's *Love Rune*.[35] If so, the fifty lines before the four-line epilogue may betoken something sacramental, justifying the generic term 'sermun' (line 2). The middle stanza holds the central exhortation to 'gode men' (lines 25–8) while the speaker scorns the feeble bread and weak ale concocted by thievish bakers and brewers. These merchants of malfeasance offer an anti-Eucharist and cheat for silver. This image, combined with the rising womb of a wayward girl, sum up the materialism and fleshliness of Adam's unrepentant children, images made right by the call to Mary and her son.

In presenting *An Orison to Our Lord* and *A Little Sooth Sermon* as specimens from the Cotton–Jesus sequence, I do not wish to suggest that either is composed by one of the notable poets found in those manuscripts – that is, by Thomas of Hales or the *Owl* poet (or even, more remotely, by Layamon or Chardri) – but *if* any more English lyrics by any of these intriguing writers, or even any lyrics floating in circles where they were admired, should have survived, Jesus and Cotton are prime spots to find them. We should examine critically each poetic document of early Middle English, seeking not only to establish milieux of origin but also to understand the sensibilities and pieties that inspired these utterances, as well as to grasp the medieval motives that impelled particular lyrics to be grouped and disseminated as collections.

---

35 And elsewhere in his one extant Anglo-French sermon. See S. Fein, 'Roll or Codex? The Diptych Layout of Thomas of Hales's *Love Rune*', *Trivium* 31 (1999), 13–23 (19).

16

Musical and Poetical Form in *Stond wel, moder, under rode*

Christiania Whitehead

Stond wel, moder, under rode[1]

'Stond wel, moder, under rode,   *cross*
Bihold thi child wyth glade mode,   *gladsome heart (mood)*
Blythe moder might thou be.'   *A happy; may*
'Sone, how may I blithe stonden?   *be happy*
5   I se thin feet, I se thin honden,
Nayled to the harde tre.'

'Moder, do wey thi wepinge;   *put away*
I thole this deth for mannes thinge,   *endure; sake*
For owen gilte thole I non.'   *for my own guilt*
10   'Sone, I fele the dethe-stounde,   *pangs of death*
The swerd is at min herte-grounde,   *the bottom of my heart*
That me by-highte Symeon.'   *which Simeon promised me*

'Moder, rew upon thy beren!   *have pity; child*
Thow washe awey tho blodi teren,

For further essays focused on the resizing and reordering of lyrics in different manuscript versions, see Katherine Zieman (Chapter 11), 'Compiling the Lyric: Richard Rolle, Textual Dynamism and Devotional Song in London, British Library, Additional MS 37049', and Anne Baden-Daintree (Chapter 10), 'Voice and Response: Lyric Rewriting of the Song of Songs'.

1   NIMEV 3211; DIMEV 5030; reproduced from Duncan, I, 91, pp. 144–5, with reduced glossing, by kind permission of Boydell & Brewer publishers. This edition represents the version of the lyric in London, British Library, Royal MS 12 E I, with variants supplied from London, British Library, Harley MS 2253. The major modern editions of *Stond wel, moder*, in the versions given in the Royal and Harley manuscripts, are: Brown XIII, pp. 87–91; C. Sisam and K. Sisam, eds, *The Oxford Book of Medieval English Verse* (Oxford, 1970), pp. 136–8; T. Silverstein, ed., *Medieval English Lyrics* (London, 1971), pp. 12–14; M. S. Luria and R. L. Hoffman, eds, *Middle English Lyrics* (New York, 1974), pp. 215–17; K. Saupe, ed., *Middle English Marian Lyrics* (Kalamazoo, MI, 1998), pp. 87–9; S. G. Fein, ed. and trans., with D. Raybin and J. Ziolowski, *The Complete Harley 2253 Manuscript, Volume 2* (Kalamazoo, MI, 2009), Booklet 5, no. 60.

15	It don me werse than mi det.'	they affect; death
	'Sone, how might I teres wernen?	restrain
	I se tho blodi flodes ernen	run
	Out of thin herte to min fet.'	
	'Moder, now I may thee seye,	tell you
20	Better is that Ich one deye	I alone die
	Than al mankin to helle go.'	
	'Sone, I se thi bodi swongen,	beaten
	Thi brest, thin hond, thi fot thurgh-stongen,	pierced through
	No selly nis though me be wo.'	it is no wonder
25	'Moder, if I dar thee telle,	
	Yif I ne dye thou gost to helle;	
	I thole this deth for thine sake.'	endure
	'Sone, thou beest me so minde,	you are so thoughtful for me
	Ne wit me nought, it is my kinde	blame me not; nature
30	That I for thee this sorwe make.'	
	'Moder, merci! Let me deyen,	
	For Adam owt of helle beyen,	in order; to buy
	And al mankin that is forloren.'	lost
	'Sone, what shal me to rede?	what am I to do?
35	Thi pine pineth me to dede,	your agony tortures me
	Let me deyen thee biforen.'	die
	'Moder, now tarst thou might leren	for the first time; learn
	What pine thole that children beren,	pain (they) suffer who
	What sorwe have that child forgon.'	(they) have who lose a child
40	'Sone, I wot, I can thee telle,	know
	Bute it be the pine of helle	unless; torment
	More sorwe ne wot I non.'	
	'Moder, rew of moder care!	have pity on a mother's sorrow
	Now thou wost of moder fare,	know; a mother's lot
45	Though thou be clene mayden-man.'	virgin
	'Sone, help at alle nede	in every necessity
	Alle tho that to me grede,	cry
	Maiden, wif, and fool womman.'	foolish
	'Moder, I may no lenger dwelle,	stay
50	The time is come I fare to helle,	go
	The thridde day I rise upon.'	shall rise
	'Sone, I wille with thee founden,	go with you
	I deye, y-wis, of thine wounden,	
	So rewful deth was never non.'	so pitiable a death
55	When He ros than fel thi sorwe,	then your sorrow vanished
	Thy blisse sprong the thridde morwe,	on the third morning
	Wel blithe moder wer thou tho.	most happy; then
	Moder, for that ilke blisse,	very

Bisech oure God oure sinnes lisse,	*to remit*
60 Thou be oure sheld ayayn oure fo.	*be thou*
Blissen be thou quen of hevene,	
Bring us out of helle levene	*hell's flames*
Thurgh thi dere sones might.	
Moder, for that heighe blode	*noble*
65 That He shadde upon the rode,	*shed*
Led us into hevene light. Amen.	

Stond wel, moder, under rode explores the emotions of Mary at the foot of the cross by placing her in dialogue with her dying son. The tension created by juxtaposing her stubborn refusal to understand or endorse Christ's sacrifice with his *lack* of passion and seemingly callous exhortations to joy, has attracted scholarly interest for many decades, and the lyric appears in practically all modern anthologies of medieval short poetry. These various editions, generally based upon a single, favoured manuscript witness, tend to occlude other variants and versions, including, in this specific instance, the musical notation that accompanies vernacular renderings of the lyric in half its extant manuscripts. Rather than revisiting the lyric's alleged origins in twelfth-century, dialogic, monastic meditations associated with St Anselm and St Bernard of Clairvaux,[2] this chapter will take a synchronic approach, seeking to bring the *liturgical* dimensions of the lyric into clearer relief, and extracting the evidence of its various manuscript witnesses and versions in order to arrive at a proposition concerning the impact of musical form upon the poem's dialogic structure and affect.

Manuscripts

Stond wel, moder, under rode was probably originally composed c.1260, in the East Midlands. It survives in six manuscripts in a number of different lengths and stanza orders, and one of the aims of this chapter will be to examine how it reads and resonates in different ways depending on whether all or only a part of the lyric is present. The earliest extant manuscript containing the lyric is Cambridge, St John's College, MS 111, produced in the early thirteenth century by a Kentish scribe.[3] It contains a selection of practical and catechetical material useful for a priest or ecclesiastical establishment, including listings of the Commandments, the Hours, the church seasons, the vices and virtues, followed by Innocent III's *De miseria conditionis humanae* and a form of exorcism. In the final folios,

---

[2] Pseudo-Anselm, *Dialogus beatae Mariae et Anselmi de Passione Domini*, PL 159: 271–90; Pseudo-Bernard of Clairvaux, *Liber de passione Christi et doloribus et planctibus matris eius*, PL 182: 1133–42. *Stond wel, moder*'s derivation from these passion meditations is reported but never developed in any detail by Brown *XIII*, p. 204; Woolf, pp. 247–8; Gray, *Themes*, p. 136; Gray, *Selection*, p. 111; J. A. W. Bennett, *Poetry of the Passion: Studies in Twelve Centuries of English Verse* (Oxford, 1982), pp. 34–6; S. Wenzel, *Preachers, Poets, and the Early English Lyric* (Princeton, 1986), p. 49.

[3] M. R. James, ed., *A Descriptive Catalogue of the Manuscripts in the Library of St John's College, Cambridge* (Cambridge, 1913), pp. 144–5.

in a small thirteenth-century hand, is a French religious poem on the Day of Judgement, succeeded by the Latin sequence *Stabat iuxta Christi crucem* (which *Stond wel, moder* is loosely based on). This Latin sequence is fitted to musical notation on a four-line stave, with the English words of *Stond wel, moder* added loosely beneath, but not perfectly reconciled with the musical notation.[4] This rendition of the lyric is unfortunately incomplete because a manuscript leaf is missing after fol. 106, breaking off after line 27; however, there is no reason not to believe that it was originally transcribed within the manuscript in its entirety.[5] The evidence of St John's, MS 111 indicates that, in its earliest extant form, *Stond wel, moder* was closely related to the Latin sequence, and to a sung performance of that sequence, in liturgical circumstances. Nonetheless, it does not seem to be the case that the *English* lyric was necessarily intended to be sung, bearing in mind the lack of close correlation with the musical notation.

Moving forward in chronological order, the next manuscript, Oxford, Bodleian Library, MS Digby 86, is one that has generated extensive critical attention.[6] Judged to date from the last quarter of the thirteenth century, it is largely comprised of religious texts in Latin, French and Middle English. For many years it was perceived as a 'friar's miscellany', that is, as a medley of materials that could be deployed to assist Franciscan and Dominican preaching,[7] but it has more recently been reassessed as a layman's commonplace book or miscellany, probably written down by Richard Grimhill II near Worcester.[8] *Stond wel, moder* appears on fol. 127, surrounded by other short religious lyrics: its most immediate contexts are fifteen signs of the day of judgement, a Life of St Eustace, the sayings of St Bernard, an '*Ubi sunt*' poem, a prayer of St Bede, and a Miracle of the Virgin.[9] Along with the other lyrics in the manuscript it is given an Anglo Norman title: *Chansoun de noustre dame*. This Digby version lacks stanzas 10–11, the final two stanzas of the lyric, which change voice from the first-person dialogue between Jesus and Mary, to the poet's second-person address to Mary. Here, the poet sketches the joy she must have felt on the day of resurrection, labels her as queen of heaven, and asks for her salvific intercession. Left without stanzas 10–11, *Stond wel, moder* reads very differently – it remains much more anguished, much more focused on present dereliction devoid of future purpose, much more unresolved. It ends without Mary being comforted in any way, or exhibiting any real understanding of the theological necessity of

---

4   Cambridge, St John's College, MS 111, fol. 106v.
5   The manuscript finishes, following the missing leaf, with a receipt in French on fol. 107, and a prayer in Latin.
6   W. D. Macray et al., *Bodleian Library Quarto Catalogues. 9, Digby Manuscripts* (Oxford, 1999 [reproducing 1883 catalogue]), cols 91–7. See also, J. Tschann and M. Parkes, intro., *Facsimile of Bodleian Library, MS Digby 86*, EETS SS, 16 (Oxford, 1996).
7   D. L. Jeffrey, *The Early English Lyric and Franciscan Spirituality* (Lincoln, 1975), pp. 203–7.
8   J. Boffey, 'Middle English Lyrics and Manuscripts', Duncan, *Companion*, pp. 1–18 (pp. 7–8).
9   Macray, *Quarto catalogues. 9, Digby Manuscripts*, MS 86, items 35–41. *Stond wel, moder* is item 39.

her son's death. To sum up: MS Digby 86 contains no hint of a *liturgical* perception of this lyric, nor any signs of musical performance. Wholly detached from its Latin predecessor, in a shortened, sharpened version, it seems to be designed for devotional reading within trilingual lay circumstances.

Digby 86 contrasts in almost every way with the next manuscript witness, British Library, Royal MS 8 F II, a fifteenth-century manuscript containing Latin biblical exegesis and moral philosophy.[10] However, we may disregard the contents and concentrate instead on the fly leaves of the codex, which have been torn from a collection of Latin sermons for church festivals (c.1300), and from a thirteenth-century lectionary. The flyleaf from the sermon collection includes a sermon on the pains and joys of the Blessed Virgin, which quotes the first stanza of *Stond wel, moder*.[11] The immediate context of this quotation is as follows:

Vnde cum in quondam cantu dicatur in persona filii ad Beatam virginem sic:[12]	
'Stond wel, moder, under rode,	cross
Bihold thi child wyth glade mode,	gladsome heart (mood)
Blythe moder might thou be.'	A happy; may
Respondetur sic in persona matris:[13]	
'Sone, how may I blithe stonden?	be happy
I se thin feet, I se thin honden,	
Nayled to the harde tre.'[14]	

The incomplete context of this quotation leaves many unanswered questions. Nonetheless, we should note that *Stond wel, moder* is already described as a former or traditional song (*quondam cantu*) by c.1300, suggesting that we may need to reconsider its conventional attribution to the mid-thirteenth century. Here, in this third manuscript witness, we find the first stanza interpolated into a sermon and voiced from the pulpit, presumably to bring dramatic immediacy and intensity to an exposition of Mary's pain at the foot of the cross. Moreover, given that the stanza plays with the oppositions of joy and grief (Christ demands Mary's joy at his redemption of mankind, while Mary remains bound in anguished contemplation of his physical suffering), it appears remarkably well suited to the homiletic and catechetical trope of the Virgin's antithetical joys and pains, and may even originally have been composed with that rhetorical commonplace in mind. The division of the stanza into two parts, and the references to speaking in the personae of the son and mother (*dicatur in persona filii ... respondetur sic in persona matris*) emphasise the dialogic and performative potential of the lyric,

---

10 See BL online MS catalogue. The manuscript contains a partial index to Gregory the Great's *Moralia in Job*, a series of lectures or sermons on St John's Gospel and Ecclesiastes, and an incomplete version of the *Moralia philosophia* of Roger Bacon.
11 The two other sermons on this leaf are an exposition of 3 Kings 19, and a sermon on the feast of the purification of Mary.
12 'Regarding which, in a song once (or formerly), the following is said in the person of the Son to the Blessed Virgin' (my translation).
13 'This is answered in this way in the person of the Mother' (my translation).
14 The passage is transcribed in Brown *XIII*, p. 204.

and we might even speculate whether it could not have been sung or spoken by two different voices in the course of the sermon. It is at times like these that the sermon begins to encroach upon the dramatic mode.

Royal MS 8 F II is succeeded chronologically by British Library, Harley MS 2253, an important compilation of religious and secular materials in English, French and Latin, which has been conventionally dated c.1340. Like Digby 86, this manuscript has attracted an enormous amount of critical and editorial attention, which cannot be fully summarised here.[15] It clearly has a connection with Leominster Priory in North Herefordshire, and was traditionally categorised as another 'friars' miscellany', but again, is now thought possibly to have been compiled to suit the reading tastes of a lay household. There are a number of lyric repetitions and continuities between Digby 86 and Harley 2253; however, in Harley, *Stond wel, moder* is situated within a short drift of religious lyrics (*Sweet Jesus, King of Bliss*; *A Spring Song on the Passion*; *Song on Jesus' Precious Blood*; *Jesus, Sweet is the Love of You*; *Stond wel, moder*; *I Sigh When I Sing*; *An Autumn Song*), which broadly adopt a more lyrical and emotional tone than the equivalent context of Digby. By contrast with this affective context, the Harley version of *Stond wel, moder* contains a couple of structural and grammatical variants that could be judged to pull in the opposite direction. The stanzaic order is changed slightly so that stanza 3 follows after stanza 6. This disrupts the crescendo of emotion through the first six stanzas towards Jesus's climactic expostulation: 'Moder, merci! Let me deyen', at the beginning of stanza 6 in the original structure, matched dramatically with Mary's corresponding wish to die before or instead of Jesus. In addition, at the close of the poem, at lines 64–5, Harley alters the object of intercessory address from Mary to Jesus, replacing 'Moder, for that heighe (*noble*) blode / That He shadde upon the rode, / Led us into hevene light' with '*Louerd*, for that heighe blode / That *þou* sheddest upon the rode, / Led us into hevene light'. The revision dilutes the Marian focus of the lyric, and considerably diminishes her final salvific force by contrast with her earlier epistemological limitations. As such, it may suggest a compiler with some degree of hesitation about the eschatological abilities attributed to Mary in the popular theology of the period. To conclude: in Harley 2253, *Stond wel, moder* occurs in a local, affective context, once again intended for trilingual devotional reading, and contains small changes that excise Mary's posthumous authority.

The next manuscript witness, British Library, Royal MS 12 E I, is the one from which the majority of editions of the lyric have been taken. Bound together with disparate fifteenth-century Latin materials, including recipes, a bilingual medicine list and a versified arithmetic, it contains an early fourteenth-century collection of Latin saints' lives (Alexius, Katherine of Alexandria, Dionysius, Dominic, Barlaam and Josephat, and so on), hymns and liturgical materials,

---

15 BL online MS catalogue. S. Fein, ed., *Studies in the Harley Manuscript; the Scribes, Contents, and Social Contexts of British Library, MS Harley 2253* (Kalamazoo, MI, 2000); S. Fein, ed. and trans., with D. Raybin and J. Ziolkowski, *The Complete Harley 2253 Manuscript, Volumes 1–3* (Kalamazoo, MI, 2014–15).

which derive from the East Midlands.[16] The manuscript is very small, measuring 5¼ x 4 inches, and towards its end, commencing at fol. 193, is a short group of three 'sacred songs', namely, *Stond wel, moder*, with musical notation; the English lyric *Quenne hic se on rode* (more widely edited as *Whan ich se on rode*), and a French lyric whose opening words have been lost, also with musical notation.[17] A couple of observations follow from this manuscript information. The fourteenth-century section of Royal 12 E I clearly has a relation to ecclesiastical liturgy and ecclesiastical space, bearing in mind its inclusion of hymns, a fragmentary office, and tables of epistles and gospel readings.[18] Juxtaposing *Stond wel, moder* with *Whan ich se on rode* accentuates this relationship. *Whan ich se* continues:

Whan ich se on rode	cross
Jhesu mi lemman,	beloved
And beside Him stonde	
Marie an Johan,	
And his rig y-swongen,	back scourged
And his side y-stongen,	pierced
For the love of man,	
Wel ow Ich to wepen ... [19]	ought

It is tempting to interpret this lyric, with its very precise visual evocations, as an affective response to the church rood screen, with its wood sculptures of Mary, Jesus and John, or to a Passion altarpiece. This may help us to think about *Stond wel, moder*, juxtaposed alongside it, as a more *performative*, more *dramatic* reponse to the rood screen, bringing the personae of Mary and Jesus to life, and supplying them with speech. In this respect, Royal 12 E I bears comparison with the torn flyleaf of Royal 8 F II, which transcribes the first stanza as a homiletic playscript. The version in Royal 12 E I is accompanied by notation. So, perhaps this lyric, or 'English sequence' as the catalogue has it, was sung within church, in the course of the mass? We will examine the character of liturgical sequences in more detail below. The difficulty with this suggestion is the tiny size of the manuscript. At 5¼ x 4 inches, it is almost impossible to envisage that it could have been used publicly or liturgically. There is no definitive solution to this, but it seems most probable that the manuscript was compiled for a priest's personal use, adjacent and supplementary to his public service in church.

The final and latest manuscript witness, Dublin, Trinity College, MS 301, has traditionally been somewhat overlooked.[20] A large-scale fourteenth-century manuscript in Midlands dialect, comprising many sections, hands, corrections

---

16 BL online manuscript catalogue.
17 The French lyric continues, '[ ] mer me estut a tute fin e mun', fol. 194v. The music of both lyrics is described briefly in A. Hughes-Hughes, *Catalogue of Manuscript Music in the British Museum*, 3 vols (London, 1964–6), I, p. 424.
18 Items 7, and 9–12, in the online catalogue description.
19 Duncan, I, 87, p. 140.
20 M. L. Colker, *Trinity College Library Dublin: Descriptive Catalogue of the Medieval and Renaissance Latin Manuscripts*, 2 vols (Aldershot, 1991), I, 559–97 (p. 593).

and notes, it contains copious Latin religious materials, including excerpts from the church fathers, *De negligentiis praelatorum*, Innocent III's *De miseria humanae conditionis*, sermons for various seasons, several items suggesting a monastic readership – for example, a short piece on the necessities of the monastic life, and an extraordinarily large number of diagrams shaping elementary didactic information such as the parts of penance, the attributes of Jesus, the symbolism of the church building and Eucharist, the four indications of royalty, and so on, into a mnemonic visual form. The diagrams suggest that the codex may have been used to assist catechetical teaching or to underpin sermon composition. From fol. 164, we enter a section of didactic materials focused on the Virgin Mary, including a number of Latin verses in her honour, and at fol. 194, *Stond wel, moder* is transcribed as the only English item in the manuscript. Like the copy in Harley 2253, this version of the lyric changes the object of address in the last three lines from 'Moder', to 'Louerd'; both manuscripts seem to be part of the same textual tradition despite their dissimilarities on other fronts. It is not easy to pin down the function of the lyric in Trinity 301, except to say that its disparate Latinate contents suggest pedagogy within a monastic or cathedral context. Nonetheless, it does give us another complete rendition of the lyric to compare with Harley and Royal 12 E I.

This brief survey of the extant manuscripts of *Stond wel, moder* reveals a diverse range of uses and settings, from homiletic and para-liturgical, with some emphasis on performance, to devotional lay reading in an affective context. As we noted earlier, Digby 86 and Harley 2253 were viewed as friars' miscellanies for many years, amassing materials for use in preaching. The more recent understanding of them as lay compilations significantly changes our perception of this lyric *away* from homiletic usage and towards devotional reading. All that really remains on the homiletic front are those flyleaves from 1300. We should also note the diversity of scribal dialects, from Kent up to the East Midlands and across to the Welsh border counties, suggesting that the lyric was widely circulated and known within central and southern England.

Music

We will now change tack to explore the *musical* aspect of this lyric in more detail. Let us first remind ourselves that *Stond wel, moder* comes accompanied by musical notation in St John's College, MS 111 and Royal MS 12 E I. Illuminatingly, in St John's College 111, it is linked closely to the Latin sequence *Stabat iuxta Christi crucem*, with the English words slotted beneath the music and words of the Latin sequence. Royal 12 E I fails to provide the Latin words; nonetheless, its musical notation of the English lyric is largely identical with the music of *Stabat iuxta Christi crucem* in important, thirteenth-century, English Missal manuscripts.[21] This leads us to the question of the musical and textual characteristics

---

21 The musical notation of these manuscripts has been extensively analysed in E. J. Dobson and F. Ll. Harrison, *Medieval English Songs* (London, 1979), pp. 300–2. They note that the

of a liturgical sequence. A sequence can be sung within the mass in between the intoned readings of the epistle and gospel, and after the responses and alleluia. It is a series of verses set to music, in which each verse falls into two equal sections sung to a repeating melody, and in which each *new* verse (always in two parts) moves to a *new* repeating melody.[22] In other words, it differs from a hymn, in which the *same* melody is repeated for each verse. Thus, if one were to picture a series of sequence verses advancing:

    ab   cd   ef   gh   ij,   the music to these verses would go

    AA   BB   CC   DD   EE

What it is important to stress here is the way in which the music pairs balance and repetition with a principle of progression and forward momentum. There is no circularity, no return to a seminal statement or refrain, such as we might find in a hymn or carol. Sequences were generally sung antiphonally, with the two parts of each verse passed backwards and forwards between the choir stalls. The anonymous sequence *Stabat iuxta Christi crucem*, possibly of French origin, seems to have been fairly widely disseminated and performed. It features amongst a number of sequences composed in honour of Mary contained in a noted Sarum missal (Paris, Bibliothèque de l'Arsenal, MS 135, s. xiii), which probably derives from Canterbury Cathedral and St Augustine's Abbey,[23] and is also included with other sequences in many manuscripts of the York Missal.[24] These Marian sequences were presumably intended to be used in the course of the Votive Mass of the Virgin, celebrated on a Saturday, which became incorporated into England monastic and cathedral calendars of worship from the thirteenth century onwards.

Let us now take a closer look at the textual content of the Latin sequence:

1.	2.
Stabat iuxta Christi crucem,	Stabat virgo spectans crucem
stabat videns vitae ducem	et utramque pati lucem,
vitae valefacere.	sed plus suam doluit.
Stabat mater, nec jam mater,	Ista stabat, hic pendabat,

---

notation in Royal 12 E I closely resembles the notation to the *Stabat iuxta Christi crucem* in a Sarum Missal (Paris, Bibliothèque de l'Arsenal, MS 135, fols 282v–83v, s.xiii), where two units are identical note for note, and four others are nearly identical. The notation in St John's College MS 111 is slightly more approximate: only one unit agrees entirely, and Dobson and Harrison cite some striking note divergences.

22   M. McGrade, 'Enriching the Gregorian Heritage', *A Cambridge Companion to Medieval Music*, ed. M. Everist (Cambridge, 2011), pp. 26–45.
23   Dobson and Harrison, *Medieval English Songs*, p. 147.
24   The sequence is also included in the Eton Choirbook (Eton College, MS 178, early s.xvi), amongst many other Marian hymns, in a six-part setting by John Browne (fl. 1490). As such, it has been recorded a number of times in recent years (The Sixteen, *The Rose and the Ostrich Feather* (1991); the Anonymous Four, *The Lily and the Lamb: Chant and Polyphony from Medieval England* (1995)).

et quid sit eventus ater
   novo novit funere.

et, quae foris hic ferebat,
   intus haec sustinuit.

3.
Intus cruci conclavatur,
intus suo jugulatur
   mater agni gladio;
intus martyr consecratur,
intus tota concrematur
   amoris incendio.

4.
Modo manus, modo latus,
modo ferro pes foratus
   oculis resumitur;
modo caput spinis sutum
cuius orbis totus nutum
   et sentit et sequitur.

5.
Os verendum litum sputis
et flagellis rupta cutis
   et tot rivi sanguinis;
probra, risus, et quae restant
orbitati tela praestant
   et dolori virginis.

(plus six more stanzas)[25]

One can immediately see that it is *not* a dialogue but a third-person observation of the spectacle of the cross, balancing the physical sight of Christ's mutilations with the internal agonies of his watching mother. With the exception of the first verse, it does *not* divide each verse in half between observation of Christ and the Virgin. In fact if one compares the Latin composition with *Stond wel, moder*, the first six stanzas differ very notably from the Middle English, although the final five are closer. The poetry of the Latin sequence is measured and sophisticated rather than immediate and anguished, incorporating wordplay and repetition that is absent from the Middle English version (repetitions of *stabat, intus, modo* and so on).

At this point we should note that there is *another* independent Middle English translation of this Latin sequence, *stod ho þere neh* [*Stood the moder under roode*], which possibly predates *Stond wel, moder*.[26] This poem, which unfortunately lacks its first stanzas, is extant in Oxford, Bodleian Library, MS Tanner 169*, pp. 175–6, a composite manuscript

---

25 Dobson and Harrison, *Medieval English Songs*, p. 146. Trans. Dobson, p. 325: 'She stood beside the cross of Christ, she stood watching the lord of life bid farewell to life. The mother stood, not now a mother, and has learnt from the recent funeral procession what the dire outcome will be. // The Virgin stood watching the cross and watching each light [i.e. the sun and Christ, 'the light of the world'] suffer, but she mourned more for her own. She stood, he hung, and the things that he suffered openly she endured within. // Within, she was nailed to the cross; within, the mother of the Lamb was killed by her own sword; within, she was consecrated a martyr; within, she was wholly consumed by the flame of love. // Now his hand, now his side, now his foot pierced with steel is observed by her eyes; now his head pricked by thorns, whose will the whole world both observes and obeys. // The revered face covered with spittle, and the skin broken by whips, and such rivers of blood; insults, laughter, and the rest are the chief weapons for the bereavement and grief of the Virgin.'

26 NIMEV *3216.5; DIMEV 5038. Brown *XIII*, no. 4, pp. 8–10.

from the Benedictine abbey at Chester.[27] The majority of this manuscript is comprised of a Latin calendar, psalter, and other late twelfth-century liturgical materials and masses. These are framed, front and back, by three thirteenth-century leaves, containing Latin hymns with musical notations and *stod ho þere neh*, also with musical notation. Since the first of the two Latin hymns is titled *In exaltatione sancte Crucis*, and since the Middle English poem is strangely headed, in a later hand, *Translacio sancte Elene* (St Helena was credited with uncovering the true cross), there would seem a thread of evidence to suggest that, at some point, this particular translation was used within a liturgical context of cross veneration. This would tally with its association with *Whan ic se on rode*, in Royal MS 12 E I. Like the Latin, *stod ho þere neh* is *not* a first-person dialogue. As such, it is actually a far closer translation of *Stabat iuxta Christi crucem*, while the music that accompanies it seems similar to the notation shared between Royal 12 E I and the Canterbury Missal.[28] Based on some identities of rhyme word, Dobson and Harrison posit that the author of *Stond wel, moder* was aware of this earlier translation and consciously modified it into dialogue form.[29]

Finally, before moving on, we should also note a *third* independent translation, *Jesu Cristes milde moder*, in British Library, Arundel MS 248, fols 154v–55, dating from the fourteenth century.[30] Here, the translation is situated at the latter end of a manuscript of Latin scriptural commentaries, proverbs, sermons and excerpts, amidst roughly fifteen hymns and sequences to the Virgin and Mary Magdalene, in Latin, French and English, all accompanied by musical notation. As with St John's College 111, and Royal 12 E I, this context clearly points to a liturgical role for the lyric within Marian masses and other offices. Like *stod ho þere neh*, this translation adheres more closely to the Latin sequence than *Stond wel, moder*. We might compare the fourth stanza of *Stabat iuxta* printed above, for example, with the equivalent stanza in *Jesu Cristes milde moder*:

Now his hed with blod bispronken,	*besprinkled*
Now his side with spere y-stongen,	*pierced*
Thou bihelde, lady fre.	*gracious*
Now his hondes sprad o rode,	
Now hise fet washen with blode	
And y-nailled to the tre.[31] (lines 19–24)	

Like the Latin sequence and *stod ho þere neh*, *Jesu Cristes milde moder* is projected from the perspective of a third party, addressing the Virgin and the suffering that she witnesses, and there is no first-person dialogue. This version also rebalances the emotional freighting of the poem so as to give slightly more emphasis to the Virgin's proleptic joy at the salvation of mankind. Rather than staying concentrated on the

---

27 No. 9995 in R. W. Hunt and F. Madan, *A Summary Catalogue of Western Manuscripts in the Bodleian Library at Oxford* (Oxford, 1953), III, p. 86. *stod ho þere neh* is in a northern dialect.
28 Dobson and Harrison, *Medieval English Songs*, pp. 253, 300.
29 At lines 37–8, both versions use the same Middle English rhymes: 'leren / beren'.
30 NIMEV 1697; DIMEV 2831. Brown XIII, no. 47, pp. 83–5. Saupe, ed., *Middle English Marian Lyrics*, pp. 85–7. Duncan, I, 90, pp. 142–3.
31 The quotation is taken from Duncan, I, 90, p. 142, with reduced glossing.

Virgin's pain for nine out of eleven stanzas, as in *Stond wel, moder* (and we should recall that the Digby 86 version never moves on from that pain), *Jesu Cristes milde moder* confines its scrutiny of the Virgin's anguish to its first seven stanzas, and uses the final four to dilate on the doctrinal purpose of the Crucifixion and its implications for Mary's more long-term emotions. Pain and joy are better balanced here, and we might recall that fragmentary Latin sermon on the pains and joys of the Virgin that reaches so instinctively towards this family of lyrics.

This brief assessment of the two *other* Middle English versions of the Latin sequence enables us to realise that, in turning *Stabat iuxta Christi crucem* into a dramatic dialogue between Jesus and Mary, the author of *Stond wel, moder* is making a conscious decision to adapt rather than translate, to diverge significantly from the Latin text, and to go against the drift of the earlier Middle English translation that he probably knew. I would suggest that this decision, interestingly and surprisingly, draws *Stond wel, moder* much *closer* to the musical form of the sequence. As we have seen, a sequence depends on a structure of musical repetition between the first and second half of each stanza, alternated between the two sides of the monastic choir. Turning the poem into a dialogue in which Jesus speaks from the cross for the first three lines of each stanza and is answered by Mary in the following three lines, is to pay much more attention to this antiphonal and choral form and to achieve a much closer imitation of the relationship of balance, reflection and equivalence that distinguishes the two musical halves of each verse.

Turning *Stabat iuxta Christi crucem* into a dialogue also rebalances the Latin poem and allows Jesus more psychological imput. Rather than restricting the lyric viewpoint to the third-party observation of Mary's emotional fluctuations, the poem becomes instead a succession of *paired* complaints, in which Mary's psychological pain at the crucifixion of her son is finely balanced and answered by Jesus's psychological torment at the sight of his mother's suffering: 'Moder, rew upon thy beren! / Thow washe awey tho blodi teren, / It don me werse than mi det' ('Mother, have pity upon your child, wash away those bloody tears, they affect me worse than my death', lines 13–15). In like fashion, Christ's theological perception of what he will achieve by dying – the salvation of all mankind – is balanced against Mary's doggedly literal perception of what is happening – I see your body beaten and pierced through (stanza 4) – and neither is allowed wholly to persuade or silence the other. In stanza 5, Christ's desire for death on behalf of mankind is balanced dramatically against Mary's desire to die on behalf of her son. In stanzas 7 and 8, while Christ uses the first half of each stanza didactically to turn Mary's newfound capacity for empathetic suffering away from him towards women suffering in childbirth, by the second half of stanza 8, Mary has learnt that lesson and is promising to intercede on their behalf. The only time that we abandon that sense of balance is in the last two stanzas, which remain purely Marian in address. Perhaps that is the reason why the Harley and Trinity Dubin manuscript group replace 'Moder' with 'Louerd' in line 64, restoring the equivalence that marks the preceding stanzas, albeit with a final change in familial register: *moder, son, moder, son, moder, louerd*.

There is a long critical history of fascination with *Stond wel, moder*. Many poetry scholars have found it exceptionally responsive to literary analysis: because of the tense psychology of the mother–son relationship; because Mary is allowed to be reproachful, even bitter – unusual emotions; because there seems to be some kind of emotional standoff going on between these two protagonists (mother, I need to die; son, what you have decided to do is making *me* die); because the game of pain of the cross then seems to open itself specifically in the direction of *womankind* ('Maiden, wif, and fool womman', line 48). I want to close by suggesting that a great deal of this lauded psychology arises from the first-person dialogic format of the lyric, and that this dialogic format emerges from the poet's very close attention to the musical form of the liturgical sequence that he is translating and adapting. Who knows, in the final count, whether *Stond wel, moder* was ever really sung all that much from that one tiny manuscript, Royal 12 E I, in which the music of the sequence is accurately paired with the Middle English words? Nonetheless, musical form lies at the root of its affective verve. That, we might say, is finally an argument for musical form creating poetic form, which in turn determines the verbal expression of feeling.

17

Tutivillus and the Policing of Speech in Oxford, Bodleian Library, MS Douce 104

Mary C. Flannery

Tutivillus, þe deuyl of hell[1]

    Tutiuillus, þe deuyl of hell,
    He wryteþ har names soþe to tel,   *their*
       ad missam garulantes.   *(who are) chattering at mass*

    Better wer be at tome for ay,   *leisure; always*
5   Þan her to serue þe deuil to pay,   *here*
       sic vana famulantes.   *serving such vain/empty things*

    Þe[s] women þat sitteþ þe church about,
    Þai beþ al of þe deuelis rowte,   *crowd*
       diuina impedientes.   *(who are) hindering divine matters*

10 But þai be stil, he wil ham quell,   *unless*
    Wiþ kene crokes draw hem to hell,   *cruel crooks*
       ad puteum autem flentes.   *wailing, nevertheless, to the pit*

    ffor his loue þat ȝou der boȝth,   *bought you dearly*
    Hold ȝou stil & Iangel noȝth,   *gossip*

For another essay focused on the materiality of the word, see Jane Griffiths (Chapter 18), 'Have This is Mind: Word and Image in Audelay's Writing'; for another essay discussing a short poem appended tactically to more canonical and sizeable works, see Michael P. Kuczynski (Chapter 4), 'Textual and Affective Stability in *All Other Love is Like the Moon*', this volume.

[1] NIMEV 3812; DIMEV 6084. Lyric reproduced from Brown *XV*, p. 277, with the addition of glosses. The translations of the Latin lines are my own. All subsequent references are to this edition, cited in the text by line number. Further editions of the lyric include T. Wright and J. O. Halliwell-Phillipps, eds, *Reliquiae antiquae*, 2 vols (London, 1845), I, 257; a version of the text printed in W. Heuser, 'With an O and an I', *Anglia* 27 (1904), 283–319 (223); R. T. Davies, ed., *Medieval English Lyrics: A Critical Anthology* (London, 1963; repr. 1987), p. 198; C. Sisam and K. Sisam, eds, *The Oxford Book of Medieval English Verse* (Oxford, 1970), pp. 484–5, and Duncan, II, 137, pp. 300–1.

15 sed prece deponentes.²	*putting aside (such activities) with prayer*
Þe blis of heuen þan may 3e wyn;	*gain*
god bryng vs al to his In,	*dwelling place*
amen! amen! dicentes.	*saying 'Amen! Amen!'*

The 18-line poem above appears at the very end of Oxford, Bodleian Library, MS Douce 104 (henceforward referred to in this chapter as 'Douce').³ This manuscript, dated by a scribal colophon to 1427, contains only one other text, apart from various marginal annotations: a Middle Hiberno-English translation of the C-Text of *Piers Plowman*.⁴ Douce is best known as the only manuscript of *Piers Plowman* to contain an extensive series of marginal illustrations accompanying the poem.⁵ It is also unique, however, as the only witness to the above short poem about Tutivillus, the devil who eavesdrops on men and women in church in order to record their sinful speech. Dwarfed by the only other text the manuscript contains, six macaronic three-line stanzas at the end of Douce warn readers not to imitate '[þ]e[s] women þat sitteþ þe church about' (line 7) but to '[h]old 3ou stil & Iangel (*gossip*) no3th' (line 14), lest Tutivillus drag them off to hell.

The Tutivillus lyric is most frequently cited in scholarly discussions of medieval anxieties concerning wayward vernacular (and usually feminine) speech, but the dynamic between the Middle English and Latin lines of the poem, and the poem's potential to also act as a warning against the misuse of liturgical Latin, have been almost entirely overlooked.⁶ This chapter considers how the lyric's macaronic form brings together two narrative traditions concerning the demon: one that envisions him as a sack-carrying demon collecting dropped syllables of botched Latin liturgy, and one that envisions him as a writing demon eavesdropping on gossipers or

---

2 In this verse, the Latin follows the English instructions concerning what *not* to do with instructions concerning what readers *should* do.

3 Douce 104 is best known to scholars of *Piers Plowman* as D. On the manuscript's dialect and likely geographical origins, see A. McIntosh and M. L. Samuels, 'Prolegomena to a study of Mediaeval Anglo-Irish', *Medium Aevum* 37 (1968), 1–11, and S. Horobin, '"In London and in Opelond": The Dialect and Circulation of the C Version of *Piers Plowman*', *Medium Aevum* 74 (2005), 248–69 (esp. 251–2).

4 The manuscript is reproduced in facsimile in D. Pearsall, intro., *Piers Plowman: A Facsimile of Bodleian Library, Oxford, MS Douce 104*, with a catalogue of the illustrations by K. L. Scott (Cambridge, 1992).

5 On these illustrations, see especially K. Scott, 'The Illustrations of *Piers Plowman* in Bodleian Library MS. Douce 104', *Yearbook of Langland Studies* 4 (1990), 1–86 (which is adapted and included at the beginning of the facsimile of Douce, on pp. xxvii–xciv). K. Kerby-Fulton and D. L. Despres attempt to discern the intentions of the manuscript's illustrator and annotator in *Iconography and the Professional Reader: The Politics of Book Production in the Douce 'Piers Plowman'* (Minneapolis, 1999).

6 K. Cawsey discusses the relationship between the Latin and English lines of the lyric in 'Tutivillus and the "Kyrkchaterars": Strategies of Control in the Middle Ages', *Studies in Philology* 102 (2005), 434–51 (447–8).

'janglers' in church in order to record their idle words for Judgement Day.[7] Although the two traditions concerning Tutivillus originally ran along two distinct but parallel narrative lines, both the content and the macaronic form of this lyric (as well as the manuscript context in which the lyric survives) bring them together in this short poem. As a consequence, the space of this unique copy of an eighteen-line lyric in alternating Middle English and Latin becomes a space in which one language disciplines another, and in which the need to police speech in *both* languages is brought to the fore. The lyric's macaronic form contributes to its function as both sermon and script, a warning against the dangers of idle speech and an example of how speech must be used mindfully in Christian worship.

Although Tutivillus was one of many 'everyday demons' believed to hover near men and women in the hope either of catching them in the act of sinning or of inspiring them to sin, he is one of the better-known and more colourful demons of medieval English literary tradition. The sin that fell under his particular jurisdiction was *vaniloquia*, or idle speech, first categorised as one of twenty-four Sins of the Tongue (under the heading of *otiosa verba*) by Guillaume Peyraut (Peraldus) in his thirteenth-century treatise *Summa de vitiis et virtutibus*.[8] As Margaret Jennings has noted in what remains the most thorough study of Tutivillus's origins and significance to date, the single demon that came to be known by the name 'Tutivillus' originated in two distinct narrative strands of sermon exempla concerning *vaniloquia*. The first story typically featured a demon who was seen writing down idle words uttered by churchgoers; the second story featured 'a sack-carrying devil who also concerns himself with unprofitable speech – this time by depositing in his bag omitted or skimmed-over syllables from the carelessly recited prayers of the religious in order that these peccadilloes might be a witness to their lack of fervor in performing ecclesiastical duties'.[9] Although these two manifestations of Tutivillus have different origins and usually appear in separate narratives, their functions are very occasionally conflated. In an exemplum related to sloth in the fifteenth-century sermon cycle *Jacob's Well*, for example, a holy man sees a devil toting a heavy sack; the devil explains, 'I bere in my sacche sylablys & woordys, ouerskyppyd and synkopyd, & verse & psalmys þe whiche þese clerkys han stolyn in þe qweere (*choir*), & haue fayled in here seruyse'. The holy man then sees that the devil carries another heavy sack full of 'ydell woordys':

> ffor þis same clerk seyth þat þe deuyl in a cherche wrote þe woordys of þe peple, whiche þei iangledyn (*gossiped*) & rownedyn (*whispered*) in cherch, & whan his

---

[7] On the two distinct narrative threads concerning Tutivillus, see M. Jennings, *Tutivillus: The Literary Career of the Recording Demon*, Texts and Studies 1977, *Studies in Philology* 74:5 (1977), 10–11.

[8] S. E. Phillips has suggested that for Peyraut, 'idle talk is the quintessential venial sin': '"Janglynge in Cherche": Gossip and the *Exemplum*', *The Hands of the Tongue: Essays on Deviant Speech*, ed. E. D. Craun (Kalamazoo, 2007), pp. 61–94 (p. 85 n. 15). Peyraut and other pastoral writers characterised *vaniloquia* as empty or unprofitable speech; see E. D. Craun, *Lies, Slander and Obscenity in Medieval English Literature: Pastoral Rhetoric and the Deviant Speaker* (Cambridge, 2005), pp. 214–15, and Phillips, '"Janglynge in Cherche"', esp. pp. 63–4.

[9] Jennings, *Tutivillus*, 10–11.

scrowe (*scroll*) was to lytel, he drewe it out, wyth his teeth, broddere; and in his drawynge he smote his heuyd a3eyns þe walle.[10]

Although this 'deuyl' is never identified, the two activities in which he is engaged – collecting botched Latin in one bag, and collecting his records of lay gossip in church in another – clearly mark him as the demon Tutivillus.[11]

While some references to a recording demon may be found in earlier material, the earliest developed treatments of a Tutivillus-like demon are datable to the thirteenth century, and the earliest identifications of this demon as Tutivillus to the late thirteenth and early fourteenth centuries.[12] The geographical and etymological origins of the name are unknown. In medieval English writings, Tutivillus's popularity and presence seem to have come to a swift peak in the fifteenth century, and declined by the end of the sixteenth century.[13] He is best known to most readers of medieval English drama for his appearances in *Mankind* (where he does his best to lead mankind astray) and in the Towneley Cycle's *Judicium* play (where he revels in his ability to lure various sinners to hell).[14]

The demon who was believed to haunt the margins of human life in the Middle Ages haunts the edges of medieval English literature as well. Both the writing and the sack-carrying versions of Tutivillus observe sinning speakers from the borders of the narrative action. In exempla concerning the writing Tutivillus, he is pictured sitting off to the side of those who are jangling in church, observed in his act of recording only by a single onlooker. He is interesting to readers of and observers within these exempla *as* a listener and observer; his role is to remind medieval churchgoers that, however unobserved they may believe themselves to be in their idle chattering, someone will always be watching and listening, ready to consign them to hell with evidence of their sinful speech. Similarly, the sack-carrying Tutivillus moves around the church monitoring the liturgy almost totally unobserved by those on whom he eavesdrops, collecting the skipped syllables dropped by the inarticulate or inattentive religious. The Latin verses by which Tutivillus was most frequently identified tag him as a collector of fragments, leftovers of Latin prayers that the religious have failed to enunciate thoroughly; thus in his *Tractatus de poenitentia* (c.1285), John of Wales warns that:

---

10 A. Brandeis, ed., *Jacob's Well: An Englisht Treatise on the Cleaning of Man's Conscience*, EETS OS 115 (London, 1900), pp. 114–15.
11 Phillips suggests that *Jacob's Well* 'is the only text that tells both [versions of the Tutivillus narrative] at the same time' ('"Janglynge in Cherche"', p. 71), but as I will show, the Tutivillus lyric also plays upon both narrative strands.
12 See Jennings, *Tutivillus*, 11–17, and the appendices to Jennings's study (84–91), which enumerate named and unnamed appearances of Tutivillus between the thirteenth and sixteenth centuries.
13 *Ibid.*, 74.
14 K. M. Ashley and G. NeCastro, eds, *Mankind*, TEAMS (Kalamazoo, 2010); M. Stevens and A. C. Cawley, eds, *The Towneley Plays*, 2 vols, EETS SS 13, 14 (Oxford, 1994).

> Fragmina verborum Titivillus colligit horum
> Quibus die mille vicibus se sarcinat ille.[15]

Tutivillus's tendency to lurk at the side – as well as his perceived interest in fragments or snippets of speech or misspeaking – translates into a marginal, fragmentary existence in medieval texts. He is rarely the centre of the action in medieval literature, but instead more of a warning sidenote.

This seems to be the function he fulfils in Douce. The manuscript, which has been dated to c.1427–28, has been most thoroughly discussed by Derek Pearsall in the introduction to the facsimile of the manuscript, as well as by Kathleen Scott in her study of the manuscript's illustrations, which is reproduced in adapted form at the beginning of the facsimile.[16] Identified as having been written in Ireland by a 'practised and perhaps "professional" scribe', the manuscript was owned by Sir James Ley (1550–1629), first Earl of Marlborough, and was later acquired by Francis Douce (1757–1834), collector and antiquarian, who bequeathed it to the Bodleian Library.[17] Despite the manuscript's extensive programme of marginal illustration, Pearsall characterises it as constructed of 'poor thick membrane' and 'not of high quality'.[18] The Tutivillus lyric has been added to the end of the manuscript in a fifteenth-century hand by someone other than the manuscript's scribe.[19] Douce seems to have attempted to transcribe the poem on what is now fol. 33a, a leaf pasted in after fol. 33 (although Pearsall notes that this transcription is 'rather inaccurate').[20]

What, then, is the above lyric doing at the end of a poem like *Piers Plowman*? One possible answer hinges on a thematic overlap between the two texts: the lyric may have been added to the end of the longer poem as a comment on or response to *Piers Plowman*'s concerns with idle or wasted speech. As J. A. Burrow has pointed out, in both the B and C texts of *Piers Plowman*, 'Langland introduces a new pair of moral topics, closely related to each other in his mind: the wasting of time and the wasting of words'.[21] In fact, Burrow notes that the C

---

15 'Tutivillus collects fragments of words / He burdens himself with a thousand a day'. My translation. London, British Library, Royal MS 10 A IX, fol. 40vb (cited in Jennings, *Tutivillus*, 16). Jennings points out that these verses originally included the word *psalmorum* instead of the more general *verborum*, doubtless a reflection of the original linking of this exemplum with monastic speech (*Tutivillus*, 15).
16 See Pearsall and Scott, eds, *Piers Plowman: A Facsimile*; Scott, 'Illustrations of *Piers Plowman*'; and Kerby-Fulton and Despres, *Iconography and the Professional Reader*.
17 A. V. C. Schmidt, '*Piers Plowman: A Facsimile of Bodleian Library, Oxford, MS Douce 104*, with an introduction by Derek Pearsall and a catalogue of the illustrations by Kathleen Scott', review, *Medium Aevum* 63 (1994), 128–30 (129). On the scribe, see D. Pearsall, 'Introduction', in Pearsall and Scott, eds, *Piers Plowman: A Facsimile*, pp. ix–xxv (p. xiv).
18 Pearsall, 'Introduction', p. x.
19 *Ibid.*, p. x; Douce 104, fol. 112v.
20 Pearsall, 'Introduction', p. x. Francis Douce, who himself produced an edition of the Towneley *Judicium* pageant in 1822, seems to have been interested in the etymological origins of the name 'Tutivillus' (Jennings, *Tutivillus*, 40).
21 J. A. Burrow, 'Wasting Time, Wasting Words in *Piers Plowman* B and C', *Yearbook of Langland Studies* 17 (2003), 191–202 (191).

text refers to the wasting of time and speech even more frequently than the B text of the poem, 'preserving most of the references in B and adding new ones'.[22] Drawing on the work of Siegfried Wenzel, Burrow argues that the attention to wasted speech is largely a product of Langland's concern with sloth or *acedia*. Such a link between sloth and idle words was made by other writers such as the author of the *Jacob's Well* exemplum cited above, which warns its audience about Tutivillus (in both his sack-carrying and recording-demon guises) in the context of a sermon against sloth. Jennings observes that medieval Tutivillus narratives frequently connect sloth with the idle speech that comprises the demon's special area of jurisdiction:[23]

> it was acknowledged that among the laity, sloth could be a cause of disturbance at church services: the slothful, it was said, 'jangle' and engage in 'harlotry' (idle talk). Among the clergy the vice caused the speeding up or abbreviating of the obligatory prayers (either Mass or Office), and a general negligence in recitation: mumbling *sotto voce* at one end of the continuum, and making loud noises rather than intelligible words at the other.[24]

Tutivillus is thus charged with policing two different kinds of slothful speech, one clerical and Latin, the other lay and vernacular. The case of idle clerical speech in church – instances when careless clergy omit, misplace, mumble or skip over bits of Latin prayers – is an explicit cause for concern in the C version of *Piers Plowman*, the text that precedes the Tutivillus lyric in Douce. Passus XIII includes verses that are highly critical of such 'overskipping' of Latin in church:

> So hit is a goky, by god! þat in þe gospel fayleth   *fool*
> Or in masse or in matynes maketh eny defaute.
>   *Qui offendit in vno in omnibus est reus.*
> For ouerskipperes also in þe sauter sayth Dauid:
>   *Psallite deo nostro, psallite; quia Rex terre deus, psallite sapienter.*
> The bishop shal be blamed before god, as y leue,
> That crouneth suche for goddes knyhtes that conne *sapienter*
> Nother syng ne rede ne seye a masse of þe day.
> Ac neuer noþer is blameless, the bischop ne þe chapeleyn,
> For *ignorancia non excusat*, as ych haue herd in bokes.
>
> (Passus XIII, lines 120–7)[25]

---

22 Ibid., 194.
23 Ibid., 193; see also S. Wenzel, *The Sin of Sloth: Acedia in Medieval Thought and Literature* (Chapel Hill, 1960, 1967), pp. 197–8, which cites medieval confession manuals that link wasted speech with wasted time as consequences of the sin of sloth.
24 Jennings, *Tutivillus*, 12.
25 *Piers Plowman by William Langland: An Edition of the C-text*, ed. D. Pearsall (London, 1978), with added gloss. The first Latin quotation in the excerpt above is taken from James 2: 10: 'Quicumque autem totam legem servaverit, offendat autem in uno, factus est omnium reus' ('And whosoever shall keep the whole law, but offend in one point, is become guilty of all'); The second echoes Psalm 46: 7–8 (varied): 'Psallite Deo nostro, psallite; psallite regi nostro, psallite: quoniam rex omnis terrae Deus, psallite sapienter' ('Sing praises to our God, sing ye; sing praises to our king, sing ye. For God is the king of all the earth: sing ye wisely'); see *Piers Plowman*, ed. Pearsall, pp. 227–8. Latin and

Here, overskipping and 'defaute' in the recitation of Latin prayers are attributed to the foolishness of ignorant priests and the irresponsibility of the bishops who appoint them. A priest who cannot 'syng ne rede ne seye a masse of þe day' *sapienter* (that is, with a thorough understanding of the Latin words he is uttering) cannot fulfil his office. This passage also echoes such medieval critiques of slothful speech as that of Jacques de Vitry (d.1240), who, in one of the earliest exempla to feature a sack-carrying predecessor of Tutivillus, describes such lazy Latin as 'stealing' from God:

> Audivi quod quidam sanctus homo, dum esset in choro, vidit diabolum quasi sacco pleno valde oneratum. Dum autem adjuraret dyabolum ut diceret ei quid portaret ait: 'Hec sunt sillabe et dictiones syncopate et versus psalmodie, que isti clerici in hiis matutinis furati sunt Deo; hec utique ad eorum accusationem diligenter reservo.' Excubate igitur diligenter in mysterio altaris ne super populum oriatur indignatio.[26]

It is possible that the writer who added the Tutivillus lyric after the end of the C version of *Piers Plowman* in Douce had such exempla in mind and inserted the lyric as a comment on the C text's critiques of idle words.

The association of Tutivillus with the policing of idle speech thus represents a possible thematic link between the two poems that sit alongside one another in Douce, despite the fact that the first poem dwarfs the second. In addition to this thematic link, however, the Tutivillus lyric's macaronic structure suggests a formal connection between the two poems, one that also plays on Tutivillus's dual narrative origins. Both *Piers Plowman* and the Tutivillus lyric rely on complex interplay between Middle English and Latin, and I would argue that the short lyric is as concerned with Latinity as is the longer poem.[27] In the remainder of this chapter, I will work through the Tutivillus lyric, focusing in particular on the interplay between the Middle English and Latin verses, and on how this interplay affects the representation of the disciplining of language and speech within the poem.

English Bible quotations are taken from the parallel-text edition of the Latin Vulgate and Douay-Rheims versions of the Bible.

26 'I have heard that a certain holy man, while he was in choir, saw a devil truly weighed down with a full sack. When, however, he commanded the demon to tell what he carried, the evil one said: "These are the syllables and syncopated words and verses of the psalms which these very clerics in their matins stole from God; you can be sure I am keeping these diligently for their accusation." Keep watch diligently, therefore, over the mystery of the altar lest indignation arise over the people.' See Jacques de Vitry, *The Exempla or Illustrative Stories from the Sermones Vulgares of Jacques de Vitry*, ed. T. F. Crane (London, 1890), p. 6, and Jennings, *Tutivillus*, 11–13, for discussion (I have adapted the English translation of de Vitry's exemplum from p. 11).

27 Langland's use of Latin has been the subject of much scholarly attention. Fiona Somerset provides a thoughtful discussion of what she terms 'multilingual Latin' in *Piers Plowman*, as well as a helpful overview of the relevant scholarship, in '"Al þe comonys with o voys atonys": Multilingual Latin and Vernacular Voice in *Piers Plowman*', *Yearbook of Langland Studies* 19 (2005), 107–36.

At first glance, the poem seems to concern the writing Tutivillus most directly. The lyric warns readers of Tutivillus's constant presence in church, where he waits to drag janglers to hell and 'wryteþ har names' of those who gossip at Mass ('ad missam garulantes', lines 2–3). This immediately suggests that the targets of the poem's critique are the usual targets of the writing demon: lay churchgoers gossiping in the vernacular, rather than clergy botching the Latin liturgy. The lyric is specific about *which* laypeople are particularly prone to gossiping in church: 'women þat sitteþ þe church about' (line 7). The trope of the generalised, unnamed 'jangling women' is a common feature of the writing Tutivillus exempla, which tend to specify 'a female presence while keeping all figures unnamed'.[28] As studies of deviant speech in medieval England have made clear, gossip was typically gendered as a female activity during this period, a connection also made by at least one fifteenth-century annotator of Douce.[29] Immediately following the Tutivillus poem on fol. 112v is a note in a formal fifteenth-century hand, which reads, 'unde beda / Qui osculetur mere*tr*icem : pulsat ianua*m* i*n*ferni / war<t?h?[es?]>' ('From Bede: He who would kiss a prostitute knocks at the door of hell / beware these').[30] Pearsall notes that, while the word appearing immediately underneath the Latin proverb might be the name of the person who wrote it down, it 'is more likely to be … an admonitory response to the poem: *war thes*, "beware of these (harlots)"'.[31] Should this interpretation of the smudged final words indeed be correct, A. V. C. Schmidt has further suggested that they and the Latin proverb they succeed might be a reference to the warning in Passus X of the C text: '*meretrix est ianua mortis.* / And 3e þat han wyues, ben war' (Passus X, lines 287–8).[32] Thus it is possible that the Tutivillus lyric's macaronic reference to jangling women in church prompted the author of the note to reflect on the C text's warnings concerning the spiritual dangers posed by women and wives.

---

28 Jennings, *Tutivillus*, 27. This likely explains the fact that one of the most recognisable artistic depictions of Tutivillus to survive in medieval art and architecture is the image of him perched between two gossiping women, occasionally with an arm around each. For examples of artistic representations of Tutivillus, see M. D. Anderson, *Drama and Imagery in English Medieval Churches* (Cambridge, 1963), pp. 173–7, and E. Lehrer, *Demons, Death and Damnation* (New York, 1971), plates 16b, 21–2, 25. In her book on gossip in late medieval England, S. E. Phillips likewise points out that, '[a]mong the Middle English versions of the [Tutivillus] narrative, Mirk's *Festial*, the *Book of the Knight of the Tower*, the *Lay Folks Mass Book*, and *Handlyng Synne* all explicitly identify the janglers as women': *Transforming Talk: The Problem with Gossip in Late Medieval England* (University Park, 2007), p. 24 n. 34.
29 See in particular, S. Bardsley, *Venomous Tongues: Speech and Gender in Late Medieval England* (Philadelphia, 2006); Phillips, *Transforming Talk*; K. Lochrie, *Covert Operations: The Medieval Uses of Secrecy* (Philadelphia, 1999), pp. 56–92.
30 My translation. The note is transcribed in Pearsall, 'Introduction', p. xi.
31 Pearsall, 'Introduction', p. xi.
32 Pearsall translates the Latin as 'a prostitute is the gateway of death' (*Piers Plowman*, ed. Pearsall, p. 193).

Given the lyric's tone in relation to '[þ]e[s] women' being pointed out around the church, the poem's perspective seems to be both masculine and clerical, the perspective of someone who here admonishes readers to shun the example of the gossiping female churchgoers. One might read the lyric as embodying the 'antagonism between idle talk and the sermon, between the priest and his congregation', which Susan Phillips has noted was a problem 'for a whole host of pastoral writers in late medieval England'.[33] Read in this light, the lyric takes up a specifically Latinate clerical position in relation to wayward vernacular gossip, a position that is achieved by means of the poem's macaronic form and particularly by the final, Latin line of its concluding stanza. The poem's English lines make up a minuscule vernacular sermon functioning largely for the benefit of lay, female churchgoers.[34] Unless these women are 'stil', Tutivillus 'wil ham quell' and '[w]iþ kene crokes (*cruel crooks*) draw hem to hell' (lines 10–11), a somewhat darker depiction of the demon and his powers than normally appears in Tutivillus narratives. The lyric's admonition to '[h]old ȝou stil & Iangel (*gossip*) noȝth' could be a general warning to all churchgoers, which uses the sinfully gossiping women as an example of behaviour that will incur damnation; but following so closely on the reflection that these women are bound for hell *unless* they reform, it seems likelier that this admonition is addressed to lay female churchgoers. The lyric's final stanza assures women that, if they cease their jangling in church, '[þ]e blis of heuen þan may ȝe wyn (*gain*)' (line 16). Two final lines bring the poem to a close on a prayerful note:

> god bryng vs al to his In,   *dwelling place*
>   amen! amen! dicentes. (lines 17–18)   *saying 'Amen! Amen!'*

These concluding lines function as a short prayer, but we might also read them as a script for correct speaking in church. With the lyric's concluding 'amen! amen!', wayward (vernacular) speech is brought back in line. Having warned against the dangers of sinful speech in church, the lyric concludes by reminding its audience of the goal that draws them to their devotions in the first place – the possibility of salvation – and then providing an approved script, a reminder of the correct words (even the correctly spoken Latin language) they ought to be using during their devotions.

But what does this suggest about the relative status of Latin and vernacular speech within the poem? In her own discussion of the Tutivillus lyric that appears in Douce, Kathy Cawsey has read Latin as the dominant language within the poem, despite its making up only one-third of the lyric's linguistic content. She views the vernacular as being 'included' within the poem, but argues that this inclusion is exclusive rather than inclusive:

---

33 Phillips, '"Janglynge in Cherche"', p. 62.
34 While lay male churchgoers might be tacitly invited to join in with the lyric's condemnation of female gossip, the readers and listeners most likely to be in on the poem's Latin jokes and barbed criticism would be clerkly and clerical readers and listeners capable of understanding the language.

Far from being inclusive, the use of the vernacular excludes certain segments of the population: the vernacular listeners/readers would understand just enough to know that they were the target of the poem, but would not understand the joke. The Latin also works like it does in John Gower's *Confessio Amantis*, where the Latin headnotes and glosses control, interpret and contain the vernacular verses in much the same way that the priests want to order and control their parishioners' speech.[35]

In Cawsey's reading of the poem, the Latin verses of the Tutivillus lyric work to exert control over a potentially threatening disorder that, she argues, is inherently bound up with vernacularity:

> Gossip is by nature vernacular – not only is it invariably in English, but it epitomizes, in a sense, all the other dangerous traits of the vernacular. It is unstructured, uncontrolled, unruly, accessible to all, communal. The action the demon takes in writing down the women's gossip betrays a desire to fix it, to control it – for like the vernacular, gossip's danger is in its fluidity, the chance for each individual to rework, gloss, and re-interpret the original message.[36]

Given the fact that the lyric describes the demon as *writing* the names of gossiping churchgoers ('[h]e wryteþ har (*their*) names', line 2), Cawsey understandably presumes the lyric's subject to be the writing incarnation of Tutivillus, whom she views as policing a specifically vernacular form of transgressive, unruly speech. On one level, one might indeed read the poem and its Latin as countering and controlling the wayward tongues of women gossiping in church. However, since Tutivillus is not only or even primarily a punisher of vernacular gossip in medieval literature, we would be remiss if we overlooked the role he was believed to play in the policing of misspoken liturgical Latin, particularly given the context in which the Tutivillus lyric survives. This manuscript context should also alert us to other possible interpretations of the satirical interplay between English and Latin in macaronic verse, whose targets – as the C text illustrates – include not only lay women, but also male clergy. If one approaches the lyric with *both* the sack-carrying narratives and the exempla concerning the writing demon in mind, and while taking account of the preceding C text's noted concern with botched Latin and idle speech, a new reading of the lyric comes into view. In this reading, the final line of the poem emerges more clearly as a script for bringing *both* English and Latin speakers to heel, with the repeated 'amen! amen!' uniting English and Latin speakers in the mindful uttering of correct speech in worship. Such a reading would also enable us to admit the C text's sharp critique of lazy and ignorant priests to our interpretation of the Tutivillus lyric, thereby complicating initial interpretations of the shorter poem as a text targeting solely, or at least primarily, the idle vernacular speech of female churchgoers. By uniting the two threads of the Tutivillus narrative within

---

35 Cawsey, 'Tutivillus and the "Kyrkchaterars"', 448.
36 *Ibid.*, 447.

a macaronic text, the lyric functions as a linguistic leveller, a warning directed at both lay speakers of the vernacular and Latin-speaking clergy.

The Tutivillus lyric in Douce 104 stands as an example of linguistic lyrical form responding to a linguistic topic: the spiritually pressing problem of how to speak correctly (if at all) in church. At first glance, the short poem seems a straightforward example of one of the many narratives concerning the version of Tutivillus who was believed to police vernacular (usually female) gossipers in church. But if one reconsiders its content in light of the macaronic form of the poem and the manuscript context in which it appears, the lyric seems, like the demon himself, to be concerning itself with *both* groups of unruly speakers, the lay and the clerical, the vernacular and the Latin. In the interplay between the lyric's two languages, it is possible to discern a creative fusion of Tutivillus's two identities as sack-carrying collector of the clergy's misspoken Latin, and as writing eavesdropper on lay gossip in church. Read from this perspective, the poem might be seen as speaking to *all* of its medieval readers, a stern reminder that no one's speech escapes the notice of the recording demon.

18

Have This in Mind: Word and Image in Audelay's Writing

Jane Griffiths

Despite recent work by Susanna Fein and others, Audelay and his writing remain relatively unfamiliar. His poems survive in a single manuscript, Oxford, Bodleian Library, MS Douce 302, which was produced during Audelay's lifetime (c.1426–31) at the Augustinian Haughmond Abbey, where he was a priest in the Lestrange chantry.[1] It consists of four main parts: a collection of poems under the title *The Counsel of Conscience*, a series of 'salutations', a collection of carols, and what Fein describes in her edition as a 'meditative close' to the manuscript as a whole.[2] Although it is likely that not all poems in the manuscript are of Audelay's own composition, it is evidently a compilation that combines Audelay's own writing with that of others in a highly purposeful way.[3] The

---

For another essay focused on wordplay, see Joel Grossman (Chapter 19), '"The Dance of the Intellect among Words": Wyatt's *In eternum* and Late Medieval Lyric Practice'; for further essays exploring the relation between word and image, see Katherine Zieman (Chapter 11), 'Compiling the Lyric: Richard Rolle, Textual Dynamism and Devotional Song in London, British Library, Additional MS 37049', and A. S. Lazikani (Chapter 2), 'Moving Lights: An Affective Reading of *On leome is in þis world ilist* and Church Wall Paintings'.

1 The manuscript has been edited as *John the Blind Audelay, Poems and Carols (Oxford, Bodleian Library MS Douce 302)*, ed. S. Fein (Kalamazoo, 2009). All quotations will be from this edition, with the addition of some glosses. For Audelay's life, see M. J. Bennett, 'John Audelay: Life Records and Heaven's Ladder', *My Wyl and my Wrytyng: Essays on John the Blind Audelay*, ed. S. Fein (Kalamazoo, 2009), pp. 30–53.
2 See further, Fein, ed., *Poems and Carols*, pp. 5–22; S. Fein, 'John Audelay and his Book: Critical Overview and Major Issues', *Wyl and Wrytyng*, ed. Fein, esp. pp. 8–13 (9).
3 For the manuscript as compilation, see Fein, 'Audelay and his Book', pp. 7–8, 24 n. 16; and cf. O. Pickering, 'The Make-Up of *Counsel of Conscience*', *Wyl and Wrytyng*, ed. Fein, pp. 112–37. For identification of those lyrics that are not Audelay's, see Fein 'Audelay and his Book' pp. 9, 12, 27–8 n. 40; for more extensive discussion of the authorship of *Three Dead Kings*, see A. Putter, 'The Language and Metre of *Pater Noster* and *Three Dead Kings*', *Review of English Studies*, NS 55 (2004), 498–526, and E. G. Stanley, 'The Verse Forms of Jon the Blynde Awdelay', *The Long Fifteenth Century: Essays for Douglas Gray*, ed. H. Cooper and S. Mapstone (Oxford, 1997), pp. 99–121: Putter argues that the poem is not by Audelay; Stanley that it is.

paratext repeatedly emphasises Audelay's close association with the manuscript; within the lyrics, too, he is frequently named, and the final colophon includes a prayer for his soul.[4] He is thus among a relatively small number of fifteenth-century authors who seek systematically to attach their name to their work. Focusing primarily on *The Counsel of Conscience*, this chapter will argue that he is also among those whose writing constitutes a practical poetics: that is, among those whose views on poetry are both governed by their experience of writing and expressed through their poems. Specifically, it will suggest that his view of poetry as spiritual instruction is reflected in the form as well as the content of his lyrics.

Although Audelay is closely associated with Douce 302, the manuscript is not a holograph; it was written by two scribes at the abbey, very possibly because Audelay himself was blind.[5] This is of more than incidental importance; the epithet 'blind' is used of him so consistently that it effectively becomes part of his name. As a result, his frequent association of blindness with spiritual failings, as in *Marcolf and Solomon* (lines 298, 629) and the *Epilogue* to *The Counsel of Conscience* (line 381), has a particular resonance; there is a strong implication that Audelay's own blindness is a punishment for the sins of his youth.[6] Yet Audelay's condition also allows him to define himself as a seer: one whose lack of physical sight enables his spiritual vision. Near the beginning of the *Epilogue* to *The Counsel of Conscience*, Audelay explicitly sets out this position, thanking God that:

> [he has] geven me wil, wit, tyme, and space,
> Throgh the Holé Gost, blynd, def to be,   *deaf*
> And say this wordis throgh his gret grace. (lines 19–21)[7]

As is made still more explicit in the strikingly unhumble humility topos that follows, Audelay considers himself to be the recipient of the word of God:

---

4   For Audelay's self-naming, see Fein, 'Audelay and his Book', p. 4, and R. Meyer-Lee, 'The Vatic Penitent: John Audelay's Self-Representation', *Wyl and Wrytyng*, ed. Fein, p. 57. For the argument that Douce 302 is atypical of its period in gathering together the works of a single author, see A. S. G. Edwards, 'Fifteenth-Century Middle English Verse Author Collections', *The English Medieval Book: Studies in Memory of Jeremy Griffiths*, ed. A. S. G. Edwards, V. Gillespie and R. Hanna (London, 2000), pp. 101–12.

5   For a brief outline of each scribe's contribution to the manuscript, see Fein, ed., *Poems and Carols*, pp. 4–5; and for a fuller discussion, see her 'Good Ends in the Audelay Manuscript', *Yearbook of English Studies* 33 (2003), 97–119.

6   *Marcolf and Solomon*: NIMEV 947; DIMEV 1559; *Epilogue*: NIMEV 1200; DIMEV 1973. For Audelay's blindness as a symbol of sin, see Fein, 'Good Ends', 100–1; Meyer-Lee, 'Vatic Penitent', pp. 56–7; and T. W. Machan, *Textual Criticism and Middle English Texts* (Charlottesville, 1994), pp. 103–4.

7   This is one of the few points in the manuscript where Audelay is referred to as deaf as well as blind; another is the carol *Dread of Death* (NIMEV 693; DIMEV 1152), lines 7–9. His want of hearing is generally not emphasised, however (cf. Fein, 'Good Ends', 98 n. 2).

> Mervel ye not of this makyng,
> Fore I me excuse – hit is not I;
> This was the Holé Gost wercheng,   *making/labour of the*
> That sayd these wordis so faythfully. (lines 495–8)

Variants of these lines are found at several other points in the *Counsel*, making Audelay the first writer in English to claim explicitly to be divinely inspired.[8] It is not just the claim to inspiration itself that is significant, however; equally important is the implication that inspiration is located specifically in words. Both his turning away from sensory perception and his insistence on the spiritual significance of the word are central tenets of the instruction he offers his readers.

The stated purpose of Audelay's work is the salvation of souls.[9] As he puts it at the end of the *Epilogue* to *The Counsel of Conscience*:

> *The Cownsel of Conseans* this boke I calle,
> Or *The Ladder of Heven*, I say, forewy: *because*
> Ther is no mon may clym up a walle
> Without a ladder, sekyrly;   *safely/certainly*
> No more may we to heven on hye
> Without treu cownsel of consians.
> Clyme up this ladder – then may ye se
> What ye schul do to Godis plesans. (lines 417–24)   *please God*

He consistently implies that the surest means of achieving this end is a practice that might best be described by the anachronistic-sounding word 'mindfulness'. Almost every poem contains the injunction to 'have this in mind', and many contain it several times; in *Marcolf and Solomon* he writes: 'Eever have mekenes in your mynd, relegyouse, I you rede' (line 300); in *True Living* 'Ever have this in thi mynd: / To the pore, loke thou be kynd' (lines 182–3), and 'Have his Passyon in thi mynd, / That dyed on cros' (lines 210–11).[10] As these examples indicate, the nature of what his readers are to hold in mind varies from case to case: it may be a virtue, a moral imperative, or an affective image. It is in the play between these variables that the special significance that Audelay attributes to the word becomes apparent. At first sight, his repeated injunction to 'have in mind' resembles the recurrent marginal instruction, *contemplacio*, in Nicholas Love's *Mirror of the Blessed Life of Jesus Christ*, and the lines from *True Living* that specifically invite the reader to focus on Christ's Passion similarly seem to imply that Audelay, like Love, is a proponent of affective piety, who seeks to foster his readers' faith by inviting them to 'contemplate' the mental images evoked by his text. Yet the lyric

---

8   Other points in *The Counsel of Conscience* where a version of these lines occurs include: *The Remedy of Nine Virtues* (NIMEV 3780.5; DIMEV 6031), lines 77–80; *Visiting the Sick and Consoling the Needy* (NIMEV 2853; DIMEV 4542), lines 378–81; *Our Lord's Epistle on Sunday* (NIMEV 2324, not in DIMEV), lines 196–9; *The Vision of St Paul* (NIMEV 3481; DIMEV 5491), lines 353–60. Audelay's claim anticipates those of Stephen Hawes and John Skelton by the best part of a century.
9   See further Fein, 'Good Ends'.
10 NIMEV 1492.5; DIMEV 2513.

that most explicitly facilitates imaginative re-creation of that event on the part of the reader, *Pope John's Passion of Our Lord*, also indicates how, for Audelay, such visualisation is ultimately at the service of the word. Although each of its stanzas describes one stage of Christ's suffering, and the early stanzas, in particular, do so with considerable emphasis on its physical detail, a level of distance is created when Audelay asserts that what he is reporting is what was witnessed by 'the holé evangelist, swete Saynt Jon' (line 76), emphasising that the images he presents are derived from previous writing.[11] The weight that this gives to the word is matched, in practice, by the way Audelay structures his material. His retelling of the Passion story is insistently interrupted by the refrain line with which each of the first seven stanzas concludes: 'And al hit was fore love of thee'. Because this recurs at the relatively short interval of eight lines, its repetition dominates the narrative; it becomes the point to which each stanza builds. The introduction of a new refrain line in the eighth stanza, one that exhorts Audelay's readers to 'have peté' of Christ's Passion, thus comes as a surprise, and in drawing attention to the point at which Audelay turns from his account of the events of the Passion to the significance they hold for his own contemporaries, it reaffirms that verbal patterning is key to Audelay's attempt to engage his readers' attention and shape their understanding. Indeed, in the concluding stanzas of the poem, what the reader is exhorted to 'have ... in mynd' (line 81) is not the Passion itself, but Audelay's injunction 'To that Lord, be never unkynd' (line 83); moreover, the recommended course of action is not imaginative, but oral: to achieve remission of sins, 'say this prayour with gret peté' (line 88). The prayer that follows summarises the events of the Passion in much abbreviated form; the implication is that the more fully imagined version of events in the first part of the poem should inform the reader's understanding as he prays. But it is nonetheless the speaking of the words of the prayer, not any attendant reimagining, that is said to be efficacious, and the most intimate link between the prayer and the preceding part of the poem is, again, through word rather than image, as the prayer's refrain lines at once echo and subtly alter those of the previous stanzas. As much as encouraging his readers to believe themselves actually present at the events he describes, Audelay makes them acutely attentive to the encounter with his verse.

A comparable redirection of affective material is found in the *Epilogue* to *The Counsel of Conscience*. Here, Audelay posits his book as the result of a kind of dream vision:

> Fore as I lay seke, in my dremyng,
> Methoght a mon to me con say:
> 'Let be thi slouth and thi slomeryng!

---

11 Something comparable occurs in *The Vision of St Paul*, where despite the emphasis on what Paul saw, Audelay's injunction to 'have mynd' does not encourage readers to visualise a scene, but to remember Audelay's own words, and it *interrupts* the record of what Paul saw (lines 93–105). For a detailed discussion of this poem in relation to its source, see R. Easting, '"Choose yourselves whither to go": John Audelay's *Vision of St Paul*', *Wyl and Wrytyng*, ed. Fein, pp. 170–90.

> Have mynd on God both nyght and day!
> Bohold and se a reuful aray –   *pitiful sight*
> Al the word on foyre brenyng!' (lines 27–32)   *on fire*

Yet although his dreaming self is instructed to 'behold and se', and although Audelay's response to what he sees is an affective one – he 'barst on wepyng' (line 42) – he once again turns 'seeing' into something verbal, suggesting that his private, affective response is inadequate until it has been turned into writing for the public good:

> With soroue of hert, to Crist I prayd:
> 'Take no venchanche, Lord!' I sayd,   *vengeance*
> 'Bot *send the pepul sum warnyng,*
>
> ...
>
> And *grawnt me, Lord, throgh thi gret grace,*
> *Sum good word that I may say*
> To thi worchip, Lord, I thee pray. (lines 43–5, 48–50; my italics)

Just as the purpose of Pope John's vision is to lead to prayer, the purpose of Audelay's vision is to lead to the writing of the word; he implies that without the act of writing the vision would not constitute a form of 'having in mind', but rather a form of sinfulness or sloth. Indeed, the *Epilogue* explains that *The Counsel of Conscience* is the very warning Audelay has prayed to be able to give:

> Beware, seris, ye han warnyng!   *sirs*
> For I say soth. No mon me blame.
> God hath me grawntid myn askeng. (lines 54–6)[12]   *request*

In other words, God has enabled him to turn his vision into the words of the *Counsel*, with their potential to benefit spiritually both the reader who follows Audelay's exhortations and their author, who salves his own soul by saving others. As Fein has argued, Audelay's writing is grounded in an intensely visual devotional culture, yet in his 'verbal/visual aesthetic' the word ultimately possesses the greatest efficacy and reality.[13]

This appears particularly clearly from the lyric that seems most directly to appeal to the reader's visual imagination: *The Meditation on the Holy Face*.[14] The last of a sequence of linked 'salutations' to five women each of whom, either literally or metaphorically, has 'borne' Christ, it is addressed to the image of Christ's face on the vernicle.[15] Audelay begins by invoking the image in visual terms:

---

12 Cf. Fein's argument that Audelay 'conflates the action of bookmaking with his religious conviction' ('Good Ends', 109).
13 S. Fein, 'Mary to Veronica: John Audelay's Sequence of Salutations to God-Bearing Women', *Speculum* 86 (2011), 964–1009 (966, 968).
14 NIMEV 3073; DIMEV 4777.
15 See further Fein, 'Mary to Veronica'.

Salve, I say, Holé Face of our Saveour,	Hail
In the wyche schynth to us an hevenly fygure,	image
An graceus on to se!	One gracious to behold
Salve, thou settis thi prynt on lynin cloth of witlé coloure,	imprint; whitish
And betoke hit Veroneca fore love and gret honoure	
Upon here sudoré. (lines 1–6)	handkerchief

In Douce 302, this meditation is accompanied by an illustration of Christ's face. The only illustration in the manuscript, it strongly resembles those attached to the lyric *O Vernicle* in a number of Arma Christi manuscripts, in particular in its detailed depiction of the 'lynin cloth' on which Christ's face appears, indicating that what it represents is not Christ's face itself, but the image of it on the vernicle.[16] These manuscripts contained a series of lyrics, frequently accompanied by illustrations of the instruments of Christ's torture, prefaced by *O Vernicle*, which emphasises that viewing the illustration of the vernicle may bring about forgiveness of sins. As Douglas Gray puts it:

> The relationship of image and words is a simple and practical one: the image gives a visual focus for the reader of the words, and the words direct the eye of the worshipper to the image.[17]

In principle, then, the illustration takes on the function of the vernicle itself, which in the fourteenth century was displayed to pilgrims to Rome on certain days during Jubilee years, with the stated effect of reducing their time in Purgatory.[18] Yet despite Audelay's punning reference to it as a visible figure of the heavenly 'fygure (*image*)' of Christ, the relatively light and sketchy illustration is visually much less dominant than the lengthy and heavily inked Latin rubric under which it appears. Moreover, the rubric draws attention to the efficacy of Audelay's lyric rather than that of the illustration, asserting:

> Quicumque hanc salutationem in honore Salvatoris per xx dies continuo devote dixerit, Bonefacius papa quartus concessit omnibus vere confessis et contritus plenam remissionem omnium peccatorem.[19]

In consequence, the presence of the illustration seems to be conventional rather than active or affective – a reflection of the practice of attaching equivalent illustrations to equivalent lyrics in Arma Christi manuscripts, rather than a prompt

---

[16] See A. Nichols, 'O Vernicle: Illustrations of an Arma Christi Poem', *Tributes to Kathleen L. Scott: English Medieval Manuscripts and Their Readers*, ed. M. Villalobos Hennessy (Turnhout, 2009), pp. 139–70 (pp. 151–2).

[17] D. Gray, 'A Middle English Illustrated Poem', *Medieval Studies for J. A. W. Bennett*, ed. P. L. Heyworth (Oxford, 1981), pp. 185–205 (pp. 187–8); cf. J. Hirsh, *The Boundaries of Faith: The Development and Transmission of Medieval Spirituality* (Leiden, 1996), pp. 129–36.

[18] Nichols, 'O Vernicle', p. 150.

[19] 'Whoever has devoutly said this salutation in honor of the Savior for twenty days in a row, Pope Boniface IV has granted to those who have truly confessed all and are contrite, full remission of all sins.' The translation is from Fein, ed., *Poems and Carols*, p. 173 n.

visually to 'have in mind' Christ's presence.[20] Moreover, Audelay almost immediately redefines the image of the face as a verbal one, apostrophising it in the first line of the second stanza: '*Salve*, the fayrnes of this *word*, a myrrore of holé men' (line 7, my italics). The change of terms is so unexpected that Fein's edition glosses 'word' as 'word', emphasising the way in which the line reverses the terms of the first line of Genesis: there, 'the word was God'; here the appearance of God is the word.

This gives an indication of the almost mystical significance that Audelay attaches to the word – something that is reflected in the form as well as the content of his writing. Through extensive formal and linguistic play, his own written words serve not only to instruct in divine truth but themselves to represent it. The first stanza of *Marcolf and Solomon* provides a good example. Like each stanza of the poem, it follows a Latin rubric, in this case *De concordia inter rectores fratres et rectores ecclesie* ('Concerning an accord between friars and secular priests'), and it states:

> God hath grauntyd grace unto oure lernyng
> Al that we fyndon fayfully wrytyn in Holé Wryt,   *find*
> That be our pacyens, princypaly, and holy wrytyng,   *through our patience*
> We schuld have consolacion and comford – byleve
> truly in hyt!   *it*
> I schal say you the soth, that wele schul ye wyt,   *know*
> Hit is Godys Word and his werke and his worchyng.   *making*
> Be the grace of the Holé Gost, togedyr hit is yknyt,   *tied together/composed*
> Redlé us to remembyr in oure redyng.   *For us to recall easily*
> And hold hit in mynde:
> Ther is no mon that saved may be,
> But he have Faythe, Hope, and Charité,
> And do as thou woldust me dud by thee,   *one did*
> To God and men, be kynde. (lines 1–13)

The relationship between the rubric and the content of the stanza is a characteristically oblique one. Taken on its own, the rubric is in line with the poem's project of clerical reform.[21] Rather than translate or 'gloss' the succinct Latin

---

20   Pictures of the vernicle in Arma Christi manuscripts did not necessarily appeal only to the sight. As representations of a relic – an object that once touched Christ – they had a talismanic function too (see Fein, ed., *Poems and Carols*, p. 293; Nichols, 'O Vernicle', p. 141 n. 19). It is possible that the drawing in Audelay's manuscript was similarly intended as a talismanic and practical representation of a powerful object, rather than a prompt to visualisation and meditation.

21   For *Marcolf and Solomon* as a poem in a broadly Langlandian tradition, see J. Simpson, 'Saving Satire after Arundel's *Constitutions*: John Audelay's *Marcol and Solomon*', *Text and Controversy from Wyclif to Bale: Essays in Honour of Anne Hudson*, ed. H. Barr and A. M. Hutchison, Medieval Church Studies 4 (Turnhout, 2004), pp. 387–404; D. Pearsall, 'Audelay's *Marcolf and Solomon* and the Langlandian Tradition', *Wyl and Wrytyng*, ed. Fein, pp. 138–52; M. Bose, 'Useless Mouths: Reformist Poetics in Audelay and Skelton', *Form and Reform: Reading Across the Fifteenth Century*, ed. S. Gayk and K. Tonry (Columbus, 2011), pp. 159–79; and (with specific reference to Audelay's poetic form),

phrase, however, Audelay's verse provides a rhetorical, interpretative response to it.[22] Its main subject is the praise of scripture: a strikingly oblique take on the rubric's reference to a concord between two different types of cleric. Still more surprising is the way in which it seeks not just to express, but to articulate and realise Audelay's understanding of the nature of Holy Writ. While the bob marks the turn from Audelay's celebration of scripture in the body of the stanza to the wheel's plain statement of the simple truth its readers should have in mind, that statement is far from being a summary of what has gone before. In the wheel, words are used as vehicles of an extra-verbal truth, but the first part of the stanza explores the potential of the word itself to act as symbolic truth, using formal device and poetic compression to demonstrate both that God's world *is* word and how Audelay's own writing can replicate that effect.

Within Audelay's characteristic thirteen-line stanza, alliteration is a key means of achieving this replication. It does not follow an entirely predictable pattern (not, for example, AA/AX). In the first line the three alliterating words all occur in the first half line, while lines 3, 4 and 7 alliterate AA/XX (and in each case the alliterating words are either adjacent, or linked in a phrase); line 5 alliterates AA/BB, line 6 XA/AA, and line 8 AAA; as a shorter line with fewer stresses, it has no 'X'. Working across both this variable alliterative pattern *and* across the end-rhyme are additional aural patterns: for example, in the third line, the shared suffix '-ly' creates a strong aural connection between 'pryncypaly' and 'holy', so that 'pryncypaly' forms an audible link between 'pacyens' and 'holy wrytyng'; in a similar way, 'Godys' in line 6 anticipates the alliterative 'grace' and 'Gost' of line 7. This kind of counterpoint finds fullest expression in the way 'wryt' (line 2), 'wrytyng' (line 3), and 'wyt' (line 5) all anticipate the extensive w-alliteration of line 6: 'Word', 'werke' and 'worchyng' (the last of which incidentally is also the rhyme for 'wrytyng' of line 2). The effect is to establish implicit analogies of sense between 'wyt', 'wryt', 'wrytyng', 'worchyng', 'Word' and 'werke': through Audelay's highly visible, highly wrought poetic workings, the stanza emphasises that for God there is no distinction between thinking and making, between the process of completing a work and the work itself – and, above all, that all of these things can be expressed in the single word 'Word'.[23]

This, of course, is a relatively local effect, but at least one significant instance of this theology of wordplay recurs throughout Audelay's book, in the form of a pun on 'word' and 'world'. Thus, in *God's Address to Sinful Men*, he writes:

S. Fein, 'A Thirteen-Line Stanza on the Abuse of Prayer from the Audelay MS', *Medium Aevum* 63 (1994), 61–74 (62).

22 For discussion and classification of more usual relationships between Latin and vernacular in macaronic writing, see E. Archibald, 'Tradition and Innovation in the Macaronic Poetry of Dunbar and Skelton', *Modern Language Quarterly* 53 (1992), 126–49 (126–9).

23 Audelay is not alone in using poetic form and wordplay as a means of apprehending and representing God's presence in the world; for parallel instances in the work of fourteenth-century writers, see C. M. Cervone, *Poetics of the Incarnation: Middle English Writing and the Leap of Love* (Philadelphia, 2012).

Leud and lerd, prest and clerke,	*unlettered and learned*
Thai schal be rewardid, ywis,	
Affter here dedis – *this word* ye mark!	*according to their*
Nolo mortem peccatoris.	*I do not desire the death of a sinner*
The valey of wepyng, *this word* I cal.	

(lines 13–17, vernacular italics mine)[24]

Here, 'word' is used first as synonym for 'phrase'; second in the sense of 'world'. Because 'word' is a standard Middle English form of 'world', in principle no pun need be intended; both 'word' and 'world' spellings are used in the manuscript, and there is not always an obvious reason for the use of the former rather than the latter.[25] But in several cases, when 'word' in the sense of 'world' occurs in juxtaposition with 'word' in its current sense, there *is* a clear implication that readers are being invited to see a pun – as, for example, in the *Epilogue* to *The Counsel of Conscience*:

And let ham never, Lord, be forelore,	*them; lost*
That prayn for Jon the Blynd Audlay.	
Into the kyngdam thou ham restore,	*them*
Unto that blis that lasteth fore ay,	*ever*
In word without end!	
Fore blessid be thai that heren *the Word*	
And don therafter here in *this word*,	
Fore in heven thou wilt hem reward,	
That here mysdedis here wil amende.[26]	*their*

(lines 5–13, my italics)

Just as in the first stanza of *Marcolf and Solomon*, alliteration and end-rhyme perform an act of 'knitting up' equivalent to that which links God's 'wyl', 'word' and 'worchyng'. Here too there is both a play on 'world' and 'word', and a play between meaning and verse-form in the way the Psalmist's statement of faith, 'wor[l]d without end', is used as bob, marking the conclusion of the main body of the stanza. As in the phrase from the Psalms of which it is a translation, the meaning of the word 'end' is consonant with its position in the line, while the phrase of which it is a part, 'world without end', opposes that sense of conclusion. This wordplay is both repeated and re-emphasised through Audelay's use of 'amende' as the final word of the wheel; by rhyming with 'end' this reaffirms that the 'end' was not an ending, while by (aurally, if not etymologically) adding 'am' to 'end' it creates a change of meaning that itself resists the very idea of ending, even as it also echoes the 'amen' that is the natural conclusion of a prayer.

---

24 NIMEV 171; DIMEV 316.
25 MED, *s.v.* 'world', *n.*
26 Other lines in which a pun is in evidence include *Marcolf and Solomon*, line 366, and *God's Address to Sinful Men*, lines 15, 259; lines in which there is not quite a pun, but where the 'word' spelling appears in close proximity to a use of 'word' in its current sense, and there is an element of play between the two, include *Seven Words of Christ on the Cross*, lines 84, 96 and *Salutation to St Bridget*, line 34.

This kind of paranomasia is not unique to Audelay – a comparable play on 'ending' occurs in the opening stanza of the York Play's *Fall of Angels*, for example, while Skelton includes a play on 'amen' and 'amende' in *Speke Parott* – but it is highly characteristic of his writing.[27] An identical use of 'World withoutyn end' occurs in *Marcolf and Solomon* (line 377), and a variant appears in *True Living*, where the word 'endyng' conspicuously does *not* signal the end of the stanza in his assertion that God counsels men:

> To do as thou woldest me dud by thee,   *one did*
> And bryng thi lyf to good endyng,
>   Here and hen. (lines 231–3)   *henceforth*

Punning thus becomes both a form of theology and a form of poetics, at once drawing attention to the inadequacy of human terms to express God's truth and seeking to approximate a divine perspective; it is the kind of play between word and form that Eleanor Cook has described as 'true seriousness ... the true sense of *serio ludere*' ('to play in earnest').[28] It is for this reason that when Audelay exhorts his readers to 'have in mind' his teaching, he appeals to the ear rather than to the eye, by means of the kind of tropes that Puttenham would later define as 'sententious': those that surprise and engage both hearing and understanding.[29] For Audelay, the visual is a prompt to the verbal, rather than an end in itself. The form as well as the content of his writing manifests his belief that he is spoken through by the Holy Ghost, and his readers are invited to apprehend God through participation in his complex wordplay. As the dense patterning of his words replicates or imitates the divine effect of which they speak, they themselves become 'things' that may be 'seen' and had in mind: they are the rungs on Audelay's ladder to salvation.

---

27 *The Fall of Angels*, lines 1–8, in *The York Plays: A Critical Edition of the York Corpus Christi Play as recorded in British Library Additional MS 35290*, ed. R. Beadle, 2 vols, EETS SS 23, 24 (Oxford, 2009, 2013 for 2011), I, 3; John Skelton, *Speke Parott*, lines 274–7, in *The Complete English Poems of John Skelton*, ed. J. Scattergood, rev. edn (Liverpool, 2015).
28 E. Cook, *Against Coercion: Games Poets Play* (Stanford, 1998), p. 186.
29 George Puttenham, *The Arte of English Poesie*, in *English Renaissance Literary Criticism*, ed. B. Vickers (Oxford, 1999), pp. 236, 253; for examples, see pp. 254–79.

19

'The Dance of the Intellect among Words': Wyatt's *In eternum* and Late Medieval Lyric Practice

Joel Grossman

Sir Thomas Wyatt, *In eternum*[1]

    Ineternum I was ons determinid
    for to have lovid and my minde affirmid
    that with my herte it shuld be confirmid
    Ineternum

5   forthwith I founde the thing that I might like
    and sought with love to warm her hert alyke
    for as me thought I shulde not se the lyke   *see*
    Ineternum.

    To trase this daunse I put my self in prease   *press*
10 Vayne hope ded lede and bad I shuld not cease
    to serve / to suffer / & still to hold my peace
    Ineternum

    With this furst Rule I ferdred me a pase   *furthered myself a pace*
    that as me thought my trowghthe had taken plase   *truth (pledge)*
15 With full assurans to stand in her grace
    in eternum

    It was nat long er I by proofe had founde

For another essay focused upon wordplay, see Jane Griffiths (Chapter 18), 'Have This in Mind: Word and Image in Audelay's Writing'; for another essay focused on lyric selfhood and authorial representation, see Denis Renevey (Chapter 14), '"Short song is good in ale": Charles d'Orléans and Authorial Intentions in the Middle English *Ballade 84*', this volume.

1   Not in NIMEV or DIMEV, as the witnesses are post-1530. The poem is TM 763 in W. A. Ringler, *Bibliography and Index of English Verse in Manuscript 1501–1558*, completed by M. Rudick and S. J. Ringler (London, 1992), p. 131. The text here is transcribed from the so-called Devonshire manuscript, London, British Library, Additional MS 17492, fol. 72v. (hereafter 'Devonshire'). All contractions have been silently expanded and 'ſ' has been replaced with 's'. Manuscript punctuation and orthography are retained. The spacing of 'In eternum' and 'ineternum' is maintained from the manuscript.

>   that feble bilding is on feble grounde
>   for in her herte this worde never sounde
> 20 Ineternum
>
>   Ineternum then from my herte I keste   *cast*
>   that I had furst determind for the best
>   nowe in the place another thought doth rest
>   Ineternum

A recent and influential cross-period study of lyric poetry edited by Marion Thain spans the period from 1580 to the present day.[2] The reasoning behind this choice of date limits seems relatively well founded: 'the OED's first recorded uses of "lyric" as an adjective or noun come from the 1580s'.[3] However, the decision not to account for the wide array of medieval 'lyric' forms, many of which are outlined in this present volume, gives the impression that the lyric poem emerged in the Renaissance as if out of a vacuum. While omitting medieval lyrics may have been a pragmatic decision, this sense of a literary and cultural vacuum prior to the Renaissance is not without an ideological bent. This reflects, of course, the long-standing notion of a rupture between medieval and Renaissance literary practice, the sense of a major epochal shift that potentially saw a 'rebirth' of Western culture and of perceptions of the self. Study of lyric poetry has demonstrated particular interest in such claims because of lyric poetry's connection to self-expression: '[i]n the first place "lyric" is held to apply to poems employing a first person speaker, and, by extension, to indicate a preoccupation with the expression of individual feeling or emotion'.[4] As David Lindley's introduction to lyric shows, such claims are problematic and far from universal.[5] However, there remains a correlation between periods perceived to demonstrate particular interest in self-expression or individualism and periods singled out by criticism as particularly relevant to the lyric. Hence the attention given to lyric poetry in the Renaissance, Romantic, modernist and postmodern periods.[6] This chapter will offer a reading of Sir Thomas Wyatt's poem *In eternum*, which queries the relationship between lyric and selfhood in the early sixteenth century, and in doing so suggests new ways of understanding the relationship between medieval and Renaissance lyric poetry.[7]

---

2   M. Thain, ed., *The Lyric Poem* (Cambridge, 2013).
3   *Ibid.*, p. 1.
4   D. Lindley, *Lyric* (London, 1985), p. 2.
5   *Ibid*, p. 3.
6   As well as Thain's collection, medieval lyric is largely absent from major cross-period studies including C. Hošek and P. A. Parker, eds, *Lyric Poetry: Beyond New Criticism* (Ithaca, 1985); J. Culler, *Theory of Lyric* (Cambridge, MA, 2015); and V. Jackson and Y. Prins, eds, *The Lyric Theory Reader: A Critical Anthology* (Baltimore, 2014). The last of these, as a collection of pre-existing critical material on theories of lyric, is revealing in that only one article out of forty-eight pays particular attention to medieval lyric.
7   The poem *In eternum* exists in two contemporary manuscripts, Wyatt's personal manuscript, London, British Library, Egerton MS 2711, fol. 46v (hereafter 'Egerton'), and the Devonshire manuscript, fol. 72v. The poem is included in the major editions of Wyatt's

Before turning to the relationship between the medieval–Renaissance divide and the disproportionate emphasis on postmedieval lyric, it is worth briefly considering a central concern of lyric theory in recent scholarship: is lyric a transhistorical category? The idea that it is has been most forcefully put forward by Jonathan Culler.[8] He argues not that there is a singular definition of lyric, but that lyric poetry frequently responds to an awareness of its own tradition. Hence, lyric poetry emphasises connections across periods rather than within them, as writers attempt to join a lively and adaptive tradition of lyric writing. Theoretically, such an approach makes room for medieval lyric by incorporating any poem that engages with this tradition, or which takes up some of the transhistorical features of lyric. In practice, however, any transhistorical lyric category will reinforce the established canon of lyric; the very notion of lyric is predetermined by those poems that have already been taken as exemplary of the tradition. Hence Culler's *Theory of Lyric* largely glosses over the Middle Ages. Several lyric studies have opposed this transhistorical approach, arguing that the term lyric can only be used 'with precise historical awareness'.[9] This opens up space for medieval lyrics that do not fit the established lyric canon.[10] But, heeding the warnings set out in Culler's transhistorical approach, this model might further encourage the sense of a divide between medieval and Renaissance and can give credence to ideas that the latter period is somehow more lyric-oriented: that lyric is relatively absent from the spirit of medieval poetry.

The sense of a cultural rupture that divides 'medieval' from 'Renaissance' stems back to early humanist debate, and continues to be discussed today. Scholarship on this issue is far too broad to be covered here, but it is important

---

poetry: G. F. Nott, ed., *The Works of Henry Howard, Earl of Surrey, and of Sir Thomas Wyatt the Elder*, 2 vols (London, 1815), II, 189–90, and in K. Muir and P. Thomson, ed., *Collected Poems of Sir Thomas Wyatt* (Liverpool, 1969), pp. 53–4 and later editions of Wyatt's poems. The Egerton copy is severely damaged, containing only the final part of each line (anywhere from two letters to four words); none of the refrains survive in the Egerton copy. A transcription of the damaged text can be found in R. Harrier, *The Canon of Sir Thomas Wyatt's Poetry* (Cambridge, MA, 1975), pp. 162–3. Unlike many of Wyatt's poems, *In eternum* is not included in Tottel's *Songes and Sonettes*, nor printed at all in the sixteenth century (presumably because Egerton was the primary source for printings of Wyatt's poetry and in the case of this poem it was damaged). Thus the Devonshire manuscript offers the only near-contemporary witness to the complete poem. However, it is likely that the Devonshire version stems – either directly or indirectly – from the now damaged poem in Egerton 2711. It occurs in the Devonshire manuscript in a section of thirty-seven poems of which at least thirty occur in Egerton. See Harrier, *The Canon of Sir Thomas Wyatt's Poetry*, p. 53.

8   See, in particular, *Theory of Lyric*, pp. 1–9; and 'Lyric, History, and Genre', Jackson and Prins, eds, *The Lyric Theory Reader*, pp. 63–77.
9   Lindley, *Lyric*, p. 84.
10 See, for example, S. Brewster, *Lyric* (London, 2009), pp. 20–3; and S. Lerer, 'The Genre of the Grave and the Origins of the Middle English Lyric', Jackson and Prins, eds, *Lyric Theory Reader*, pp. 104–13. These discuss Old and Middle English lyric respectively, but occur within works devoted to broader approaches to lyric.

to note some key trends that have contributed to the absence of medieval short and occasional verse in many discussions of lyric, and which have tied the Renaissance lyric output to anti- or postmedieval cultural shifts.[11] Humanist claims, beginning with Petrarch, that Renaissance scholars were reaching back to classical culture across a 'dark' age were reinforced in the nineteenth century by the likes of Michelet and Burckhardt, who re-established ideas of Renaissance rebirth and the discovery of the individual. These ideas continue to exert themselves in modern scholarship, which – perhaps too frequently and uncritically – has a tendency to accept the 'newness' of the Renaissance. In particular, new historicism has tended to commit to 'reproducing aspects of the ideology which gave us the term "Renaissance"'.[12] That is, the Renaissance is often taken as marking a clear separation from the medieval, whether it be in terms of a new sense of the self, of history, of theology, or, indeed, of literary undertaking. Greenblatt's seminal *Renaissance Self-Fashioning* does not deny Burckhardtian ideas but views such changes dialectically.[13] Thus, the increased sense of self in the Renaissance becomes, also, a self-awareness and self-consciousness that enables the individual increasingly to fashion or construct their identity. It is not surprising that, for Greenblatt, Wyatt's poetry manifests 'inwardness', 'personal crisis' and a literary 'enactment ... of Wyatt's [psychological] condition'.[14]

This idea of a Renaissance break from the medieval sense of self has perhaps been most cogently argued in recent years by Thomas Greene in *The Light in Troy*.[15] In this work, Greene posits a new understanding of history begun by Petrarch (if not Dante); previously '[n]o one ... was fully sensitive to the fact of radical cultural change that would be glimpsed by Dante and then faced in all its overwhelming force by Renaissance humanism' because earlier texts 'lack historical self-consciousness'.[16] Complicating and expanding on the truism that medieval history and literature were anachronistic, Greene argues that it is only with the Renaissance that texts demonstrate an understanding of history as a series of dislocations, rather than as a continuum. Hence, '[t]o say that Petrarch "discovered" history means, in effect, that he was the first to notice that classical antiquity was very different from his own medieval world'.[17] Greene suggests

---

11 An important recent discussion and rebuttal of this scholarly preference can be found in A. C. Spearing, *Textual Subjectivity: The Encoding of Subjectivity in Medieval Narratives and Lyrics* (Oxford, 2005). See, in particular, Spearing's suggestion that medieval lyric is 'virtually undiscussed' by most modern scholars 'for whom post-classical lyric seems to begin with Petrarch' (p. 175).
12 D. Aers, 'A Whisper in the Ear of Early Modernists; or, Reflections on Literary Critics Writing the "History of the Subject"', *Culture and History 1350–1600: Essays on English Communities, Identities and Writing*, ed. D. Aers (London, 1992), pp. 177–202 (p. 192).
13 S. Greenblatt, *Renaissance Self-Fashioning: From More to Shakespeare* (Chicago, 1980), p. 1.
14 Ibid., pp. 127, 135.
15 T. Greene, *The Light in Troy: Imitation and Discovery in Renaissance Poetry* (New Haven, 1982).
16 Ibid., p. 17.
17 Ibid., p. 90.

that in doing so, Petrarch allowed a new sense of 'self-discovery' because 'he recognised *the possibility of a cultural alternative*': because Petrarch accepts that history is not contingent, his poetry, 'the first poetry deliberately to dramatise the passage of history, would dramatise a descent into a selfhood unsure of its status'.[18] The interrelated ideas of historical- and self-discovery are thus tied to the invention of the lyric self; as such, scholarly emphasis on lyric speakers' subjectivity has given the impression that lyric, like selfhood, was (re)discovered in the Renaissance.

Thomas Wyatt, whose poem *In eternum* is the focus of this chapter, occurs directly on the cusp between medieval and Renaissance, as far as academic scholarship is concerned, and he is often taken to be the first truly lyric poet in English (though the present volume should suggest otherwise). Produced from the late 1520s until his death in 1542, Wyatt's lyrics clearly predate the 1580 mark taken by Thain as the starting point for her collection.[19] So Wyatt's perceived position as the first English lyricist relies on a more fundamental rejection of the medieval lyric than simply a pragmatic choice of dating. As Greene puts it, '[Wyatt and the Earl of Surrey] must have been aware of themselves as attempting something new, as filling a vacuum', and of their poems as 'crossings of a cultural rupture'.[20] In part, this chapter attempts to redress this emphasis on the 'newness' of the Renaissance lyric, to rebut the idea that any clear division can be created between short poetry of the medieval period, and 'lyric' as an inherently postmedieval phenomenon. More than this, however, it questions the emphasis on subjectivity and selfhood as essential lyric qualities, qualities further reinforced in the Romantic period where 'a more vigorous conception of the individual subject made it possible to conceive of lyric as mimetic: mimetic of the experience of the subject'.[21] I will suggest here that Wyatt's *In eternum* offers lyricism of a very different sort, less concerned with the individual subject than with an appeal to an intellectual perception that transcends individual expression: this is a poetry that dismisses the mimetic experience of the external world in favour of 'the dance of the intellect among words'.[22]

The Third Lyric Category: '*melos*', '*opsis*' and '*logopoeia*'

In Northrop Frye's influential series of essays *Anatomy of Criticism*, he suggests two opposing categories at the heart of the lyric, derived immediately from Ezra Pound but ultimately from Aristotle. On the one hand is the aural, *melos* (or what Pound terms *melopoeia*), which he relates to the subconscious desire of

---

18 *Ibid.*, pp. 90, 101.
19 See p. 262 above.
20 Greene, *The Light in Troy*, p. 245.
21 Culler, 'Lyric, History, and Genre', p. 66. Though Culler is focused here on Hegelian categorisation of lyric, Greene's argument demonstrates similar positions in current Renaissance scholarship.
22 Ezra Pound, 'How to Read', *Literary Essays of Ezra Pound*, ed. T. S. Eliot (London, 1954), pp. 15–40 (p. 25). For the full quotation see p. 267 below.

'babble', or pure sound association.²³ At the other end of the spectrum is the visual, *opsis* (Pound's *phanopoeia*), related to the subconscious desire of 'doodle', the relation of ideas by image (including the metaphoricity of poetic language).²⁴ Whatever the value of Frye's categories, they have something to tell us about how twentieth- and twenty-first-century criticism comprehends the broad range of poetry covered by the term 'lyric', and more specifically how the lyric poetry of Thomas Wyatt has been understood. For Frye, Wyatt's poetry sits very strongly in the realm of *melos*, or the musical side of the lyric spectrum. This view is reiterated in Andrew Welsh's 1978 re-examination of Frye's categories, where he suggests that the 'roughness' of Wyatt's verse creates a 'speech-melos' that prioritises the musicality of everyday speech over the artificiality of 'smoothly' metrical poetic lines.²⁵ Anthropologically, Welsh suggests, *melos* is derived from charm, the 'magic incantation carried on the singsong voice of a magician at work'.²⁶ Putting less stress on the precise understanding of words themselves, charm-melos emphasises 'coincidences of the sound pattern'. If 'primitive cosmologies' used such 'babble' or nonsensical sound pattern to manipulate 'the hidden forces in nature', so too, according to Welsh, Wyatt wrote love poems that are 'at root a charm aimed at casting a spell and pulling the beloved irresistibly toward the lover'.²⁷

I suggest that foregrounding the mystical, subconscious power of words over precision of language and poetic construction is a fundamental misreading of Wyatt's poetry. Were Wyatt to be defined according to one of Frye's categories, he displays far more characteristics of *opsis*, where 'we find the greatest drive toward the utter precision of the word' rather than the 'lull' or 'distraction' of *melos*.²⁸ The *melos*-reading of Wyatt appears to stem from the popular image of the early Tudor poet as a musician, singing his love poems both for entertainment and even as genuine acts of courtship.²⁹ (Indeed, such imaginings as the BBC series *The Tudors* generally depict Wyatt wandering the court of Henry VIII with lute in hand.) This image of Wyatt is related to the problematic articulations of lyric outlined in the introduction to this chapter. Read as *melos*, Wyatt's poetry becomes the mimetic expression of his (or his speaker's) subjective experience of love, whereby 'the lyric poet absorbs into himself the external world and stamps it with inner consciousness'.³⁰ The poem is seen as individual and personal at the expense of being a rhetorical, intellectual or artificial exercise. This sense of lyric subjectivity, of the external world becoming an extension or projection of the

---

23   N. Frye, *Anatomy of Criticism: Four Essays* (Princeton, 1957), p. 244.
24   Ibid.
25   A. Welsh, *Roots of Lyric* (Princeton, 1978), pp. 244–5.
26   Ibid., p. 135.
27   Ibid., p. 242.
28   Pound, 'How to Read', p. 25.
29   For this view, see Welsh, *Roots of Lyric*, p. 233.
30   Culler, 'Lyric, History, and Genre', p. 66.

lyric consciousness, foregrounds the sensory experience; the poem is something *felt* by both speaker and reader.

It is not the purpose of this chapter, however, to read Wyatt's lyric practice as *opsis*. What is more telling, I suggest, is that both of Frye's categories of *opsis* and *melos* appeal to the senses – the aural and visual – and in doing so inherently imply something of the mimetic relationship between internal and external worlds so central to understanding of the lyric from the Renaissance onwards. Reading all lyric as sensory implies an emphasis on expressionism and/or impressionism, on the relationship between the self and the external world, which is not only problematic in the case of Wyatt or the medieval lyric, but does not necessarily hold for Renaissance practice with its emphasis on artifice and construction. (It is, I think, naive to read lyrics by the likes of Sidney, Donne, or countless other Renaissance poets, as mimetic expressions of the self.) Most telling about Frye's categories is what is conspicuously absent, a third category outlined by Pound: *logopoeia*. Pound defines this as:

> the 'dance of the intellect among words', that is to say, it employs words not only for their direct meaning, but it takes count in a special way of habits and usage, of the context we *expect* to find with the word, of its known acceptances, and of ironical play.[31]

Logopoeia, then, plays with language as metatextual, something that responds to an entire tradition of usage. It is less concerned with individual expression than it is with literary tradition and construction, with poetry as the play of linguistic and literary history and expectation. Implicit is the sense that language is not the property of the individual but the group: it cannot express an individual so much as construct one.

The remainder of this chapter will read Wyatt's poem *In eternum* as a manifestation of this third category of lyric: *logopoeia* or 'the dance of the intellect among words'. In doing so, it will suggest that rather than presenting a mimetic relationship to the world, both perceived and expressed through the senses, the poem offers a conflict between an idealised intellectual perception and a debased (and wordly) sensory perception. If Wyatt's poem concerns subjective experience, it is only to the extent that it presents such experience as undesirable and corrupt in contrast to the idealised and transcendent relationships made possible by escaping the sensory realm entirely.

In eternum: the *Logopoesis* of the Refrain

The central site of conflict between sensory and intellectual perception in Wyatt's *In eternum* is the refrain. In purely aural terms a refrain is a repetition, a recurring sound that binds the poem together, repeating its central ideas and images, and formalising them into a pattern. However, despite a constancy of sound and sight, with each repetition a change occurs. This is in part because the reader's

---

[31] Pound, 'How to Read', p. 25.

expectations are programmed by the formal repetition, and in part because the meaning of the phrase builds up, it accretes. This process of accretion is *logopoeia*'s play of the intellect upon words: each repetition creates a comparison with every other use, which retrospectively alters the refrain's semantic possibilities. Whilst aurally (and visually) the refrain is always constant, by formalising the repetition a poem demands an attention to language as dependent on context, and so creates an 'ironical play' (Pound's key element of *logopoeia*) between the fixed phrase and its shifting meaning.

Whilst this process is inherent in the refrain form, Wyatt's poem highlights these ironic possibilities with its choice of refrain phrase: *'in eternum'*. On first reading, the refrain might seem the perfect way to enact the eternity it expresses: the continual reiteration of *'eternum'* might be taken as a mimetic expression of eternity itself. Yet, the very possibility of repeating the phrase exposes this expression of atemporality to a temporal system: the phrase recurs at precise intervals, but the possibility that it might not recur, that it will cease when the poem ends, delimits the eternity that the phrase conveys. It is perhaps not surprising, then, that the eternity expressed in the opening stanza soon undergoes an ironic inversion, as the variability of time and human actions fails to live up to the eternity promised.

If we take the opening three stanzas at face value as expressions of the eternity of the speaker's love (we will return to the opening later), then in the fourth stanza this eternity begins to look unstable: 'that as me thought my trowghthe had taken plase / With full assurans to stond in her grace / In eternum' (lines 14–16). The phrases 'as me thought' and 'with full assurans' act as dramatic asides by a speaker who retrospectively knows that these assurances were false and not 'as [he] thought' at the time. In the next stanza the transformation is complete:

> It was nat long er I by proofe had founde
> That feble bilding is one feble grounde
> For in her herte this worde did never sounde
> Ineternum.   (lines 17–20)

The stanza begins with an ironic bathos; eternity has now become 'not long'. More than just something long-lasting becoming ironically and unfortunately short, the exposure of eternity to temporality makes the concept entirely redundant. In other words, if *'eternum'* can end at all then it must never have existed in the first place (the length is irrelevant), and so 'this worde did never sounde'. There is an ironic play here between 'never' and the 'forever' of *'eternum'*; perhaps the speaker is attempting to hold on to forever's atemporality by turning to its negative form, 'never'. The refrain now takes on new possibilities, not only is *'eternum'* the word that never sounded, but the lack of sounding is itself continued *'in eternum'*; having never existed, the very lack of eternity becomes eternal, an eternal absence.

By the final stanza the meaning of the refrain phrase has undergone a complete reversal as the eternity of the love between the speaker and his lover (now shown to be an imagined eternity) is replaced: 'Nowe in the place another thought doth rest / Ineternum' (lines 23–4). If the refrain appears to promise stability in its constancy of words and sounds, semantically it has produced the opposite effect as eternal love is replaced by the 'other thought' of eternal hatred or animosity. The refrain form in this poem manifests *logopoeia* rather than the sensory categories of *melos* and *opsis*. The ironical play of the refrain phrase stems from the dislocation of its semantic possibilities from the aural and visual constancy of the phrase itself. Throughout the poem the reader is asked to understand the phrase not as having a 'direct meaning' but to take account of the 'habits and usage, of the context we *expect* to find … of ironical play'.[32] Given that aurally and visually the refrain phrase never changes, these shifts in meaning must be understood as happening on the abstract, intellectual level, rather than the sensory.

If this is the case structurally in the poem, *In eternum* more deeply concerns the speaker's problematic attempt to negotiate the worlds of the intellect and the senses: of eternal love as an abstract concept and 'eternal' love in his experience of a particular relationship. It is in this conflict, and especially in the negation of the speaker's individual experience, that I suggest this poem may more broadly undermine conceptions of lyric as inherently concerned with subjectivity and the 'discovery of the self'.

Reading the refrain retrospectively – with the knowledge that the form will undermine the word '*eternum*' – reveals that the poem's sense of eternity has always been insecure. In the opening lines the speaker claims that 'In eternum I was ons determinid / for to have lovid and my minde affirmid' (lines 1–2). This sense of determination, the possibility that eternal love was a decision made by the speaker, exposes its temporality; far from being without beginning or end, 'eternal' love came to the speaker 'ons', and so has a beginning point that counteracts any sense that this is truly eternal. This limitation is figured in the language-use itself, which necessarily marks the tense of an apparently tenseless concept. At the same time this opening sets up a conflict between the speaker's 'minde' that 'affirmid' his love and his heart that 'confirmid' it. Are we to take these two similar statements as repetitions of the same basic idea, or, like the refrain, does this repetition create a conflict within an apparently stable concept?

A clue is found in stanza five as the speaker's sense of eternal love begins to unravel: 'For in her herte this worde did never sounde' (line 19). Though, as love complaint, the line attacks the strength of the lady's 'trowghthe' (line 14), on a philosophical level it exposes the gap between the metaphysical *idea* of eternity and its 'sounde' in the 'herte'. It is telling that even in the 'herte' the word is expressed in aural terms; it has already shifted from an abstract concept to a linguistic signifier. In the real world, the word 'eternum' can never enact the idea it expresses because even before being spoken aloud it has taken on the slipperiness of human language (a language system that occurs as aural sounds or visual letters even before it is expressed in speech or writing). Exposure to the sensory realm of language immediately undermines the concept as it exists in

---

32   *Ibid.*, p. 25.

the intellectual realm. In this poem, subjective experience, the experience of the heart, is figured through the senses because the subject understands their experience through language, transforming ideas into aural and visual signs. Similarly, in the opening stanza, the shift from 'mynde' to 'herte' seems to express a move from '*eternum*' as a concept that transcends the limitations of human experience to '*eternum*' as the speaker's 'determinid' impulse of love confirmed by his 'herte'. From its very expression in the poem as a particular speaker's love for a particular woman, the transcendent possibilities of eternity are made impossible.

The final stanza returns to these images and ideas:

> In eternum then from my herte I keste
> that I had furst determind for the best
> nowe in the place another thought doth rest
> Ineternum   (lines 21–4)

Just as determination led to the apparently eternal love, so it ends it, sealing the lack of any genuine eternity in the love depicted. With the final change of heart the refrain is once more brought back with its most explicit irony yet: it has not only failed to last eternally, but has been retrospectively revealed as transient from its first utterance. What this final stanza seems to express so pessimistically is not one woman's rejection of Wyatt's speaker, but the impossibility of transcendent or eternal love once it enters the realm of human experience. If *In eternum* might be read as depicting the speaker's subjective experiences in love, the poem itself constantly works to dismiss the subjective, human or sensory sphere in favour of a transcendent or abstract notion of eternity, an eternity that ceases to exist by its very expression in language.

Conclusion: Re-Joining Medieval and Renaissance Lyricism

The aim of this chapter has not been to redefine Wyatt's poetry as more medieval than is usually argued, nor to argue that medieval lyric is less concerned with subjectivity than its Renaissance successors. Instead this chapter hopes to reinforce critical arguments that have increasingly complicated or rejected ideas of subjectivity and personal expression as the central features of lyric. In its position on the boundaries between the received periods of medieval and Renaissance, Wyatt's *In eternum* might offer a point of interaction between the concerns of this volume and those found in studies of Renaissance lyric rather than pushing the two periods further apart. In Heather Dubrow's essay on 'Lyric Forms' in the Renaissance, she warns against excessive generalisations about lyric, even within a singular period. However, her study outlines some broad considerations relating to Renaissance lyric:

> the connection between lyric and song is central. One can also assert with confidence that Renaissance lyrics variously qualify and challenge definitions that emphasize an isolated speaker overheard rather than participate in social

interactions ... In an age fascinated by rhetoric, the lyric poet is typically a consummate rhetorician.[33]

Though approaching lyric from quite different perspectives to this chapter's reading of *In eternum*, Dubrow's questioning of lyrical assumptions opens up a space for comparison to medieval lyric concerns.

Indeed, what is most surprising about Dubrow's conclusions is that they needed to be stated at all. No one who has read Sidney's *Defence of Poesie* would be astonished by the idea that Renaissance poets expected their works to be socially productive or to display rhetorical skill. It would be much more difficult to find in the *Defence* a version of poetry that presents lyric as purely subjective experience or 'an isolated speaker overheard'. It is not just medieval literature that challenges perceived notions of lyric. Just as many of the lyrics in this volume will not conform to definitions of lyric that begin with the Renaissance, so too readings of later lyric poetry may have been skewed by a retrospective definition of what 'lyric' actually entails. The difficulty of assimilating Wyatt's *In eternum* to some of the received notions of Renaissance lyric does not mean that Renaissance lyric bears little resemblance to earlier lyric practice; instead, it suggests that these received notions are themselves problematic, based on preconceived ideas of what 'Renaissance', and indeed 'lyric', actually entail. If scholars of Renaissance and later poetry are seeking to understand the emergence of lyric, they need look no further than the medieval practices outlined in this volume, which demonstrate a rich and varied tradition already present in English literary culture.

---

33 H. Dubrow, 'Lyric Forms', Jackson and Prins, eds, *The Lyric Theory Reader*, pp. 114–28 (p. 127).

Afterword: The Study of Medieval Lyrics in 1960s Oxford and Today

John C. Hirsh

Detailed and considered analysis of medieval English lyrics is of relatively recent date, whether because of the lyrics' overall inaccessibility to earlier generations of scholars, their putatively dubious theology, or what was sometimes taken to be their limited literary accomplishment. Early collections there were, however, and although these often supplied an introduction, textual and historical notes, and sometimes even translations of the older and more difficult texts, their focus tended to be upon fact, not interpretation, and the text was usually read as a written and static unity, so that when versions were compared, it was usually to determine precedence. Surprisingly little in the way of comment and less in that of context allowed for critical judgement or textual conjecture (practices that endured an unexpectedly long time), though in the best of these, R. T. Davies's *Medieval English Lyrics: A Critical Anthology* (published in 1963), familiar to a generation of students – the formal aspects of the individual lyric, though not its crafting – were taken into account.

***

This critical nonchalance came to an end in the late 1960s, when three Oxford medievalists, Douglas Gray of Pembroke and for a time of Lincoln, Rosemary Woolf, soon to be of Somerville, and Peter Dronke, an Oxford lecturer who would shortly move to Cambridge, began to inquire seriously into the nature and effect of the medieval lyric in English and in Latin, and to argue emphatically for their intellectual importance and their literary interest, regarding them as of great interest as any other writing produced at the time, not excepting Chaucer.[1]

---

1   Professor Douglas Gray died, peacefully and in his sleep, on the night of 8 December 2017. Six months earlier he had contributed to, read, and expressed approval of the following account, which appears here exactly as he last saw it, with the addition of these few sentences. It is now dedicated to his memory, as an expression of esteem and gratitude for an extraordinarily learned, understanding and kind man, whom it was my privilege to know as a teacher and friend for fifty years.

The first study to emerge from this new scrutiny was Rosemary (Estelle) Woolf's pioneering book, published without subtitle, *The English Religious Lyric in the Middle Ages* (Oxford, 1968), a work that occupied its accomplished author for many years and through one publishing deferral; it remains the work for which she is now best known. In fact, Woolf (1925–78), who had been the first woman in her family to attend university, was educated at St Hugh's College, Oxford and received a B. Litt. in 1949. Her academic career began at University College, Hull in 1948, but she returned to a fellowship at Somerville College, Oxford in 1961. Throughout her career she both was, and was known to be, an extraordinarily able medievalist, widely knowledgeable and, informed by her understanding of the set texts of the Oxford examination syllabus as it then was, able to address Old English as well as Middle English texts, a circumstance that influenced her work on the lyric. But particularly in her last years, her work showed a reflective if academic resonance that seemed to have sprung at least in part from her investment in the tradition of Latin and English meditative religiousness to which I have been alluding.

It was in her academic work that the question of lyrical spirituality first appeared, if often incidentally, informed both by her Jewish family background and her understanding of Christianity, nurtured in her Anglican primary school, that functioned powerfully *in extremis*, while maintaining a social and devotional stability that was apparent in practice. Though she was not usually inclined to discuss issues of spirituality as such, they resonate throughout her work in inference and indirection, as they do elsewhere, since such lyrics as she addressed remain one of the most manifestly religious, often devout, series of texts to have come down to us from the late medieval period. But the serious interrogation of religious attitudes remains one of those topics of which even the most practised scholars can fight shy, if only because its presence can become totalising, and bend all other interests to it. As a result, throughout her career Woolf nudged at such issues from the outside, focusing less on what was new than on the poet's willing acceptance of, and engagement with, an articulate Christian tradition that he followed willingly, and that was itself a way of addressing effective – not necessarily affective – spiritual engagement with his art.

No strict traditionalist, she herself was as alive to modern artistic forms as to medieval, and while she was teaching at Oxford, her successful and well-known father, C. M. Woolf (1879–1942), was deeply involved, among other enterprises, in the burgeoning British film industry, primarily through distribution and management, while her brothers, Sir John Woolf (1913–99) and James Woolf (1920–66), also worked in the film industry, Sir John becoming a highly successful producer. It may not be too much to conjecture that this circumstance may have informed her interest in things visual, and to suggest that the extent of her originality, and the evident courage needed to engage with such a new and unfamiliar project, are easily underestimated.

In the same year that *The English Religious Lyric* was published there also appeared two works by a brilliant young student of comparative medieval literature named Peter Dronke, otherwise Ernst Peter Michael Dronke, which would inform the study of the lyric deeply, both in Latin and in the vernacular. These were the two-volume second edition of *Medieval Latin and the Rise of European Love-Lyric* (Oxford, 1968), and the first edition of *The Medieval Lyric* (London, 1968), a work that passed through four editions, addressing lyrics in several languages, especially Latin, in terms that were critically sophisticated, well informed and highly imaginative. Although both informed the study of the lyric in those early years, in the second work Dronke would make passing remarks that usefully informed specific English texts – suggesting, for example, that *Maiden in the Mor* may have been a song associated with dance – while generally assuming that literary significance and sophistication are the main motivators for studying literature of any sort, not then universal givens among those studying the medieval lyric. Throughout his career Dronke's readings did not pass uncontested, but it was a dour scholar indeed who was not engaged by his critical energy, his evident and extensive learning and his commitment to the understanding and the revelation that really great poetry provides.

Dronke's family background and outlook was European and Catholic, developed during the years he spent in New Zealand, having moved there out of necessity from Cologne in 1939, where his father had been a lawyer and then a judge. With his Jewish mother and sister, but without his father, Peter had gone, aged five, first to Britain, then, when his father had been able to join them, the reunited family had continued on to New Zealand as planned, appallingly losing many of their possessions in transit. It was in New Zealand that young Peter first distinguished himself academically, winning the first of many awards and, following the wishes of his converted mother, attending Sacred Heart Catholic High School (now College) in Auckland. From there he went on to Victoria University College (or 'Vic') in Wellington, one of the constituent colleges of the University of New Zealand, from which he graduated in 1954. He was thereupon awarded a travelling scholarship that took him to read English at Magdalen College, Oxford, in the following year.

Completing his studies in Oxford in 1957, he accepted a fellowship that took him to Rome, where, the fellowship renewed, he spent much of the next two years, meeting and becoming friends with the great Dante scholar and philosopher Bruno Nardi (1884–1968), whose interests and values corresponded to his own, and whose insistence on the importance of medieval philosophy for reading Dante came to inform his thinking deeply. Nardi had rejected any idealist reading of Dante, opting instead for a realist position rooted in a reading of a wide range of medieval philosophers, not identifying Dante with any one of them, but showing how, understood together, they could inform a reading of his text. It was a considered and nuanced position, at once philosophical and literary, and one that spoke to Dronke's own literary and philosophical position at the time, and also addressed the complicated religious and social challenges that had come before.

After his time in Rome, Dronke returned to Oxford to lecture and to teach, and one of his series of college lectures, given at Merton in 1960, is of particular interest. The lecture began at 11a.m. and ran for an hour, addressed to an audience of a dozen or so undergraduates and six or eight graduates and senior members, including, as it happened, Rosemary Woolf, on study leave from Hull where she was then teaching. It was there that she and Dronke met for the first time. Of the three scholars considered here, Dronke and Woolf had the most divergent approaches, she focused on the poet's willing acceptance of religious and literary tradition, he on poetic originality and creativity, but they both were concerned as well with the nature of the genre, however differently they described it. It may have been that Douglas Gray sometimes attended Dronke's lectures as well, and though he had already met Woolf in other contexts it is very possible that, sometimes at least, he would have appeared. After the lectures most of the senior members would repair to the bar of the nearby and respectable Eastgate Hotel, there to discuss, among other things, what they were working on, and it is probable that it was at the Eastgate that Dronke, Woolf and, assuming his attendance, Gray, first came together and discussed their mutual but varied interests in the medieval lyric, and the direction their work was taking.

Because the area that Dronke had identified for himself was medieval Latin literature, a field that does not appear in most undergraduate or even graduate curriculums, academic positions were (and are) few and far between, but a lectureship in the subject came up in Cambridge in 1961, to which he was appointed; his wife Ursula, then an English fellow at Somerville and already a distinguished scholar of Old Norse literature, chose to move with him, and it was her now-vacated fellowship that was then awarded to Rosemary Woolf, and that allowed her return to Oxford. Over the years Dronke prospered at Cambridge, being elected to a fellowship at Clare Hall in 1964, to a personal Readership in 1979, and to a personal Chair in 1989. He was elected Fellow of the British Academy in 1984.

It was at Victoria University College that Dronke cemented a friendship with the third Oxford scholar whom I have already mentioned, Douglas Gray, who had been born in Melbourne to a family originally from Durham, that had subsequently moved to Australia, and then to New Zealand, where young Douglas had lived from the age of seven. He graduated from Wellington College before entering 'Vic', which he left with a master's degree in 1952, coming, after having lectured there for two years, to Merton College, Oxford, on a scholarship to read English, in 1954. Subsequently, and after five years spent as a lecturer at Pembroke and Lincoln, he was elected to a fellowship at Pembroke in 1961, and when I met him in the late 1960s he was the senior English fellow there, though in 1980 he would become the first J. R. R. Tolkien Professor of Medieval English Literature and Language at Oxford, attached to Lady Margaret Hall. In 1989 he was elected to the British Academy.

Both men had by then developed a friendship as well with Professor Joseph Trapp, CBE (1925–2005), whose lectures they had attended in Wellington, and who had left New Zealand for Britain in 1951, teaching first in Reading, but afterwards moving to London, where in due course he became Director of the Warburg Institute. Before that, and for many years, he was its long-term, markedly academic and very learned librarian. One aspect of the Warburg not shared with other institute libraries concerns its most open of shelves, among which readers were and are encouraged not only to roam freely so as to locate a sought book, but also to investigate others as well, often on the same shelf, that could suggest new directions. It was through Trapp that the Warburg, though then as now best known for art history, made available to these scholars a tradition of a culturally based literary criticism, for medieval lyrics among other texts, both by expediting the facility with which both men, Dronke in particular, crossed national boundaries, and through the informed cultural connections that are present throughout Gray's work. Both men were, from their beginnings in Britain, indebted to their association with what, for many working scholars in those days, was Joe Trapp's Warburg.

It is important in this context to understand that Gray's interest in the medieval lyric, like Dronke's, began in Wellington, where he had been Dronke's senior by two years. Following his graduation, Gray had lectured to students on medieval lyrics, romances, and certain other texts, employing a cyclostyled (mimeographed) anthology of the lyrics he had himself edited in order to do so. The work anticipated one he would prepare years later in Oxford for the Clarendon Medieval and Tudor Series, *A Selection of Religious Lyrics* (Oxford, 1975; repr. Exeter, 1992). Throughout, his interest in the lyric was more literary than religious, though religious interests figured incidentally, reaching back to the days when his father had embraced an evangelical church that did not engage him, so that he adopted instead traditionally Anglican teachings and practices, informed by a study of their medieval antecedents. Soon after I met him in Oxford, and sensing that our interests coincided, he very kindly took me to a church not far from his home where together we examined such evidence of medieval practice as could still be found there. No doubt it was such interests that led to his later reputation as a particularly devout Anglican, a description that somewhat understates the nature of his religious inquiry.

The focus among this early triad of scholars was upon the brilliant literary craftsmanship and evident and powerful originality of this then undervalued genre, which they were among the first to argue included texts as good as anything written in English during the medieval period, not excepting Chaucer – an insight some commentators have yet to embrace. But a consideration of religiousness occasionally appears in their work, usually in connection with individual utterances or (particularly in Woolf) in devout and meditative attitudes. Still, such concerns were rarely the central issue, and the actual usefulness of such issues, particularly in analysis, could be ambiguous.

Dronke and Gray shared an intellectual and felt interest in a kind of criticism that privileged creative originality, not, as I have said, an interest widely shared with very many other medievalists at the time. But it also involved a considered understanding that medieval creativity emerged from circumstances often requiring an author to be in dialogue with his tradition, a phrase and a concept derived at least in part from a widely admired Oxford, New Zealand and finally Catholic medievalist, J. A. W. Bennett (1911–81), who became Professor of Medieval and Renaissance Literature at Cambridge in 1964. Like the scholars I have been describing, and in part because of his influence, many members of this group, but Gray and Dronke in particular, tended to view originality as having emerged when the medieval poet, usually quite consciously, departed, sometimes delicately, from the literary, iconographic and even the scriptural conventions that he shared with his reader, acting in the interests of a new meaning when he did so – so that, to take an uncontested example, Adam's sin becomes worthy of celebration not only because it brought Christ to redeem humankind, but also because without it Mary, the best of humankind and the real subject of the poem, would not have become Queen of Heaven – a designation that was of meaning and importance in the period.

All three of these scholars knew each other – and Professors Bennett and Trapp – particularly well, and all three were well aware of the projects each one had in hand. The result was that when Gray's pioneering study, *Themes and Images in the Medieval English Religious Lyric* (London, 1972) appeared, the medieval English lyric seemed almost to have been opened anew to reader and specialist alike. Woolf's focus on the sometimes elaborate literary and meditative traditions added a depth that had escaped earlier critics, while Dronke's comparativist perspective placed English medieval lyrics in a European tradition as never before, while also acknowledging their uniqueness. Gray's work, while responsive to both of them, read tradition with a less heavy hand (unlike Woolf, he was sometimes reluctant to fix a lyric's century of composition on the basis of style), and though attuned to European influences, he was not less interested in the concept of an originality that responded as much to immediate cultural circumstance as to intellectual influence.

The fact that these three scholars interacted as they did had a certain effect on their individual readings, which sometimes informed subsequent readings too, though I am of course aware that literary criticism of lyrical texts did not actually begin in Oxford, and there were subsequent scholars who wrote without reference to the sort of criticism that I have been discussing. But to those who were alert to these influences, this particular triad was not without its interest. Thus, for example, even if Woolf's meditative thesis was not specifically cited, its effect could sometimes be felt, not invariably to the benefit of the text in question. Gray's influence emerged, in some quarters at least and over time, both from the title I have cited, and also from his anthology of medieval religious lyrics, whose commentary and notes set a gold standard of what could be accomplished, even though it was criticised for its evident and extensive learning by the editor of an earlier anthology who, like many another, fought shy of cultural commentary.

But the volumes and other studies that this generation of scholars produced had the effect of privileging both the status of the lyric among students of medieval literature generally and, as time went by, of developing respect for its several and increasingly evident accomplishments. Even when specific reference to these studies and these scholars has not registered – as in some contributions to the present collection – their effect can sometimes be felt in a like responsiveness to the texts, issues and criticism that first engaged them, so that their studies and disagreements, including those between and among themselves, indirectly nurtured what was to follow. In any case, it was in no small part because of their witness that the critical drought came to an end. Serious examination could continue, if in many different ways, and from many different hands.

***

There is no straight line between the treatment of the medieval lyric that developed in Oxford in the late 1960s and this collection of essays, or indeed with many of the directions that the study of the lyric has subsequently taken, but even so, there may be said to have been a certain passing of the torch to many of those whose essays appear here. *Middle English Lyrics: New Readings of Short Poems* is both indebted to, but also departs from, the readings and the ways of reading that I have been discussing above, now usually designated as 'literary criticism', though it is interesting to note how often the scholars I have been writing about are cited, and how important a role literary criticism continues to play in our discourse. To be sure, there were critical readings that preceded the developments in Oxford, one of the more useful being Stephen Manning's *Wisdom and Number: Toward a Critical Appraisal of the Middle English Religious Lyric*.[2] As Manning and many other studies cited in Rosemary Greentree's extensive and annotated bibliography make plain,[3] these pointed in many different directions – vernacular theology, patristic commentary, new criticism, historical analysis – in such now familiar works such as Sarah Appleton Weber's reflective *Theology and Poetry in the Middle English Lyric*;[4] Edmund Reiss's exegetical, *The Art of the Middle English Lyric*;[5] Siegfried Wenzel's historical treatment of the interaction with the sermon, *Preachers, Poets and the Early English Lyric*;[6] and Karin Boklund-Lagopoulou's *'I have a yong suster': Popular Song and the Middle English Lyric*,[7] which is important as having began a long deferred rapprochement between literary theory and the lyric that continues today, including in this collection.

---

[2] S. Manning, *Wisdom and Number: Toward a Critical Appraisal of the Middle English Religious Lyric* (Lincoln, NE, 1962).
[3] R. Greentree, *The Middle English Lyric and Short Poem* (Cambridge, 2001).
[4] S. A. Weber, *Theology and Poetry in the Middle English Lyric: A Study of Sacred History and Aesthetic Form* (Columbus, OH, 1969).
[5] E. Reiss, *The Art of the Middle English Lyric: Essays in Criticism* (Athens, GA, 1972).
[6] S. Wenzel, *Preachers, Poets and the Early English Lyric* (Princeton, 1986).
[7] K. Boklund-Lagopoulou, *'I have a yong suster': Popular Song and the Middle English Lyric* (Dublin, 2002).

But one aspect of *New Readings* that sets it apart from studies that, like it, seek to deepen our understanding of the genre by an examination of individual authors, texts, circumstance and themes, are the four categories that the editors have designated so as to indicate the direction individual authors have taken. These categories, or others like them, have indeed been in evidence in earlier studies, but often without the critical nuance present here, and without the commitment to addressing the ways in which the lyrics proceeded. Throughout, attention to detail, including both bibliographical and manuscript detail, has been extensive, but there is also a general understanding that as a genre the lyric is a more dynamic art form than is generally acknowledged, and that change, development and innovation between and among the versions of any particular text, not a single preferred reading, is the critic's business, a point forcefully made at the start of this volume in Thomas G. Duncan's study of editing issues. Taken as a whole, this anthology offers a way of reading medieval lyrics that, in scope and accomplishment at least, if not in method, is not entirely unlike the ones I have been describing.

The first of the larger categories that appears here, 'Affect', concerns a quality that is at the heart of all poetry, but that has often been taken in the medieval religious lyric to allude to its largely devout context. Affective practices thus have long been understood to inform a large number of religious lyrics, many attached to Rosemary Woolf's constructions and also to her understanding both of Old English, and of the role and effect of devout meditation. These practices are by now so often assumed that they are only rarely interrogated, though the first study under 'Affect' offers reason to inquire how far they may have mitigated such powerful emotions as the kind of fear A. S. Lazikani describes, and how far the subject in prayer experienced not only compassion and consolation but also confidence as his or her engagement deepened. Daniel McCann's perceptive and thoughtful evocation of what amounts to the tone of many lyrics focuses upon the nature and effect of a sweetness that can develop into grief and sorrow, but lead to a penitential awareness of the pain and suffering that the world supplies, so as to end in bliss and joy. This use of affective feeling can have both secular and devout resonance, as religious lyrics reflect philosophical reflection through natural imagery while also encoding affective resonances, as Michael P. Kuczynski, freshly inspired by the sure use of an u/v lamp, perceptively proposes.

Affective emotion does not separate easily from emotion, even when sustained by the familiar and totalising narrative of Christ's passion, but neither should it be associated automatically with meditation, as it sometimes is. It is in the nature of Christianity, medieval and modern alike, to evoke a response, and to do so even when no question has been proposed. That response sometimes accounts for the origin, sometimes acts as the backbone, to many a lyric, and as such indicates a certain religiousness that, too often, awaits description. Affective practice, whether meditative or not, is often a means rather than an end, a way rather than a destination, but the questions it raises are central to the genre, and as such the best entry into a collection such as this one.

Afterword

The context of 'Affect' leads naturally to that of 'Visuality', though its meaning too is somewhat more elastic than first appears. Again, and thanks in part to Rosemary Woolf, the first and still usual connotation is meditative and devout, what the Christian subject considers and perceives while in prayer, and it is one of the accomplishments of the present collection to extend its meaning outwards, and indicate a variety of associated practices and devotions that have nothing to do with Christ's passion. The several manifestations of the Blessed Virgin include, as Annie Sutherland quite brilliantly indicates in her reading of lyric landscapes, her role as transfigured Queen of Heaven, where she reigns fair and bright, at once beautiful and regal – all adjectives that invoke the visual as they construct meaning. Visuality can also define the nature of Christ's passion, not only in terms of traditional meditation, but, as Hetta Howes notes, it can also serve a teaching function. This is relevant because it can also move the discourse concerning visuality away from the tradition of meditation to something more painterly, as Natalie Jones's study of the context and effectiveness of Christ's five wounds, and Anne Marie D'Arcy's learned and wide-ranging examination of material culture and aureate diction – issues that also engaged both Woolf and Gray – make plain. In one way or another visuality is central to poetry, and without it neither Milton nor Keats would have realised their very different effects. This same sort of grandeur can also be found in religious poems of the kind examined here, which often powerfully pull the subject reader onto another path. As Mary Wellesley rightly points out in her reading of Lydgate's little-studied poem on Mary's joys and sorrows (fifteen in this version), joy no less than sorrow is often the result, further widening the lyrical distance between the passion narratives and their associated meditations.

The third section is designated '*Mouvance*, Transformation', and is in some ways the most interesting of the four, engaging textual and interpretive issues that have been sounded elsewhere, but rarely with the critical sophistication and cultural nuance that appears here. In some ways it is this section that departs most clearly from traditional readings, and reveals what may be the most innovative contributions to the collection. Anne Baden-Daintree's considered study of the lyrical 'rewriting' of the Song of Songs provides a fine opening for the several plastic and expansive issues present throughout.

Echoing Paul Zumthor's suggestion that *mouvance* is observable as a product of oral transmission, where orality prevails over the fixity of a written text, Katherine Zieman brilliantly indicates the boundaries of poetry, arguing that the modes of communication can, in some contexts, take precedence over content, particularly (to greatly simplify her argument) when they encode other devout texts that contain differences attributable, at least in part, to oral transmission. In this context Ardis Butterfield's concept of 'textual dynamism' also can inform our reading, allowing for a greater latitude of 'horizontal' influences, from such sources as music and literary convention, than is often taken into account.[8] Given the kinds of readings and influences privileged in this section, it seems the correct phrase to appropriate in order to describe the newer ways of identifying ideas concerning the development of a powerful, sometimes even paramystical religiousness (not a word or an issue sounded here), involving Richard Rolle and others, and articulated in the lyric best of all.

Within this section too, appears a larger cultural understanding of Church and Christian, addressed in Elizabeth Robertson's Hegelian approach to the gendered reading, in the context of war, of the lyrics that speak to Criseyde's feelings about love in Chaucer's *Troilus and Criseyde*, and Julia Boffey's perceptive identification of other issues in an even more Chaucerian John Lydgate, who gains in depth and originality in her treatment of his shorter poems. Denis Renevey's sharp engagement with Charles d'Orléans points in a different direction, treating, *inter alia*, the persona of the poet in a single English poem, and so engaging issues of authorship and composition, as well as literary influence and (importantly) structural difference, as he does so. The sense of *mouvance* present (if in varying degrees) throughout the section speaks in different ways to the new dynamic present in the collection as a whole.

The final section appears in some ways more theoretically traditional, though paradoxically it is also one of the more imaginative, addressing individual lyrics, as is the custom, but doing so in a way that extends the examination of their variations in new directions. The chapters in this section consider the transmission of lyrics as written words but are also alive to the potentialities of words sung and words spoken, as instanced in Mary C. Flannery's perceptive discussion of a poem warning against idle speech. Susanna Fein's typically learned treatment of two (and more) lyrics in Oxford, Jesus College, MS 29 moves the treatment of lyrics towards a discussion of their meaning, perhaps even towards their spirituality, a concern about which I have already spoken, but one that, taken as a whole, this volume can be read as encouraging, if guardedly. Christiania Whitehead's fine treatment of the well-known lyric *Stond wel, moder, under rode*, reads the six versions of the lyric in their manuscript context, linking them to the variations in the textual content throughout, so as to consider the ways in which the lyric is thus effectively transformed. This is the first study to consider such variation, but what makes this examination particularly interesting is the attention given to music, and throughout, the confident opposition of texts, attitudes and meanings, so as to demonstrate their generic diversity and stylistic variation.

This same confidence appears as well in Jane Griffiths's perceptive and smart treatment of John Audelay, which reads him in a larger intellectual context than is usual, and identifies usually unnoticed literary and religious attitudes that thus

---

[8] A. Butterfield, 'The Construction of Textual Form: Cross-lingual Citation in Some Medieval Lyrics', *Citation, Intertextuality and Memory in the Middle Ages and Renaissance*, ed. Y. Plumley, G. di Bacco and S. Jossa (Exeter, 2011), pp. 41–57 (p. 55).

become evident throughout his *oeuvre*. Like Whitehead, her reading is nuanced and perceptive, connected, as throughout the collection, to other texts and other attitudes, so that the poet who emerges at the end gains not only in complexity but also in stature. A most interesting final chapter by Joel Grossman contrasts Renaissance lyrics with medieval, indicating, among other things, evident differences in rhetorical and social strategies that inform the persona and offer, in authors like Sir Thomas Wyatt and Henry Howard, Earl of Surrey, what almost amounts to a new, but not entirely new, genre, one that is associated with the person of the poet, who himself may be said to emerge from, or at least to echo, previously existing lyrics.

***

Among the changes that have informed recent studies and that are present as well in this collection is the studied criticism of earlier bibliographical practice, and thus the setting aside of print-oriented language generally, in order to move to concerns associated with the plastic form of the medieval lyric. It is thus concerned with oral practice and with reader reception, practices in which the reader's or the reciter's response, informed by an understood continuation (or rejection) of past practice, call into question any too static a reading of text, content and meaning.

When all is said and done, the medieval lyric remains the single most widely known and still-practised literary art form to come down to us from the late Middle Ages – as its present-day imitators, in their own way, often wildly attest. But the great advantage of this anthology is that it resolutely sets aside the assumption that such lyrics were confined by tradition, or were in any way static, in the ways of other written texts, or best studied through a manuscript stemma, in which our first concern is ever to identify and examine whatever it is that constitutes the 'best version'. On the contrary, what emerges here is the sure realisation that the medieval lyric was and is a living, dynamic entity, often married to song and to music generally, in which every version of a text is of real interest, and in which context as well as content is key. Informed as it was by everything that it touched or that touched it – visual and plastic art, music, theology and previous lyrics among them – it stands as it always has, as the single most important, dynamic and widespread literary accomplishment of late medieval Britain, of late medieval Europe.

Author's Note

I am indebted to Professor Emeritus Helen Cooper of Cambridge, and to J. R. R. Tolkien Professor Vincent Gillespie of Oxford, for perceptive comment on what I have written, and to certain other sympathetic informants for their encouragement and support. But most of all I am indebted both to my teacher, mentor and friend of many years, J. R. R. Tolkien Professor Emeritus Douglas Gray, for discussion of these and related matters over many years, but in particular for a conversation that we had in Tackley on 9 June 2017, when my work was in progress, and to Professor Emeritus Peter Dronke, who very kindly allowed a similar conversation in Cambridge on 22 June of the same year. The focus and direction offered here, of course, are entirely my own, and I alone am responsible for any errors or omissions, but it was those meetings that reminded me of what had transpired in Oxford half a century ago, and that best informed my narrative.

Bibliography

Manuscripts and Early Printed Books
Cambridge, St John's College, MS 111
Cambridge, Trinity College, MS B. 14. 39
——MS O. 2. 40
——MS R. 3. 21
Cambridge, University Library, MS Hh. 4. 12
Dublin, Trinity College, MS 301
Edinburgh, National Library of Scotland, Advocates' MS 18. 7. 21 ('John of Grimestone's preaching book')
London, BL, Additional MS 20059
——Additional MS 27909
——Additional MS 37049
——Additional MS 46919
——Additional MS 60577 ('The Winchester anthology')
——Arundel MS 248
——Cotton MS Appendix XXVII
——Cotton MS Caligula A IX
——Cotton MS Nero A XIV
——Cotton MS Titus D XVIII
——Harley MS 2253
——Printed Book IB. 55242
——Royal MS 2 F VIII
——Royal MS 8 F II
——Royal MS 12 E I
——Sloane MS 2593
London, Lambeth Palace Library, MS 557
Maidstone Museum, MS A. 13
New Haven, Yale University, Beinecke Library, Takamiya MS 15
Oxford, Balliol College, MS 354 ('Richard Hill's book')
Oxford, BodL, MS Arch. Selden. supra 52
——MS Bodley 649
——MS Digby 86
——MS Douce 104
——MS Douce 302
——MS Eng. poet. a. 1 (the Vernon MS)

——MS Eng. poet. e.1
——MS Rawlinson C. 670
——MS Rawlinson G. 22
——MS Tanner 169
Oxford, Jesus College, MS 29
Paris, Bibliothèque de l'Arsenal, MS 135
Warminster, Longleat House, MS 29
Windsor, Eton College, MS 36
Windsor, Eton College, MS 178

Digital Manuscript Facsimiles

British Library Digitised Manuscripts (http://www.bl.uk/manuscripts/BriefDisplay.aspx): Additional MS 37049, Additional MS 60577, Harley MS 2253

Trinity College, Cambridge, Wren Digital Library (https://www.trin.cam.ac.uk/library/wren-digital-library/): Trinity College, MS B. 14. 39, MS O. 2. 40, MS R. 3. 21

Yale University, Beinecke Digital Collections (https://brbl-dl.library.yale.edu/vufind/): Takamiya MS 15

Primary Works

Allen, H. E., ed., *Writings Ascribed to Richard Rolle, Hermit of Hampole, and Materials for his Biography* (New York, 1927)

Allt, P. and R. K. Alspach, eds, *The Variorum Edition of the Poems of W. B. Yeats*, 2nd edn (London, 1957)

Andrew, M. and R. Waldron, eds, *The Poems of the Pearl Manuscript: 'Pearl', 'Cleanness', 'Patience', 'Sir Gawain and the Green Knight'*, 5th edn (Exeter, 2007)

Arn, M-J., ed., *Fortunes Stabilnes: Charles of Orléans's English Book of Love: A Critical Edition* (New York, 1994)

——and J. Fox, eds, *Poetry of Charles d'Orléans and His Circle: A Critical Edition of BnF MS. Fr. 25458, Charles d'Orléans's Personal Manuscript* (Tempe, AZ, 2010)

Ashley, K. M. and G. NeCastro, eds, *Mankind* (Kalamazoo, 2010)

Ayto, J. and A. Barratt, eds, *Aelred of Rievaulx's 'De Institutione Inclusarum': Two English Versions*, EETS OS 287 (Oxford, 1984)

Barr, H., ed., *The Digby Poems: A New Edition of the Lyrics* (Exeter, 2009)

Barratt, A., ed., *The Book of Tribulation* (Heidelberg, 1983)

——ed., *Women's Writing in Middle English*, 2nd edn (Oxford, 2013)

Bawcutt, P., ed., *The Poems of William Dunbar*, 2 vols (Glasgow, 1998)

Bazzi, P., ed., Thomas Aquinas, *Quaestiones Disputatae, Volumen II* (Rome, 1965)

Beadle, R., ed., *The York Plays: A Critical Edition of the York Corpus Christi Play as Recorded in British Library Additional MS 35290*, 2 vols, EETS SS 23 and 24 (Oxford, 2009 and 2013 for 2011)

Bergen, H., ed., *Lydgate's Troy Book*, 4 vols, EETS ES 97, 103, 106, 126 (London, 1906–35)

——ed., John Lydgate, *Fall of Princes*, 4 vols, EETS ES 121, 122, 123, 124 (London, 1924–27)

Birch, W. de Gray, ed., Adam of Dryburgh, *Sermones Fratris Adae, Ordinis Praemonstratensis* (Edinburgh, 1901)

Bliss, A. J., ed., Thomas Chestre, *Sir Launfal* (London, 1960)

——ed., *Sir Orfeo*, 2nd edn (Oxford 1966)

Blunt, J. H., ed., *The Myroure of Oure Ladye*, EETS ES 19 (London, 1873)

Borgnet, A., ed., *Alberti Magni Opera Omnia*, 38 vols (Paris, 1890–99)

Bibliography

Brandeis, A., ed., *Jacob's Well: An English Treatise on the Cleansing of Man's Conscience*, EETS OS 115 (London, 1901)
Brett, R. L. and A. R. Jones, ed., *Wordsworth and Coleridge: Lyrical Ballads* (London, 2005)
Browne, M. and A. Fernandez, ed. and trans., Thomas Aquinas, *Summa Theologiae* (New York, 1963)
Cartlidge, N., ed. and trans., *The Owl and the Nightingale: Text and Translation* (Exeter, 2001)
——trans., *The Works of Chardri: Three Poems in the French of Thirteenth-Century England: 'The Life of Seven Sleepers', 'The Life of St. Josaphaz', and 'The Little Debate'*, French of England Translation Series 9 (Tempe, AZ, 2015)
Chambers, E. K. and F. Sidgwick, eds, *Early English Lyrics: Amorous, Divine, Moral, and Trivial* (London, 1907)
Cohen, J. M., ed., *The Penguin Book of Spanish Verse* (Harmondsworth, 1956)
Crane, T. F., ed., *The Exempla or Illustrative Stories from the Sermones Vulgares of Jacques de Vitry* (London, 1890)
Davies, R. T., ed., *Medieval English Lyrics: A Critical Anthology* (London, 1964)
Deanesly, M., ed., *The Incendium Amoris of Richard Rolle of Hampole* (Manchester, 1915)
Dobson, E. J. and F. Ll. Harrison, *Medieval English Songs* (London, 1979)
Duncan, T. G., ed., *Medieval English Lyrics 1200–1400* (Harmondsworth, 1995)
——ed., *Late Medieval English Lyrics and Carols 1400–1530* (Harmondsworth, 2000)
Duncan-Jones, K. and H. R. Woudhuysen, eds, *Shakespeare's Poems: Venus and Adonis, the Rape of Lucrece and the Shorter Poems* (London, 2007)
Erdmann, A. and E. Ekwall, eds, *Lydgate's Siege of Thebes*, 2 vols, EETS ES 108 and 125 (London, 1911 and 1930)
Fallows, D., ed., *The Henry VIII Book (British Library, Add. MS 31922)*, DIAMM facsimiles 4 (Oxford, 2014)
Fein, S. G., ed., *Moral Love Songs and Laments* (Kalamazoo, MI, 1998)
——ed., *John the Blind Audelay, Poems and Carols (Oxford, Bodleian Library MS Douce 302)* (Kalamazoo, MI, 2009)
——ed. and trans., with D. Raybin and J. Ziolkowski, *The Complete Harley 2253 Manuscript*, 3 vols (Kalamazoo, MI, 2014–15)
Feiss, H., ed., *On Love: A Selection of Works of Hugh, Adam, Achard, Richard, and Godfrey of St Victor*, Victorine Texts in Translation 2 (Turnhout, 2012)
Furnivall, F. J., ed., *Political, Religious and Love Poems from Lambeth 306 and Other Sources*, EETS OS 15 (London, 1866)
——ed., *Hymns to the Virgin and Christ and Other Religious Poems*, EETS OS 24 (London, 1867)
——ed., *The Minor Poems of the Vernon Manuscript, Part 2*, EETS OS 117 (Oxford, 1901, repr. 1973)
Glasscoe, M., ed., *Julian of Norwich, A Revelation of Divine Love* (Exeter, 1976)
Gordon, E. V., ed., *Pearl* (Oxford, 1953)
Hailbach-Reinisch, M., ed., Pseudo-Melito of Sardis, *Ein neuer 'Transitus Mariae' des Pseudo-Melito* (Rome, 1962)
Hall, J., ed., *Selections from Early Middle English, 1130–1250*, 2 parts in 3 vols (Oxford, 1920, repr. 1951)
Hanna, R., ed., *Richard Rolle: Uncollected Prose and Verse*, EETS OS 329 (Oxford, 2007)
——and S. Wood, eds, *Richard Morris's Prick of Conscience*, EETS OS 342 (Oxford, 2013)
Harrison, J. E., ed., *The Complete Works of Edgar Allan Poe*, 17 vols (New York, 1902)
Hegel, G. W. F., trans. T. M. Knox, *Aesthetics: Lectures on Fine Art* (Oxford, 1975)
Hill, G., *Tenebrae* (London, 1978)

Hirsh, J. C., ed., *Medieval Lyric: Middle English Lyrics, Ballads and Carols* (Oxford, 2005)
Hodgson, P. and G. M. Liegey, eds, *The Orcherd of Syon*, EETS OS 258 (Oxford, 1966)
Horstmann, C., ed., *Altenglische Legenden: Neue Folge* (Heilbronn, 1881)
——ed., *Yorkshire Writers*, 2 vols (London and New York, 1895–96)
Hunt, T., ed., *'Cher alme': Texts of Anglo-Norman Piety*, trans. J. Bliss (Tempe, AZ, 2010)
Innes, M. M., trans., Ovid, *Metamorphoses* (London, 1955)
Innes-Parker, C., ed. and trans., *The Wooing of Our Lord and the Wooing Group Prayers* (Peterborough, Ontario, 2015)
Jeffrey, D. and B. Levy, eds, *The Anglo-Norman Lyric* (Turnhout, 1990)
Jollès, B., ed. and trans., *Quatorze proses du XIIe siècle à la louange de Marie* (Turnhout, 1994)
Kail, J., ed. *Twenty-six Political and Other Poems*, EETS OS 124 (1904)
Kane, G., ed., *Piers Plowman: The A-Version* (London, 1960)
——and E. T. Donaldson, eds, *Piers Plowman: The B Version* (London, 1975)
Karwasińska, J., ed., *Bruno of Querfurt, S. Adalberti Pragensis episcopi et martyris vita altera* (Warsaw, 1969)
Ker, N. R., intro., *The Owl and the Nightingale Reproduced in Facsimile from the Surviving Manuscripts Jesus College Oxford 29 and British Museum Cotton Caligula A.ix*, EETS OS 251 (London, 1963)
Kirchberger, C., trans., *Richard of Saint Victor, Selected Writings on Contemplation* (New York, 1957)
Lauritis, J. A., R. A. Klinefelter and V. Gallagher, eds, *A Critical Edition of John Lydgate's Life of Our Lady*, Duquesne Studies, Philological Series 2 (Pittsburgh, 1961)
Luria, M. S. and R. L. Hoffman, eds, *Middle English Lyrics* (New York and London, 1974)
MacCracken, H. N., ed., *The Minor Poems of John Lydgate*, 2 vols, EETS ES 107, OS 192 (London, 1911, 1934)
Milanesi, C., ed., *Benvenuto Cellini, I Trattati dell'oreficeria e della scultura* (Florence, 1857)
Millett, B., ed., *Ancrene Wisse: A Corrected Edition of the Text in Cambridge, Corpus Christi College, MS 402, with Variants from other Manuscripts*, 2 vols, EETS OS 325 and 326 (Oxford, 2005)
Mone, F.-J., ed., *Lateinische Hymnen des Mittelalters*, 3 vols (Freiburg, 1853–55)
Moon, H. M., ed., *Þe Life of Soule: An Edition with Commentary* (Salzburg, 1978)
Morris, R., ed., *Old English Homilies of the 12th and 13th Centuries*, 2 vols, EETS OS 29, 34 (1867 and 1868; repr. 1988)
Morris, R., ed., *An Old English Miscellany*, EETS OS 49 (London, 1872)
Mountain, W. J. and F. Glorie, eds, Augustine of Hippo, *De Trinitate*, 2 vols (Turnhout, 1968)
Mühlethaler, J.-C., ed., *Charles d'Orléans, Ballades et Rondeaux. Edition du manuscrit 25458 du fonds français de la Bibliothèque nationale de Paris* (Paris, 1992)
Muir, K. and P. Thomson, eds, *Collected Poems of Sir Thomas Wyatt* (Liverpool, 1969)
Nott, G. F., ed., *The Works of Henry Howard, Earl of Surrey, and of Sir Thomas Wyatt the Elder*, 2 vols (London, 1815)
O'Donnell, J. J., ed., *Augustine: Confessions, Volume II; Commentary, Books 1–7* (Oxford, 2013)
O'Farrell-Tate, U., ed., *The Abridged English Metrical Brut*, Middle English Texts 32 (Heidelberg, 2002)
Ogilvie-Thomson, S. J., ed., *Richard Rolle: Prose and Verse*, EETS OS 293 (Oxford, 1988)
Oliver, R., ed., *Poems without Names: The English Lyric 1200–1500* (Berkeley, CA, 1970)
Paulino, F. F. and R. Osório, eds, *Tesouros Artísticos da Misericórdia do Porto* (Porto, 1995)

Pearsall, D., ed., *Piers Plowman by William Langland: An Edition of the C-Text* (London, 1978)
——intro., *Piers Plowman: A Facsimile of Bodleian Library, Oxford, MS Douce 104*, with a catalogue of the illustrations by K. L. Scott (Cambridge, 1992)
Rebholz, R. A., ed., *Sir Thomas Wyatt: The Complete Poems* (New Haven, 1978)
Regan, R., trans., Thomas Aquinas, *On Evil* (Oxford, 2003)
Reimer, S. R., ed., *The Works of William Herebert* (Toronto, 1987)
Reinsch, R., ed., 'La vie de Tobie de Guillaume le Clerc de Normandie', *Archiv für das Studium der Neueren Sprachen und Literaturen* 62 (1879), 375–96
Rettig, J. W., trans., St Augustine, *Tractates on the Gospel of John 112–24 and Tractates on the First Epistle of John*, Fathers of the Church 92 (Washington, DC, 1995)
Rigg, A. G., ed., *The Poems of Walter of Wimborne* (Toronto, 1978)
Russell, G. and G. Kane, eds, *Piers Plowman: The C Version* (London, 1997)
Saiani, A., ed. and trans., John of Garland, *Epithalamium beate Marie virginis* (Florence, 1995)
Sakari, A., ed., *Doctrinal Sauvage, publié d'après tous les manuscrits*, Studia Philologica Jyväskyläensia 3 (Jyväskylä, 1967)
Saupe, K., ed., *Middle English Marian Lyrics* (Kalamazoo, MI, 1998)
Scattergood, J., ed., *The Complete English Poems of John Skelton*, revised edn (Liverpool, 2015)
Schmitt. F. S., ed., *S. Anselmi Cantuariensis Archiepiscopi Opera Omnia*, 6 vols (Edinburgh, 1940–61)
Scudder, H. E., ed., *The Complete Poetical Works of Henry Wadsworth Longfellow* (New York, 1902)
Shepherd, G., ed., Sir Philip Sidney, *An Apology for Poetry or the Defence of Poesy*, revised by R. W. Maslen, 3rd edn (Manchester, 2002)
Silverstein, T., ed., *Medieval English Lyrics* (London, 1971)
Sinclair, J. D., trans., *The Divine Comedy of Dante Alighieri II: Purgatorio, and III: Paradiso*, 3 vols (Oxford, 1961)
Sisam, C. and K. Sisam, eds, *The Oxford Book of Medieval English Verse* (Oxford, 1970)
Spector, S., ed., *The N-Town Play: Cotton Vespasian D.8*, 2 vols, EETS SS 11 and 12 (Oxford, 1991)
Steele, R. and M. Day, eds, *The English Poems of Charles d'Orléans*, EETS OS 215 and 220, rev. edn in one volume (London, 1970)
Stevens, J. E., ed., *Medieval Carols*, Musica Britannica 4 (London, 1958)
——ed., *Music at the Court of Henry VIII*, Musica Britannica 18 (London, 1962)
——ed., *Early Tudor Songs and Carols*, Musica Britannica 36 (London, 1975)
Stevens, M. and A. C. Cawley, eds, *The Towneley Plays*, 2 vols, EETS SS 13 and 14 (Oxford, 1994)
Stone, B., ed. and trans., *Medieval English Verse* (London, 1964)
Thompson, W. M., ed., *þe Wohunge of Ure Lauerd*, EETS OS 241 (London, 1958 for 1955)
Tischendorff, C. von, ed., *Apocalypses apocryphae* (Leipzig, 1866)
Tolkien, J. R. R. and E. V. Gordon, eds, *Sir Gawain and the Green Knight*, 2nd edn rev. Norman Davis (Oxford, 1967)
Tschann, J. and M. Parkes, intro., *Facsimile of Bodleian Library, MS Digby 86*, EETS SS 16 (Oxford, 1996)
Vandenbrouke, F., ed., Richard Rolle, *Le Chant d'Amour: Melos Amoris I*, Sources Chrétiennes 168 (Paris, 1971)
Vickers, B., ed., *English Renaissance Literary Criticism* (Oxford, 1999)
Ward, B., S. L. G., trans., *The Prayers and Meditation of Saint Anselm with the Proslogion* (Harmondsworth, 1973)

Weber, R., et al., eds, *Biblia sacra iuxta vulgata versionem*, rev. R. Gryson, 5th edn (Stuttgart, 2007)

Whitehead, C., D. Renevey and A. Mouron, eds, *'The Doctrine of the Hert': A Critical Edition with Introduction and Commentary* (Exeter, 2010)

Wilson, E., intro., *The Winchester Anthology: A Facsimile of British Library Additional Manuscript 60577* (Cambridge, 1981)

Windeatt, B., ed., Geoffrey Chaucer, *Troilus and Criseyde: A New Edition of 'The Book of Troilus'* (London, 1984)

Wogan-Browne, J., N. Watson, A. Taylor and R. Evans, eds, *The Idea of the Vernacular: An Anthology of Middle English Literary Theory 1280–1520* (Exeter, 1999)

——T. Fenster and D. Russell, eds, *Vernacular Literary Theory from the French of Medieval England: Texts and Translations, c.1120–c.1450* (Cambridge, 2016)

Wright, T., ed., *The Owl and the Nightingale: An Early English Poem attributed to Nicholas of Guildford, with some shorter poems from the same manuscript*, Percy Society 11 (London, 1843)

——ed., *The Seven Sages* (London, 1845)

——and J. O. Halliwell-Phillipps, eds, *Reliquiae Antiquae*, 2 vols (London, 1845)

Zupitza, J., ed., *Alt- und mittelenglisches Uebungsbuch mit einem Wörterbuch*, 12th edn, ed. A. Eichler (Vienna, 1922)

Secondary Works

Adnès, P., 'Pénitence', *Dictionnaire de spiritualité: ascétique et mystique, doctrine et historique*, ed. M. Viller et al., 17 vols (Paris, 1937–95), XII, pp. 943–1010

Adorno, T., 'On Lyric Poetry and Society', *Notes to Literature, Volume One*, trans. S. W. Nicholsen (New York, 1958), pp. 36–54

Aers, D., 'Criseyde: Woman in Medieval Society', *Critical Essays on Chaucer's Troilus and Criseyde and His Major Early Poems*, ed. C. D. Benson (Toronto, 1991), pp. 128–48

——'A Whisper in the Ear of Early Modernists; or, Reflections on Literary Critics Writing the "History of the Subject"', *Culture and History 1350–1600: Essays on English Communities, Identities and Writing*, ed. D. Aers (London, 1992), pp. 177–202

Alföldy, G., 'Augustus und die Inschriften: Tradition und Innovation. Die Geburt der imperialen Epigraphik', *Gymnasium* 98 (2001), 289–324

Amsler, M., *Affective Literacies: Writing and Multilingualism in the Late Middle Ages* (Turnhout, 2011)

Anderson, M. D., *Drama and Imagery in English Medieval Churches* (Cambridge, 1963)

Archibald, E., 'Tradition and Innovation in the Macaronic Poetry of Dunbar and Skelton', *Modern Language Quarterly* 53 (1992), 126–49

Arn, M.-J., 'Poetic Form as Mirror of Meaning in the English Poems of Charles of Orleans', *Philological Quarterly* 69 (1990), 13–29

——'Charles of Orleans: Translator?', *The Medieval Translator* 4, ed. R. Ellis and R. Evans (Exeter, 1994), 125–35

——ed., *Charles d'Orléans in England 1415–1440* (Cambridge, 2000)

——'Two Manuscripts, One Mind: Charles d'Orléans and the Production of Manuscripts in Two Languages (Paris, BN, MS fr. 25458 and London, BL MS Harley 682)', Arn, ed., *Charles d'Orléans in England*, pp. 61–78

Astell, A. W., *The Song of Songs in the Middle Ages* (Ithaca and London, 1990)

Avery, S., *The Dimensional Structure of Consciousness: A Physical Basis for Immaterialism* (Lexington, KY, 1995)

Bibliography

Bahr, A., 'Miscellaneity and Variance in the Medieval Book', *The Medieval Manuscript Book: Cultural Approaches*, ed. M. Johnston and M. Van Dussen (Cambridge, 2016), pp. 181–98

Barclay Lloyd, J. E., 'Das *goldene Gewand* der Muttergottes in der Bildersprache mittelalterlicher und frühchristlicher Mosaiken in Rom', *Römische Quartalschrift* 85 (1990), 66–85

Bardsley, S., *Venomous Tongues: Speech and Gender in Late Medieval England* (Philadelphia, 2006)

Barratt, A., 'The Prymer and its Influence on Fifteenth-Century English Passion Lyrics', *Medium Aevum* 44 (1975), 264–79

Baumstark, R., ed., *Das Goldene Rössl: Ein Meisterwerk der Pariser Hofkunst um 1400* (Munich, 1995)

Belting, H., *The Image and its Public in the Middle Ages: Form and Function of Early Paintings of the Passion*, trans. M. Bartusis and R. Meyer (New Rochelle, NY, 1990)

Bennett, M. J., 'John Audelay: Life Records and Heaven's Ladder', Fein, ed., *My Wyl and my Wrytyng*, pp. 30–53

Bernard, E. and H. Wanley, *Catalogi librorum manuscriptorum Angliae et Hiberniae in unum collecti cum indice alphabetico*, 2 vols (Oxford, 1697)

Bertelli, C., *La Madonna di Santa Maria in Trastevere* (Rome, 1961)

Bestul, T. H., 'Chaucer's *Parson's Tale* and the Late Medieval Tradition of Religious Meditation', *Speculum* 64 (1989), 600–19

Bimson, M. and I. C. Freestone, '"Rouge Clair" and other Late 14th Century Enamels on the Royal Gold Cup of the Kings of France and England', *Annales du 9e Congres de l'Association Internationale pour l'histoire du Verre, Nancy 1983* (Liège, 1985), pp. 209–22

Binski, P., *Medieval Death: Ritual and Representation* (London, 1996)

Boffey, J., 'Middle English Lyrics: Texts and Interpretation', *Medieval Literature: Texts and Interpretation*, ed. T. W. Machan (Binghamton, NY, 1991), pp. 121–38

——'Charles of Orleans Reading Chaucer's Dream Visions', *Medievalitas: Reading the Middle Ages. The J. A. W. Bennett Memorial Lectures, Ninth Series, Perugia*, ed. A. Torti (Cambridge, 1996), pp. 43–62

——'Middle English Lyrics and Manuscripts', Duncan, *Companion*, pp. 1–18

——and J. J. Thompson, 'Anthologies and Miscellanies: Production and Choice of Texts', *Book Production and Publishing in Britain 1375–1475*, ed. J. Griffiths and D. Pearsall (Cambridge, 1989), pp. 279–316

——and A. S. G. Edwards, 'Towards a Taxonomy of Middle English Manuscript Assemblages', *Insular Books: Vernacular Manuscript Miscellanies in Late Medieval Britain*, ed. M. Connolly and R. Radulescu (Oxford, 2015), pp. 263–79

Borthwick, Sister M. C., 'Antigone's Song as "Mirour" in Chaucer's *Troilus and Criseyde*', *Modern Language Quarterly* 22 (1961), 227–35

Bose, M., 'Useless Mouths: Reformist Poetics in Audelay and Skelton', *Form and Reform: Reading Across the Fifteenth Century*, ed. S. Gayk and K. Tonry (Columbus, 2011), pp. 159–79

Brantley, J., *Reading in the Wilderness: Private Devotion and Public Performance in Late Medieval England* (London and Chicago, 2007)

Breeze, A., 'Two Bardic Themes: the Virgin and Child, and Ave-Eva', *Medium Aevum* 63 (1994), 17–33

Brewster, S., *Lyric* (London, 2009)

British Library Catalogue of Additions to the Manuscripts: 1946–1950, 2 vols (London, 1959)

Brooks, C., *The Well Wrought Urn: Studies in the Structure of Poetry* (New York, 1947)

Buettner, B., 'Past's Presents: New Year's Gifts at the Valois Courts ca. 1400', *Art Bulletin* 83 (2001), 598–625

Burrow, J. A., 'Poems without Contexts: the Poems of Bodl. Rawl. D. 913', *Essays in Criticism* 29 (1979), 6–32, reprinted in Burrow, *Essays in Middle English Literature* (Oxford, 1974), pp. 1–26

—— 'Wasting Time, Wasting Words in *Piers Plowman* B and C', *Yearbook of Langland Studies* 17 (2003), 191–202

Butterfield, A., 'Interpolated Lyric in Medieval Narrative Poetry', unpublished Ph.D. thesis, Cambridge, 1987

—— *The Familiar Enemy: Chaucer, Language and Nation in the Hundred Years War* (Oxford, 2009)

—— 'The Construction of Textual Form: Cross-Lingual Citation in the Medieval Insular Lyric', *Citation, Intertextuality and Memory in the Middle Ages and Renaissance: Text, Music and Image from Machaut to Ariosto*, ed. Y. Plumley, G. Di Bacco and S. Jossa (Exeter, 2011), pp. 41–57

—— 'Why Medieval Lyric?' *English Literary History* 82 (2015), 319–43

Campbell, M., 'English *basse taille* Enamels', *Annali della Scuola Normale Superiore di Pisa* 4 (1997), 37–46

Carruthers, M., *The Book of Memory: A Study of Memory in Medieval Culture* (Cambridge, 1990)

—— *The Craft of Thought: Meditation, Rhetoric and the Making of Images 400–1200* (Cambridge, 1998)

—— *The Experience of Beauty in the Middle Ages* (Oxford, 2013)

Cartlidge, N., 'The Composition and Social Context of Oxford, Jesus College, MS 29 (II) and London, British Library, MS Cotton Caligula A.ix', *Medium Ævum* 66 (1997), 250–69

—— 'Imagining X: A Lost Early Vernacular Miscellany', *Imagining the Book*, ed. S. Kelly and J. J. Thompson (Turnhout, 2005), pp. 31–44

Cawsey, K., 'Tutivillus and the "Kyrkchaterars": Strategies of Control in the Middle Ages', *Studies in Philology* 102 (2005), 434–51

Cervone, C. M., *Poetics of the Incarnation: Middle English Writing and the Leap of Love* (Philadelphia, 2012)

Cherry, J., 'The Dunstable Swan Jewel', *Journal of the British Archaeological Association* 32 (1969), 38–53

—— *The Holy Thorn Reliquary* (London, 2010)

Chewning, S. M., ed., *The Milieu and Context of the Wooing Group* (Cardiff, 2009)

Cioffi, C. A., '"Dolce color d'orïental zaffiro": A Gloss on "Purgatorio" 1.13', *Modern Philology* 82 (1985), 355–64

Clayton, M., *The Cult of the Virgin Mary in Anglo-Saxon England* (Cambridge, 1990)

Colker, M. L., *Trinity College Library Dublin: Descriptive Catalogue of the Medieval and Renaissance Latin Manuscripts*, 2 vols (Aldershot, 1991)

Connolly, M., *John Shirley: Book Production and the Noble Household in Fifteenth-Century England* (Aldershot, 1998)

Constantinescu, R., 'Alcuin et les "Libelli precum" de l'époque carolingienne', *Revue d'histoire de la spiritualité* 50 (1974), 17–56

Cook, E., *Against Coercion: Games Poets Play* (Stanford, 1998)

Cooper, L. H. and A. Denny-Brown, eds, *Lydgate Matters: Poetry and Material Culture in the Fifteenth Century* (Basingstoke, 2008)

Copeland, R., 'The Middle English *Candet Nudatum Pectus* and Norms of Early Vernacular Translation Practice', *Leeds Studies in English* 15 (1984), 57–81

Cornell, C., '"Purtreture" and "Holsom Stories": John Lydgate's Accommodation of Image and Text in Three Religious Lyrics', *Florilegium* 10 (1988-91), 167-78

Crane, S., 'Charles d'Orléans: Self-Translation', in *The Medieval Translator* 8, ed. R. Voaden (Turnhout, 2003), 169-77

Craun, E. D., *Lies, Slander and Obscenity in Medieval English Literature: Pastoral Rhetoric and the Deviant Speaker* (Cambridge, 2005)

Critten, R., 'The Political Valence of Charles d'Orléans's English Poetry', *Modern Philology* 111 (2014), 339-64

Culler, J., 'Lyric, History, and Genre', *The Lyric Theory Reader: A Critical Anthology*, ed. V. Jackson and Y. Prins (Baltimore, 2014), pp. 63-76

——*Theory of the Lyric* (Cambridge, MA, and London, 2015)

Curtius, E. R., *Literature and the Latin Middle Ages*, trans. W. R. Trask (New York, 1953)

de Certeau, M., *The Practice of Everyday Life*, trans. S. Rendall (Berkeley, CA, 1984)

Deeming, H., *Song in British Sources, c.1150-1300* (London, 2013)

Dillon, E., *The Sense of Sound: Musical Meaning in France, 1260-1300* (Oxford, 2012)

——'Unwriting Medieval Song', *New Literary History* 46 (2015), 595-622

Dinshaw, C., *Chaucer's Sexual Poetics* (Madison, WI, 1989)

Donaldson, E. T., 'The Manuscripts of Chaucer's Works and Their Use', *Geoffrey Chaucer: The Writer and his Background*, ed. D. Brewer (London, 1974), pp. 85-108

Dronke, P., *Medieval Latin and the Rise of the European Love-Lyric* (Oxford, 1965)

Dubrow, H., 'Lyric Forms', Jackson and Prins, eds, *The Lyric Theory Reader*, pp. 114-28

Duffy, E., *The Stripping of the Altars: Traditional Religion in England, c.1400-1580* (New Haven and London, 1995)

——*Marking the Hours: English People and Their Prayers 1240-1570* (New Haven, 2006)

Duncan, T. G., 'Textual Notes on Two Early Middle English Lyrics', *Neuphilologische Mitteilungen* 93 (1992), 109-20

——'Two Middle English Penitential Lyrics: Sound and Scansion', *Late-Medieval Religious Texts and Their Transmission*, ed. A. J. Minnis (Cambridge, 1994), pp. 55-65

Easting, R., '"Choose yourselves whither to go": John Audelay's *Vision of St Paul*', Fein, ed., *My Wyl and my Wrytyng*, pp. 170-90

Edwards, A. S. G., 'Lydgate Manuscripts: Some Directions for Future Research', *Manuscripts and Readers in Fifteenth-Century England*, ed. D. Pearsall (Cambridge, 1983), pp. 15-26

——'Lydgate Scholarship: Progress and Prospects', *Fifteenth-Century Studies: Recent Essays*, ed. R. F. Yeager (Hamden, 1984), pp. 29-47

——'Fifteenth-Century Middle English Verse Author Collections', *The English Medieval Book*, ed. A. S. G. Edwards, V. Gillespie and R. Hanna (London, 2000), pp. 101-12

——'Editing and Manuscript Form: Middle English Verse Written as Prose', *English Studies in Canada* 27: 1-2 (2001), 15-28

——'John Shirley, John Lydgate, and the Motives of Compilation', *Studies in the Age of Chaucer* 38 (2016), 245-54

Fallows, D., *A Catalogue of Polyphonic Songs* (Oxford, 1999)

Farvolden, P. and S. R. Reimer, 'Of Arms and the Manuscript: The Date and Provenance of Harley 2255', *Journal of the Early Book Society for the Study of Manuscripts and Printing History* 8 (2005), 239-60

Fein, S. G., 'A Thirteen-Line Stanza on the Abuse of Prayer from the Audelay MS', *Medium Aevum* 63 (1994), 61-74

——'Roll or Codex? The Diptych Layout of Thomas of Hales's *Love Rune*', *Trivium* 31 (1999), 13-23

——ed., *Studies in the Harley Manuscript; The Scribes, Contents, and Social Contexts of British Library, MS Harley 2253*, TEAMS (Kalamazoo, MI, 2000)

——'Good Ends in the Audelay Manuscript', *Yearbook of English Studies* 33 (2003), 97-119

——ed., *My Wyl and my Wrytyng: Essays on John the Blind Audelay* (Kalamazoo, MI, 2009)
——'John Audelay and his Book: Critical Overview and Major Issues', Fein, ed., *My Wyl and my Wrytyng*, pp. 3–29
——'Mary to Veronica: John Audelay's Sequence of Salutations to God-Bearing Women', *Speculum* 86 (2011), 964–1009
——'The Fillers of the Auchinleck Manuscript and the Literary Culture of the West Midlands', *Makers and Users of Medieval Books: Essays in Honour of A. S. G. Edwards*, ed. C. M. Meale and D. Pearsall (Cambridge, 2014), pp. 60–77
——, ed., *The Auchinleck Manuscript: New Perspectives* (York, 2016)
Flannery, M. C., 'The Concept of Shame in Late-Medieval English Literature', *Literature Compass* 9 (2012), 166–82
Fleming, J., *Classical Imitation and Interpretation in Chaucer's 'Troilus'* (Lincoln, NE, 1990)
Fletcher, A. J., 'The Lyric in the Sermon', Duncan, *Companion*, pp. 189–209
Fokkelman, J. P., 'Genesis', *The Literary Guide to the Bible*, ed. R. Alter and F. Kermode (London, 1987), pp. 36–55
——'Exodus', *The Literary Guide to the Bible*, ed. R. Alter and F. Kermode (London, 1987), pp. 56–65
Forshall, J., ed., *Catalogue of Manuscripts in the British Museum*, 3 vols (London, 1834–41)
Foucault, M., *Technologies of the Self: A Seminar with Michel Foucault*, ed. L. H. Martin, H. Gutman and P. H. Hutton (Amherst, 1988)
Frankis, J., 'The Social Context of Vernacular Writing in Thirteenth Century England: The Evidence of the Manuscripts', *Thirteenth Century England I: Proceedings of the Newcastle upon Tyne Conference 1985*, ed. P. R. Coss and S. D. Lloyd (Woodbridge, 1986), pp. 175–84
Frye, N., *Anatomy of Criticism: Four Essays* (Princeton, 1957)
Fuller, D., 'Lyrics, Sacred and Secular', *A Companion to Medieval Poetry*, ed. Corinne Saunders (Chichester, 2010), pp. 258–76
Fumo, J. C., *The Legacy of Apollo: Antiquity, Authority and Chaucerian Poetics* (Toronto, 2010)
Gattinger, E., *Die Lyrik Lydgates*, Wiener Beiträge zur Englischen Philologie 4 (Vienna, 1896)
Gavrilyuk, P. and S. Coakley, eds, *The Spiritual Senses: Perceiving God in Western Christianity* (Cambridge, 2012)
Gayk, S., 'Images of Pity: The Regulatory Aesthetics of John Lydgate's Religious Lyrics', *Studies in the Age of Chaucer* 28 (2006), 175–203
Gerhardt, C., *Die Metamorphosen des Pelikans: Exempel und Auslegung in der mittelalterlichen Literatur* (Frankfurt am Main, 1979)
Gillespie, V., 'Moral and Penitential Lyrics', Duncan, *Companion*, pp. 68–95
——*Looking in Holy Books: Essays on Late Medieval Religious Writing in England* (Turnhout, 2011)
——'The Colours of Contemplation: Less Light on Julian of Norwich', *The Medieval Mystical Tradition in England, VIII*, ed. E. A. Jones (Cambridge, 2013), pp. 7–28
——'The Senses in Literature: The Textures of Perception', *A Cultural History of the Senses in the Middle Ages*, ed. R. G. Newhauser (London, 2014), pp. 155–73
——'Songs of the Threshold: *Enargeia* and the Psalter', *The Psalms and Medieval English Literature From the Conversion to the Reformation*, ed. T. Atkin and F. Leneghan (Cambridge, 2017), pp. 271–97
Gougaud, L., *Dévotions et pratiques ascétiques du moyen âge* (Paris, 1925)
Gray, D., 'The Five Wounds of Our Lord', *Notes and Queries* 208 (1963), 50–1, 82–9, 127–34, 163–8

——'A Middle English Illustrated Poem', *Medieval Studies for J. A. W. Bennett*, ed P. L. Heyworth (Oxford, 1981), pp. 185–205
——'The Medieval Religious Lyric', *The Blackwell Companion to the Bible in English Literature*, ed. by R. Lemon, E. Mason, J. Roberts and C. Rowland (Chichester, 2009), pp. 76–84
——*Simple Forms: Essays on Medieval English Popular Literature* (Oxford, 2015)
Greenblatt, S., *Renaissance Self-Fashioning: From More to Shakespeare* (Chicago, 1980)
Greene, R., et al., eds, *Princeton Encyclopedia of Poetry and Poetics*, 4th edn (Princeton, 2012)
Greene, T., *The Light in Troy: Imitation and Discovery in Renaissance Poetry* (New Haven, 1982)
Greentree, R., *Annotated Bibliographies of Old and Middle English Literature, VII: The Middle English Lyric and Short Poem* (Cambridge, 2001)
Hage, S. J., *Let There Be Light: Physics, Philosophy, and the Dimensional Structure of Consciousness* (New York, 2013)
Hamburger, J., *Nuns as Artists: The Visual Culture of a Medieval Convent* (Berkeley, 1997)
Hammond, E. P., 'Two British Museum Manuscripts: A Contribution to the Bibliography of John Lydgate', *Anglia* 28 (1905), 1–28
——'Two Tapestry Poems by Lydgate', *Englische Studien* 43 (1910–11), 10–26
Hand, J. M., *Women, Manuscripts and Identity in Northern Europe, 1350–1550* (Farnham, 2013)
Hanna, R., 'The Origins and Production of Westminster School MS 3', *Studies in Bibliography* 41 (1988), 197–218
——*A Descriptive Catalogue of the Western Manuscripts of St John's College, Oxford* (Oxford, 2002)
——'Takamiya MS 15: Some Liminal Observations', *The Medieval Book and a Modern Collector: Essays in Honour of Toshiyuki Takamiya*, ed. T. Matsuda, R. A. Linenthal and J. Scahill (Cambridge, 2004), pp. 125–34
——*The English Manuscripts of Richard Rolle: A Descriptive Catalogue* (Exeter, 2010)
——'Editing "Middle English Lyrics": The Case of *Candet Nudatum Pectus*', *Medium Aevum* 80 (2011), 189–200
Hargreaves, H., 'Lydgate's *A Rams' Horn*', *Chaucer Review* 10 (1976), 255–9
Harrier, R., *The Canon of Sir Thomas Wyatt's Poetry* (Cambridge, MA, 1975)
Heffernan, T., 'Early Middle English Sermons and Homilies', *A Manual of the Writings in Middle English 1050–1500*, Vol. 11, ed. P. G. Beidler (New Haven, 2005), pp. 3996–4056
Heslop, T. A., 'The English Origins of the Coronation of the Virgin', *Burlington Magazine* 147 (2005), 790–7
Heuser, W., 'With an O and an I', *Anglia* 27 (1904), 283–319
Hill, B., 'The History of Jesus College, Oxford MS. 29', *Medium Ævum* 32 (1963), 203–13
——'Oxford, Jesus College MS 29, Part II: Contents, Technical Matters, Compilation, and Its History to c.1695', *Notes and Queries* 50 (2003), 268–76
Hill, C. S., *Consciousness* (Leiden, 2009)
Hillier, R. M., 'The Wreath, the Rock and the Winepress: Passion Iconography in Milton's *Paradise Regain'd*', *Literature and Theology* 22 (2008), 387–405
Hirsh, J. C., *The Boundaries of Faith: The Development and Transmission of Medieval Spirituality* (Leiden, 1996)
Hirschbiegel, J., *Étrennes: Untersuchungen zum höfischen Geschenkverkehr im spätmittelalterlichen Frankreich zur Zeit König Karls VI (1380–1422)* (Munich, 2003)
Holsinger, B., 'Liturgy', Strohm, ed., *Middle English*, pp. 295–314
Horobin, S., '"In London and in Opelond": The Dialect and Circulation of the C Version of *Piers Plowman*', *Medium Aevum* 74 (2005), 248–69

Hošek, C. and P. A. Parker, eds, *Lyric Poetry: Beyond New Criticism* (Ithaca, NY, 1985)
Howes, H. E., 'In Search of Clearer Water: An Exploration of Water Imagery in Late Medieval Devotional Prose', Unpublished Ph.D. thesis, Queen Mary University of London, 2016
Hughes-Hughes, A., *Catalogue of Manuscript Music in the British Museum*, 3 vols (London, 1964–66)
Hunt, R. W. and F. F. Madan, *A Summary Catalogue of Western Manuscripts in the Bodleian Library at Oxford* (Oxford, 1953)
Hunt, T., 'Insular Trilingual Compilations', *Codices Miscellanearum*, ed. R. Jansen-Sieben and H. van Dijk, Archives et Bibliothèques de Belgique 60 (Brussels, 1999), 51–70
Hyland, P., *An Introduction to Shakespeare's Poems* (London, 2002)
Jackson, V. and Y. Prins, eds, *The Lyric Theory Reader: A Critical Anthology* (Baltimore, 2014)
Jahner, J., 'The Poetry of the Second Barons' War: Some Manuscript Contexts', *English Manuscript Studies, 1100–1700*, 17 (2013), 201–22
James, M. R., *A Descriptive Catalogue of the Manuscripts in the Library of Eton College* (Cambridge, 1895)
——*The Western Manuscripts in the Library of Trinity College, Cambridge: A Descriptive Catalogue*, 4 vols (Cambridge, 1900–04)
——*A Descriptive Catalogue of the Manuscripts in the Library of St John's College, Cambridge* (Cambridge, 1913)
Jefferson, J., A. Putter and M. Stokes, *Studies in the Metres of Alliterative Verse* (Oxford, 2007)
——and A. Putter, eds, *Approaches to the Metres of Alliterative Verse* (Leeds, 2009)
Jeffrey, D. L., *The Early English Lyric and Franciscan Spirituality* (Lincoln, NE, 1975)
Jennings, M., *Tutivillus: The Literary Career of the Recording Demon*, Texts and Studies 1977, *Studies in Philology* 74:5 (1977)
Johnson, H., *The Grammar of Good Friday: Macaronic Sermons of Late Medieval England* (Turnhout, 2012)
Jolliffe, P. S., *A Check-List of Middle English Prose Writings of Spiritual Guidance* (Toronto, 1974)
Katzenellenbogen, A., *The Sculptural Programs of Chartres Cathedral: Christ, Mary, Ecclesia* (Baltimore, 1959)
Kehnel, A., 'Poets, Preachers and Friars Revisited: Fourteenth-Century Multilingual Franciscan Manuscripts', *The Beginnings of Standardization: Language and Culture in Fourteenth-Century England*, ed. U. Schaefer (Frankfurt am Main, 2006), pp. 91–114
Kelly, D., *Medieval Imagination: Rhetoric and the Poetry of Courtly Love* (London, 1978)
Ker, N. R., *Medieval Manuscripts in British Libraries, II, Abbotsford–Keele* (Oxford, 1977)
Kerby-Fulton, K. and D. L. Despres, *Iconography and the Professional Reader: The Politics of Book Production in the Douce 'Piers Plowman'* (Minneapolis, 1999)
Kern, P., *Trinität, Maria, Inkarnation: Studien zur Thematik der deutschen. Dichtung des späteren Mittelalters* (Berlin, 1972)
King, P., 'Rules of Exchange in Medieval Plays and Play Manuscripts', *Literature as Dialogue: Invitations Offered and Negotiated*, ed. R. D. Sell (Amsterdam, 2014), pp. 177–96
Kinney, C. R., 'Who Made this Song?: The Engendering of Lyric Counterplots in *Troilus and Criseyde*', *Studies in Philology* 89 (1991), 272–92
Kirwin, G. F., 'Queenship of Mary: Queen-Mother', *Marian Library Studies* 28 (2007), 37–320
Kitzinger, E., 'A Virgin's Face: Antiquarianism in Twelfth-Century Art', *Art Bulletin* 62 (1980), 6–19

Bibliography

Knight, S., *Rymyng craftily: Meaning in Chaucer's Poetry* (Sydney and London, 1973)

Kovâcs, É., 'Le Reliquaire de l'ordre du Saint-Esprit. La "dot" d' Anne de Bretagne', *Revue du Louvre* 31 (1981), 246–51

Kowalik, B., *Betwixt 'engelaunde' and 'englene londe': Dialogic Poetics in Early English Religious Lyric* (Bern, 2010)

Krebber, G. B. and G. Kotting, 'Jean Bellegambe en zijn Mystiek Bad vor Anchin', *Oud Holland* 104 (1990), 123–39

Kuczynski, M. P., 'Theological Sophistication and the Middle English Religious Lyric: A Polemic', *Chaucer Review* 45 (2011), 321–39

La Favia, L. M., *The Man of Sorrows: its Origins and Development in Trecento Florentine Painting* (Rome, 1980)

Lawrence, M., 'Maria Regina', *Art Bulletin* 7 (1925), 150–61

Lawton, D., 'Dullness and the Fifteenth Century', *English Literary History* 54 (1987), 761–99

——'Voice After Arundel', *After Arundel: Religious Writing in Fifteenth-Century England*, ed. V. Gillespie and K. Ghosh (Turnhout, 2011), 133–51

——'Public Interiorities', *A Handbook of Middle English Studies*, ed. M. Turner (Chichester, 2013), pp. 93–107

Lazikani, A. S., *Cultivating the Heart: Feeling and Emotion in Twelfth- and Thirteenth-Century Religious Texts* (Cardiff, 2015)

Leach, E. E., *Sung Birds: Music, Nature and Poetry in the Later Middle Ages* (Ithaca, NY, 2007)

——and H. Deeming, *Manuscripts and Medieval Song: Inscription, Performance, Context* (Cambridge, 2015)

Leclercq, J., *The Love of Learning and the Desire for God*, 3rd edn (New York, 1982)

Lehrer, E., *Demons, Death and Damnation* (New York, 1971)

Lerer, S., 'Artifice and Artistry in *Sir Orfeo*', *Speculum* 60 (1985), 92–109

——'The Genre of the Grave and the Origins of the Middle English Lyric', Jackson and Prins, eds, *The Lyric Theory Reader*, pp. 104–13

Levine, C., *Forms: Whole, Rhythm, Hierarchy, Network* (Princeton, 2015)

Lewis, C. S., *English Literature in the Sixteenth Century, Excluding Drama* (Oxford, 1954)

Lindley, D., *Lyric* (London, 1985)

Lochrie, K., *Covert Operations: The Medieval Uses of Secrecy* (Philadelphia, 1999)

MacCracken, H. N., 'New Stanzas by Dunbar', *Modern Language Notes* 24 (1909), 110–11

McAvoy, L. H., 'Bathing in Blood: The Medicinal Cures of Anchoritic Devotion', *Medicine, Religion and Gender in Medieval Culture*, ed. N. K. Yoshikawa (Cambridge, 2015) pp. 85–102

McGovern-Mouron, A., 'The Desert of Religion in British Library Cotton Faustina B VI, Pars II', *The Mystical Tradition and the Carthusians*, ed. J. Hogg (Salzburg, 1997), pp. 149–62

McGrade, M., 'Enriching the Gregorian Heritage', *A Cambridge Companion to Medieval Music*, ed. M. Everist (Cambridge, 2011), pp. 26–45

McGuire, B. P., 'c.1080–1215: Culture and History', *The Cambridge Companion to Medieval English Mysticism*, ed. S. Fanous and V. Gillespie (Cambridge, 2011), pp. 29–47

McIntosh, A. and M. L. Samuels, 'Prolegomena to a Study of Mediaeval Anglo-Irish', *Medium Aevum* 37 (1968), 1–11

——M. L. Samuels and M. Benskin, eds, *A Linguistic Atlas of Late Mediaeval English*, 4 vols (Aberdeen, 1986)

McNamer, S., 'Feeling', Strohm, ed., *Middle English*, pp. 241–57

——*Affective Meditation and the Invention of Medieval Compassion* (Philadelphia, 2010)

McTaggart, A., *Shame and Guilt in Chaucer* (New York, 2012)

Machan, T. W., *Textual Criticism and Middle English Texts* (Charlottesville, 1994)
Macray, W. D., et al., *Bodleian Library Quarto Catalogues. 9, Digby Manuscripts* (Oxford, 1999 [reproducing 1883 catalogue])
Mâle, E., *L'Art religieux du XIIe siècle en France*, 4th edn (Paris, 1940)
——ed. H. Bober, *Religious Art in France, the Late Middle Ages: A Study of Medieval Iconography and its Sources*, trans. M. Matthews (Princeton, 1984)
——ed. H. Bober, *Religious Art in France: The Thirteenth Century*, trans. M. Mathews (Princeton, 1984)
Mann, J., 'Troilus's Swoon', *Critical Essays on Chaucer's 'Troilus and Criseyde' and his Major Early Poems*, ed. C. D. Benson (Toronto, 1991), pp. 149–64
Mannyng, S., *Wisdom and Number* (Lincoln, NE, 1962)
Marrow, J. H., *Passion Iconography in Northern European Art of the Late Middle Ages and Early Renaissance: A Study of the Transformation of Sacred Metaphor into Descriptive Narrative* (Kortrijk, 1979)
Martz, L., *The Poetry of Meditation: A Study of English Religious Literature of the Seventeenth Century* (New Haven, 1954)
Matter, E. A., *The Voice of My Beloved: The Song of Songs in Western Medieval Christianity* (Philadelphia, 1990)
Meersseman, G. G., *Der Hymnos Akathistos im Abendland*, 2 vols (Freiburg, 1958–60)
Mellon, J., *The Virgin Mary in the Perceptions of Women: Mother, Protector and Queen Since the Middle Ages* (Jefferson, NC, 2008)
Meyer-Lee, R., *Poets and Power from Chaucer to Wyatt* (Cambridge, 2007)
——'The Vatic Penitent: John Audelay's Self-Representation', Fein, ed., *My Wyl and my Wrytyng*, pp. 54–85
Minnis, A. J., *Medieval Theory of Authorship: Scholastic Literary Attitudes in the Late Middle Ages*, 2nd edn (Aldershot, 1988)
Mooney, L. R., 'Lydgate's "Kings of England" and Another Verse Chronicle of the Kings', *Viator* 20 (1989), 255–89
——Scribes and Booklets of Trinity College, Cambridge, Manuscripts R. 3.19 and R 3.21', *Middle English Poetry: Texts and Traditions*, ed. A. J. Minnis (York, 2001), pp. 241–66
Morgan, N., 'An SS Collar in the Devotional Context of the Shield of the Five Wounds', *The Lancastrian Court: Proceedings of the 2001 Harlaxton Symposium*, ed. J. Stratford (Donington, 2003), pp. 147–62
Mortimer, N., *John Lydgate's 'Fall of Princes': Narrative Tragedy in its Literary and Political Contexts* (Oxford, 2005)
Naughton, J., 'A Minimally-Intrusive Presence: Portraits in Illustrations for Prayers to the Virgin', *Medieval Texts and Images: Studies of Manuscripts from the Middle Ages*, ed. M. Manion and B. J. Muir (Chur, 1991), 111–26
Nelson, I., *Lyric Tactics: Poetry, Genre, and Practice in Later Medieval England* (Philadelphia, 2016)
Nichols, A. E., 'O Vernicle: Illustrations of an Arma Christi Poem', *Tributes to Kathleen L. Scott: English Medieval Manuscripts and Their Readers*, ed. M. V. Hennessy (Turnhout, 2009), pp. 139–70
Nilgen, U., 'Maria Regina: ein politischer Kultbildtypus?', *Römisches Jarbuch für Kunstgeschichte* 19 (1981), 1–33
O'Kane, M., 'Picturing "The Man of Sorrows": the Passion-Filled Afterlives of a Biblical Icon', *Religion and the Arts* 9 (2005), 62–100
Onions, C. T., ed., *The Oxford Dictionary of English Etymology* (Oxford, 1966)
Ouy, G., 'Un poème mystique de Charles d'Orléans: le *Canticum amoris*', *Studi francesi* 7 (1959), 64–84

—'Charles d'Orléans and his Brother Jean d'Angoulême in England: What their Manuscripts Have to Tell', Arn, ed., *Charles d'Orléans in England*, pp. 47–60

—*La librairie des frères captifs: les manuscrits de Charles d'Orléans et Jean d'Angoulême*, Texte, codex et contexte, 4 (Turnhout, 2007)

Panofsky, E., *Early Netherlandish Painting: Its Origins and Character*, 2 vols (Cambridge, MA, 1953)

Parkes, M. B., 'The Influence of the Concepts of *Ordinatio* and *Compilatio* on the Development of the Book', in *Medieval Learning and the Book: Essays Presented to Richard William Hunt*, ed. J. J. G. Alexander and M. T. Gibson (Oxford, 1976), pp. 115–41

—*Pause and Effect: A History of Punctuation in the West* (Aldershot, 1992)

Patterson, L. W., *Chaucer and the Subject of History* (Madison, WI, 1991)

Paulino, F. F. and R. Osório eds, *Tesouros Artísticos da Misericórdia do Porto* (Porto, 1995)

Pearsall, D., *John Lydgate* (London, 1970)

—*Old English and Middle English Poetry* (London, 1977)

—'Chaucer and Lydgate', *Chaucer Traditions: Studies in Honour of Derek Brewer*, ed. R. Morse and B. Windeatt (Cambridge, 1990), pp. 39–53

—'Audelay's *Marcolf and Solomon* and the Langlandian Tradition', Fein, ed., *My Wyl and my Wrytyng*, pp. 138–52

Pelikan, J., *Mary Through the Centuries: Her Place in the History of Culture* (New Haven and London, 1996)

Petrina, A., 'One Bowl, Two Eaters: Medieval Eating Habits in the "Babees' Books"', *A Garland of True Plain Words: saggi in onore di Paola Bottalla*, ed. A. Oboe and A. Scacchi (Padua, 2012), pp. 231–47

—'Creative *ymagynacioun* and Canon Constraints in the Fifteenth Century: James I and Charles d'Orléans', *Inspiration and Technique: Ancient to Modern Views on Beauty and Art*, ed. J. Roe and M. Stanco (Bern, 2007), pp. 107–25

Pezzini, D., '"How Resoun Schal Be Keper of þe Soule": Una Tradizione del Quattrocento Inglese Dalle Rivelazioni (VII, 5) di S. Brigida di Svezia', *Aevum* 60 (1986), 253–81

Phillips, H., '"Almighty and al merciable Queene": Marian Titles and Marian Lyrics', *Medieval Women: Texts and Contexts in Late Medieval Britain. Essays for Felicity Riddy*, ed. J. Wogan-Browne et al. (Turnhout, 2000), pp. 83–99

Phillips, Susan E., '"Janglynge in Cherche": Gossip and the *Exemplum*', *The Hands of the Tongue: Essays on Deviant Speech*, ed. E. D. Craun (Kalamazoo, 2007), pp. 61–94

—*Transforming Talk: The Problem with Gossip in Late Medieval England* (University Park, PA, 2007)

Pickering, O., 'The Make-Up of Counsel of Conscience', Fein, ed., *My Wyl and my Wrytyng*, pp. 112–37

Poirion, D., *Le poète et le prince : L'évolution du lyrisme courtois de Guillaume de Machaut à Charles d'Orléans* (Paris, 1965)

Pound, E., 'How to Read', *Literary Essays of Ezra Pound*, ed. T. S. Eliot (London, 1954), pp. 15–40

Putter, A., 'The Language and Metre of *Pater Noster* and *Three Dead Kings*', *Review of English Studies* 55 (2004), 498–526

Rahner, H., 'Flumina de ventre Christi: Die patristiche Auslegung von Joh. 7, 37.38', *Biblica* 22 (1941), 269–302, 362–403

Raskolnikov, M., 'Confessional Literature, Vernacular Psychology, and the History of the Self in Middle English', *Literature Compass* 2 (2005), 1–20

Reichl, K., *Religiöse Dichtung im Englischen Hochmittelalter: Untersuchung und Edition der Handschrift B. 14.39 des Trinity College in Cambridge* (Munich, 1973)

Reiss, E., *The Art of the Middle English Lyric* (Athens, GA, 1972)

Renevey, D., 'Enclosed Desires: A Study of the Wooing Group', *Mysticism and Spirituality in Medieval England*, ed. W. F. Pollard and R. Boenig (Cambridge, 1997), pp. 39–62
—— 'Name Above Names: The Devotion to the Name of Jesus from Richard Rolle to Walter Hilton's *Scale of Perfection* I', *The Medieval Mystical Tradition – England, Ireland and Wales: Exeter Symposium VI*, ed. M. Glasscoe (Cambridge, 1999), pp. 103–22
Rentz, E. K., *Imagining the Parish in Late Medieval England* (Columbus, OH, 2015)
Rézeau, P., *Les prières aux saints en français à la fin du moyen age: introduction, les prières à plusieurs saints* (Geneva, 1982)
Riccioni, S., 'The Word in the Image: An Epiconographic Analysis of Mosaics of the Reform in Rome (Twelfth-Century)', *Inscriptions in Liturgical Spaces*, ed. K. B. Aavitsland and T. K. Seim (Rome, 2011), pp. 85–137
Riehle, W., *The Middle English Mystics*, trans. B. Standring (London, 1981)
Robilliard, J.-A., 'Face (dévotion à la Sainte Face)', *Dictionnaire de spiritualité: ascétique et mystique, doctrine et historique*, ed. M. Viller et al., 17 vols (Paris, 1937–95), V, pp. 26–33
Rosewell, R., *Medieval Wall Paintings in English and Welsh Churches* (Woodbridge, 2008)
Ross, E. M., *The Grief of God: Images of the Suffering Jesus in Late Medieval England* (Oxford, 1997)
Rubin, M., *Mother of God: A History of the Virgin Mary* (London, 2010)
Rust, M. D., 'The ABC of Aristotle', *Medieval Literature for Children*, ed. D. T. Kline (London, 2003), pp. 63–7
—— *Imaginary Worlds in Medieval Books: Exploring the Manuscript Matrix* (New York, 2007)
Salzer, A., *Die Sinnbilder und Beiworte Mariens in der deutschen Literatur und lateinischen Hymnenpoesie des Mittelalters* (Linz, 1898)
Sawyer, D., 'Codicological Evidence of Reading in Late Medieval England, with Particular Reference to Practical Pastoral Verse', unpublished D.Phil. thesis, University of Oxford, 2016
Scaramuzzi, D., '"*Totius Trinitatis* Nobile Triclinium". Maria e la Trinità', *Rivista di Scienze Religiose* 1 (1987), 257–91
Schirmer, W. F., *John Lydgate: A Study in the Culture of the XVth Century*, trans. A. E. Keep (Westport, CT, 1961)
Schmidt, A. V. C., review of '*Piers Plowman: A Facsimile of Bodleian Library, Oxford, MS Douce 104*, with an introduction by Derek Pearsall and a catalogue of the illustrations by K. Scott', *Medium Aevum* 63 (1994), 128–30
Schönborn, C., *God's Human Face: The Christ-Icon*, trans. L. Krauth (San Francisco, 1994)
Scott, K., 'The Illustrations of *Piers Plowman* in Bodleian Library MS. Douce 104', *Yearbook of Langland Studies* 4 (1990), 1–86
Simpson, J., *Reform and Cultural Revolution: The Oxford English Literary History, Volume 2: 1350–1547* (Oxford, 2002)
—— 'Saving Satire after Arundel's *Constitutions*: John Audelay's *Marcof and Solomon*', *Text and Controversy from Wyclif to Bale: Essays in Honour of Anne Hudson*, ed. H. Barr and A. M. Hutchison, Medieval Church Studies 4 (Turnhout, 2004), pp. 387–404
Sisam, C., 'The Broken Leaf in MS. Jesus College, Oxford, 29', *Review of English Studies*, NS 5 (1954), 337–43
Smith, K. A., *Art, Identity and Devotion in Fourteenth-Century England* (London, 2003)
Smith, M. A., *From Sight to Light: the Passage from Ancient to Modern Optics* (Chicago, 2015)
Smith, R. M., 'Three Obscure English Proverbs', *Modern Language Notes* 65 (1950), 441–7
Solopova, E., 'Layout, Punctuation, and Stanza Patterns in the English Verse', Fein, ed., *Studies in the Harley Manuscript*, pp. 377–89

Somerset, F., '"Al þe comonys with o voys atonys": Multilingual Latin and Vernacular Voice in *Piers Plowman*', *Yearbook of Langland Studies* 19 (2005), 107–36

Spearing, A. C., 'Prison, Writing, Absence: Representing the Subject in the English Poems of Charles d'Orléans', *Modern Language Quarterly* 53 (1992), 83–99

——*The Medieval Poet as Voyeur: Looking and Listening in Medieval Love-Narratives* (Cambridge, 1993)

——*Textual Subjectivity: The Encoding of Subjectivity in Medieval Narratives and Lyrics* (Oxford, 2005)

Spitzer, L., '*Explication de texte* Applied to Three Great Middle English Poems', *Archivum Linguisticum* 3 (1951), 1–22, 157–65

Stanbury, S., 'The Virgin's Gaze: Spectacle and Transgression in Middle English Lyrics of the Passion', *PMLA* 106 (1991), 1083–93

Stanley, E. G., 'The Verse Forms of Jon the Blynde Awdelay', *The Long Fifteenth Century: Essays for Douglas Gray*, ed. H. Cooper and S. Mapstone (Oxford, 1997), pp. 99–121

Stevens, J. E., *Music and Poetry in the Early Tudor Period* (London, 1961, repr. Cambridge, 1979)

——*The Old Sound and the New: An Inaugural Lecture* (Cambridge, 1982)

——*Words and Music in the Middle Ages: Song, Narrative, Dance and Drama, 1050–1350* (Cambridge, 1986)

Stratford, J., *Richard II and the English Royal Treasure* (Woodbridge, 2013)

Strohm, P., ed., *Middle English: Twenty-First Century Approaches to Literature* (Oxford, 2007)

Stroll, M., 'Maria Regina: Papal Symbol', *Queens and Queenship in Medieval Europe*, ed. A. J. Duggan (Woodbridge, 1997), pp. 173–203

Summers, J., *Late-Medieval Prison Writing and the Politics of Autobiography* (Oxford, 2004)

Taburet-Delahaye, E. and F. Avril, eds, *Paris 1400. Les arts sous Charles VI* (Paris, 2004)

Takamiya, T., 'Richard and Robert as False Executors in Late Medieval England', *Anglistik* 8 (1997), 49–59

——'"On the Evils of Covetousness": an Unrecorded Middle English Poem', *New Science Out of Old Books: Studies in Manuscripts and Early Printed Books in Honour of A. I. Doyle*, ed. R. Beadle and A. J. Piper (Aldershot, 1995), pp. 189–206

Taylor, K., 'Proverbs and the Authentication of Convention in *Troilus and Criseyde*', *Chaucer's Troilus: Essays in Criticism*, ed. S. A. Barney (London, 1980), pp. 277–96

Thain, M., ed., *The Lyric Poem* (Cambridge, 2013)

Timmerman, A., 'A View of the Eucharist on the Eve of the Protestant Reformation', *A Companion to the Eucharist in the Reformation*, ed. L. P. Wandel (Leiden, 2014), pp. 365–98

Trigg, S., *Shame and Honor: A Vulgar History of the Order of the Garter* (Philadelphia, 2012)

Tristram, P., *Figures of Life and Death in Medieval English Literature* (London, 1976)

Tronzo, W., 'Apse Decoration, the Liturgy, and the Perception of Art in Medieval Rome. S. Maria in Trastevere and S. Maria Maggiore', *Italian Church Decoration of the Middle Ages and Early Renaissance: Functions, Form and Regional Tradition*, ed. W. Tronzo (Baltimore, 1989), pp. 167–93

Underhill, E., 'The Fountain of Life: An Iconographic Study', *Burlington Magazine* 17 (1910), 99–109

Underwood, P., 'The Fountain of Life in Manuscripts of the Gospels', *Dumbarton Oak Papers* 5 (1950), 41–138

Vanuxem, J., 'Autour du triomphe de la Vierge du portail de la cathédrale de Senlis. Les portails détruits de la cathédrale de Cambrai et de Saint-Nicolas d'Amiens', *Bulletin monumental* 103 (1945), 89–102

Verdier, P., 'Suger a-t-il été en France le créateur du thème iconographique du couronnement de la Vierge?', *Gesta* 15 (1976), 227–36

——*Le couronnement de la Vierge. Les origines et les premiers développements d'un thème iconographique* (Montreal and Paris, 1980)

Walther, H., *Initia Carminum ac Versuum Medii Aevi Posterioris Latinorum* (Göttingen, 1959)

Watson, N., *Richard Rolle and the Invention of Authority* (Cambridge, 1991)

Wellen, G. A., 'Sponsa Christi: Het absismozaiek van de Santa Maria in Trastevere te Rome en het Hooglied', in *Feestbundel F. van der Meer*, ed. E. F. van der Grinten et al. (Amsterdam and Brussels, 1966), pp. 148–59

Wellesley, M., 'Static "Menyng" and Transitory "Melodye" in Lydgate's *Seying of The Nightingale*', in *Stasis in the Medieval West: Questioning Change and Continuity*, ed. M. Bintley et al., The New Middle Ages (New York, 2017), pp. 231–51

Welsh, A., *Roots of Lyric* (Princeton, 1978)

Wenzel, S., *The Sin of Sloth: Acedia in Medieval Thought and Literature* (Chapel Hill, 1960)

——*Verses in Sermons: 'Fasciculus Morum' and its Middle English Poems* (Cambridge, MA, 1978)

——*Preachers, Poets, and the Early English Lyric* (Princeton, 1986)

Whitehead, C., 'Middle English Religious Lyrics', Duncan, *Companion*, pp. 96–119

Whiting, B. J., *Proverbs, Sentences and Proverbial Phrases From English Writings Mainly Before 1500* (Cambridge, MA, 1968)

Wilson, E., *A Descriptive Index of the English Lyrics in John of Grimestone's Preaching Book*, Medium Aevum Monographs NS 2 (Oxford, 1973)

Wimsatt, W. K., *The Verbal Icon: Studies in the Meaning of Poetry* (Lexington, KY, 1954)

Windeatt, B., *Oxford Guides to Chaucer: Troilus and Criseyde* (Oxford, 1992)

Woolf, R., 'The Theme of Christ the Lover-Knight in Medieval English Literature', *Review of English Studies* 13 (1962), 1–16

Yoshikawa, N. K., 'Mysticism and Medicine: Holy Communion in the *Vita of Marie d'Oignies* and *The Book of Margery Kempe*', *Poetica* 72 (2009), 109–22

Zarnecki, G., 'The Coronation of the Virgin on a Capital from Reading Abbey', *Journal of the Warburg and Courtauld Institutes* 13 (1950), 1–12

Zeeman, N., 'Imaginative Theory', Strohm, ed., *Middle English*, pp. 222–40

——'The Theory of Passionate Song', *Medieval Latin and Middle English Literature: Essays in Honour of Jill Mann*, ed. C. Cannon and M. Nolan (Cambridge, 2011), pp. 231–51

Zieman, K., *Singing the New Song: Literacy and Liturgy in Late Medieval England* (Philadelphia, 2008)

——'The Perils of *Canor*: Mystical Authority, Alliteration, and Extragrammatical Meaning in Rolle, the *Cloud-Author*, and Hilton', *Yearbook of Langland Studies* 22 (2008), 133–66

Zumthor, P., *Essai de poétique médiévale* (Paris, 1972), trans. Philip Bennett, *Towards a Medieval Poetics* (Minneapolis, 1992)

Index of Manuscripts

Aberdeen, University Library, MS 25 (the Burnet Psalter), 117
Cambridge, Fitzwilliam Museum, MS McLean 125n, 134, 182
Cambridge, Jesus College, MS 56, 125n
Cambridge, St John's College, MS 111, 229–30, 234
Cambridge, Trinity College, MS B. 14. 39, 31–44, 218n
Cambridge, Trinity College, MS O. 2. 40, 25, 26
Cambridge, Trinity College, MS R. 3. 20, 197
Cambridge, Trinity College, MS R. 3. 21, 125n, 134, 135–6
Cambridge, University Library, MS Dd. 14. 2, 199n
Cambridge, University Library, MS Hh. 4. 12, 146n
Chantilly, Musée Condé, MS 65 (*Les Très Riches Heures du Duc de Berry*), 114
Dublin, Trinity College, MS 301, 233–4
Edinburgh, National Library of Scotland, Advocates' MS 18. 7. 21, 4, 18, 141–57
London, British Library, Printed Book IB. 55242, 25
London, British Library, Additional MS 17492, 261–71
London, British Library, Additional MS 20059, 109–21
London, British Library, Additional MS 27909, 20–1
London, British Library, Additional MS 37049, 7, 158–73
London, British Library, Additional MS 46919, 87–98
London, British Library, Additional MS 60577, 189–200
London, British Library, Arundel MS 248, 237
London, British Library, Arundel MS 286, 99–108
London, British Library, Cotton MS Appendix XXVII, 125n
London, British Library, Cotton MS Faustina B VI, 170
London, British Library, Cotton MS Caligula A IX, 217–20
London, British Library, Cotton MS Nero A XIV, 73–86
London, British Library, Cotton MS Titus D XVIII, 75n
London, British Library, Egerton MS 2711, 262n
London, British Library, Egerton MS 3883, 130
London, British Library, Harley MS 682, 201–10
London, British Library, Harley MS 2251, 196–7
London, British Library, Harley MS 2253, 8, 9, 19, 38, 79, 222, 224, 227n, 232, 234
London, British Library, Harley MS 2255, 122–37
London, British Library, Royal MS 2 F VIII, 19
London, British Library, Royal MS 8 F II, 232, 233
London, British Library, Royal MS 10 A IX, 244n
London, British Library, Royal MS 12 E I, 227–39
London, British Library, Royal MS A XXVII, 76n
London, British Library, Sloane MS 2593, 22–4
London, Lambeth Palace, MS 557, 143, 147–9, 152

Index of Manuscripts

London, Lambeth Palace, MS 853, 142
Maidstone Museum, MS A. 13, 218n
New Haven, Yale University, Beinecke Library, Takamiya MS 15, 149–52
Oxford, Balliol College, MS 354, 25
Oxford, Bodleian Library, MS Arch. Selden. supra 52, 19–20
Oxford, Bodleian Library, MS Bodley 649, 154n
Oxford, Bodleian Library, MS Bodley 686, 125n
Oxford, Bodleian Library, MS Digby 86, 218n, 230-2, 234, 237
Oxford, Bodleian Library, MS Digby 102, 4, 193
Oxford, Bodleian Library, MS Douce 104, 9, 240–50
Oxford, Bodleian Library, MS Douce 302, 9, 251–60
Oxford, Bodleian Library, MS Eng. poet. a. 1 (the Vernon MS), 45, 47, 193
Oxford, Bodleian Library, MS Eng. poet. e. 1, 25
Oxford, Bodleian Library, MS Rawlinson C. 670, 152n
Oxford, Bodleian Library, MS Rawlinson G. 22, 15
Oxford, Bodleian Library, MS Tanner 169*, 236–7
Oxford, Jesus College, MS 29 (II), 9, 213–26,
Oxford, St John's College, MS 209, 199n
Paris, Bibliothèque de l'Arsenal, MS 135, 235–6
Paris, Bibliothèque nationale de France, MS fr. 25458, 9, 202, 206
Warminster, Longleat House 29, 166n
Windsor, Eton College, MS 36, 57–69
Windsor, Eton College, MS 178, 235n

General Index

This is an index of primary authors, titles of works, and places. It does not include references to recent and contemporary scholars and critics. Individual lyrics discussed in the essays are indexed here under author, if known, and otherwise (under 'Lyrics') alphabetically by their first line or conventional title. Manuscripts are separately indexed above on pp. 303–4.

ABC of Aristotle, 193–4
Adam of Dryburgh, 120
Adam of St Victor, 121
Aelred of Rievaulx, *De institutio inclusarum*, 93–4, 97
Akathistos (hymn to the Virgin), 116–19, 121n
Alan of Lille, *Compendiosa in Cantica Canticorum ad laudem Deiparae Virginis Mariae elucidatio*, 118n
Albertus Magnus, *Mariale* (ascribed to), 118
Alcuin of York, *De laude Dei*, 116
Alma Redemptoris Mater, 119n
Ambrose, St, 111
Ancrene Wisse, 75, 97–8
Ambrose, St, *Liber de Paradiso*, 103n
Anselm, St, 35–7, 101, 229
　De veritate, 36
　Meditatio ad concitandum timorem (Meditation I), 43
　Meditatio redemptionis humanae, 37, 44
　Prayers to the Virgin, 80, 84
　see also: pseudo-Anselm
Aristotle, 203, 207–9, 265–6
　Nichomachean Ethics, 194
Ashampstead, Berkshire, St Clement's Church, 44
Assisa panis Anglie, 219
Audelay, John, 4, 9, 11, 251–60
　Counsel of Conscience, 252–60
　Dread of death, 252n
　Epilogue, 252–5, 259
　God's Address to Sinful Men, 258–9

Marcolf and Solomon, 252–3, 257, 259–60
Meditation on the Holy Face, 255–6
Our Lord's Epistle on Sunday, 253n
Pope John's Passion of Our Lord, 254
Remedy of Nine Virtues, 253n
Salutation to St Bridget, 259n
Seven Words of Christ on the Cross, 259n
True Living, 253
Vision of St Paul, 253n, 254n
Visiting the Sick and Consoling the Needy, 253n
Augustine of Hippo, St, 35–6
　Confessions, 66
　De Trinitate, 35–6
　Tractates on the First Epistle of John, 103n
　Tractates on the Gospel of John, 103–4
Autpert, Ambrose, *De Assumptione sanctae Mariae*, 119n
Ave, caput gloriosum, 105n
Ave mundi spes Maria, 116–17
Ave regina celorum, 117
Ave virgo mater Christi, 120n

Bacon, Roger, *Moralia philosophia*, 231n
Basil of Seleucia, *Oratio 39, In Sanctissimae Deiparae Annuntiationem*, 118n
Baudelaire, Charles, 113
Bede, Venerable, 59, 247
　Historia ecclesiastica, 85
Belchamp Walter, Essex, St Mary's Church, 42n
Beowulf, 13

General Index

Bernard of Clairvaux, St, 41, 117, 229
    Sayings, 230
    see also: pseudo-Bernard
Bernard van Orley, 104n
Bible
    Canticles/Song of Songs, 37, 41, 43, 49, 67, 113, 114–20, 141–57
    I Corinthians, 103n, 114
    Daniel, 34
    Ecclesiastes, 231n
    Exodus, 34, 103n, 117
    Ezekiel, 103n
    Genesis, 34, 97n, 103
    Hebrews, 39
    Isaiah, 40, 89–98, 103, 107n, 117
    James, 245n
    Jeremiah, 64
    Job, 34n
    John, 34, 103, 104, 231n
    Kings, 115n, 231n
    Luke, 42, 44n, 107n
    Mark, 66
    Matthew, 43, 44n, 59, 62, 68–9, 107n, 118
    Psalms, 34n, 39, 49, 103, 105, 106, 113, 115, 245n
    Revelation, 43n, 44n, 82, 107n, 141n, 145
    Romans, 66, 117
    Samuel, 133n
    I Thessalonians, 199
    Wisdom, 118, 133n
Boccaccio, 177
Boethius, *Consolation of Philosophy*, 195–8
Bokenham, Osbern, *Legendys of Hooly Wummen*, 207n
Bonaventure, St, 101
Book of the Knight of the Tower, 247n
Book of Tribulacyon, 100
Bridget, St, *Revelation*, 101n
Britten, Benjamin, 3
Browne, John, 235n
Bruno of Querfurt, *S. Adalberti Pragensis episcopi et martyris vita altera*, 116n
Bruno of Segni, *Expositio in Exodum*, 117
Burgh, Benedict (with John Lydgate), *Secrees of Old Philisoffres*, 134–5
Bury St Edmunds, Benedictine abbey, 135

Canterbury Cathedral, 235
    St Augustine's Abbey, 235
Canticum amoris, 203–4
Catherine of Siena, *Dialogue*, 97

Cellini, Benvenuto, 113
Chardri, 218n, 226
    Life of St Josaphaz, 218
    Life of the Seven Sleepers, 218
    Little Debate, 219
Charles d'Orléans, poems in English (*Fortunes Stabilnes*) and French, 4, 7, 8, 9, 11, 201–10
    Ballade 40, 204
    Ballade 52, 204
    Balade 72, 205
    Ballade 73, 206
    Ballade 75 (*Je meurs de soif en couste fontaine*), 206
    Ballade 76, 205–6
    Ballade 83, 204–6, 210n
    Ballade 84 (*But for bi cause that deynte lo is leef*), 8, 201–10
    La Departie d'Amours en balades, 205
    Songe en complainte, 205
Charles VI of France, 112
Charter of Christ, 172n
Chaucer, Geoffrey, 4, 11, 17–18, 95n, 113, 114, 127, 133, 137
    Antigone's Song, 174–88
    Book of the Duchess, 4
    Canterbury Tales, 17, 203–4
        'Knight's Tale', 195–8
        'Monk's Tale', 198
        'Prioress's Tale', 131, 133n
        'Second Nun's Tale', 111, 131, 133n
    Fortune, 195, 198
    Gentilesse, 195
    Parliament of Fowls, 127, 133
    Troilus and Criseyde, 10, 17, 131, 174–88
    Truth, 195
Chester, Benedictine abbey, 236
Christ
    his blood, 51, 90, 97, 104, 107–8, 142
    his body, 40–1, 92, 97
    as bridegroom, 67, 141–57
    his face, 39, 93, 256–7
    as fountain of life, 99–108
    as gardener, 50
    Holy Name, 46n, 47, 167–70, 171
    Incarnation, 38, 50, 117–19, 223
    as judge, 92–3
    as knight, 89–90, 102, 154
    his love, 52, 65–9, 146
    as man, 92–3
    as Man of Sorrows, 44, 52

General Index

Miles Christi, 102
  his nativity, 6, 52
  his Passion, 31–44, 49, 51–4, 59, 62, 77, 87–98, 99–108, 142, 146–7, 158–73, 223, 253–4
  as physician, 90
  proclamation as *Theotokos*, 117
  as vine, 102, 107
  as winepress, 89–98, 107
  his wounds, 41, 54–5, 66–7, 99–108
Christine de Pizan, 114
Chronicle, English prose, 218
Chrysippus of Jerusalem, *Oratio in Sanctam Mariam Deiparam*, 119–20
Conrad of Haimburg, *Annulus Beatae Virginis Mariae*, 117n

Dante, 264, 275
  Purgatorio and *Paradiso*, 117
De negligentiis praelatorum, 234
Deschamps, Eustache, 114
Desert of Religion, 170
Dickinson, Emily, 6
Digby lyrics, 2, 4, 193
Doctrinale Sauvage, 219
Doctrine of the Hert, 98
Donne, John, 267
Dunbar, William, *The Golden Targe*, 113–14

East Midlands, 229, 233
Edmund, St, 111
Eleven Pains of Hell, 219–20
Eugenius of Toledo, *Epitaphium*, 31, 118n
Eustace, St, life of, 230

Fairstead, Essex, St Mary's Church, 37
Fasciculus morum, 152n
Fifteen Oes, 91
Forrest, William, 113
Frith, John, *Pistle to the reader*, 200n

Galen, 203
Gaude, amplissimum Verbi tabernaculum, 119n
Gawain poet, 112
Glossa ordinaria, 92
Godfrey of Admont, 117n
Gower, John, *Confessio Amantis*, 203, 249
Great Tew, Oxfordshire, St Mary's Church, 41
Gregory the Great, St, 85
  Moralia in Job, 231n
Grimestone, John, 4, 141–57
Grimhill, Richard, 230
Guienne and Normandy, 204
Gussage, Dorset, St Andrew's Church, 38, 40

Harley lyrics, 2, 8–9, 13, 221, 224
Haughmond Abbey, 251
Hegel, Georg, 6, 176, 265n
Herebert, William, 4
  Quis est iste qui uenit de Edom?, 87–98
Hill, Geoffrey, 155–6
Hoccleve, Thomas, 4
Hoffmansthal, Hugo von, 113
Howard, Henry, Earl of Surrey, 265
Humphrey, Duke of Gloucester, 196
Hymnus Acathistus, 118n, 119n

Ignatius of Antioch, 111
Innocent III, *Ave Mundi spes Maria*, 116
  De miseria conditionis humanae, 229, 234
Ipomedon, 79n
Isabella of Bavaria, 112

Jacob's Well, 97, 242–3, 245
Jacques de Vitry, 246
James IV of Scotland, 114
Jean, Duc de Berry, 112
Jerome, St, 117
Jesse, Tree of, 117
Jesu dulcis memoria, 47
Joan of Navarre, 112
John the Baptist, St, 130
John the Evangelist, St, 38–41
  see also: Augustine of Hippo
John V, Duke of Brittany, 112
John Chrysostom, *Homiliae in Joannem*, 103n
John of Garland, *Epithalamium beata Mariae virginis*, 118
John of Grimestone, *see* Grimestone
John of Howden, *Philomela*, 203
John of Wales, *Tractatus de poenitentia*, 243–4
Joseph the Hymnographer, *Mariale*, 118n
Julian of Norwich, 47–8, 96

Katherine, St, 130

Layamon, *Brut*, 218, 219, 226

General Index

Langland, William, *Piers Plowman*, 14, 67–9, 203, 241–50
Lay Folks' Mass Book, 247n
Leominster Priory, Herefordshire, 232
Life of Soul, 100
Lope de Vega, 155–6
Love, Nicholas, *Mirror of the Blessed Life of Jesus Christ*, 253
Lydgate, John, 4, 11, 110, 165
    Ballade at the Reverence of Our Lady, 111n, 113
    Dietary, 198
    Doctrine for pestilence, 198
    Dolerous Pyte of Crystes Passioun, 127–8
    Exposition of the Pater Noster, 111n
    Fall of Princes, 111, 196, 198
    Fifteen Joys and Sorrows of Mary, 7, 122–37
    Fifteen Joys of Our Lady, 130
    Invocation to St Anne, 111n
    Legend of St Margarete, 111
    Life of Our Lady, 118–19, 131, 133n
    Lives of Saints Edmund and Fremund, 111
    Mumming for the Mercers, 111n
    Pageant of Knowledge, 198
    Secrees of Old Philisoffres (with Benedict Burgh), 134–5
    Seying of the Nightingale, 127n
    Siege of Thebes, 112n
    Sodein fal of princes in oure dayes, 198
    Testament, 111
    Thoroughfare of Woe, 189–200
    Tied with a lyne, 198
    Treatise for Laundresses, 198
    Troy Book, 111
    Verses on the Kings of England, 197–8
Lyrics
    A Call for a Song, 26n
    A Little Sooth Sermon, 215–17, 224–6
    A wayle whyte as whalles bon, 22n
    Adam lay i-bowndyn, 22–4
    Allas, allas! Wel yvel y sped, 147
    All other love is like the moon, 57–69
    Alle þat gos and rydys, loket opon me, 148
    Almyghty God, fadir of hevene, 25
    An Autumn Song, 232
    On God Ureisun of Ure Lefdi, 42, 73–86
    On leome is in þis world ilist, 31–44, 78n
    On Lofsong of Ure Lefdi, 75n, 76, 78
    On Lofsong of Ure Louerde, 75n, 76, 78
    An Orison to Our Lady, 218
    An Orison to Our Lord, 213–23
    On wel swuþe god ureisun of god almihti, 40, 75n
    Annunciation, 218
    Annunciation of the Virgin Mary, 219
    Antiphon of St Thomas the Martyr, 219
    Byhalde merveylis: a mayde ys moder, 193
    Blow, northerne wynd, 3n, 79
    Crist is offred for mannis sake, 141n
    Death, 219
    Death's Wither-Clench, 218
    Doomsday, 219
    Duty of Christians, 219–20
    Edi beo þu, heuene quene, 78–9
    Fragment on Doomsday, 219
    Freers, freers, wo ye be, 26–7
    Herkneþ alle gode men and stylle sitteþ adun, 215–22, 224–6
    Ichot a burde in boure bryht, 3n
    I knaw no þinge þat so inwardly þi luf to God wyl brynge, 159–73
    I sigh when I sing, 232
    I syng of a myden þat is makeles, 3n
    I syt and synge of luf langyng, 170
    In a pistel þat Poul wrouȝt, 199
    In a tabernacle of a tour, 142
    In a valey of þis restles mynde, 142, 146
    Is ther any good man here, 26n
    Jesu Cristes milde moder, 237–8
    Jesus, sweet is the love of you, 232
    Ihesus woundes so wide, 99–108
    Lestenyt lordynges boþe elde and ȝynge, 3n
    Louerd Crist, ich þe grete, 213–23
    Maiden in the mor, 275
    Man be ware and be no fool, 199
    Miri it is while sumer i-last, 15–16
    Man in the Moon, 224
    Moral Ode, 217–18, 220
    My folk, now answerë mei, 18–19
    Nou goth sonne vnder wod, 78n
    Now I se blosmë sprynge, 19
    O Vernicle, 256
    On Serving Christ, 219
    Penitence for Wasted Life, 20–1
    Prayer of St Bede, 230
    Proverbs of Alfred, 217, 219
    Satire on the Retinues of the Great, 224
    Seven Joys of Our Lady Saint Mary, 218
    Signs of Death, 218
    Sinners Beware, 218

Song on Jesus' Precious Blood, 232
Spring Song on the Passion, 232
Stod ho þere neh [Stood the moder under roode], 236
Stond wel, moder, under rode, 227–39
Surge mea sponsa, 142
Sweet Jesus, King of Bliss, 232
Ten Abuses, 219
The infinite power essenciall, 109–21
þe luf of God, whoso will lere, 158–72
þe milde Lomb isprad o rode, 78n
Thayr ys no myrth under the sky, 19–20
Three Sorrowful Things, 219
Tutiuillus, þe deuyl of hell, 240–50
Ubi sunt poem, 230
Ureisun of God Almihti, 76, 77n, 78
Vndo þi dore, my spuse dere, 141–57
Weal, 218
Weping hath myn wongës wet, 13
When Holy Church Is Overcome, 218
Whan ich se on rode/Quenne hic se on rode, 233
Whan netilles in wynter bere rosis rede, 24–5
Uuere beþ þey biforen vs weren, 82
Whils I satte in a chapel in my prayere, 158–72
Will and Wit, 217–19
Womman Jon I take to þe, 142n
Woman of Samaria, 218
see also: Audelay, Charles d'Orléans, Chaucer, Herebert, Lydgate, Minot, Rolle, Skelton, Thomas of Hales, Wyatt

Mallarmé, Stéphane, 113
Malory, Sir Thomas, *Le Morte d'Arthur*, 95n
Mankind, 243
Mannyng, Robert, *Handlyng Synne*, 247n
Marbod of Rennes, *Oratio ad Sanctam Mariam*, 78
Marot, Clément, 114
Martin of Troppa, 59, 68
Mary
  Annunciation, 129
  Assumption, 112, 114, 115, 142, 153
  Coronation, 112, 115, 120
  at the Crucifixion, 41–4, 51–2, 77, 227–39
  cult in England, 77–8
  depictions of, 116n, 118
  floral symbolism, 42, 117
  joys and sorrows, 122–37, 231
  Marian antiphons, 118
  Mediatrix, 65, 84, 120–1
  miracle of, 230
  names of, 142
  pietà, 135–6
  petition to, 225
  proclamation as *Theotokos*, 117
  Purification, 231n
  queen of Heaven, 78–9, 109–21
  as spiritual vineyard, 113
  in Tree of Jesse motif, 117
  Triumph, 112, 115
  weeping blood, 42
Meditation of the Hours, 38, 43
Michelet, Jules, 264
Minot, Laurence, 4
Mirk, John, *Festial*, 247n
Myroure of Our Ladye, 117n

N-Town play, 120
Novalis, 113
North Cove, Suffolk, St Botolph's Church, 40

Oddington, Gloucestershire, St Andrew's Church, 43
Orcherd of Syon, 97
Ovid, 177, 180, 186–8
Owl and the Nightingale, 217–20, 226

Passion of Jesus Christ, 218, 220
Paul, St, 66
Pearl, 97, 105, 113, 121n
Peter Damian, 155
Peter of Celle, *Sermo 6*, 118n
Petrarch, Francesco, 180, 264–5
Peyraut (Peraldus), Guillame, *Summa de vitiis et virtutibus*, 242
Poe, Edgar Allen, *The Raven*, 193
Pound, Ezra, 265–8
Prick of Conscience, 203n
pseudo-Anselm, *Dialogus beatae Mariae et Anselmi de passione Domini*, 41, 229
  De passione Christi, 40
pseudo-Augustine, *Candet nudatum pectus*, 166n
pseudo-Bernard, *Liber de passione Christi et doloribus et planctibus Matris ejus*, 41, 229
pseudo-Hugh of St Victor, *De bestiis et aliis rebus*, 121n

General Index

pseudo-Ildefonsus of Toledo, *Libellus de Corona virginis*, 117n, 121
pseudo-Melito, *Transitus Mariae*, 119–20
Puttenham, George, *Art of English Poesie*, 126, 260

Quedington, Gloucestershire, St Swithin's Church, 115n
Qui est hic qui pulsat ad ostium?, 155
Quinze Joies de la Vierge, 129

Radbertus of Corbie, *De Assumptione sanctae Mariae virginis*, 119n
Reading Abbey, 115n
Regina Caeli, 119
Rhabanus Maurus, 59
Richard of Saint Laurent, *Mariale*, 118
Richard of St Victor, 101
  De quatuor gradibus violentae caritatis, 48
Rolle, Richard, 4, 11, 45–56, 101n, 150, 158–73
  Commandment, 158–60, 168
  Ego Dormio, 158–73
  Form of Living, 158–73
  I knaw no þinge þat so inwardly, 159–73
  Incendium amoris, 158–60, 170, 172
  Melos amoris, 120, 121n
  Swete Ihesu, now wol I synge, 45–56
  þe luf of God, whoso will lere, 158–73
  Whils I satte in a chapel in my prayere, 159–73
Ryman, James, 4

Saints' lives, Latin collection, 232
Salutatio ad latus domini, 107n
Salve Regina, 119
Shakespeare, William, *Rape of Lucrece*, 131
Shires of England, 219–20
Shirley, John, 196–7
Sidney, Sir Philip, 267
  Defence of Poesie, 271
Sir Gawain and the Green Knight, 95n, 203
Sir Launfal, 113
Sir Orfeo, 112
Skelton, John, 4
  Garland of Laurel, 4–5
  Speke Parrott, 260
South Newington, Oxfordshire, church of St Peter ad vincula, 42
Stabat iuxta Christi crucem, 230–9

Stöcklin, Ulrich, von Rottach, *Super Ave Maria* and *De Beata Maria Virgine*, 117n
Swetstock, John, 154

Theopano, Empress, 116
Thomas Aquinas,
  De malo, 68
  De spiritualabis creaturis, 59
  Quaestiones disputatae, 59
  De spiritualibis creaturis, 59
  Summa Theologicae, 64–5
Thomas of Hales, *Love Rune*, 217, 219, 222, 226
Three Dead Kings, 251n
Tobie, extract from, 219–20
Towneley Cycle, *Judicium* play, 243
Trastevere, Rome, Church of Santa Maria, 115
Treatise on the Passion, 99–108
Tutivillus, 240–50

Usk, Thomas, *Testament of Love*, 206n

Vaughan Williams, Ralph, 3
Vegetius, *De re militari*, 59, 62
Vernon lyrics, 193, 199
Virgin, Miracle of, 230
Virginity, Treatise on, 100

Walter of Wimborne, 120
Walton, John, translation of Boethius, *De consolatione Philosophiae*, 206n
Warwickshire, 101
West Chiltington, Sussex, St Mary's Church, 41, 42
West Midlands, 217, 222
William of Nassington, *Speculum vitae*, 143, 150
Winchester, St Swithun's Priory, 197
Wissington, Suffolk, St Mary's Church, 36–7
Wooing Group, 39, 40, 42, 75, 76n
Wohunge of Ure Lauerd, 75n
Worcester, 230
Wordsworth, William, *Preface to Lyrical Ballads*, 58
Wyatt, Sir Thomas, 8, 261–71
  Ineternum I was ons determinid, 261–71

Yeats, William Butler,
  'Sailing to Byzantium', 111n
  'The Gift of Harun Al-Rashid', 111
York plays, *Fall of Angels*, 260

www.ingramcontent.com/pod-product-compliance
Lightning Source LLC
Chambersburg PA
CBHW051559230426
43668CB00013B/1913